NOEL & COLE

THE SOPHISTICATES

STEPHEN CITRON

Hal Leonard books are available at your local bookstore,
or you may order them **www.musicdispatch.com**
or call Music Dispatch at
1-800-637-2852

780.922

Published by Hal Leonard Corporation
7777 West Bluemound Road
P.O. Box 13819
Milwaukee, WI 53213, USA

Trade Book Division Editorial Offices
151 West 46th Street, 8th Floor
New York, NY 10036

Cover photos:
Noel Coward: © Bettmann/Corbis
Cole Porter: © Culver Pictures, Inc./Superstock

Library of Congress Control Number: 2004117539
ISBN 0-634-09302-9

Printed in the United States of America

10 9 8 7 6 5 4 3 2 1

Visit Hal Leonard online at:
www.halleonard.com

NOEL & COLE

THE SOPHISTICATES

COVENTRY LIBRARIES

**Please return this book on or before
the last date stamped below.**

PS130553 Disk 4 2005

To renew this book take it to any of
the City Libraries before
the date due for return

Cole Porter and Noel Coward

Contents

Acknowledgements

N O BOOK that sets out to be a musical biography can ever have been written without the help of a great many individuals. Since this is a dual one, I must amend that last sentence to read 'a great, great many'.

Let me first tip my hat (because he was the first born of these two giants) to those who helped me with the Cole Porter material, then to the people who had input into the Noel Coward pages and lastly let me thank those without whose help this book would not have left my piano desk and computer.

In Peru, Indiana, Cole's family – James Omar and Lousse Cole and Joanna Cole Lamberton – answered my questions about their cousin and supplied pictures which have not, I believe, been published before. Mary James, at the Miami County Historical Society, copied photos, letters, even menus so that I could understand Cole and Linda Porter's lifestyle better, while Charlet Smith at the Peru Library gave me almost more information than I needed about the early Coles and Porters. Doris and Vernon Zumhagen filled me in on life in Peru while Susan Wolf in the Peru High School Library showed me their extensive collection of memorabilia.

My deep thanks to Robert H. Montgomery, Jr., attorney for the Cole Porter Musical and Literary Property Trust and to Florence Leeds, executive secretary of the trusts. Not only did they provide me with the raw materials, copies of every score and letter Porter wrote but they offered me working space and great consideration during the months of research in New York. Thanks also to Rose-Marie Bartley in their office, for secretarial assistance.

Richard Warren, Jr. and his assistant, David Finley at the Sterling Library, Yale University went out of their way to photocopy reviews and to play me every scrap of Porter's music that has been recorded while the entire staff of the Yale Beniecke Rare Book Library brought forth the total Porter oeuvre for me to study. I should also like to thank local librarians Julia MacKenzie at Fairfield and Meg McCrery at the Pequot Library for their assistance.

The Noel Coward Estate is ably managed by Mr. Graham Payn who I have seen several times in conjunction with this book. I am grateful for our interviews during which he dug down into his memory and tried to let me see the unknown Coward, and for the loan of several heretofore unpublished pictures. I also received invaluable assistance from Joan Hirst, who took over Lorn Lorraine's awesome job and manages it as well as her dynamic predecessor. Martin Tickner has not only done a superb job editing Coward's verse but it is a veritable mine of Cowardiana. Thanks for an illuminating interview go to Norman Hackforth who was Noel's piano accompanist, nay collaborator, over half of his life, and also to Jon Wynne-Tyson, whose mother was Coward's first lyricist.

I should also like to thank Chappell & Company and Warner Brothers Inc. who publish the Coward and Porter songs. Caroline Underwood helped me locate many Coward songs and Malcolm Billingsley photocopied all the manuscripts. My thanks also to the above mentioned publisher for permission to quote from the Porter and coward catalogue.

My appreciation also to Madeline Gilford, whose late husband Jack was an irreplaceable international treasure. She supplied information on Coward's *Look After Lulu*, in which Jack appeared. Frances Gershwin Godowsky recreated the atmosphere of Paris in the '20s for me during a long interview when she told me about her appearances in Porter's *La Revue des Ambassadeurs*; Timothy Gray who wrote the book and lyrics for *High Spirits* gave me much information on that show's genesis while Mitch Douglas who manages most of the best theatrical and literary lights in America let me explore his splendid collection of tapes and videos.

Michael Kerker at ASCAP)American Society of Composers, Authors, and Publishers) was a tremendous help in supplying complete lists of Porter and Coward published work as was Dorothy Swerdlove, Curator of the Billy Rose Collection of the New York Public Library.

My thanks go also to Porter authority Robert Kimball and to Coward experts Sheridan Morley, Ruth Leon and Ned Sherrin for stories and anecdotes; and to Bobby Short, the ideal interpreter of songs of both masters.

Deep appreciation also goes to my publisher, Christopher Sinclair-Stevenson Ltd, to Hilary Rubinstein, my British agent and the entire staff at A.P. Watt and to Sally Slaney who has a knack for ferreting out unusual Porter and Coward photos. Michael Edwards and Robert Jorgen helped in the proofing of this book, to them and to Thomas Z. Shepard whose 'eagle eye' is second only to his multi-musical talents, my gratitude.

My further gratitude goes to the theatrical and musical artists listed below who talked to me on the telephone or answered my questionnaires. Their names are listed alphabetically below:

Louis Aborn, Billie Allen, Robert Anederson, Theodore Chapin, Fred Ebb, Ian Marshall Fisher, Morton Gottlieb, Adolph Green, Benny Green, Stanley Green, Tammy Grimes, William Hammerstein, Wally Harper, Kitty Carlisle Hart, George Hetherington, Florence Henderson, Luther Henderson, Celeste Holm, Evan Hunter, Paula Laurence, Victor Lee Leslie, David Le Vine, Peter Lipscomb, Cameron Macintosh, Vivian Matalon, Barry Norman, Rex Reed, Helena Scott, Rose Tobias Shaw, Dinah Sheridan, Jeffrey Simmons, Elaine Stritch, Charles Strouse, Jule Styne, Ion Trewin, Simon Trewin, Fran and Barry Weisler, Kevin White.

To my son, Alexander Citron, my thanks for copying manuscript and letters as well as his deep involvement in every stage of the creation of this book; to Dr. Leonard Diamond further thanks for his thorough explanation of Porter's and Coward's psychology as related to their artistic temperament.

Last of all, to my wife, Anne Edwards, who is never too busy to put aside the novel or biography she is writing to listen to a passage hot off the computer or to a Coward or Porter marvel I have just discovered – and who has the considerable talent of being able to give constructive advice lovingly – my deepest thanks and devotion.

New Milford, Connecticut
January 1992

Introduction

Now in the first decade of the twenty-first century, one can look back on the fifteen years since the original publication of *Noel & Cole: The Sophisticates* and remark that their œuvres—instead of declining in critical esteem or becoming rarely performed—are still as vital and as popular as ever. Cole Porter's songs seem to be everywhere. With new interpretations by jazz artists, to fresh recordings by crossover singers, and background music in the movies, one can hardly go to a film that is set in the past without hearing Cole's "Just of Those Things" or "Night and Day" in the background. Nor can one watch a PBS saga of castellated British family life unaccompanied by a nostalgic Coward waltz. And where would subscription theatre be without *Blithe Spirit, Private Lives*, and *Design for Living*, Coward's popular comedies? They are still staples of regional theatre, just as Porter's *Anything Goes* and *Kiss Me, Kate* and sometimes *Can-Can* and *Silk Stockings* rival the popularity of *Hello, Dolly!, Cats*, and *42nd Street*, in reconceptions and touring productions.

By some fortunate design, Noel Coward and Cole Porter, both homosexuals and both geniuses, managed to be born into and become icons of the Art Deco era, a time of sleek chromium, elegant motor cars, smoking jackets, short skirts, and easy morality. They championed it as they maintained their own liberal mindset. Now that an age similar to Deco is in vogue their influence is even more strongly felt. Noel's *Brief Encounter* and Cole's "gossamer wings" have metamorphosed into code words for gay bars. Their eagerness to try anything and everything at least once has become a mantra for sophisticated young people everywhere.

Far more germane, in view of the importance of the republications of their musical, lyrical, and dramatic works in this book, is their influence on today's world and that their output refused to date. Time has finally caught up with these prescient men for whom no tabu was taboo. To their credit, it must be noted that it took two generations to do that, so far ahead of the public ethos were they.

In contrast to the leading lights of the contemporary musical scene, the purveyors of hip-hop, rap, and acid rock, Noel and Cole were far more shocking than Emimem and the Beastie Boys, but they had no need to use profanity or indulge in political correctness. Cole's lyrics remain avant garde and his music harmonically intriguing, while the subjects of some of Noel's plays—drugs, blackmail (*Suite in Three Keys*), older woman with a younger man, even incest as in *The Vortex*, and ménage à trois in *Design for Living* are the stuff of shocking drama today.

But it was all handled so deftly.

I am convinced that could Noel and Cole look down on us today, they would grimace at the heavy-handedness of our songs and the mistreatment accorded to love affairs, the stock-in-trade of popular music. To paraphrase Cole in "Ours":

The high gods above
Look down and laugh at our love
And to say to themselves, 'How tawdry it's grown.'
They've seen our cars
In front of so many bars;
When we should be under the stars
Together but alone.

Noel too dealt lightly with sex, but would save his best ripostes for the Foreign Service, where he could write about beastial sex in an utterly amusing way. This is quite different form the seriousness of Edward Albee's *The Goat, or Who Is Sylvia?* Look at the few lines from "I Wonder What Happened to Him."

Have you had any word
Of that bloke in the "Third"
Was it Southerly, Sedgwick, or Sym?
They had him thrown out of the club in Bombay.
For apart of his mess bills exceeding his pay,
He took to pig-sticking in quite the wrong way.
I wonder what happened to him.

Cole could also introduce anything. Sex for money ("Love for Sale," "I'm a Gigolo"), sadism ("Why Do You Want to Hurt Me So?"), transvestism ("A Skipper from Heaven Above"), nor was he afraid of displaying how own homosexuality and sophistication in a most disarming way as when the naïve subject of "I'm Unlucky at Gambling" takes her croupier to the movies:

I took the croupier to a picture show
And though I snuggled close when the lights were low.
The croupier impressed me as rather slow.
I said, "I like John Gilbert a lot, don't you?"
He didn't answer, but when the show was through
I realized that he liked John Gilbert too.

As a chronicler of musical theatre, I cannot resist the opportunity the new edition of this book affords me to compare my subjects' work to contemporary musical. Just a cursory look at what Cole or Noel could put into a musical show, say, *Anything Goes* with "All Through the Night," "I Get a Kick Out of You," "You're the Top," "Anything Goes," and "Blow, Gabriel, Blow" for starters, and Noel's magnificent score for *Ace of Clubs*, which included "Sail Away," "Josephine," "Three Juvenile Delinquents," "I Like America," and "Chase Me," among other gems. One can only contrast these with the current crop on Broadway: a musical adaptation of a fairy tale, like *Beauty and the Beast*, and its counterpart, *The Phantom of the Opera*, a second-rate movie musicalized into *Hairspray*, a *Wizard of Oz* spinoff like *Wicked*, or a Puccini rocker like *Rent*. The Sophisticates would be disappointed at the paucity of good songs. One can imagine them watching a current musical, squirming in their seats, having a hard time—in Cole's words—"fighting the old ennui."

As a final note to this preamble, I would like to thank Christopher Sinclair-Stevenson and Sheldon Mayer of Oxford University Press, the original publishers, for their help. And a hearty handshake goes out to John Cerullo, publisher of Hal Leonard Corporation, who saw the need for this book, too long absent, to make its reappearance.

Stephen Citron
Beverly Hills, California
January 2005

Prelude

I N 1955 when Cole Porter was hard at work writing *Silk Stockings*, a musicalization of the Soviet-Parisian comedy *Ninotchka*, he asked his friend of many years, Noel[1] Coward, to mail him any Russian-sounding rhymes he might be able to invent for a particularly troublesome comedy song, 'Siberia.' Noel obliged by sending a packet of rhymes for 'ski,' 'off' and 'ievitch.' At the last minute he added one more, saying 'I got carried away for a moment with:

> 'If the atmosphere gets cornier
> We can all sing Ortchitchornia.'

only I can't spell Ortchitchornia which put me off, but probably you can – if not there's always Serge Oblensky or Natasha or Valentina.'

Of course these were 'white Russians' married to wealthy Americans and society friends of both Porter and Coward, who would remember Mother Russia only as it was before the Revolution. Educated refugees, they would certainly know how to spell its prominent folk-songs. But, for a comic song about the hardship of being sentenced to live in Siberia, they as well as Cole would certainly be at a loss. Porter remembered that area quite well as an elegant place, the home of the landed gentry and their servants, as he had been a guest at a Prince's estate some years before the revolution. It remained for Cy Feuer the show's co-producer to feed him concepts like, 'in USSR Siberia there are no bills to pay because there are no postal deliveries; no nasty telephone calls because there are no phones; no icecubes necessary in your vodka, they're on your front lawn, etc.' With this added input, Cole was able to come up with a showstopper in the second act of his musical.

Although Feuer found Cole's outdated concept amusingly parochial, Noel understood it completely, for they travelled in the same sets, knew the same elegant citified people, and if you asked either to describe the other in a single word, he would probably have used 'urbane.' In fact, that word might have been invented to describe these two personalities who wrote the most intellectual songs of the mid-twentieth century. Other terms like 'old-world,' 'sophisticated,' 'cosmopolitan,' 'polished,' 'suave,' 'cultivated,' 'refined' and 'elegant' might apply, but they would be equally applicable to their numerous contemporaries who were writing songs in the second quarter of the twentieth century for an especial breed of knowledgeable theatre audiences.

---

[1] Throughout this book the dieresis over the 'e' will be omitted even though Coward taught himself at fourteen to emphasize his distinctive signature with a flourish and double dots. To this writer it is an archaic crutch reminding a speaker to say 'Noel' in two syllables. Written, it seems an unnecessary encumbrance resembling flyspecks on the page.

Although neither of them was born in an urban centre (Noel was born in the Middlesex town of Teddington and Cole came from a small village in Indiana), once they hit London or New York – they knew that was where they belonged. And, since their audiences were invariably in the metropolises, vice (their favourite topic) versa.

Other sassy cosmopolites were well known at the time they were creating their biggest successes throughout the '30s and '40s. Lorenz Hart was setting big-city words to Richard Rodgers' flowing melodies. Howard Dietz was doing the same for Arthur Schwartz's intense ones. Kern, the doyen master melodist, was being de-operetta-ized by Harbach (and later by Hammerstein). Each of these teams was considered highly sophisticated. And there were other individuals, less well-known: Marc Blitzstein, Ivor Novello, Alec Wilder, Bart Howard and John Latouche among them, whose music or lyrics might be considered elitist. But only Coward and Porter had their worldly urbanity in common.

Although born an ocean apart, they had other things in common as well. Both had ineffectual fathers and strong, determined and ambitious mothers who were highly musical. Each woman had lost her first-born son in infancy and throughout Cole's and Noel's childhood (although both boys were extremely healthy children) their mothers hovered over them and feared unnecessarily for their sons' health.

Kate Porter and Violet Coward steered their young sons early into creative and performing lives. Kate did so because she was a frustrated singer and Violet because she hoped to rise above the penny-pinching boarding-house-keeper life she had been born into. Because of this interdependence, each youth was to revere his mother, have night terrors about losing her while writing off his milquetoast father who left breadwinning and discipline to the distaff side. Coming from such a classically twisted psychological situation it is not surprising that both Noel and Cole were homosexual. With their raising of women, especially strong, determined and opinionated women, to such an exalted pedestal, perhaps bisexual would be a more apt description of their libidinous behaviour. For, if one allows that true love need not necessarily have a sexual release, then both Noel and Cole were deeply in love with women. Noel was as heavily dependent upon his relationships with Gladys Calthrop, Lorn Loraine and especially Gertrude Lawrence as Cole was on his with Linda Thomas (to whom he was married in 1919). Platonic or sexual as these alliances might have been, it is certain that neither man could have achieved what he did without the intense transference, involvement and support of these women.

They were both Francophiles (perhaps Parisophiles would be a better-word for they cared not a whit for Bordeaux or Provence), who learned to speak the language fluently out of love for its sound – not snobbery. Each frequently wrote in French and made things gallic – with typical naughtiness, brevity and wit – the theme of many of their works.[2] Again, their urbanity made them content to be working and creating in Paris as well as New York and London. Additionally, in a field totally dominated by teams writing music and lyrics, each of these men was a master of both words and music. Neither needed or wanted a collaborator.

Each man loved to travel and because of this frequently could be found sending in his songs or plays from sunny or exotic resorts. Because of this the uninitiated considered them hedonistic dilettantes, when actually both took their work very seriously and believed in the adage that the show must go on – *when announced*, even if they had to spend sleepless nights to complete their immense contribution to the project.

They were both well versed in the techniques of songwriting. Noel was self-taught while Cole was given violin, piano and composition instruction from his early days. But the fact that they each developed an unerring sense of how to set *words* to music for maximum effect came from their desire to perform. Since they revelled in and developed the 'list song' to its peak and because the sound of applause was their goal, to attain it they never forgot what most of their contemporaries never learned – that, if one writes several choruses, *each succeeding one must be more amusing*, or boredom sets in. Precociously singing for friends and schoolmates from an early age, they learned from watching their listeners' faces when their prosody was coming across and when, by a puzzled look, they had missed the mark.

Fiercely independent, neither man could stand being importuned by an individual he considered his inferior: Cole in the social arena and Noel in the theatrical. Noel's song 'Don't Put Your Daughter on the Stage, Mrs. Worthington' was written in response to the scores of letters he received from misguided would-be stage mothers. It was more than a mere song. It was a philosophy. When he told Mrs. Worthington

'The profession is overcrowded and the struggle's pretty tough,
And admitting the fact she's burning to act,
That isn't quite enough.
She has nice hands, to give the wretched girl her due,
But don't you think her bust is too developed for her age?'

he was being tactfully honest, but later when he informed the mother that her daughter is doomed to theatrical failure with

<hr>

[2] Porter wrote *Mayfair and Montmarte* (1922), *Paris* (1928), *Fifty Million Frenchmen* (1929), *The Battle of Paris* (Film, 1929), *Du Barry Was a Lady* (1939), and *Can-Can* (1953). Coward wrote *The Marquise* (1927), *Private Lives* (1930), *Conversation Piece* (1933), *Ways & Means* (1936), *Operette* (1937), *Quadrille* (1951) and starred in his own play, *Present Laughter (Joyeux Chagrins)*, and translated Feydeau's farce, *Occupe-toi d'Amélie* into *Look After Lulu*.

'Though they said at the school of acting she was lovely as Peer Gynt,
I'm afraid on the whole an ingenue role would emphasise her squint.
She's a big girl, and though her teeth are fairly good,
She's not the type I ever would
Be eager to engage.'

he has dropped total tact in favour of bluntness.

Cole, for his part, much in demand by dowager hostesses as an entertaining week-end guest, was obliged to write thank yous for these largely boring times. Always well-mannered, he wrote a polite word, but this is what he would have liked to send to his typical bête noire, a Mrs. Lowsborough-Goodby ...

'Thank you so much, Mrs. Lowsborough-Goodby ...
For the clinging perfume
And that damp little room,
For the cocktails so hot
And the bath that was not.
For those guests so amusing and mentally bracing
Who talked about racing and racing and racing.
For the ptomaine I got from your famous tinned salmon,
For the fortune I lost when you taught me backgammon ...'

They both adored shocking audiences. But they were conversant enough with language and rhyme to be able to accomplish this through wit and innuendo. Love and sex in all its forms – healthy and perverse, for money or for sheer pleasure – were their frequent concepts. Gigolos, courtesans, prostitutes, pimps, lesbians, nymphomaniacs, the under- and oversexed were the protagonists in many of their songs. Both flourished in a hot-house drawing-room atmosphere and neither wrote much or well about open air, nature or space.

Nor did either's work seem to wave a social flag. It was not for them to write of race riots in Alabama or anti-Protestant upheavals in Ireland. Perhaps that is part of the reason their oeuvre refuses to date. Agitprop is only vital to today. Nothing is so dead as yesterday's news. Communism to Noel and Cole was merely a picturesque panorama in Russia. They did not try to dissect it, and when they mentioned it in song it was only to poke fun at. Their people were more content to enthuse from balconies overlooking the Riviera or to sing while crossing the Atlantic on the *Ile de France*.

Perhaps, simply because of each man's brilliance with the printed word or lyric, history has overlooked their remarkable music. Their words have unjustly overshadowed their considerable contributions to twentieth-century popular song. Cole's rhythmic vitality, subtle changes of key, sinuous minor-major melodies and Noel's way of using the whole-tone scale, refreshing operetta melodies, and creating perky tunes that go to unexpected places or heartbreaking ones with a blues feeling are still fresh. Their melodies are much played today and one has only to be trapped in a lift with Muzak or take tea while listening to a continental hotel string ensemble, to realize how valid their wordless music remains.

In the matter of religion, with a quality that set them apart, they were intense social animals who took their Episcopalianism or Church of England with a grain of salt. And in the field of song-writing, largely dominated, at least in America, by Jewish composers and lyricists, they were the only outstandingly successful Christians.

Lastly, and by incredible coincidence, each had four letters in his first name[3] and six in his surname. And each died in his seventy-third year. (Cole was born in 1891 and died in 1964 and Noel, who was born in 1899, died in 1973.)

But they were not twins.

Noel came from a middle-class British family while Cole was born into provincial American pioneering stock possessed of great wealth. Perhaps that explains Noel's early commercial success and Cole, who never lacked for money, having the nonchalance to wait until he was almost in his thirties before he had a major hit. Although Coward's success enabled him to live well, with a house in the country, a residence cum studio in London and a villa in Jamaica, his lifestyle could in no way be compared to the lavish Porters' who simultaneously rented a fourteen-room apartment on Park Avenue in Manhattan and a palazzo in Venice while maintaining a suite in London's Ritz Hotel. This, in addition to owning a large house in Paris, and later a 200-acre country estate in Williamstown, Massachusetts. When Cole's fame called him to Hollywood, they rented Richard Barthelmess's movie star showplace in Beverly Hills. Noel was well-to-do, but Cole, who hated the word 'rich', was wealthy.

Then there is the matter of their looks. Noel was angelic as a child, handsome and lean as a boy, ardent, winning and tall as an ingenu and debonairly suave for the rest of his life. Cole, on the other hand, was quite short, had a slight frame, an open roundish face and was slightly bug-eyed. When asked why he allowed the studio to cast Cary Grant to impersonate him in his film biography, *Night and Day*, with the availability of Fred Astaire who looked more Porterish, he answered candidly, 'would *you* turn down Cary Grant?'

As for their careers, they differed in that respect as well. Noel, besides writing words and music was, of course, an actor, a revue artist as well as a superb interpreter of songs, and is most remembered today as a playwright. But he was a total man of the theatre while Cole never cared to involve himself in the play as a whole. Porter expected his librettists to finish the play and then

---

[3] Sensitive to the rhythms inherent in words, they often reminded each other that their first names almost rhymed, and addressed each other as 'Noley' and 'Coley.'

call him in just to write the songs. In the large-scale collaborative effort of the musical Porter only cared to execute the words and music (no small task) and, although the librettos of almost every project he worked upon are so far-fetched as to make the shows unrevivable, each one has come to be known today as a 'Cole Porter musical.'

Although both of these men lived a great part of their lives in foreign lands they were unquestionably 'native sons'. By looks, stance, voice and attitude, Noel could never have been mistaken for anyone other than British and Cole, despite hand-made Savile Row suits and Lanvin shirts was quintes-sentially American. However they held different attitudes towards the count-ries they had been born into. Cole often denigrated his compatriots while Noel was fiercely pro-British. If Coward were to vilify, he would aim a tongue-in-cheek barb at his beloved French, saving his acidity for the Germans. As in 'Mad Dogs and Englishmen', he could do no more than poke gentle fun at his countrymen.

Coward was fiercely patriotic. Having been too young for involvement in the First World War, he manoeuvred his career heroically to serve his country and immersed himself in World War II. Working behind the lines in propaganda, producing artistic movies, entertaining troops often in dangerous war zones and performing at fund-raising rallies, these became his primary concerns. Playwriting and songwriting took a back seat until the conflict was over.

Cole, on the other hand, had a short involvement with World War I during which he served in the Duryea Relief Organization and then enlisted for a mere three months in the French army as a foreigner – serving behind the lines. Although it is everywhere reported that he joined the French Foreign Legion, the truth is that this is a romantic figment of Porter's imagination. Once the war had ended, Cole resumed his picaresque existence, his travels and his own kind of escape musical, hewing for the rest of his life to the same kind of fantasy libretto that was still seemingly unaware of the changes that had been introduced in the American musical theatre by the production of realistic works like *Pal Joey* and *Oklahoma*.

The legacy Cole Porter and Noel Coward left was a body of work that seems to grow more adventuresome and daring with the passing years, for, if they wrote of a rarefied world, they wrote truly of it and honestly. And in that way they mirrored the early to middle decades of the twentieth century faithfully. Cole wrote of the rich, the social register and the sexually liberated – things he understood very well; while Noel wrote of peers, travel, shopgirls, London pride and pubs. The two are even more contemporary today than is F. Scott Fitzgerald for they lived, they personified, the age while Fitzgerald simply *wrote of* it.

The critic James Agate accused Noel of writing aimless drawing room comedy and in particular singled out one of his great successes, *Blithe Spirit*, which he labelled 'common'. Then he hastily withdrew the remark, saying 'I am wrong to attribute commonness to Noel. This is uncritical. The proper thing to say is that the age is common, and that Noel's plays mirror the age.'

Of course, Agate is wrong even in his denial. The first half of the twentieth century was no more common than today seems when compared to yesterday. In retrospect, as the century winds down, that time seems freer, more impassioned and adventuresome than the recent past. And both Noel Coward and Cole Porter, highly uncommon men, were chronicling it in their uniquely personal, urbane style.

COLE
1891 - 1909

THE LITTLE BOY in the velvet suit with lace cuffs, playing a selection first on the violin and then turning his attention to perform an encore on piano, was not a prodigy. Even here in Marion, Indiana, the bucolic heartland of America at an annual Conservatory of Music recital in the late 1890s, that was obvious. But his relish, confidence and élan when he turned to the keyboard had to be evident to the assembly, the farmers and shopkeepers, relatives and friends who comprised the audience. No one in that crowded hall could doubt that Cole Porter, eight years old, and already competent on two instruments, was the star of the show.

At the age of five, he had begun informal piano lessons with his mother. Two years later Kate Cole Porter engaged a professional keyboard teacher for him. Once she became aware her son had what she called 'a gift for music', she felt he might fulfil her own lifelong dream – to become a professional musician. To attain that goal, Kate felt it was imperative that he first master the violin. But since there was no one capable to teach any stringed instrument in their small hometown, Peru, the child was taken for weekly lessons to the county seat, Marion, some thirty miles east of his home, and an hour's journey by slow train.

For anyone with a strong sensitivity to pitch, tuning and playing a stringed instrument is often a painful experience, and for young Cole this was compounded by the fact that his frame, and necessarily his hand, was small and the violin he played in this provincial music school (contrary to the way youngsters were taught in sophisticated metropolitan conservatories) was full-size. His being naturally left-handed was another obstacle, for he was forced to hold frets and execute difficult fingerwork with his awkward right hand. And so the lessons were an onerous task for Cole Porter – especially since, by the time he was nine, he was obliged to travel alone every Saturday for his conservatory instruction.

Contrast this with his inborn love of harmony and how easily it could be created on the piano, as well as the fact that the keyboard instrument, requiring only occasional tuning, was not offensive to his ear. It is easy to see why the young musician was more at home here. But superseding all consider-ations of Cole's natural gift for the keyboard was his mother's involvement and her supervision of his daily two-hour piano practice. When the scales and arpeggios became tiring, Kate Cole would break the routine by listening to whatever simple melodies her son had composed and then she would take over the keyboard, accompanying herself in a song or two. Moments like these became even more important than whatever inherent love Cole may have had for the piano. For through them he achieved a deep familial bonding that was never to be broken throughout both their lifetimes.

The mature Cole Porter was to look back on his public appearances at the Marion Conservatory (or on those for which the entire Conservatory Orchestra would be transported to perform in Peru) with loathing, and of these recital appearances would recall that he 'adored playing the piano as much as he abhorred the screeching violin.' But he had to allow that the pleasure his musical accomplishments on both instruments afforded his mother, who kept a scrapbook dating from his very earliest recital programme, made such an ordeal worthwhile.

Approval from the distaff side of his family was an obvious necessity for the boy; not so with his male kinsfolk. He had only occasional rapport with his father, Samuel Fenwick Porter, who had come to Peru from Vevey, Indiana, opened a drug store, courted and married his mother in 1884, some said for her fortune. Only rarely would Samuel be uninhibited enough to share his favourite hobby, reading poetry, with his young son, and even more occasionally would he show Cole a few of the poems he himself had written.[1] Both Cole's and his father's sensitivity were frowned upon by Sam's father-in-

[1] James Cole, heir to the Cole Porter estate, and his closest family member, when interviewed, said that 'the Coles are devoid of any poetic or musical talents, so we decided long ago that his [Cole's] talent had to come from the Porters.'

Porter, aged eight

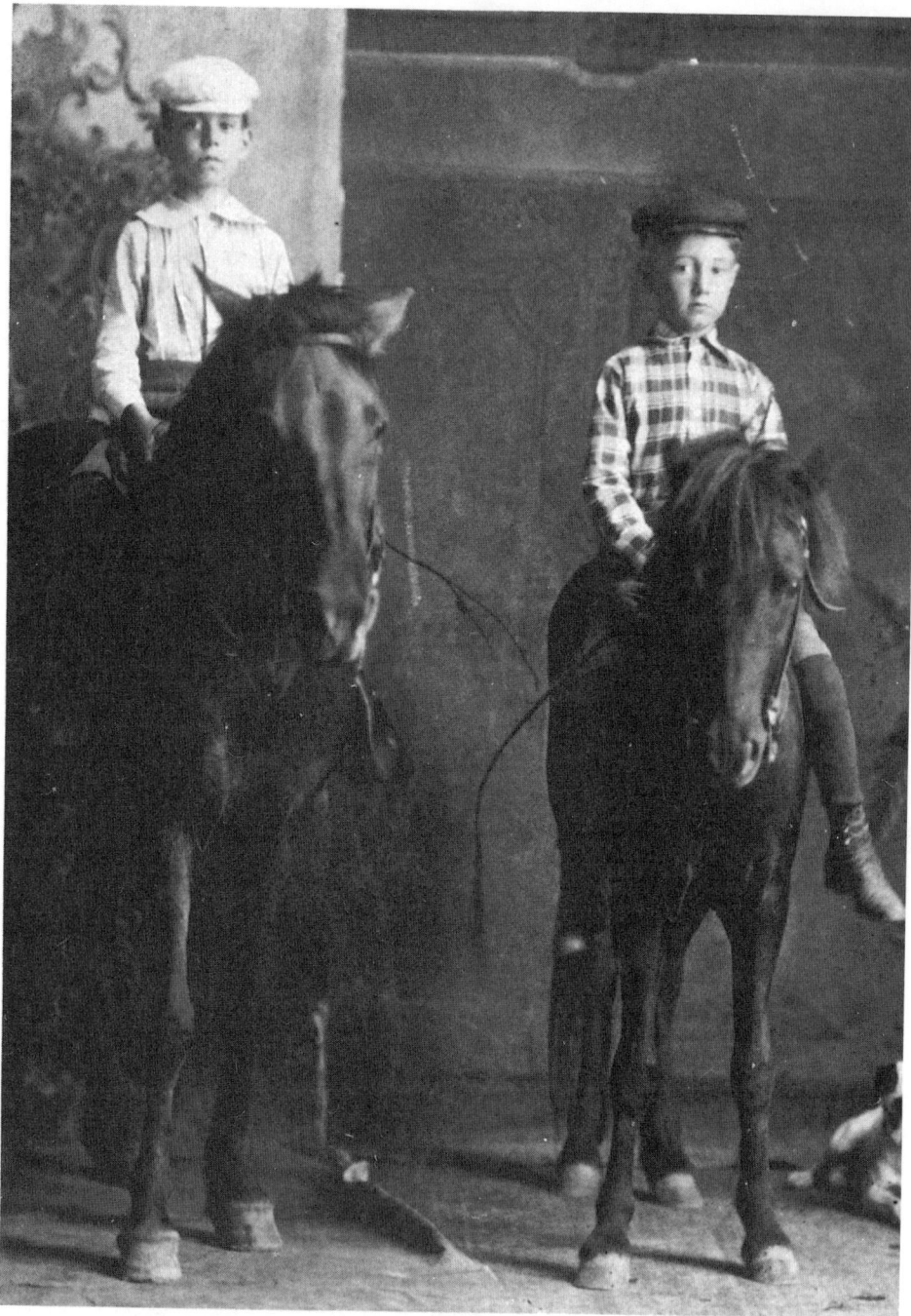

Porter (left), aged eleven, with his cousin Louis

law, James Omar Cole – Peru's most powerful civic leader and one of Indiana's richest citizens.

Nor was there any warmth between grandfather and grandson. James Omar, who was known to family and friends as J.O., was a gruff man who, having been left a fairly sizeable fortune, decided his mission in life was to increase his legacy. To do that, he joined the rush to California in 1849, but soon realized there was more money to be made from the miners than the gold in 'them thar hills'. He opened a general store, selling the prospectors the equipment they needed for gold panning, and soon amassed the then-considerable fortune of $30,000 with which he returned to his home in Peru. Opening a brewery, and an ice plant, and investing in real estate in Illinois, Ohio, Kentucky and West Virginia, he soon expanded his fortune to an estate which, at the time of Cole's birth, was worth many millions of dollars.

J. O., being deeply involved in his extensive real estate holdings and investments, was totally uninterested in artistic matters. Money, he felt, bore with it a heavy, full-time responsibility leaving no time for men, and certainly men in *his* family, to indulge in such frivolities as music or poetry. The arts were a fitting 'accomplishment' only for the women of the household, and even then never as professionals. No, Cole would be a lawyer and would learn to handle the large fortune that would one day be his.

While J. O. was imperious enough to predetermine the careers of his son[2] and grandson, he was tender and indulgent with the females of the family. He is reputed to have sat for hours at the bedside of his ailing wife, Rachel, gazing at what he called 'her flawless face'. He even considered Kate quite beautiful, although her photographs attest that she was indeed plain. He continued his daughter's handsome allowance partly because 'he loved to spoil his women', but mostly because his druggist son-in-law could not keep her in the style to which her father had accustomed her. Of course, that allowed him to feel he had the right to voice the opinion that he considered the intense musical training Cole was receiving a waste of time, money and energy. He had disapproved strenuously of his only daughter's marriage and took every opportunity to denigrate Samuel Porter. Kate, depending all her life on her father's largesse, also eventually came to hold her father's emasculating opinion of her husband.[3]

Thus it was that in 1901, when Cole was ten and wrote 'The Song of the Birds', he dedicated it to his mother, his only champion. In his maturity he was

[2] Because of J. O.'s deep belief in his daughter Kate's ambition and intelligence, Louis Cole (1865-1903) was more or less shunted aside. Louis's son, Jules Omar, and then his grandson James Omar were eventually to inherit half of the sizeable and flourishing Cole Porter estate whose songs, still under world copyright, bring in considerable sums annually.
[3] The gulf had widened into a chasm by 1910 when the Porters moved into the large house called 'Westleigh' (a gift from J. O.). Kate chose a large open room on the second floor which overlooked the rolling fields for her bedroom. She reserved an equally splendid one on the other side of the house for young Cole's visits. Samuel Porter slept in a small dingy one in the rear.

to refer to this first opus as 'my noxious operetta'. Actually the piece has nothing to do with operetta but is a rather extended wordless example of childish programme music whose titles often seem to have little connection with the music they represent. But still he deserves high marks for what he was able to put down on scoring paper with obviously painstaking care. Taken in toto, 'The Song of the Birds' creates a story that paints a revealing musical and psychological portrait of an imaginative, though not wildly talented, ten-year-old.

The piece is in F major and its six sections are:

1. **'Mother's Cooing'**, a chorale using simple I, IV and V harmonies.[4]
2. **'The Young Ones Learning to Sing'**, which uses the tritone,[5] Alberti bass[6], a high register and indeed sounds rather birdlike.
3. **'One Bird Falls From the Nest'**, a rather sad, Victorian-sounding melody constructed of two bar phrases.
4. **'The Cuckoo Tells the Mother Where the Bird Is'**, changes the key to C minor. Although the obvious cuckoo (G-D) sound is prevalent this section sounds like an intrusion.
5. **'The Bird is Found'**, would seem to call for a joyous climax, but again (although written in 6/8) we are given a saccharine melody, this time a waltz.
6. **'They Fly Away'** is a rather bombastic finale replete with tremolos[7] and a long V, I cadence.[8]

Cole's next extant work, his first published composition, was to be written eighteen months later. 'The Bobolink Waltz', again in the key of F is another 'bird' piano piece.

For a hundred dollars, doting and encouraging Kate Porter had a hundred copies of the composition copyrighted and published by a vanity press in Chicago. She proudly distributed them to friends and relatives. With its oom-pah-pah bass and boring scalelike melody, it is no improvement over 'The Song of the Birds', shows very little talent, even for an eleven-year-old, and bears no resemblance to the kind of music Cole was to write only a few years in the future. One could dismiss it as totally unimportant had it not the distinction of being Cole Porter's first professionally printed work. Its publication also points out Kate Cole's strong belief in her son's talent and is another example of the proud – some would say suffocating – nurturing he received from his mother.

---

[4] It is obvious from this manuscript that this first important composition was recopied (perhaps several times) by young Cole. And by examination one can see the precision and care, already part of his personality, that would later become a hallmark of every Porter manuscript. In typical and endearing ten-year-old fashion, rather than re-do the 114-measure manuscript to insert bar six that was inadvertently omitted, he inserted a carat between bars five and seven. Near the top of the page he drew staff lines with a pointing arrow and printed the legend 'measure left out at mark (V)'.

[5] See Musical Terms Appendix.   [7] See Musical Terms Appendix.
[6] See Musical Terms Appendix.   [8] See Musical Terms Appendix.

By 1905, when Cole was fourteen and had completed the eighth grade in Peru Grammar School, Kate had decided he would be sent to a fine Eastern prep school where he would get a classical education and mingle with wealthy boys possibly from the Eastern social register. J. O. had other ideas; he felt his grandson was too weak and 'sissified', and wanted Cole to be sent to a military academy to toughen him up. But Kate would not consider such a proposal. J. O. then suggested a business school where he would learn to manage the family interests, or even that he be taken out of school to learn new ways of farming the thousands of acres his grandfather owned.[9] Again he was overruled, and Worcester Academy in Massachusetts – an obvious springboard to matriculation in an Ivy League college – was chosen.

This bitter argument was not without its ramifications with Cole caught in the middle. The decision in favour of Worcester was to drive a wedge so deep between his mother and grandfather that they did not speak to each other for two years. And yet it was to be Cole's salvation. Once he left Peru for the East, except for brief visits at holiday times, he was never to return to the nest again.

Cole quickly entered into the spirit of life at Worcester and relished being on his own. So rarely did he mention his family and life in Peru that most of his classmates in the Academy thought he was an orphan. Small for his age, witty and with a quick and endearing smile, he was befriended by students and faculty alike.

Cole's records at Worcester Academy have listed his birth date erroneously as 1893 which would have made him twelve that year, the youngest in the class. Actually he was fourteen, the deception having been foisted many years before by Kate in the attempt to make her son seem a prodigy. The mix-up happened when Cole was six and Kate became interested in spiritualism in an attempt to divine her son's future. She was told by the local seer that fame would be his if his initials spelled out any common word, whereupon Kate, as the daughter of the most powerful man in Peru, marched down to the town's Hall of Records, cowed the clerk into giving her access to her son's birth certificate, and added the middle name of Albert (after his maternal great-grandfather), thereby spelling out the common word CAP.[10] While she was there she changed his birthdate as well, probably realizing that, since he had already begun playing the piano and was small for his age, a four-year-old performing even an easy piece in the local recital might be accepted as a *wunderkind* whereas a six-year-old beginner was merely that, a beginner.

[9] One can understand, if not condone, J. O.'s concern for the management of the fortune he had built up. His only son Louis had died unexpectedly during a hernia operation that year at the age of thirty-eight.
[10] Madeline P. Smith, Porter's secretary for the last seventeen years of his life, remembered: 'He carried a very small flat silver box containing saccharin. It had been given him by his mother and engraved C. A. P. on the cover. But he so disliked his middle name, Albert, that he had long since discarded it [the name], and had had the "A" erased.'

Kate could not have chosen a more suitable prep school than Worcester for the artistic, rich, malleable and slightly snobbish Cole. In his freshman year, 1905, Worcester Academy catered to a smallish and select student body of 240 boys and maintained a large ratio of teachers to students: 21 professors. The headmaster was Harvard-trained Daniel Webster Abercrombie whose professed aim was to convert his youthful charges into young gentlemen. Here at Worcester he followed the curricula of the best British schools. The school required at least three years' study and proficiency in English, mathematics, Greek, Latin, French, history and science.

Additionally, Dr. Abercrombie, who headed Worcester's Greek department, tried to imbue his young students with a love of beauty. Cole often repeated a favourite phrase of his mentor's, 'there is always enough money in the world – never enough beauty.'

The headmaster's influence on the emergent Cole cannot be over-emphasized for Dr. Abercrombie was known to mesmerize his classes with the recounting of the ancient Greek myths and to illuminate the rhythms and poetry of the great classical writers with a rare narrative gift. The mature Cole was often to credit Dr. Abercrombie with making him realize the match between the rhythm of words in a good song and the beat of the music. Cole's later mastery of setting words to music is a testament to how well he learned that lesson.

Of Dr. Abercrombie's snobbery, too, there is little doubt. His words could be mistaken for a mature Cole Porter lyric. It was he who coined 'democracy is not a levelling down, but a levelling up,' and 'a gentleman never eats. He breakfasts, he lunches, he dines, but he *never* eats.'

If Dr. Abercrombie charmed Cole, so did the reverse apply. Cole took copious notes in Abercrombie's class – and this was not mere apple polishing, for Cole had a real love for and was an excellent student not only of Greek but of all languages.

In the course of Worcester's freshman year all students are invited to tea at the Headmaster's house, and once Cole had been a guest there he worked his considerable charm on Mrs. Abercrombie as well. Seated at the piano and performing salon pieces by MacDowell and Nevin, his musical accomplishments were even more appreciated here at the Academy than they had been in Indiana. Always more comfortable with adults than he was with his peers, he was soon a regular.

Since Kate had insisted that, in order to keep up with his (and her) musical aspirations, he have a piano in his room it was there that Cole entertained his classmates. Not good at any sport, this, he found, was the best way to ingratiate himself with boys of his age. The kind of songs he played here were quite different from those he performed in staid faculty parlours.

Although the copies have been lost some of his classmates remembered the risqué 'Bearded Lady', the smutty 'Tattooed Gentleman' and 'Fi-Fi-Fifi', so full of the innuendoes that would become his trademark. Here then, in Worcester, Massachusetts, is where the first of the suggestive songs for which Cole Porter would become famous were born.

Summers in those Academy years were spent at Camp Wynchmere, a nautical camp off the coast of Portland, Maine. Perhaps because of the rift between his mother and grandfather, or because of the dullness of life in a hick town like Peru, or, as some have suggested, a boyhood crush on Donald Baxter MacMillan who coached the Worcester Academy athletic teams and ran the camp, Cole went directly from school to camp and back to school.

Even at camp, though, he was a loner and MacMillan was disappointed that he was unable to 'toughen him up'. Of Cole's two summers at Wynchmere, MacMillan was to recall that 'he slept in a tent with some other boys, but during the day he'd come to my cottage. I had an old piano there. He'd have stayed at that all the time if we'd let him. Swimming and boating – that was just an interruption. The time there didn't toughen him up a whit. Everything was music with Cole. All the big athletes liked him ... even if he couldn't play ball, he could play the piano. Truth is ... he was a little soft. Never thought he'd amount to much.'

Perhaps MacMillan was only thinking of athletic prowess in his assessment of Cole, but by the time he was a senior at Worcester Cole was in demand to perform for faculty and student groups. From a loner Cole had blossomed into a leader in many activities. He starred in the class play, was a member of the Mandolin Club, pianist for the Glee Club, editor of the school paper, alternate in the Inter-City Debate and had won the $25 Dexter Speaking Award for his recitation of Wordsworth's poetry. Although he was a good student, Cole was much too involved in these activities to be bothered preparing for his college entrance examinations, and so he failed the preliminary test for Yale. He wanted to stay in New Haven and take a crammer's course but, the rift between father and daughter having been repaired, J. O. called him home.

That summer he did very little studying but spent most of his time playing the piano on the *Peerless*, the excursion boat that toured nearby Lake Maxinkuckee. Many of the tourists he entertained with drinking songs, Gilbert and Sullivan and bar-room ballads never forgot him. Most thought he was a professional entertainer hired by the steam-ship line. Unfortunately, for the next decade of his life, Cole was too torn between dilettantism – the reluctance to take money for his work – and the desire to feel professional, to be paid. This was to cause him much anxiety. Perhaps if he had truly needed a job he might have turned professional, as did Gershwin, Kern, Berlin and

Coward, and found his true songwriting niche and the acceptance of his peers he had sought so desperately many years earlier.

When he returned to Worcester for his senior year, although he did not slacken the pace of his non-academic activities, he managed somehow to make excellent grades and to pass his second and last chance examination for Yale. Emulating Dr. Abercrombie and combining his recent victory in debating with his love of oratory he was chosen valedictorian of his class, whereupon he wired his mother who duly saw to it that an announcement was put into the *Peru Republican*, emphasizing his youthfulness.[11]

By this time, J. O. mollified and justifiably proud of Cole's record at Worcester, in one of his rare expansive moods offered his grandson any present he wished. Cole had always dreamed of a trip abroad but thought this might be beyond the reach of what J. O. had in mind. The Academy was organizing a trip through the French Alps, followed by a tour of Switzerland and Germany, but Cole hoped for more than that. He had been drawn to Paris since he was a child, when his mother had hired a French seamstress to be his first piano teacher. He admired the sound of the language, the supposed sexuality and sophistication of the people. Now he might have an opportunity to stay in the city of his dreams with a French family (ostensibly to master the language) before he entered Yale. He telegraphed Kate to intercede for him.

'THE NEWS [about the valedictory] WE ALL REJOICE IN,' she wired back, 'THIS FIXES THE PARIS TRIP.'

In Paris he stayed with a bourgeois family named Delarue at 29 rue Boissonade, who added to their income by taking in exchange students, and during those six weeks Cole did indeed master the language.

The journey and the experience of living abroad bolstered his desire for total independence. But, more than that, it whetted his appetite for even more travel. If Worcester had represented his first solo flight away from the nest, this uncovering of places unknown to him was to become a deep passion and he indulged in it, alone or with a retinue, until he became a recluse, towards the end of his life. From his teens, there was hardly a year when he did not travel or a part of the globe which he did not visit, take notes on and chronicle in lyrics and song.

In an age before travel became popular or the general public knew much of foreign lands, Cole Porter's songs were to introduce his audiences to the rhythms, language and customs that he uncovered in these exotic parts of the world.

---

[11] Cole was well aware of his mother's subterfuge regarding his birth certificate. One might assume he relished joining Yale at the precocious age of sixteen rather than the normal eighteen. Entering the Schola Cantorum in Paris several years later, he gave his birth-date as 1895, making him two years younger still. Late in his life he was always evasive when asked when he had been born, wriggling out of the problem with 'I've lied about my age so often, I don't know *when* I was born.'

NOEL
1899-1917

WHILE HE WAS IN PARIS, Cole kept a diary and took voluminous notes about the buildings and paintings he saw. But, most importantly of all, the eighteen-year-old revelled in his freedom.

This was not the case with young Noel Coward. He loved being surrounded by his family: his aunts and uncles, grandparents, father and especially his mother. Fears of losing her plagued his nights, and with his dramatic nature he was later to recall these obsessions:

> The dramatic scenes I visualised were terrifying; first the fatal telegram arriving at the house, my aunt and uncle calling me into the drawing-room on the first floor to break the news, then a tear-sodden journey in the train, and Auntie Vida meeting me at Fratton Junction, very small and morose, in black. Then, as a fitting climax, I imagined the front bedroom enshrouded in funereal twilight with blinds down and Mother lying still and dead under a sheet like a waxwork.

Noel and his mother always possessed an amazing empathy. His father, Arthur Sabin Coward, was musical, possessed a light tenor voice, and, realizing his son's early interest in the stage, helped to build scenery for his toy theatres. But it was his mother who encouraged him and coached him in his singing when he was still a very small boy.

She began taking him from the age of five to the theatre, mostly to musicals. In those days sixpence bought a booklet of all the songs in the show, and since Noel had a tremendous musical memory, absolute pitch, a sweet voice, and was enchanted by what he saw, with the aid of the lyric booklet he was able to make his way straight through the score of the shows when they returned home.

Enthralled with the theatre, amassing and collecting sheaves of programmes, there is no doubt Violet had a strongly artistic nature. It passed to her, no doubt, from her father, Henry Gordon Veitch, who although he was a commissioned captain in Queen Victoria's navy, and not particularly musical, was an extremely accomplished and sensitive painter of landscapes. She, in turn, transmitted this talent on to her son, for by middle age Noel had become an extremely capable amateur painter.

Violet Veitch never knew her father, for he took sick and died in Madeira a few months before she was born. It was then that her mother, her sister Vida, and retarded sister Borby all moved to Teddington, a sleepy, middle-class village in Middlesex. There, in 1890, as a member of the St Alban's church choir, she met Arthur Coward who had a good job as a clerk in the distinguished music publishing firm of Metzler. All Arthur's family were stalwarts of the St. Alban's choir. Not only did the ten Coward children form the basis of this singing group, but his brother James played the organ; his sister Hilda, who sang most of the solos, was later to gain the soubriquet of 'the Twickenham Nightingale'.

Violet and Arthur's romance blossomed through the choir rehearsals, performances and amateur theatricals, mostly Gilbert and Sullivan, in which they were involved. Appropriately enough, they were married in the church where they had met, on October 8, 1890.

A year after their marriage, a son Russell Arthur Blackmore Coward, was born, but the child who looks rather frail and angelic in his one remaining misty photograph died at the age of six. During those six years fortune was to play harshly with Arthur, for he lost his job at Metzler. Then he was demoted to eke out a meagre existence as an itinerant piano salesman for a newly-formed company called Paynes. English pianos were a quality item then and Paynes, trying to increase its territorial empire, often sent Arthur away on extended selling trips, sometimes as far as Italy.

Violet Coward did not conceive another child until April 1899, and there in Teddington, on December 16, 1899, a fortnight before the advent of the twentieth century, Noel Pierce Coward was born: Noel because of the holiday season; Pierce, after Jessie Pierce, his godmother and an upstanding member of the church.

Noel was, as previously noted, healthy, precocious and very self-sufficient, but Violet – understandably, since she had lost her first-born – would not let him out of her sight. If they went to the theatre, she held his hand tightly; for such an independent child this confinement was sheer torture. His mother was to relent somewhat when in 1905 they moved to a small house in Surrey and his brother Eric was born. Now, with another youngster at home, she let go the reins a bit and, when Noel was six, took him to Miss Willington's academy where at the end of term he would have his first taste of life behind the footlights.

Dressed in a white sailor suit, accompanying himself on the piano, and singing 'Coo' from *The Country Girl*, he was greeted with thunderous approval. Applause was the 'sweetest music' to the young Noel Coward. It became his reason for preferring secular performances among strangers to those in the church where he could wallow in the approval of loving aunts and uncles. That night the audience clapped so vociferously he was obliged (with tremendous joy) to repeat his number. But, even though young Noel remembered how outstanding that performance was, he was not given a prize, for, as his mother tried to explain, at school the prizes were reserved for those who had made the most progress throughout the year, not for sheer excellence of singing. Though

Coward, aged five

he was disappointed, the tearful child may have realized at that early age the
difference between rewards for plodding academic study and the demands of
artistic life, for he was soon to choose the latter. Certainly Coward was a
perfectionist throughout his theatrical life – and gave no high marks for mere
'improvement' to anyone he ever worked with.[1]

[1] From his earliest days Coward would not allow a single syllable in a playscript or a note of his songs to be changed. This
author's favourite story of the playwright-director's refusal to have the rhythm of his speech altered one iota occurred when
he was directing Edith Evans in a revival of *Hay Fever*. Dame Edith, as she looked out of the stage window, persisted in
saying, "On a very clear day you can see Marlow", instead of, "On a clear day you can see Marlow." After a few weeks of
patient correction, Coward eventually stopped the scene and told her, 'Edith, the line is "On a clear day you can see
Marlow." On a *very* clear day you can see Marlow and Beaumont and Fletcher.'

By the time Noel was nine he was singing regularly and happily in church and at garden parties run by one of his mother's sisters, where there would be stalls, amusements, a band and – what he missed in church – applause. There, as part of the programme he could sing three or four solos as well as dance. 'It must have been surprising,' he wrote, 'and I should think nauseating, to see a little boy of nine in a white sailor suit flitting about a small wooden stage, employing with instinctive accuracy the gestures and tricks of a professional soubrette, but they seemed to love it and encored me vociferously ... I do not mean that I wasn't good ... I was certainly good. My assurance was nothing short of petrifying.'

As the above example displays, Coward's voluminous writings and autobiographies, indicating his seemingly total recall, are a good source of information on his early life. Luckily they are augmented by the notes his mother kept, for like Kate Cole Violet Coward never threw away a scrap of her son's early work and carefully retained even the most childish letter Noel wrote her. Additionally, she recorded all her recollections in a diary, so we know that at even this early age, when the question of Noel's going on the stage came up, he was so eager, there seemed no reason to wait. Since his singing was accomplished, but his dancing weak, it was soon decided he would be sent to a dancing academy run by Janet Thomas. Of course the youngster enjoyed the private lessons with Miss Thomas and later ones with Miss Thomas's assistant Alice Hall who put him through all the ballet steps including en pointe (for which he wore block-toe shoes).

Even before he had finished his dancing course, his mother read an interview, what today's show business calls 'a plant', in the *Daily Mirror* concerning an all-children fairy play, *The Goldfish*. Miss Lila Field, who was organizing a children's theatre to present her own plays, mentioned that 'to get bright children between ten and fourteen has been [a] far from easy task.' Miss Field continued: 'I have got sufficient girls at last but am still badly in need of five or six boys.' Violet Coward at once wrote for an appointment.

Two weeks later, a well-scrubbed Noel Coward sang 'Liza Ann' for Miss Field and since there was no piano in the studio did the dance he had practised daily while his mother la-la'ed the tune. Miss Field said he would do admirably for the part of Prince Mussel, and would engage him at a fee of a guinea and a half a week. 'Then', as Noel recounts, 'mother became sadly red and said she was afraid we couldn't afford to pay that. Miss Field laughed and said the guinea and a half a week was what I should receive.'

Prince Mussel, court jester to King Starfish, was obviously the plum role. He sang an impassioned number climaxing in a high B flat exposing his unrequited love for the Queen, and Noel adored this third act solo because, as he gloated, 'I was invariably encored. Sometimes twice.'

There is little doubt Lila Field knew talent when she saw it for three other of her 'Wonder Children' had successful careers: Ninette de Valois, who was to go on to fame with the Royal Ballet, Micheál Mac Liammóir with the Abbey Theatre, and June Tripp, later the star of Twenties musicals. But Miss Field, always on her uppers, did not prove to be as forthcoming in the accounts department as she promised, and Noel was only paid one week's salary for several weeks of performances.

When *The Goldfish* finally closed Noel was fortunate enought to be given a small part, actually a one-liner in Sir Charles Hawtrey's company's production of *The Great Name*. Noel, at the age of eleven, had his first exposure to an actor with true talent and was always in the wings, often underfoot, once chattering so much that he made Hawtrey miss an entrance. Eager for an association with any star, he collected seventeen signatures from his idol before the actor, assuming his apprentice was selling the autographs, refused to sign any more. But Noel's ardour was not wasted on Hawtrey and, by the time *The Great Name* closed, the actor had coached him to deliver the most amusing Cockney lines in his next production, *Where The Rainbow Ends.*

Noel appeared three times in what was to become a Christmas perennial before growing out of his roles and moving on to play Slightly in Charles Frohman's production of *Peter Pan*. But for almost a decade he was in and out of Hawtrey's company. The mature Coward attributed his proficiency in the art of playing light comedy, notably the techniques of voice placement, effective use of the hands, natural laughter, and especially his timing – so admired in his later cabaret appearances – to Hawtrey's training. Although the Coward family may have felt acting was not a suitable profession for so young a boy, there is little doubt that Noel adored those years. In his autobiography he was to recall:

> In between the matinee and evening performances the stage had an even greater allure for me with only a few working lights left on here and there, it appeared vaster and more mysterious, like an empty echoing cathedral smelling faintly of dust. Sometimes the safety curtain was not lowered, and I used to stand down on the edge of the footlights singing shrilly into the shadowy auditorium. I also danced in silence. Occasionally a cleaner appeared with a broom and pail, or a stage hand walked across the stage, but they never paid any attention me. An empty theatre is romantic, every actor knows the feeling of it: complete silence emphasised rather than broken by the dim traffic noises outside ... As a rule there are a few exit lights left burning, casting blue shadows across the rows of empty seats. It seems incredible that within an hour or two this stillness will awake to garish red-and-gilt splendour, and be shattered by the sibilance of hundreds of voices, and the exciting discords and trills of the orchestra tuning up.

His mother alone understood her son's need and by the time he was twelve considered him a professional, allowing him to take two days off from school to make the rounds of the agencies. But even she was not without guilt and was constantly plagued by lecturing in-laws for allowing Noel to sacrifice his academic training and enter so precarious a profession as acting.

Violet Coward's resolve was strengthened when she received the approbation of the thought-reader Anna Eva Fay, then appearing at the Coliseum. Fay's act consisted of answering questions members of her audience submitted on slips of paper handed to the theatre ushers. Violet had been talked into attending the performance by a friend whose husband, an electrical engineer, had been robbed of a valuable roll of copper wire. The friend inquired about the wire's whereabouts but Miss Fay ignored the prosaic and finite question. Yet, when she was handed one that read, 'Do you advise me to keep my son, Noel Coward, on the stage? Violet Coward,' the seeress seemingly went into a trance and shouted from the platform, 'Mrs. Coward, Mrs. Coward, you ask about your son. Keep him where he is! He has great talent and will have a wonderful career!'

Whether the act was a hoax or not, it was enough for Violet Coward to allow thirteen-year-old Noel to leave home and tour with Basil Dean's production of *Hannele*.

Although he never wrote about it, the pubescent Coward seems to have acquired part of his sexual suavity from two girls in his acting troupes. In the cast the first year he appeared in *Where the Rainbow Ends* was Esmé Wynne, described by Coward as a 'podgy brown-haired little girl with a bleating voice'. Esmé was to become his bosom companion, playwriting and songwriting collaborator for the next ten years, and her son, Jon Wynne-Tyson, implies that his mother's relationship with Coward went beyond the platonic.

The other young actress whose career, affection and relationship were to involve Noel more deeply throughout his life was Gertrude Lawrence, two years older and far more worldly. When they met on a train Noel writes, 'She gave me an orange and told me a few mildly dirty stories, and I loved her from then onwards.' Cole Lesley, Coward's secretary-biographer, says Noel once confessed that during this engagement of *Hannele* 'Gertie took him to the bedroom and demonstrated, more practically, the facts of life.'

By the time he turned fourteen, and after the *Peter Pan* tour, Noel seems to have explored other avenues. He became attached, first to a man with whom he camped out in the woods, and later more lastingly to a thirty-year-old painter, Philip Streatfield, who had a studio in Chelsea.

In her notes on Noel's early years, Violet Coward does not mention the Streatfield relationship or the fortnight motor jaunt this odd couple took ostensibly to look for a house they would share, but she was careful to keep the sensitive portrait Philip drew of her son along with the letters he sent her from Polperro. During this time and certainly under Philip's influence Noel began

Philip Streatfield's drawing
of Coward, aged fourteen

to develop a glib stream of consciousness manner in his writing. Fortunately he quickly grew out of the precious, almost 'flapper' style apparent in the following letter to 'mummysnooks':

I *am* enjoying myself so much it really is perfectly Heavenly here. Donald Bain has got the most ripping pair of field-glasses that ever happened in this wide universe and the next! We are right opposite the 'Eddinstone Lighthouse' and it looks so tall and white standing straight up in the sun. We havent had such very lovely weather its generally been a leetle beet to cold a wind to be really nice but we bathe from a sandy cove about a mile along the cliffs and then lie in the sun and dry. I am now the colour of a boiled lobster with which these shores abound (not to say sharks! O-o-ee-r-r Auntie!). This house is perfectly ripping so beautifully furnished and its about 300 feet above the sea and I climb right down every morning to catch fish for my aquarium which is a clear pool in the rocks. Philip has bought me a net with which to catch le denizens de la deep (Bow-wow!) . . . I received le sweater et le lettre all right and it fits me Tres Chic!!! (More bow-wows!) I haven't been very homesick but I have been a little (bless you) I shall have to stopppp now as I am going to wallow in Bacon and eggs so goodbye and love to Daddy and Eric and Florrie and Tinker and any old thing you like to mench! Hope you are well as

leaves me at pres. Your everevereverevereverever loving Noel P.S. I will write every
Saturday.

Unfortunately this idyllic summer was to be violently disrupted when, on
August 4, war with Germany was declared. Philip sent Noel home at once,
while he prepared to be called up for military service. Throughout the conflict,
however, Philip's influence on his young charge was not to be abandoned. He
wrote to his friend, Mrs. Astley-Cooper, who responded by inviting the
teenager to spend the summer of 1915 with her at her country estate, Hambleton Hall.

    Noel remembered all he learned that summer: hunting, from Captain
Astley-Cooper; how a proper country house was organized and run, from
the Astley-Coopers' butler, Fred; wit and drawing-room banter, from
Mrs. Astley-Cooper herself. This was to be his first taste of luxurious living:
servants to light the fire in his bedroom, deep baths encased in shiny brown
wood, and having his evening clothes laid out for him. When guests came over
for dinner, the excitement multiplied. 'A flurry of wheels in the drive
announced them,' he enthused, 'and the murmur of different voices echoed up
from the hall as I grandly descended the polished oak staircase, very careful
not to slip in my new polished patent-leather shoes.' Noel's masterful sense of
salon dialogue certainly originated in Hambleton Hall.[2]

    For most of that year Noel would have difficulty finding work, first
because he had reached the awkward stage, too old to play boys, yet not
mature enough for men's roles, and secondly because London theatre-going
was now greatly curtailed for, in the words of Mrs. Coward, 'the war had
started and nobody felt gay any more.' At last before Christmas 1915, he was
taken on for yet another production of *Where The Rainbow Ends*, this time,
since he had outgrown the part of the Pageboy, in the role of the Slacker – half
man, half dragon. He made the most of his costume, complete with tail,
applying green sequins to his eyelids, yellow and blue stains on his cheeks, and
emitting a hysterical laugh on his exit that never failed to elicit a sustained
round of applause.

    Esmé Wynne was also in this company and when the *Rainbow* engage-
ment concluded they were both engaged to star in another revival, a touring
one of *Charley's Aunt*. Esmé played Amy to Noel's Charley; and, since the
production was done on the cheap, Noel, Esmé and another of the company, a
girl named Norah Howard, frequently shared rooms together. 'Podj', as Esmé
called Noel, and 'Stoj', his retaliatory name for her, were, as Noel wrote,
'inseparable. We stole chocolates from sweet-shops and cakes of soap from

---

[2] Coward was to remain friendly with and frequently visit Mrs. Astley-Cooper for another decade. He was forever grateful
to her for introducing him in 1921 to Gladys Calthrop, the brilliant set and costume designer who would be involved in so
many of his shows. And he never forgot Philip Streatfield who died in 1916 of an unknown disease.

chemists; we extracted, with the aid of bent hair-pins and latchkeys, packets of "Snake Charmer" cigarettes from slot machines and smoked them publicly with outward flamboyance and inward nausea. We explored the West End, the East End, the suburbs and near country with minute thoroughness. We even had baths together for the simple reason that we didn't wish to waste a moment's companionship and because it seemed affected to stop short in the middle of some vital discussion for such a paltry reason as conventional modesty.' When they were not onstage together, he could be found pounding on the piano in whatever boarding house they occupied, while she diligently rattled away at her typewriter.

Early in their relationship they had amused themselves by exchanging clothes, and Esmé was later to recall 'the sight of Noel dashing across Clapham High Road after a large straw hat which the wind had blown from his head, his short dark hair protruding ridiculously from the hole in his girl's wig, his large patent-leather shoes flapping wildly below the knee-length skirts of my blue gingham dress.'[3]

Once Noel realized there was something unwholesome about serious transvestism the thought of dressing in women's clothes which he was forced to do at every performance of *Charley's Aunt* became repellent. 'In my opinion,' he was to say, 'of all the parts ... "Charley" is the worst.' Because 'Charley' feeds everybody else their lines he gets none of the laughs – and much less applause (the paramount ingredient in any performance). Noel had grown into a tall juvenile and was no longer amused by stage drag, although he knew it was a comic business, with a tradition descended from Shakespeare.

Esmé and Noel were both grateful for the opportunity touring gave them to be together, to read quantities of romantic poetry to each other and to collaborate on songs.

In what he called his 'Vegetable Verse', the earliest lines show a remarkable sense of humour, although Esmé's contributions were to be far less frivolous. She was soon to take over the language department of their collaboration – relegating Noel to the role of composer alone. The couplets, 'Verse to an Onion' and 'Love Ditty to a Turnip'[4] below are much more to be

[3] Cross dressing was an early Coward affectation and one that was considered a harmless diversion by Noel's mother, his aunt and Esmé. A letter written by seven-year-old Noel to his mother from his Aunt Laura's house in Cornwall, where apparently Noel's first experience occurred, includes the following: 'I had some little boys over to tea yesterday afternoon, and I dressed up in a short dress and danced to them and sung to them and we all went round the lake ...'

Aunt Laura's children, Walter and Connie Bulteel, encouraged this 'harmless' sport, for some years later they gave a party where, according to Cole Lesley, 'the idea had been that Noel should deceive the other guests that evening for as long as he could; Noel was tall and with whatever make-up there was in those days he appeared older and succeeded so well that one young man became besotted and over ardent during a walk in the garden.' After the young man appeared the next morning Walter and Connie lied and told him that their friend had already left but promised to forward his note to 'her'. The letter asked for a photograph and was signed, 'With best love, yours ever.' Connie and Walter naively commented to Leslie that they 'thought Noel had been wonderful in carrying the joke right through to the end, and it was no surprise to them that he later became such a brilliant actor.'

[4] This is surely a lighthearted take-off of Esmé's maudlin love songs. No musical settings of any of these verses has ever been found.

admired than their heavy-handed over-romantic early songs, part of a series called 'Songs of the Sea'.

In A Voice Of Soft Staccato
We Will Speak Of The Tomato

The Sinful AspaRAGus
To Iniquity Will Drag Us

I had a little Onion
Its smell was rather strong
But it couldn't help its odour,
'Twas its nature that was wrong
It was coarse and avaricious
Peculiarly pernicious
And disgustingly suspicious –
Pas Bon.

Oh Turnip turn
Those lovely eyes once more
To me
And let true love be ours
Eternally
Others I have loved before
But none
As much as thou, Thou art
My Moon, my Sun
My Star of Stars from out
The Heavens above
Come Turnip Mine
And Let us yield ... to Love

The Esmé-Noel duo was soon to turn into a trio when John Eakins, a handsome youthful actor as stage-struck and romantic as his friends, joined their troupe. When John later got a part in *The Best of Luck* in the West End, that only strengthened the bond between himself and Noel. They would dress alike, go to the theatre together, and always end up sipping tea and people-watching at the palm court of the Royal Hotel. This relationship was to come to an abrupt end with John Eakins's sudden death from spinal meningitis at the age of eighteen, in 1917. Noel wrote that their friendship was one of 'unalloyed

Coward (left) with Esmé Wynne and John Eakins, 1915

happiness' and the young actor's demise coming so soon after Philip Streat-field's was to make Coward say 'never again' to memories of someone he had loved.

Yet, throughout Coward's life, loss could not dampen his spirits or his overpowering ambition for very long, and it was around this time that Noel composed both music and lyrics for his first fully integrated song – 'Forbidden Fruit'.[5] In his introduction to *The Noel Coward Songbook*, Coward states that 'the worldly cynicism of which I have so often been accused in later years is already seen to be rearing its ugly head.' Then he goes on to discuss the lyrics for the song which, incidentally, was not published until thirty-eight years later. To this writer, its musical rhythms, phrase lengths and especially its melodic sophistication are all harbingers of a more mature Coward, and would suggest that, although the lyric may have been written when he was sixteen, the music must have come afterwards. In any case and, since the printed copy lacks a copyright date, on the assumption that 'Forbidden Fruit' was written by anyone remotely near his teens, makes it an even more amazing work.

Heartened by this success, early the next year Noel took his songs around to various publishers and soon received his first contract to write lyrics for the publishing firm of Herman Darewski. Although he filled several notebooks with his work over the next three years, and was paid £50 the first year, £75 the second and £100 for the final year of the contract, the young lyricist was sadly disappointed that none of his efforts was set to music, nor were they ever published.

With a contract as a lyricist and as an accepted fledgling member of London's acting community, Noel, however, was to feel no remorse at the age of seventeen, when his wealthy contemporaries were going up to Oxford or Cambridge. Noel was exactly where he wanted to be, and eventually was to trumpet his feelings about *not* going to school, in a verse called 'The Boy Actor'.

> I can remember. I can remember.
> The months of November and December,
> Although climatically cold and damp,
> Meant more to me than Aladdin's lamp.
> I see myself, having got a job,
> Walking on wings along the Strand,
> Uncertain whether to laugh or sob
> And clutching tightly my mother's hand,
> I never cared who scored the goal
> Or which side won the silver cup,
> I never learned to bat or bowl
> But I heard the curtain going up.

[5] See Musical Analysis Appendix

Porter, aged eighteen,
1909

COLE
1909-1917

BEFORE HE MOVED to New Haven to begin his freshman year at Yale, Kate took Cole on a shopping spree in Peru and Indianapolis. They bought a large and varied wardrobe which they felt would be suitable for an elegant Ivy League college. What they actually came out with was a garish assortment of checked suits, pink and yellow shirts and salmon ties. Two weeks later Cole moved into Garland's Rooming House at 242 York Street, bringing with him an enormous amount of luggage and a battered upright piano.

With his hair parted gigolo-fashion down the middle and wearing his outlandish clothes, Cole hardly fitted the varsity-sweater-by-day and blue-serge-by-night look of a Yale man. Gerald Murphy, later to become a member of the bohemian expatriate Parisian set and Cole's collaborator on his only ballet, expressed the feelings of most of his classmates when he remembered that 'Cole looked just like a westerner all dressed up for the East.' But soon, in spite of his jazzy outfit and small town background, because of the amusing songs he would sing for any who would listen, Cole came to be accepted, even welcomed, by the established student leaders.

The friends he sought out were not the academic types he had chosen at Worcester. Certainly, during his first years, academic grades or even the star athletes did not intrigue him. The young men – and there were many in those days – who fascinated Cole were what he called the 'rich-rich'; those with a long history of having money, rather than those who were self-made 'rich', meaning nouveau. If they were not of the 'old money' group his chums had to have notable standing in 'society'. Most of his friends had both: Vanderbilt Webb, who lived in a Fifth Avenue mansion; Edgar Montillion Woolley who, later, known as Monty Woolley, was to have a successful stage and movie career; Mark Hanna, son of a Cleveland industrialist; Howard Sturges, a member of one of Rhode Island's most distinguished families. They all had grown up surrounded by servants, were accustomed to Baccarat crystal, Tiffany silver, Spode china and driving Isotas or Rolls-Royces. Cole learned of these 'necessities' from them. Whatever innate snobbery he may have possessed before his Yale days was now full-blown and out in the open.

To further ensure his place in this charmed circle, he began to include in his lyrics the names of friends and those whose friendship he sought. This trait was to endear him to café society throughout his career, for what better way had that tight little coterie to be flattered than to be rhymed and sung about?

Now, when Cole wanted to gain membership to the Yale Dramatic Society whose president was Lawrence W. Cornwall, he wrote 'That Zip Cornwall Cooch'. Cornwall had grown a large moustache and as this Charleston-type dance song's lyrics indicate Cole's song is written in unmistakable adulation.

That Zip Cornwall Cooch   Aristocratic slide.
That Zip Cornwall Mooch   Gee, but it's great,
Give it a dash,   Leave it to fate,
Wear a moustache,   Glide along the campus
Everybody's fallin' for it   And you'll never be late
Hear the college callin' for it. When you do that Zip Cornwall Cooch.
Oh, that dramatic glide

Writing tunes with amusing lyrics, performing them with great dash nightly for all the other students who roomed at Garland would seem to have been a full-time occupation. But Cole joined practically every club the university offered. At one time or another during his New Haven days he was a member of the Whiffenpoofs, the Hogans, the Grill Room Grizzlies, the Pundits, the Mince Pie Club, the Wigwam and Wrangler Debating Club, the Corinthian Yacht Club, the Dramatic Association, the University Club, and the Elizabethan Club. Early in his sophomore year, he was handily elected into the most prestigious fraternity, Delta Kappa Epsilon, and the next year into the Scroll and Key, Yale's elite secret society.

His acceptance into all of these organizations coupled with his outstanding record at prep school and his recent European tour seem to have given him a confidence in the worth of his own work that he formerly lacked. Never again, as at Worcester Academy, would any of his songs be lost. From that September 1909, for the rest of his life, Cole was to keep every bit of music and lyric he wrote.[1] As singer-pianist-conductor of the Yale Glee Club he was in a position to get performances of any songs he turned out and, heady with the sound of a group of his peers singing his own music and lyrics, he turned out a great many.

It was here at Yale that the quest for professionality began, and in this freshman year he got Remick, a New York publisher, to buy 'Bridget McGuire', a rather charming waltz whose lyric concerns an Irish scullery maid and her beau.

Irish songs were all the rage at that time but 'Bridget McGuire' was never picked up by any well-known singer and languished in Remick's catalogue. In spite of its Irish blarney, it contains a glimmer of the Porter charm to come when Pat woos Bridget with: 'You're far too delicious to wash and wipe dishes.'

[1] Ten years later, studying counterpoint at the Schola Cantorum in Paris, a bored Cole Porter would doodle on the margins of his pages of non-creative exercises. Even these scraps were filed away.

The assurance he gained with being 'published' spurred Cole to enter Yale's football-song competition. He was to win hands down with 'Bingo Eli Yale', which is still a Yale stalwart today. Throughout his college years he was to follow that with many more campus classics. 'Morey's', 'Hail to Yale', 'Eli' and 'I Want to Be a Yale Boy', standards all, were and are still sung at games and smokers. Certainly Cole's work brought a vital rhythm and spirited language to the previously staid college anthem. 'Bingo, bingo, bingo, that's the lingo' and 'Bull dog, bull dog, bow, wow, wow' are the kind of succinct, cheering phrases he introduced. They caught on very quickly.

'A Football King' spread his fame all over the campus and led to his being chosen to head Yale's football song selection committee. Its original title, 'If I Were Only A Football Man', was perhaps too autobiographical and too full of yearning to be used, and that earlier lyric contained phrases that were a bit too recherché for the undergraduates. From language like 'My talk would be so corpuscular/ Even my verbs would be muscular/ And mine would be such downs/ As to bring home the touchdowns', one gets the idea that Cole would polish a lyric until it gleamed perhaps too blindingly for the situation.

Now Cole wanted even more involvement with some of his idols who were the football heroes, in spite of the fact that he was never very adept at sports. Perhaps because he was only five and a half feet tall and knew how to project his voice, he made a perfect cheerleader.

All these activities left him very little time for his studies, and he almost flunked out of school. Luckily, the university, perhaps realizing they had a student whose work would add lustre to the campus's activities, gave him three hours' academic credit for his extracurricular work, thereby erasing his failing average and permitting him to remain.

Delta Kappa Epsilon was not only the most prestigious fraternity at Yale, but its members were the richest, most social, and certainly the most artistic. DKE had a reputation for presenting coruscating and witty campus shows for their smokers. From his sophomore year when Cole became a 'Deeke', he was to be in charge of all their dramatic and musical presentations and to be the author of many of them.

In 1911 fraternity brother T. Galliard Thomas II wrote the book and Cole music and lyrics for a musical called *Cora*. For this show Cole would produce the first of many songs dealing with love for sale ('The Cocotte', 'Gigolo', 'My Heart Belongs To Daddy', etc.). Here is the irreverent hit song of the score, 'Hello, Miss Chapel Street', a duet for a Yalie and streetwalker:

HE: Hello, Miss Chapel Street,
  You look very sweet tonight.
SHE: Great damn, I'm sweet as sugar jam
  And how is lovey-dovey,
  Little Willie wise boy?

HE: I'm not so well,
  I'm low as hell,
  For I can barely walk about a bit, dear.
  Since we quit, dear
  I'm not feeling very fit.

SHE: Well-a, well-a, who's to blame?
  I waited for an hour in the pouring rain,
HE: But you didn't wait till eight.
SHE: I had a date with a freshman.
HE: What's that you say,
  You had a date with a freshman?
SHE: Yesh, man.
HE: On my word,
  But that's absurd.
SHE: That's enough funny stuff:
  Cut the rough!
HE: When can we have a party for two, dear?
SHE: That's up to you, anytime will do.
HE: Will you meet me tonight alone?
  For I've an awful lot of love
  That's simply hunting for a home.

SHE: Well, I'll be there
  A-waiting on the square.
HE: We'll have a drunken revel.
SHE: Good night, you little devil.
HE: We mustn't raise a riot.
SHE: Then kiss me on the quiet.
  Bring a low-necked hack and a bottle
  of rye,
HE: Oh, won't I!
  Goodbye.

Buttering up Lawrence Cornwall, President of the Yale Dramatic Association, paid off the following spring. Cole, again with book by T. Galliard Thomas, was chosen to do the score for *And The Villain Still Pursued Her*, a witless melodrama whose only distinction is that it introduced Monty Woolley (as the villain). But it whetted Cole's appetite for having more than one performance of a show, for this one, under the aegis of the YDA, not only was seen in New Haven but was shown at the Yale Club in New York as well.

Cora and *And the Villain Still Pursued Her* might be considered preparation for Porter's best and most ambitious work as an undergraduate songwriter – *The Pot of Gold*. This time there was a new librettist – Ahmet Jenks, who had won the Yale Dramatic Association prize for best play by a university member.

Through voluminous letters back and forth that summer he and Cole hammered out the convoluted plot which takes place in front of the unit set of a rundown hotel. Put simply, it concerns the hero's (played by Cole) struggle to win the beautiful daughter of the hotelkeeper. To do this, he must turn round the fortunes of the hotel. (By the final curtain he accomplishes this with a scandal involving his rich uncle, two Russian nihilists and several assorted eccentrics.)

Jenks's letters to Cole during the show's creation are lost, but a few quotes from Cole's reveal with what confidence, seriousness and maturity he attacked the project:

'I wish we could make this play a little masterpiece in its own foolish way. Take it horribly seriously and I will join you. It really is important for after all, it can never happen again.'

Of the quality of his work he wrote: 'The recitatif I have written combines the splendour of Wagner and the decadence of Strauss. As for the title *The Pot of Gold* being trite, I think it is truly wonderful. A title is good only when it means nothing until the fall of the final curtain.'[2] And later, 'You speak of three acts. I beg you – Don't. Three would be interminable.' Requesting his collaborator to provide a schedule which would leave time for him to write an overture, incidental music and an entr'acte, Cole wrote, 'I must have most of this play in black and white by October 1st.' Finally at the end of the summer he wrote, with a prescience worthy of a post-*Oklahoma* integrated songwriter, 'Finish the second act. I can do nothing until you do. You see my only means of making the songs relevant is by writing verses which give the idea of belonging to the person who sings them.'

Cole both starred in and directed the show which was done with great style and much expense. *The Pot of Gold* had such a tremendous success that William Lyon Phelps, Professor of Drama and sometime critic, wrote, 'The Dramatic Club is very fortunate in having one man who is a real genius and who writes words and music of such a high order ...' While another critic, Jack Crawford, being more forthright than Professor Phelps, hoped the students would not attempt to surpass Cole's effort 'lest it lead to more lavish and time consuming productions.'

Although no standards emerged from this musical, from its very overture, a delightful canon at the octave, one feels a surpassing musical and lyrical integrity. There is a soft-shoe, 'Longing For Dear Old Broadway', which compares favourably with the songs of George M. Cohan, two comic numbers whose titles give away their concepts – 'My Salvation Army Queen', and 'She Was a Fair Young Mermaid' – and, perhaps the hit of the show, 'My Houseboat On the Thames', which, while having a hurdy-gurdy tune, has a chorus lyric too delicious to be overlooked.

On my houseboat on the Thames	But when you're bored and feeling
It's a jolly ripping vessel to relax on,	undone
For it's deuced dull and deadly	We can wander up to London,
Anglo-Saxon.	On my houseboat,
We'll have Punch on board, I think,	On my houseboat,
One to read and one to drink.	On my houseboat on the Thames.

Shortly before graduation in spring 1913, Cole produced yet another, his last show as an undergraduate, *The Kaleidoscope*. The concept of this near-revue is the dream of a boy intending to enter college. He dreams of the prom of the past in the first act and of the prom of the future in the second.

Although the *Yale Daily News* termed Cole's production a 'complete success ... the music being superior to that of most Broadway productions', *The Kaleidoscope* is rather tame. Perhaps a few lines from its most interesting song, 'A Member of the Yale Elizabethan Club', while obviously influenced by

[2] By the end of the play the hotel, called The Rainbow, becomes financially successful. (Cole's letter notwithstanding, it seems to this writer that anyone witnessing a play called *The Pot of Gold* which takes place in a hotel called The Rainbow would put two and two together long before the final curtain.)

Gilbert and Sullivan and rather sophomoric, are worth noting in that they presage what was to be a lifelong involvement with the bard and to reach full flower in 'Brush Up Your Shakespeare' from *Kiss Me, Kate*.

'... I delight in being chatty
All the critics sing my praises.
With New Haven's literati.

In illuminated phrases.
On the subject of a brand new binding
As a literary light, I'm blinding.'

And later, in the chorus –

'For I give support
To the latest college sporto,
Tea by the quart
And editions by the quarto.'

With a host of college songs, appearances and tours with the glee club and four complete musicals to his credit, one has to marvel that Cole graduated at all. But even more astounding is that, in spite of his miserable academic record, he was accepted for the coming fall into Harvard Law School. He was unique, of that there is no doubt, for in his graduating class of almost three hundred he was voted the most entertaining, one of the most eccentric, the second most original and came in fifth in a poll of students who had done the most for Yale.

Cole's time at Yale was to be one of great growth and he was to hold on to relationships and friendships born there, attend reunions and correspond with many in his class in the years to come.

Kate did not hesitate to crow to her friends about the first member of the family to attain a degree from a famous Eastern college and to announce

Porter (left) with
T. Larason, putting
together the college show,
Paranoia

that fact in the Peru paper. The article also mentioned that Cole would be entering Harvard in the fall to study law. With the ammunition that as a lawyer he would be following along the path of manager of his estate and supervisor of land development that J. O. had envisaged for his grandson, Kate also prevailed upon her father to repeat his magnanimous gesture of offering Cole a trip to Paris upon his graduation from Worcester. This time her son would also tour the British countryside and meet up with his classmates in London.

Cole Porter's address for the next year was 404 Cragie Hall, Cambridge, Massachusetts, but it was merely the place where his books and piano and he himself could be found from Monday to Friday. His heart however was far from Harvard and after an initial two months with his nose to the grindstone he made his way almost every weekend to the Yale Club in New York. Cole had realized by early winter that he had no gift for the law and that he had a considerable one for songwriting. Encouraged by his being in great demand to organize and write Yale alumni smokers he turned his mind away from contracts, torts and civil procedures to the quest for a musical collaborator.

The one he found was Thomas Larason Riggs, Phi Beta Kappa at Yale and now taking graduate courses in English literature at Harvard. Riggs and Porter had known each other slightly at Yale when they both were members of the Scroll and Key fraternity. Although Riggs was a bit verbose and stiff enough to sign his name as T. Larason Riggs, he was a specialist in mythology and epic poetry and just the kind of collaborator Porter needed, and they decided to room together so as to speed their joint venture. Cole alone remained responsible for the music while Riggs hammered out the libretto; they both contributed to the lyrics. Because of that, for the only time in Porter's long career 'book, music and lyrics by Cole Porter *and* T. Larason Riggs' headed the credit lists of all their mutual efforts.

Together they produced yet another Yale Dramatic Association smoker with a typically nonsensical plot. Called *Paranoia*, the name they gave to a mythical Balkan country, or *Chester of the Y.D.A.*, the jejune argument concerns a Yale man (Chester) who marries Paranoia's beautiful princess Vodka and ends up as the country's ruler.

Dismissable, except for three numbers which would later be rewritten for the team's first Broadway show, *Paranoia* was to contain a song that would provide Cole's first recording. That musical scene was the delightful 'I've a Shooting Box in Scotland'.[3] Its lyric would presage Porter's own lifestyle by mentioning homes all over the world. The other numbers were 'The Language of Flowers' which was to be the prototype for Porter's first hit, 'An Old

---

[3] See number 1 in the analysis appendix.

Fashioned Garden', and 'Prithee, Come Crusading With Me', with an interminable lyric saluting the bloodthirsty Middle Ages in prolix style (it was
probably by Riggs). 'I Want To Row On the Crew', a leftover from Cole's
recent Yale days, which was resurrected and used in the 1988 revival of
Anything Goes, was also in the show.

Although not nearly as inspired as *The Pot of Gold*, *Paranoia* was so
successful that Cole, Thomas and the large cast of Yale graduates and undergraduates were soon off and running with their next project. By the end of
Cole's first year in Cambridge the team had completed an incongruous
burlesque of Mexican revolutionaries pitted against Yale undergraduates.
Called *We're All Dressed Up and Don't Know Huerta[4] Go*, its plot hinges on how
a group of rebels captures the US capitol. The insurgents' big mistake is to
move the government to New Haven where, in the second act, it is saved by
heroic Yale students.

Cole, who long ago had realized he abhorred his classes in law, closed
his textbooks, this time for good, and devoted all his energy to trying to hold
the Dramatic Association together. He even insisted they tour, and *We're All
Dressed Up and Don't Know Huerta Go* had its first presentation under the aegis
of the YDA at the annual dinner of the Associated Yale Clubs 500 miles away
in Cincinnati, Ohio.

Again, as at Yale, Cole's grades were to be unacceptable to the Harvard
administration, but this time the deus ex machina was the magnanimous dean
of Harvard Law School, Ezra Ripley Thayer. He had heard Cole sing his songs
at an impromptu function and was so convinced that the young law student
was a big fish swimming in a totally wrong pond that he helped arrange a
transfer to the Graduate School of Arts and Sciences for the coming year
(perhaps thereby also saving the reputation of Harvard Law).

Fearful lest J. O. learn of his grandson's dismal record at law and curtail
the generous allowance which supported a lavish lifestyle, Cole told only his
mother of the transfer and swore her to secrecy. Kate, for her part, rather
revelled in the conspiracy. With her now-burgeoning scrapbooks and with her
belief in her son's musical talents she must have enjoyed the mother-son bond
this confidence proclaimed. What he certainly would not have told his mother
was that he had registered for only two classes at the music school: a snap
course in music appreciation and one in basic harmony.

For his second year at Harvard, Cole, Riggs, Dean Acheson[5] and a
number of Scroll and Key alumni from New Haven rented a house off campus
and hired a houseman-butler to care for them. By now Cole had acquired a

---

[4] Victoriano Huerta (1854-1916), the tyrannical dictator, had recently taken over the Mexican government by force.
[5] US Secretary of State in the Eisenhower administration.

certain veneer, a modicum of elegance, and had exchanged his flamboyant wardrobe for a more sombre one. Accompanying himself, and singing in his high-pitched rather nasal voice, most evenings would be spent listening to Cole perform his latest numbers. He spent the days writing songs with Riggs, hoping for the big break – to have one of their numbers interpolated into a Broadway show.

They had every right to dream, for this was a time when shows were assembled with little care for length or plot. Librettos possessed an elastic story line and even composers of stature were subject to the whims of powerful producers who sought the insurance of as many hits per show as they were able to buy.

Between his creative sessions with Riggs, Cole could often be found in New York or Easthampton charming the social set and a continually widening circle of influential and wealthy friends. They, too, were enchanted by his sparkling songs, his manner and manners. One of those he captivated was Elizabeth 'Bessie' Marbury,[6] a literary agent now riding high as a theatrical producer. It was she who had backed the Princess Theatre[7] shows of Kern and Bolton – intimate small-budget musicals that contrasted mightily with the big Ziegfeld extravaganzas – which were now Broadway's reigning hits. She could afford to place her pet young composers and lyricists where they would be seen and heard, and she was soon instrumental in having Cole's 'Esmerelda,' a rather soupy song rhyming girls names, interpolated into the Romberg revue, *Hands Up*. The show was a miserable hodge-podge which lasted all of fifty-two performances, but on July 22, 1915 an ecstatic Cole Porter had his first song performed on a Broadway stage. This was followed three months later by 'Two Big Eyes', a waltz he had written to lyrics by John Golden,[8] presented as part of the Jerome Kern musical, *Miss Information*.

'Two Big Eyes' and *Miss Information* flopped as badly as his previous interpolation, but Cole could not help but crow to Kate. Hoping somewhat to mitigate the blow when J. O. found out Cole was no longer enrolled in Harvard Law, he wired his mother to 'tell Granddad that Lew Fields gave me fifty dollars for each song I sold him.' By December that year, he once again telegraphed: 'Tell Granddad unless something extraordinary happens show will go into rehearsal in a few weeks.'

[6] David Grafton, in his oral biography of Cole Porter, entitled *Red, Hot and Rich*, gives a thumb-nail biography of Elizabeth Marbury, calling her 'a hopelessly plain lesbian who tended toward stoutness and wore her straight, brown hair in a tight knot on top of her head. For forty years she was the lover of internationally famed interior decorator Elsie de Wolfe. Eventually she left Elsie for the much-younger Anne Morgan, daughter of financier J. P. Morgan. Later in life she became a powerhouse in the Democratic Party and a friend of First Lady Eleanor Roosevelt, Governor Al Smith and Mayor Jimmy Walker.'

[7] So named because of the intimate theatre that was their venue.

[8] Although he had very little talent for either words or music, Golden wrote both, somehow managing to collaborate with some of the theatre's most creative people. Shortly after he turned out the score for his 1916 fiasco, *So Long, Letty*, he was to give up the creative side altogether and become one of Broadway's best-known producers. The Golden Theater on West 45th Street stands today as an ideal house for the intimate musical.

The show he referred to was *See America First* which was intended to be a spoof on the current vogue for the flag-waving musicals of George M. Cohan as well as a Gilbert and Sullivan take-off. Unfortunately, in the rush to put this production together, Cole dipped into his trunk and for much of the score re-used the multi-varied, and not really inspired, songs he had written for *Paranoia*. The libretto owed a great debt to European operetta, and the intended parody on solid Americanism did not mix with the satire on British fantasy. Riggs's impossible plot (somewhat derivative of *We're All Dressed Up*) was only one of the liabilities of this resounding flop which miraculously managed to eke out sixteen performances. Its convoluted story concerns an American senator who leaves the effete East so that his daughter, an amorous Anglophile, can find a red-blooded husband in the Wild West. By the long arm of coincidence, she meets a British duke disguised as a cowboy on a sagebrush plain. Of course, at the final curtain, the lovers win parental approval when the duke saves the whole cast from bandits.

The sophomoric libretto notwithstanding, not only was Miss Marbury's production done on the cheap, but it was under-rehearsed. To make matters worse the producer made the unfortunate mistake of casting for the leading lady an amateur with a long social pedigree but a voice that was inaudible beyond the second row. Dorothy Bigelow (spelled Dorothie for her brief stage career) may have filled the theatre during previews with her café society friends, but on the opening night she and the show were drawn and slaughtered by the critics.

Clifton Webb, who would have a long and distinguished career in the theatre and films, was among the professionals trapped at the Maxine Elliott Theatre in *See America First*. Famous for his acid remarks, he would comment about this show in which he made his debut: 'I played a cowboy and an autumn flower. Others had roles not so believable.'

The New York Tribune, noting that the show was more like college smoker material than Broadway fare, proclaimed: 'Gotham is a big town and it may be that the sisters, aunts and cousins of its Yalemen will be sufficient to guarantee prosperity for *See America First*. That is its best chance.' *The Journal-American* called it 'the newest and the worst musical in town'. But *Variety* summed it up most succinctly: '*See America First* last!'

In spite of these devastating reviews, Cole was not discouraged. He scored a personal coup when G. Schirmer, the prestigious music house, agreed to publish thirteen numbers, practically the entire score, throwing in for good measure 'When I Used To Lead the Ballet', a Fannie Brice-type tune, originally written for *The Pot of Gold*. Shortly afterwards 'I've a Shooting Box in Scotland',[9] *See America First's* best song, was selected to be recorded by the Joseph C. Smith Orchestra. It was to be Cole's first commercial recording.

Again Cole crowed to Kate of how he thought he might have a chance to make his way as a professional songwriter and this time J. O., believing that his grandson would never return to the law and to managing the family business, set up a trust by which Cole would receive a one-half interest in the real estate holdings in West Virginia and Kentucky. J. O. did not give the money outright, but, reconciled that Cole was determined to have a musical career and might never earn a living, stipulated that upon his grandfather's death a handsome yearly income was to come to his grandson for the rest of his life. Since J. O. Cole was by then in his mid-eighties, it could be assumed it would not be long until Cole came into his multi-millions.

Accepted now by ASCAP as a 'professional' songwriter yet without a show to write, for the first time in his life Cole was at a loose end. He moved from Harvard to New York's Yale Club before eventually settling down in an apartment on East Nineteenth Street. He wrote to tell his family that he had come to Gotham to study composition with Pietro Yon, an eminent Italian composer, and indeed he applied himself during his days with some seriousness to his exercises in counterpoint. But the party scene proved irresistible and Cole's apartment soon turned into a setting for glittering gatherings rather than for concentrated musical study.

He might have continued these soirées indefinitely had the United States not declared war on Germany on April 6, 1917. One month after that proclamation Congress passed the Selective Service Act authorizing President Wilson to draft a million men between the ages of twenty-one and thirty. Cole would reach his twenty-sixth birthday in June (his twenty-fourth according to all school records). Either way, he would be a prime candidate for service.

Porter, however, never registered for the draft. Apparently he expected and received the same charmed-life, the face-above-the-crowd treatment from the army that he enjoyed in his social circle. Soon he had allied himself with a group called the Duryea Relief Party.

This organization, founded by a society matron, Nina Larre Smith Duryea, helped to distribute food to the people in villages far behind the lines in wartime France. And Cole was to be Mrs. Duryea's personal assistant and adjutant.

Thus it was that in July 1917, with a specially- constructed zither – this one having a custom-made piano keyboard – strapped to his back, dressed in a tailor-made uniform, Cole Porter set sail for a new adventure in his beloved France. His experiences during the next few months would not be unlike what used to be called 'The Grand Tour'.

[9] See Musical Analysis Appendix.

NOEL
1917-1921

COLE was almost twenty-six years old when his country belatedly entered the Great War in 1917, but Noel was a mere fourteen and a half in 1914. He would remember those war years as filled with 'air raids, darkened streets, familiar names in the casualty lists, concerts for the wounded, food rations, coupons, and the universal smear of khaki over everything.' It was a personal and catastrophic affront. Not only did the war serve to take food out of the mouths of his parents and baby brother Eric whom he was helping to support, but, much more disastrously, it delayed him getting on with his career.

When he had at last landed a good part in Gilbert Miller's production of *The Saving Grace* (directed by his former mentor, Charles Hawtrey), he recalled, with some degree of paranoia, how the director would stop the action during air-raids and 'by advancing to the footlights tell the audience that the warning had been given, and that if those present who wished to take shelter would kindly leave as quietly as possible, the play would proceed. Whereupon a few usually shuffled out and we continued, with forced brightness ... The full fury of the raids invariably occurred during my love scene with Emily Brooke and ... not only robbed us of the attention of the audience but destroyed any subtle nuances, for in order that any of the words be heard at all we had to bellow like bulls. On several occasions small pieces of shrapnel fell through the roof over the stage and tinkled on the canvas ceiling immediately over our heads.'

It was no wonder, since he had already had a taste of success, that Coward was impatient to get his career moving into high gear. The two years leading to *The Saving Grace* and his eventual conscription into the army showed him at his most eclectic. Patches of acceptance shone through the doldrums of rejection, but ambition had filled him with ideas and inspired him to the accomplishment of ideals. He had taken on himself the responsibility of supporting his family. Happily, they had all moved from the suburbs to Ebury Street in London where his mother was now taking in lodgers. Noel had installed himself comfortably on the top floor in a comfortable studio where he was able to write voluminously – turning out stories, novels and plays by the yard. No part was too small, and no salary too little, as long as he kept working. He had appeared in *The Light Blues* in London and *Wild Heather* on tour, briefly tried dancing at a cabaret restaurant, played a Sandhurst cadet in a another musical, *The Happy Family*, made his first movie appearance (a walk-on in *Hearts of the World*, a D. W. Griffith anti-German propaganda film). On the way, his winning personality had allowed him to become friendly with the Gish sisters, the stars of the film. Later, he presented himself to the pianist-singer Ivy St. Helier, who taught him something about harmonic introductions to his songs, and still later he was to sit at the feet of the reigning matinée idol, Ivor Novello. That was in 1917 when Coward was on tour and extremely envious of Novello who had already penned the reigning hit of the war, 'Keep the Home Fires Burning'.[1] But his major accomplishment was the professional production of a play he wrote with Esmé Wynne, *The Last Chapter*, later renamed *Ida Collaborates*. The comedy, which opened in Aldershot in 1917, was no worse than many of the plays that toured the provinces at that time. Its story, a light romance about a charwoman's daughter and her unrequited passion for a famous author, was to borrow heavily from Shaw among others.

Then in January 1918, came the dreaded grey envelope: a summons from the Army. He was to report immediately to Camberwell Swimming Baths.

Noel's army career, spent in the training corps of the Artists' Rifles, which had nothing artistic about it, lasted only ten months and was completely undistinguished. Shortly after forming up he was confined to bed for six weeks in the First London General Hospital recuperating from concussion he suffered when he tripped while running along a wooden path. On his return to the regiment, he was put on light duties, but the violent headaches which were intermittent after the concussion returned. Soon, inexplicably, he found himself in an epileptic ward at Colchester Hospital. Finally he was given his discharge and a small stipend for the next six months.

What Noel was later to call his 'wasted year' in the Army was not entirely misspent. During his enforced idleness in the various hospitals he read much, especially the works of G. B. Stern and Sheila Kaye–Smith, to both of whom he wrote ardent fan letters. And he began to create his own novel, *Cats and Dogs*, of which he was later to say, 'It taught me two things – one that it wasn't good enough for publication and the other was that I had the knack of bright dialogue.'

Back in civilian clothes, the standard navy blue auditioning suit, sporting matching shirt, tie, socks and handkerchief, Noel, who soon would become the fashion plate that sophisticated males on both sides of the Atlantic tried to emulate, was later to admit: 'I had not learned then that an exact duplication of colours ill becomes the well-dressed man. My bearing was a blend of assurance and professional vivacity; the fact that my bowels were as water I hope was not

---

[1] Noel tried to write his own war song to Doris Joel's music. Entitled 'When You Come Home On Leave', with uninspired lines like 'Waiting to greet you with a smile/To charm away your pain/And make you feel again/ That life is going to be worth while', he was later to call the song 'a pot boiler'.

apparent to anybody. I used to walk on to the stage, bow politely in the direction of the stalls and say "good morning" sometimes owing to nerves a trifle more loudly than I had intended. Then having banished the accompanist with a lordly gesture, I sat down at the piano on a stool that was invariably either too low or too high, and rattled off a few authoritative introductory chords, inwardly appalled by the tone and quality of the piano, but preserving an air of insouciance. I then swivelled round sharply, announced my song and started it before anyone had time to stop me.'

Trying out for a role in the Grossmith and Laurillard production of the Bolton and Kern's *Oh, Joy*[2] he became piqued when the producers were so immersed in conversation that no one paid any attention to his singing. 'I stopped dead,' he recounted, 'and waited until their voices had died into silence. Then with what I hoped was icy dignity, I said that I saw no point in wasting my time singing to them if thy continued to waste their time not listening to me. There was a horrified gasp from those waiting at the side of the stage, and the stage manager nervously rustled a lot of papers.' Noel's hauteur seems to have worked, for George Grossmith walked down to the orchestra rail and invited him to start his song again from the beginning. When he had finished, he was engaged at a salary of twelve pounds a week. The actual part he was to play would be decided upon later, but in the meantime he was told he 'could rest assured that [his] remarkable talents should have full range'.

Unfortunately, by the time the show got into rehearsal, the 'full range' section of the oral contract was forgotten and Noel found himself assigned to the chorus. Hardly a shrinking violet, as he says, 'I took a taxi to the Grossmith and Laurillard offices in Golden Square where I demanded to see Mr. Laurillard ... I think I must have roared very loudly indeed, for he looked startled, and kept on waving his hand in the air, apparently in an effort to dam the spate of words pouring on to his head ... at last he admitted there had indeed been a mistake, as there was no part suitable for me in *Oh, Joy*.' Laurillard then proceeded to mollify Noel by telling him his splendid performance in *The Saving Grace* had convinced him that the young actor could go farther than 'musical comedy', and offered him a plum part in a new play that was scheduled to go into rehearsal in two months.

Scandal, as the play was called, turned into a further disaster for the young actor. First of all, contrary to what Laurillard had promised, his part was small and nebulous, with only brief appearances at the beginnings of Acts I and II, but, more importantly, his outspokenness and dissatisfaction put most of the older actors in the company violently against him. In his memoirs, he admits to behaving 'badly and making hen noises whenever Millie Hylton

[2] *Oh, Boy*, its American title, was considered too parochial for British tastes.

came on to the stage. I also heartily detested Gladys Ffolliot, who had overheard me say to someone that her dog Daphne smelt like a drain. The truth of this statement in no way mitigated her rage, and she complained about me to the management whenever possible. Claire Greet lodged a few complaints too.'

The stars of *Scandal*, Kyrle Bellew and Arthur Bourchier, who admired Noel as an actor, but deplored his cruel imitations of the older actresses, asked him in for a talk. They told him that personal harmony was essential within any acting troupe and warned him that he was about to be sacked. In order to save face (a most important convention in the theatre), they suggested he should give two weeks' notice on the grounds that the rudeness of the older members of the company made it impossible for him to continue in the part without great emotional strain. Grossmith and Laurillard went one better. When he arrived at the theatre the evening they received his letter, his pay was handed him and he was given only half an hour to collect his things and to leave the premises.

No sooner was he at liberty than he again went back to collaborate with Esmé Wynne and they produced a comedy *Woman and Whisky* in which she toured. But the urge to write a more dramatic play and to work without a collaborator had bitten Noel and he conceive an idea for a melodrama he called *The Last Trick* which was built on the motive of revenge. Always a quick worker, it took him only a few days to get his first solo play on paper, whereupon he took it to Gilbert Miller, then a fledging scout for his famous theatrical father, Henry. Over luncheon Gilbert affirmed what Noel already knew – his natural gift for dialogue – but deplored the construction of the piece. He quoted his eminent father's words in a simile that Coward was always to remember. 'The construction of a play is as important as the foundation of a house, whereas the dialogue, however good, can only be considered as interior decoration.' But Gilbert Miller took the play to New York with him.[3]

Taking the advice of Mr. Miller senior seriously to heart Noel's next effort *The Rat Trap* had a carefully thought out construction. Built on a premise that would be quite acceptable to the women's lib movement of the '80s and beyond, it concerned a woman novelist of genuine talent married to a playwright of limited endowment, a most successful hack at turning out boulevard comedies. After three strong acts and two bold argumentative scenes, (sketches for the knock-down, drag-out fights in *Private Lives*?), the wife walks out to continue her blossoming career. Coward was later to admit that

[3] In August 1919 Coward had a cablegram from Gilbert Miller saying that Al Woods wanted to option *The Last Trick* for $500. Noel agreed to this and to Wood's offer a few days later to buy the play outright for the then enormous additional sum of $1500. By 1921, after several rewrites Wood told Coward it was still unproduceable. The play has never been staged.

The Rat Trap, written in 1918, but not produced until 1926, was Coward's second solo play. Left to right: Joyce Kennedy, Raymond Massey, Elizabeth Pollock, Robert Harris and Mary Robinson

'the last act is a shambles', due to his reaching for the happy ending in which the couple are reunited because of impending parenthood.[4]

Most of the next year was spent in enforced unemployment although the two thousand American dollars went far enough to allow him to pay some of the back rent due on Ebury Street, buy himself a new wardrobe, a second-hand grand piano at Harrods, and to lunch frequently at the Ivy where he could hob-nob with eminent theatre folk. But, though he found no part to play, Noel, always ambitious, wrote several unproduced plays and worked on lyrics for an opera *Crissa* with Doris Joel (libretto) and Max Darewski (music). By late autumn Darewski announced he was going to America to make arrangements for its production there. His expectations were decidedly premature, for both Noel and Doris soon abandoned *Crissa*, and it was never completed.

Always keeping several projects going at once, in August Noel was given the role of Ralph in *The Knight of the Burning Pestle*, a comedy by

---

[4] Although written in 1918, *The Rat Trap* was not produced until 1926 in London. Noel saw none of its twelve performances at the Everyman Theatre in Hampstead, for he was then touring in the United States.

Coward, with Esmé Wynne
in *I'll Leave It To You*, 1920

Beaumont and Fletcher. He was not very good in this mannered form of acting
and thenceforth turned away from its artificiality. But, shortly after, Gilbert
Miller returned from America and suggested the plot of a light comedy that he
wanted Noel to write for Charles Hawtrey, *I'll Leave It To You*.[5] Noel included a
fine juvenile role for himself and an ingénue one for Esmé. Miller, true to his
promise, produced the play in Manchester, but, although it received excellent
notices there, Hawtrey and Miller felt it was too slim to succeed in the West
End. Determined that his first production should not peter out in Manchester,
Noel gained the support of Lady Wyndham who presented it for a month's
run at the New Theatre in London.

The press hailed Noel as a 'Playwright of Promise', and although he had
not yet turned twenty (his father was obliged to sign the contract papers for
him) he sensed the import of this first success. Now he found fans waiting for
him outside the stage door and recalled the time only a decade before when he

[5] The title, a brilliant invention, is a typical two-edged Coward sword, a concept he was to use frequently in his lyrics. It
refers to the plot of a rich uncle who vows he will leave his money to five ne'er-do-well nieces and nephews only if they snap
to and make something of their lives; as well as to Act I's curtain line when these indolent creatures ask how they are to
manage to do this and the uncle counters, 'I'll leave it to *you!*'

had stood in the alley waiting for Pavlova, Gertie Millar or Lily Elsie to appear. Thereafter he never refused to give his autograph because, as he was later to say: 'When I was young I wanted more than anything to be a star; when I became one I realised it brought certain obligations. As long as there are people who wait for my autograph, I shall give it. And, if the day ever comes when no one waits, I shall miss it dreadfully.'

But *I'll Leave It To You* fared less well in London than it had in Manchester and, although still involved in playwriting, Noel was soon obliged to resume his work as an actor, appearing again in the dreaded *Knight of the Burning Pestle*, and later in a silly comedy called *Polly with a Past*.

At the age of twenty-one, and early in the 1920s, a decade he was to personify and dominate, Noel was so eager to have another hit that he even stole from himself. He revamped his early unpublished novel, *Cats and Dogs*, which concerns the adventures of a brother and sister using glib dialogue and fast repartee. The play itself bears a great similarity to his idol Bernard Shaw's *You Never Can Tell*. Now Noel changed the brother and sister into twins – making it even *more* like Shaw's work.

Hoping to get his comedy produced, Noel sent the play to the Vedrenne Management who, perhaps fearing a suit for plagiarism, passed it on to Shaw. GBS was encouraging to the point of writing notes for improving scenes in the margin of the manuscript. He congratulated Coward on his play and only obliquely hinted that the work might be borrowed. His letter ended with:

> I have no doubt that you will succeed if you persevere, and take care never to fall into a breach of essential good manners, and above all, never to see or read my plays. Unless you can get clean away from me you will begin as a back number, and be hopelessly out of it when you are forty.
>
> Faithfully,
> G. Bernard Shaw

The play was finally presented a year later and attained a substantial run, but what impressed Coward enormously was 'the brilliance in the trouble that the great man had taken in going minutely over the work of a comparatively unknown young writer'.

Yet again, as engagements ended and promises of productions of his work evaporated, he was to find himself at a loose end. He had heard Paul Whiteman and his jazz orchestra when they visited London and was impressed with their vitality. Now it was only a question of time before he would set his sights on the New World – America and the wonders of Broadway. He remembered Mary Robinson's exciting descriptions of New York, and was further entranced when he met Jeanne Eagels at a party and they discussed the vitality of American acting, but what clinched his resolve was his friend Jeffery Amherst's announcement that he was sailing on the *Aquitania* with a request, not an invitation, for Noël to join him. In a typical Cowardian gesture, instead of buying a third-class round trip ticket, he spent almost all his money on a first-class one-way, calculating he would sell a song or a play and would somehow be able to get his passage home when, and especially if, the time came when that might be necessary.

It was a time when American musicals frequently held sway in London and Viennese and British operettas succeeded on Broadway. Actors, producers, singers, writers frequently criss-crossed the Atlantic, for success in one country almost guaranteed there was money to be made abroad. The world was rapidly growing smaller. Travel on a liner was an elegant and comfortable experience, one no sophisticated playwright worth his salt could do without. And they were absolutely safe since President Harding had declared a 'ban on war'.

Noel's westward crossing was to become habitual throughout his life, and he was to become a sworn Americophile just as Cole Porter, a decade before, had headed eastward and found the experience of living in a foreign land changed forever the way he looked at music and lyrics. Although Coward was almost a decade younger than Porter, by mid-1921 each of them had produced one mild flop and had the word 'promising' attached to his name. They seem to have caught up with each other.

COLE
1917-1924

I
T WOULD MAKE A GOOD STORY, and one Cole enjoyed telling all his life: that the fiasco known as *See America First* drove Thomas Riggs into the priesthood and himself into the French Foreign Legion. Riggs actually did give up the theatre shortly after the show folded, converted to Roman Catholicism and eventually became a chaplain at Yale. Cole's war record remains a perpetual mystery.

For, although he tried to extend, becloud and glamourize his involvement, Cole distributed supplies for the Duryea Relief for a mere three months, until October 1917. At this point he 'is reported' to have joined the American Aviation Headquarters in the recruiting department. The reports stem directly from Cole; there is no record of his enlisting in this or any other branch of the forces other than what he himself told his family and schoolfriends.

More reliable interviewees deny Cole's involvement in the war to end all wars. Archibald MacLeish who had been in the cast of one of Cole's smokers at Yale, tells of running into him in Paris during the days when MacLeish had been granted leave after the second battle of the Marne. He says that Cole was then 'comfortably settled in a house of his own'. And Sir Rex Benson recalled visiting Cole one evening in Paris and hearing him play and sing some of his old songs.

If Cole did indeed help out at the recruiting office, it would certainly have been as a volunteer, and his duties would have had to be ended by cocktail time for many of his friends stated that he could be found most evenings in boulevard cafés or at elegant soirées. Monty Woolley said that 'during this period Cole had more changes of uniform than Maréchal Foch and wore them with complete disregard to regulation. One night he might be a captain of the Zouaves, the next an aide-de-camp.'

Cole told Ed Sullivan in an interview that he switched to the French 32nd Field Artillery, which he liked to call 'the foreign legion'. Truth to tell, it was not foreign in the romanticized sense of lovelorn or disreputable soldiers serving in the North African desert, but foreign only to an American in that it was a military group stationed in Paris. If Cole's story is true he would have come under its jurisdiction because simply by joining the French army he would become a foreigner serving for pay. Cole goes on to say that after service at the Field Artillery office he was detailed to the Bureau of the United States Military Attaché, where he spent a year, always in Paris, and from which he was discharged in April 1919.

After the war, Cole often bragged that he had received the Croix de

Guerre for heroism, but there is nothing on record to show he was ever decorated, and Kate's scrapbook which seems to contain every shred of information about her son holds no enlistment, no medals, no citations and no discharge papers.

Most biographers have come to believe that Cole never joined the army, but rented a house and spent the wartime years based in Paris. He wrote to his mother that when he was working with the Duryea group he came across an old French farm woman living in an *abri*. Feeling sorry for her because her husband and son had been killed by the Germans, but also being of a practical nature, he asked her if she could cook. 'And she said, "Oh, Monsieur, of course I can cook." So I said, "Pack up your things and jump on this motor." So here she is living in the house with us ... cooking delicious omelettes, rabbit chops and compotes. And she has forgotten her troubles and we have forgotten ours!'

Who the 'us' are, how he managed to live in a house instead of a barracks, where he got the ingredients for this clever cook to prepare tempting meals he does not say. Of course he enjoyed his year in Paris, not simply because he loved the city, but because of its proximity to London. He was able to travel there as a civilian and to sell some songs to the composer-lyricist Melville Gideon. Gideon often bought songs from fledgling writers, rewrote them and placed them in the many escapist revues then popular in wartime London. Two of Cole's collaborations with Gideon, 'Altogether Too Fond of You' and 'Alone With You', were interpolated into the English production of Jerome Kern's *Very Good, Eddie* which his old friend Bessie Marbury produced.

As far as his war record goes, Cole, who was able all through his life to lie about his age, may not have felt any compunction about falsifying it. One can see from many of his dealings in the future that the way he looked in the eyes of his social set was so vital that he had no scruples in foisting on the world the make-believe in regard to his service record, his marriage and his love affairs.

Cole formed a great many friendships in that year, 1918, and became especially close to two Yale alumni: Monty Woolley and Howard Sturges.[1] He and Cole were never lovers, but Monty was always the comedian and his ironic wit, not unlike Cole's, allowed them both to laugh at each other's jokes. Howard, on the other hand, a musician manqué, seemed born to adulate and serve his friends. Both these friendships sustained Cole and helped him in his lifelong climb up the social ladder.

[1] Woolley, who was commissioned a lieutenant in the US Army, spent most of 1918 in Paris. Sturges, who had graduated from Yale the year before Cole entered, would have been too old for the draft. Immensely rich, alcoholic and a self-proclaimed homosexual, he rented a town house in a fashionable quarter of the French capital and held court there, surrounding himself with friends, musicians and all the luxuries of life.

All in all, Cole breezed through the war years with the same easy nonchalance with which he had skimmed his way through the universities, except that he did not have the all-consuming drive to take the war as seriously as he had, for example, a Delta Kappa Epsilon smoker. Not every young man has to slog through mud so as not to be considered a coward, but Cole, certainly aware of the carnage around him, fought no battles, entertained no troops, wrote not a single patriotic song that might have inspired the Allies as much as he had stirred his Yale classmates on to victory.

The hand-made zither he had brought with him to France or his piano keyboard were always at the service of a considerable group of expatriate Americans and deposed Tsarist royalty who sat out the conflict in their comfortable houses in Paris. War was a tiresome annoyance to them, limiting their supply of red meat and caviar. Fortunately there was a young, lively, brittle and rather good-looking court jester who could lift his rather pinched nasal voice and lead them all in song. Egged on by their laughter and gossip, he might be encouraged to sing loud enough to help them drown out the annoyance of this dreary war. Cole Porter could be found during those years and in the ensuing peace wherever the fun and games were.

It was at about that time he came to know the woman who, along with his mother, would become the most important female in his life: the beautiful American divorcee, Linda Lee Thomas. Tall, with sapphire-blue eyes, a pink and white complexion and flaxen hair, she was known to stop conversation cold when she entered a salon or restaurant. Listed in the Porter family records as having been born in 1883[2], by 1910, according to society column reports, she was reputed to be the most beautiful woman in America. A decade later fashion magazines called her one of the most beautiful women in the world. Famous for her exquisite taste in furnishings, antiques, objets d'art and clothing, she dressed with surpassing originality. Women of chic copied the fashion she introduced: the simple black dress highlighted by one exquisite piece of jewellery.

Born Linda Lee into an impoverished but socially respected family in Louisville, Kentucky, at eighteen she met and married Edward Thomas whose immensely wealthy family owned the *New York Morning Telegram*. At their marriage he gave his bride a 'cottage' in Newport, a mansion in Palm Beach, a town house on 57th Street in New York, as well as a box at the opera, a yacht and an enviable collection of diamonds, rubies and pearls. Thomas was a sportsman, playboy and heavy drinker. Bullheaded and aggressive, he was certainly the wrong match for a sensitive personality like Linda. (He holds the

[2] Linda's true birth-date is more mysterious than Cole's. The Porter family bible records her birth-date as 1883 (making her eight years older than Cole), while David Grafton's biography states she was born in 1881. Still another source claims she was not ten years older than Cole, but fourteen. At her request her date of birth was not etched on her gravestone.

Linda Lee Thomas in 1910 (left) and in 1919

dubious record of being the first person to have killed someone while drinking and driving an automobile.) When inebriated he would become abusive and, although Linda's divorce was granted on grounds of incompatibility, there is no doubt that she was a battered wife, if not physically, at least psychologically.

This incompatibility was temporarily suspended in 1908 when Thomas smashed his kneecap in another car accident. Linda insisted that the leg be saved, and a short-lived truce was declared. Because of a bronchial condition from which Linda suffered, she would make frequent trips to the dry climate of Colorado during which Thomas's philandering would escalate. After a large number of Thomas's liaisons had made headlines, Linda sought an unconditional divorce. It was granted without question. This time she named the well-known showgirl, Teddie Gerard.[3]

Because Thomas's parents wished to avoid any additional notoriety nothing was said about returning Linda's important collection of jewellery and they settled stocks, bonds and other assets worth a million dollars upon her. Now she would be known in Parisian circles as the 'alimony millionairess'.

When they met at the Harriman wedding at the Ritz, Cole was at the piano accompanying a singer in his own songs. He was immediately taken with

[3] Several years later, the George Eells biography of Cole relates that, when Cole was introduced to Teddie at a London party, she said, 'I don't know whether I should meet you or not. You see, I was your wife's ex-husband's mistress.' Cole promptly kissed her hand.

Linda's beauty. She, in her turn, was charmed, as so many older women before her had been, by Cole's open manner, his saucy music and impertinent lyrics. Soon they began meeting, for champagne cocktails, at the only bar that was de rigueur for well-heeled expatriates in Paris, that at the Ritz. There they would gossip, laugh and strip away all the glamour, reminding each other that she was simply a Kentucky girl while he was a mid-Western farmboy. Although most of their friends felt this relationship was heading for disaster, the Gerald Murphys, for example, being among those who feared that, with Cole's growing attachment to Linda, his sybaritic tendencies would triumph over his creative ones, the couple were unswayed. And Linda's friends noticed with dismay that she gradually began dropping her host of rich admirers now that she was so taken with the young man from Indiana – an unlikely suitor for the worldly, gay divorcee.

In those early years of insecurity Cole came to admire Linda's confidence in the world she had created around her. Although he wore diamond-studded gold garters and kept a ready stock of Perrier-Jouet champagne on ice, he was aware that he had much to learn about the truly luxurious life he yearned for. Linda seemed to embody it all, and she was an adoring and patient teacher. She introduced him and guided him through the social protocol of rooms full of royalty, tycoons, statesmen and entertainers.

There is no doubt that Linda had an inborn sense of taste. The walls of her house at 3 rue de la Baume boasted old Chinese scrolls as well as important abstract paintings. The finest contemporary furniture stood beside French and English antiques. And she was a brilliant hostess. Even the French admired her knowledge of wine and haute cuisine. Because Cole trusted so implicitly her unerring sense of what was good, and she had such an abiding faith in his talent, he began to believe even more strongly in himself. Through her insistence he developed the habit of writing a song – or at least part of a song – every day of his life.

Linda was disciplined to a remarkable degree and expected the same from her friends and guests. When she fixed a dinner party for eight o'clock, she expected her guests to arrive at the appointed hour and those who were tardy missed the meal. Cole was the only one who need not be on time because, as she said, 'génius oblige'. Gradually, even Cole abandoned his bohemian habit of coming to meals at odd hours and adhered to Linda's schedule. Through her he developed an even more rigid feeling for the importance of punctuality and was known to leave a restaurant at five past one when a luncheon partner with whom he had a one o'clock rendez-vous failed to appear.

Early in 1919 Cole and Linda decided to marry. There is no doubt their tastes were so similar that they fitted neatly into each other's lives and, deriving such happiness from the relationship, wanted to make it a permanent one.

Their mutual interest in concerts, opera, musical theatre, painting, decoration, the social world, and all the trappings of life, made them comfortable with each other. Maintaining separate bedrooms actually helped in what was essentially a sexless relationship, for Linda, after her brutalizing marriage to Thomas, could not have been very interested in the erotic aspect of their relationship.[4] And Cole, whose occasional homosexual peccadilloes could be overlooked, was the ideal husband-son-child she sought.

Cole's reason for wanting to tie the knot was less obvious, but one must understand that this was a man who had always yearned to have it all. In a period when homosexuality was a passport into some artistic circles, but unacceptable outside the Venice-Paris salons, Linda became what Hollywood circles were calling 'the beard'. She was also Cole's confidante, his never-disapproving mother, his patroness and, at that time, his breadwinner.

Once they had come to their decision, despite his iconoclasm and over Linda's objections, Cole retained enough of his middle-class mores to feel he should contribute heavily to his household's upkeep. He sailed for America, intending to hurry to Peru and to plead with his grandfather to increase his $100-a-month[5] allowance.

It was a fortunate crossing, for on the liner Cole came to know Raymond Hitchcock. Hitchcock was a lanky, rasp-voiced comic who had recently turned producer. He had great faith in what he termed the new 'zippy' revue form, and had produced a successful one called *Hitchy-Koo of 1917*, which launched him into a series of annual productions. Despite his theory that the revue would soon outstrip the dramatic book musical in popularity, his 1918 edition of *Hitchy-Koo* had met with only limited success. Now, returning from England with slim pickings in songs for his proposed new edition, he was bowled over by Cole's fresh and witty material. After listening to a dozen numbers, the producer is reputed to have applauded and said, 'I'll take the lot!'

Thus it was that, after late summer try outs in Atlantic City, Porter's second score for Broadway came into being. *Hitchy-Koo* was not greatly successful at the box office, but proved to be a personally critical and monetary success for Cole. The *New York Times* critic, besides calling it 'the best revue in town', announced, 'The music and lyrics are the work of Cole Porter, who has made a particularly clever job of the lyrics and a good tinkling one of the music.' Perhaps more important in making Cole's name better known was the unexpected success of 'Old-Fashioned Garden', a song he had written at the behest of the frugal backers, Abe Erlanger and Charles Dillingham, who had

[4] Some biographers have suggested that Linda was lesbian because of her close relationship with Elsie de Wolfe, but this writer has found no evidence to corroborate that assertion.
[5] Although it seems a paltry sum today, because of the exchange rate of the dollar to franc one could live extremely well in post-war Paris on $100 per month.

acquired some slightly used flower costumes from an unsuccessful edition of *The Ziegfeld Follies*.

But, looked at through contemporary eyes, the 'Old-Fashioned Garden' flower number was the weakest, least adventurous song in a highly personal score that contained such lyric gems as 'I Introduced' (It's entirely due to me/Though few people know it/ That dear old Mister Chandon/ Met that dear old Mister Moët); 'That Black and White Baby of Mine' (She's got a black and white shack/And a new Cadillac/In a black and white design. /All she thinks black and white/She even drinks Black and White/That black and white baby of mine); and 'Since Ma Got the Craze Espagnol' (She rants round the home/Simply clad in a comb/Shouting, 'I'm Isabella,/ Where's that Ferdinand fella?').

Perhaps the most self-revelatory number Cole could have written at that period of his life is 'My Cozy Little Corner in the Ritz',[6] the bar where he and Linda could be found almost daily. I quote the self-mocking refrain:

I simply adorn a secluded corner,
A cozy corner in the Ritz Hotel.
When I wander each afternoon for tea
'Cause I like to see the kings
And let the queens see me.
In my corner, my dear little corner
Where I gather up the spicy bits.

And if you want to meet the girl
That's got the latest complexion on her,
If you'd like to see the fellow
That your favorite prima donna
Cashes checks on,
Just put your specs on
And try my cosy little corner in the Ritz.

Not every song in *Hitchy-Koo of 1919* breaks musical ground, but even the flops display occasional rhythmic touches and harmonic ones that presage the great songwriter to come. And in the truly successful four listed above Cole's personal voice is unmistakeable.

The 1919–20 Broadway season had reached its nadir. The New York public had embraced jazz, preferring to go dancing rather than sit in the theatre. With all that was going on around it, one is surprised at *Hitchy-Koo's* excellent gross of $16,000 in its first week. Perhaps even more astounding, in a market where the Charleston and jazz were the rage, was to watch 'Old Fashioned Garden' emerging as a hit. Eventually it sold a then-record-breaking 100,000 sheet music copies.[7]

As the money came in gradually, it was not a fortune, but this sudden recognition greatly increased Cole's belief in himself and made him yearn more strongly for marriage and a home of his own. Yet, when he approached

[6] At that time the Ritz had two bars, a men's bar on the left (a frequent gathering place for homosexuals) where, as Beverley Nichols noted, 'Cole Porter, looking like a startled leprechaun, could sip a Pernod and cast his dark, syrupy little eyes to the white and gold ceiling, and think out his devastating little rhymes', and a mixed bar on the right. Once the Cole-Linda liaison was a fait accompli, the couple switched from the left to the right-hand one.
[7] The song failed miserably in England, perhaps because the British, more horticulturally canny, could not believe Cole's lyric which implied that phlox, hollyhocks, violets, eglantines, columbines and marigolds bloomed simultaneously in the singer's garden.

his grand-father with the request for which he had travelled across the ocean, he was flatly rebuffed. J. O. presumably was angry with his grandson for several reasons: that he had served in the French, instead of the US, army, that even after the war he chose to live abroad, that he wanted to marry when he had not the means to support a wife. But what rankled most was Cole's lack of interest in managing the family fortune. As she had done so many times before, his mother, believing that Linda's love would be a stabilizing influence on her son's life, came to the rescue and, without telling her father, shared her own considerable income with Cole.

Kate's allowance plus the advances he requested and got from his new publisher Max Dreyfus and a $10,000 loan (eventually paid back) from his Yale friend, William Crocker, seemed to justify going ahead with the wedding, and on December 18, 1919, Cole and Linda were married in the local *mairie*.

A short, discreet announcement appeared in the following day's Paris *Herald*, but Walter Winchell, the gossip columnist for New York's *Herald-Tribune*, proclaimed: 'Boy with one million weds Girl with two million.'

Their honeymoon took them to the Côte d'Azur and the Italian Riviera and established a pattern of extensive and frequent travel in the decade following their marriage. The Porters voyaged frequently, usually with a host of friends, Linda's personal maid and Cole's valet. All this initially was made possible by Linda's money, later by Cole's inheritance and still later by his own success.

Now Cole needed either a job or a show. Since neither was in the offing, his thoughts turned once again to improving his musical technique. Although Linda adored Cole's witty popular songs, in his and especially in her world of nights at the opera and afternoons in the concert hall, a career in serious music might have been more socially acceptable. Wanting to give her new husband everything she could, to turn him into more than a perpetual parlour entertainer, she tried to get Igor Stravinsky to teach Cole harmony. When that failed she offered to pay her literary acquaintances, George Bernard Shaw, John Galsworthy and Arnold Bennett, handsomely for a libretto that Cole might fashion into an opera.

After all Linda's efforts misfired, Cole enrolled at the Schola Cantorum, selecting courses in harmony, counterpoint, composition and orchestration. His lessons with Pietro Yon had given him a reasonably firm foundation in harmony and enabled him now to move into the study of advanced harmony and contemporary theory. But his knowledge of counterpoint was rudimentary and he knew very little about serious composition. And nothing of orchestration.

The Schola Cantorum, which was guided by the principles of the established, but academic composer Vincent d'Indy, was very far from avant-

garde, and although Cole stayed at the conservatory for several months and
actually produced a creditable orchestration of the first movement of Schu-
mann's G Minor piano sonata he wearied of the work and abandoned it in the
middle of the second movement. Sensing a stronger urge to write popular
music that would amuse himself and his friends, he perhaps convinced himself
that most of Broadway's popular composers left the orchestration of their
songs to specialists.

For the next three years while Cole wrote many popular songs he
thought no more about serious music. Then, in 1923, he made a herculean (and
final) effort to return to the field of composition when he accepted the
invitation of his friend Gerald Murphy to collaborate on a ballet for the Ballet
Suédois's Paris season. Murphy wrote the satirical scenario and designed the
sets for the eighteen-minute piece, which burlesqued the jazz age, *Within the
Quota*. Cole wrote a dissonant and clanguorous score, and arranged it for three
pianos (at least one too many). He also engaged Charles Koechlin, the impres-
sionistic French composer best-known for *Les Bandar-Log*, to orchestrate the
ballet. The work was mildly successful in France, and was given sixty-nine
performances when the company took the programme to America, although
possibly a large part of the evening's acclaim was due to its companion on the
bill: Darius Milhaud's immediately successful *La Création du Monde*. Yet, had
the violent jazz rhythms Cole wrote into his score not been blunted by
Koechlin's tender orchestration, his ballet might have had a longer life. After
the Ballet Suédois company dispersed and *Within The Quota* was put on the
shelf Cole left concert composition, this time forever. It is curious that Cole,
who was so fastidious about keeping every one of his scores and every scrap of
his early musical exercises, claimed throughout his life that the manuscript
(and all the sketches) for *Within the Quota* were irretrievably lost. He must have
been uneasy about the work's inherent worth, and his place in the world of
serious composers.[8]

Shortly after the newly-weds returned from their honeymoon, they decided
that Linda's Paris house was too confining. She bought instead a showplace at
13 rue Monsieur in the fashionable Invalides section for a reputed quarter of a
million dollars. This was to be the *Colporteurs'*, as they were called by French
society, base for the rest of their lives. Years later their fourteen room
apartment in New York's Waldorf Towers would be the subject of articles and
photographs in fashion and decorating magazines, but for beauty, chic and

---

[8] After Cole's death the manuscript was found among the papers and scores he had willed to Yale University. The news
prompted the American Ballet Theater to undertake a new production to be choreographed by Keith Lee stressing the
nostalgia of the work. Changing the title to *Times Past* and a new and more vital orchestration by William Balcom helped a
little, but *Within the Quota* still received lukewarm reviews at its reincarnation in 1970, almost fifty years following the
première. After that one season, the American Ballet Theater dropped it permanently from its repertoire.

The grand salon, 13 rue Monsieur, Paris

avant-garde decoration nothing compared to the house in the rue Monsieur. Its imposing entrance with a black and white checkerboard marble floor, the grand circular staircase, taffeta hangings, red lacquer armchairs, the much-photographed platinum wallpaper in one room and the zebra-skin floor covering in another, would set trends in interior design throughout the '20s. It was even whispered that Elsie de Wolfe, favourite decorator of the moneyed social set, copied Linda's style.

Once the decorating was complete, Cole and Linda's restlessness impelled them into a two-year odyssey of travel. During that time Cole had occasional songs interpolated into revues presented in England and America. 'I Never Realized'[9], written with Melville Gideon, was published at last and

[9] A mystery surrounding the authorship of 'I Never Realized' was solved by Fred Lounsberry, editor-author of *103 Lyrics of Cole Porter*. Lounsberry's curiosity was piqued in 1960 when he received a flyer from Vogel Publishing who bombarded the music world with publicity hawking the song, the only Cole Porter one in their catalogue.

Lounsberry wrote to Cole: 'I thought you'd be amused by [the flyer] ... for aside from "See America First", which you wrote with T. Larason Riggs, unless you count Shakespeare – "I Am Ashamed That Women Are So Simple", – it is the only time I can recall you came to write a song with a collaborator ... My hunch some time ago was that Melville Gideon was a made-up name for a gag. Was this correct? ...'

Cole answered the next day saying that he had sold the song 'to Melville Gideon who was a well-known songwriter in London when I was in the French Army. I sold it for a very small sum, but I needed the money. Then Gideon took the song, changed some of the words and had it published under his own name, giving me no credit.' To set the record straight, Melville Gideon, who also wrote melodies to Noel Coward's early songs, certainly gave every one of his collaborators credit for their lyrics.

sold a fair amount of copies; and 'Chelsea', whose title was later changed to 'Washington Square', (it sounds like a prototype for Sandy Wilson's 'A Room in Bloomsbury') brought in considerable royalties from the sale of sheet copies.

Then Cole caused a bit of a stir with 'The Blue Boy Blues', a charming number sung by the subject of the famous Gainsborough painting who wonders what will become of him now that he has been sold to an American collector and is being moved to the Wild West. The same show, Charles Cochran's revue, *Mayfair and Montmartre*, featured a spoof whose title 'Olga Come Back To the Volga' says it all.

This was essentially the sum total of the songs he was able to place in production, yet Cole continued to work daily on material, sending songs in to his publisher from wherever he was, sometimes receiving acceptances, but mostly rejections, and always putting the unaccepted material in his files. Of course, because of Linda's wealth they were able to afford these extended travels. But the safari was not quite as sybaritic as it sounds, for Cole was to write sketches, collect themes, absorb rhythms, and live experiences that would eventually find their expression in his work.

Early in 1922 Cole went back to New York to assemble the score intended for yet another edition of *Hitchy-Koo* on Broadway. He would include many of the songs he had written and performed for friends in the past two years. What he turned out – which has with the passage of time only grown fresher and more alluring – was, in the words of Deems Taylor, certainly 'too tricky and much too sophisticated to have any popular success'. Cole's esoteric score coupled with the fact that Hitchcock's antics had worn thin by this time may be the reason *Hitchy-Koo of 1922* folded in Philadelphia, taking 'My Spanish Shawl', 'The American Punch', 'Play Me a Tune', 'Love Letter Words', 'The Harbor Deep Down in My Heart', 'Old Fashioned Waltz', 'The Bandit Band' and 'The Sponge'[10] with it. Cole, never one to throw away good material, did not let the demise of this, the last, edition of *Hitchy-Koo* scuttle his songs. He recycled 'The American Punch' which was interpolated into Sigmund Romberg's score to *The Dancing Girl*, serving as a much-needed first act finale. As for the other *Hitchy-Koo* material, he was able to fit almost all of it into forthcoming revues.

Supervising *The Dancing Girl*, catching up on plays, seeing friends as well as prospective producers who might use his material, kept Cole and Linda in New York that spring. It was there, on the evening of February 3, 1923 that they learned the J.O. had succumbed to pneumonia and died shortly after his ninety-fourth birthday.

[10] See Song Appendix under 'The Scampi'.

Hurrying to Peru to comfort Kate, they arrived in time to witness the spartan Episcopalian funeral J.O. had requested which seemed in direct contrast to the millions his estate had amassed. Upon his grandfather's death the trust he had set up for Cole became active and the Porters soon learned that enormous sums of money from the operation of mines and timberlands on the family properties in West Virginia and Kentucky would come directly to Cole. But his fortune did not end there. J.O. left approximately a million dollars in cash, which would be split between Kate and his late son Louis's offspring. Kate, who was left the Westleigh house as well, and whose wants were few, decided to give half her share of the cash to Cole, netting him a quarter of a million dollars in the days before income and estate taxes.[11]

With Cole's fortune added to Linda's already ample one, the Porters now embarked on an even more lavish lifestyle. The legendary Elsa Maxwell, freeloader, confidante and party-giver for rich Americans and minor royals, had been employed by the Italian government to develop Venice's unattractive sand-bar, the Lido, into a watering place for café society. Cole and Linda who had a perpetual love-hate relationship with the substantial Miss Maxwell firmly believed she could transform the Lido into a place where boredom could not exist. They rented the Palazzo Barbaro, a four-storey mansion on the Grand Canal, and with friends, maids, valets and their own collection of art treasures spent their first summer there. A year later, in 1926, as their social set widened, Cole and Linda found the Palazzo Barbaro too confining and took instead the imposing Palazzo Rezzonico – eminently suitable for the large parties they frequently gave.

Elsa was right. She publicized the Lido so well that soon such people as Talullah Bankhead, Fanny Brice, Diana Cooper, Sir Charles Mendl, and Elsie de Wolfe flocked there. Even Noel Coward, who had just written the successful revue, *London Calling*, and had starred in his own play *The Vortex*, spent some weeks basking in the Adriatic sun. He brought along his handsome lover-manager Jack Wilson who had the reputation of being 'ready for anything'.

In addition to indiscriminate sexual experimentation, heavy drinking was commonplace, and hashish, opium and cocaine were tried by most members of this Lido set. Cole, always the sensualist, wanted to experience every possible thrill. However, since he was intensely concerned about his appearance, when he saw signs that the dissipation was beginning to show in his face, he had the power to curtail the use of drugs and to begin a regimen of exercise and diet until his smooth-faced, boyish looks returned.

The season the Porters spent at the Palazzo Papadopoli was even more glittering. Elsa had so publicized the resort that the *crème de la crème* of English,

[11] Kate kept her money in the bank, Cole spent his on travel, but Louis's heirs invested theirs in stocks, which reportedly became valueless after the 1929 crash.

Porter, with Sturges and Linda in the Palazzo Barbaro, Venice

French and Italian nobility, (with a few White Russians thrown in) were in Venice. Artur Rubinstein, Grace Moore, and George Gershwin partied with the Porters. So too did Irving Berlin, whom Cole admired tremendously. When Cole asked him why no producer would give him a show to write, he advised him that producers would never take a chance on him, 'till you settle down at Broadway and Forty-second street'.

As the tempo of life on the Grand Canal quickened, the Porters invited Sergei Diaghilev to bring his ballet company to their palazzo, where he staged an extravagant evening of dance in the garden. One of the ballets premiered that evening was *Les Matelots*. It is based on a scenario by Boris Kochno with choreography by Massine, and Cole was involved in recreating the music on the piano when it was whistled by Kochno as George Auric's score had not yet been sent on to Venice.

Kochno, a handsome ballet enthusiast, was not only Diaghilev's second in command but he had been the impresario's lover for the past four years. For the only time in his life, Cole fell desperately in love. Porter, then in his mid 30s wrote impassioned letters to the twenty-one year old Russian Adonis: 'All night I keep awakening thinking of you, and all day I wait for your arrival. Ah, Boris how you have complicated my life! And how happy I am for it.'[12]

The intense relationship continued for a month and then Kochno lost interest. Cole, however, poured out his undiminished love in letters throughout the autumn and winter of 1925, but as it was unrequited and impossible – Cole would never desert Linda, nor could Boris leave Diaghilev, the kingpin of his career – Porter closed his heart to further entanglements. For the rest of his life Cole only gave himself to unincumbering, purely sexual brief encounters. Noel Coward, writing one of his last plays, A Song at Twilight (whose plot revolves about a married man's attempt to retrieve a sheaf of his homosexual letters) seems to have been inspired by the Porter-Kochno affair, a situation he was well aware of, having often visited the Porters in Venice.

At autumn's approach all these birds of paradise returned to their nests while Cole and Linda were off to find further titillation in Paris, London, New York or Antibes. When this paled, they would embark on a trip up the Nile or a cruise in the Mediterranean. Lunches, nightly parties, costume balls, lavish dinners, intermittent affairs and international intrigue seemed to fill their days and dawns. Somewhere in between Cole would be asked by John Murray Anderson to contribute songs to a new edition of his Greenwich Village Follies he was preparing to feature the maudlin Dolly Sisters, and Cole obliged by taking out many of the songs he had written in the previous two years. Additionally, he wrote 'Two Little Babes in the Wood' (a charming waltz whose lyric spoofs a fairy tale) especially for the sibling stars. The tune has a tongue-in-cheek sentimentality that sounds downright ironic today – an effect that must have been wasted on the show's audience, and its lyric begins to sound like the mature clean-cut Porter. After the first verse and chorus in which Cole tells us how the orphans' avaricious trustee left the girls to die in the wood, he continues with:

Verse 2
They were lying there in the freezing air
When fortunately there appeared
A rich, old man in a big sedan
And a very, very fancy beard.
He saw those girls and cheered.
Then he drove them down to New York
    town
Where he covered them with useful things,
Such as bonds and stocks and Paris frocks
And oriental pearls in strings,
And a showcase full of rings.

Chorus 2
Now those two little babes in the wood
Are the talk of the whole neighborhood
For they've too many cars, too many
    clothes,
Too many parties and too many beaux.
They have found that the fountain of youth
Is a mixture of gin and vermouth,
And the whole town's agreed
That the last thing in speed
Is the two little babes in the wood.

[12] Kochno had a long career as he went on to create ballets for the Ballet Russe de Monte Carlo after Diaghilev's death in 1929. These letters which give the details of his relationship with Porter, only surfaced after Kochno's death in 1990.

In a theatre season that included lavish revues like *George White's Scandals*, *The Ziegfeld Follies*, *The Earl Carroll Vanities*, and the smash-hit operetta *Rose Marie*, *The Greenwich Village Follies*, in spite of Cole's interesting score, was no more than second-rate entertainment. The critics did not care for it and the public who were accustomed to the Dolly Sister's mushy material could not accept their singing Porterian risqué lyrics. With the show playing to half-empty houses, Anderson made a frantic attempt to keep it running by replacing 'Two Little Babes in the Wood'[13] as well as the fourteen other fine songs Cole had contributed, among them 'Brittany', 'My Long Ago Girl', and a song that has since become a standard, 'I'm In Love Again'.

After this crushing disappointment, Cole plunged more frantically than ever into party-giving and party-going. It would not be until four years later, shortly before his thirty-seventh birthday, that he would get down to serious work and start one of the musical theatre's most glowing careers.

[13] Because of the censorship at the time, when 'Two Little Babes in the Wood' was published in sheet copy, the lyrics to the second verse and chorus (printed above) were deleted, giving the would-be amateur singer a harmless waltz that missed the whole point of the song.

NOEL
1921 - 1924

'THERE WILL ALWAYS be a stinging enchantment in this arrival. Even now, when I know it so well in every aspect, my heart jumps a little. Then it was entirely new to me.' So Coward recalled his first impression of New York in 1921. 'We slid gently past Battery Park, still green with early summer. The skyscrapers moved gracefully aside to show still further vistas, and, a long way below us, platoons of straw hats passed by on ferry-boats. As we drew near the dock, several fussy little tugs came out to meet us and finally, after tremendous efforts, succeeded in coaxing and nuzzling us alongside.'

It was certainly an impetuous thing to have done, to have set sail with a bundle of manuscripts, a one-way ticket and only seventeen pounds to spare, but Noel was counting on the experience of his gregarious friend Jeffery and the kindness of strangers. And there, waving on the dock, as a welcoming group: Naps Alington (who was actually waiting to take Jeffery in), Gabrielle Enthoven, who painted cubist portraits and shared a studio in Greenwich Village with Cecile Sartoris, an avant garde composer, and, perhaps the most notorious member of the party, Teddie Gerrard, sometime showgirl and marriage-wrecker extraordinaire who now reportedly was being 'kept' by Linda Porter's ex-lover. Noel had enjoyed Naps's friendship and admired Teddie's scandalous behaviour in London. He at once got on famously with the other two. But the producers Noel was hoping to interest in his plays were either out of town for the summer or about to vacate the sweltering metropolis. Theatres along the Great White Way, in these pre-air-conditioned days, were invariably dark from June to September.

Seventeen pounds, even at five dollars to the pound, do not go very far, yet somehow, through sheer force of will, and with a great deal of charm, Noel eked his way through that humid summer. Gabrielle and Cecile took him into their studio; *Vanity Fair* bought excerpts from a book he and Lorn Macnaughtan had put together on theatre before leaving England, and they paid him a few dollars; and then, when all his funds ran dry, he borrowed – owing everyone from his theatrical friends to the studio cleaning woman and the corner grocer. At last, when he was at his nadir, the editor of *Metropolitan Magazine* invited him to lunch and inquired whether he would be interested in turning the plot of *I'll Leave It To You* into a short story for five hundred dollars. As Noel puts it, recalling those penniless days, 'I reflected gleefully on the way home, that for five hundred dollars I would gladly consider turning *War and Peace* into a music-hall sketch.'

Puffed with his success, Noel almost immediately sold *Metropolitan Magazine* another adaptation, this time a short story based on *The Young Idea*, his play that so closely resembled Shaw's. But the magazine either didn't notice the similarity or didn't care and paid him a further five hundred dollars. Now, although much of the money went to repay his debts, and as a dutiful son he sent Violet enough to help pay the rent on Ebury Street, there was still enough left over for him to enjoy and see something of New York theatre.

What he observed, and what he was to bring to his writing for the rest of his life, was the rapid tempo at which American actors spoke their dialogue. In the first act audiences might be mystified by the clipped speech and the speed of the repartee, but by the third they had caught on and were enjoying the brisk pace.

As autumn approached and the thermometer dropped slightly, Noel was to realize that he or his plays would not make much of an impression on New York until his name was better known in the West End of London.

Luckily, through friends, he was given a free cabin and on October 31, with £10 in his pocket, set sail on a much smaller ship, the S. S. *Cedric*, to return to Britain. Although horribly seasick, he was to recall in his journal how his mind reviewed the events of the previous six months.

> I saw a brave tragic youth trudging through the hot streets to his accustomed bench in Battery Park, friendless and alone, gazing out over the sea to where Green England lay, and sharing, perhaps, a crust with some kindly negro.
>
> I saw the same gallant figure attired in deep evening dress attending the smartest first nights, with not even a nickel in his trouser pocket to pay his subway fare home.
>
> I sorted out my new friends with genuine pleasure, Lynn [Fontanne] and Alfred [Lunt], Cecile and Gabrielle, Alec Woollcott, Lester [Donahue, the pianist Noel knew in London and whose piano he could compose on in New York], Laurette [Taylor], Beatrice and George Kaufman, the Astaires ...

Noel's impecuniousness did not disappear once he was back in England. To make matters worse, he found his mother run-down and looking very pale; the strain of running a house full of boarders was obviously too much for her. Feeling financially responsible yet at a frustratingly awkward stage in his career – too well known to be able to accept little roles, but not famous enough to command big ones – he asked Ned Lathom, who had in the past bought some songs from him, for a loan. Happily, with Lathom's two hundred pounds ('gift – not a loan') he was able to leave his father in charge of the Ebury Street boarding house and rent a small cottage in the country where his mother could rest. He planned to come down every weekend to write. By the following spring he had completed a new play, *The Queen was in the Parlour*.

At long last, that June, his career began to move into high gear. Robert Courtneidge took an option on *The Young Idea*, to be produced in the autumn, and, since there is nothing so reassuring as a contract in one's pocket, the young playwright quickly acquired some new clothes and while waiting for rehearsals to begin moved back into the social whirl. At one of Lady Colefax's soirées he met Elsa Maxwell, who was charmed by Noel's songs and manner; it was not long before she persuaded her rich patroness, Dorothy Fellows-Gordon, better known as 'Dickie', to invite Noel to be their guest for a fortnight in Venice. Ostensibly he was to be their chaperon, or as he says 'a gigolo unimpaired by amatory obligations', but café society whispered he was their beard.

No sooner had Noel returned to Britain than Courtneidge, true to his promise, rehearsed and opened *The Young Idea* in Bristol. Reviews and business were good and after a short tour of the provinces the play would have opened in London – except, that since the autumn of 1922 was a particularly active West End season, no theatres were available. The West End engagement was postponed until after Christmas, when the pantomime season would be over. Noel went to Davos, in Switzerland, to stay with Ned Lathom, who was recuperating from a bout of tuberculosis.

Lathom, who greatly appreciated Coward's music, lyrics and mordant satire, was an aficionado of sophisticated songs and sketches. (It was well known in theatre circles that he single-handedly financed André Charlot's

In *The Young Idea*, 1923, with, left to right:
Kate Cutler, Herbert Marshall and Ann Trevor

revue *A to Z*).[1] He made Noel play all he had written, and after he had listened several times announced that he believed there was enough for that rare commodity, a one-man revue. Noel was exhilarated. His experience was not unlike Cole Porter's when Raymond Hitchcock jumped out of his chair on the *Mauretania* and told Cole he'd take all the songs for *Hitchy-Koo of 1919*. But, of course, in Coward's case there was Charlot to convince.

André Charlot, Britain's best known producer of intimate revues, had been active since the mid-1910s. A Charlot presentation had a built-in audience and a cachet of sophistication. Where Ziegfeld and Charles Cochran mounted lavish productions, Charlot's were smaller, his costuming and lighting sensitive, his comedy topical and his songs and dances highly original. Ned Lathom was rich enough to summon, not invite, Charlot, and after a series of cigar-smoke-laden conferences, during which the impresario was as enthusiastic as his host had been, *London Calling*, after the newly-established BBC's catchphrase, was born.

Throughout Christmas, every morning, Noel worked on sketches and new songs, presenting them to the two showmen in the afternoon. Evenings were spent enlarging Noel's already burgeoning social contacts. New entries in that season's engagement book were Clifton Webb, Teddie Thompson, Gladys Cooper, Dick Wyndham, Edward Molyneux, and Maxine Elliott. Many of them were to become theatrical collaborators, all were to remain fast friends.

In mid-January, while the skiing season was in full bloom, Noel, who had by now become part of the *haut monde*, returned to London for the imminent opening of *The Young Idea*. The play, although well reviewed (it had especial praise from Charles Cochran), inexplicably expired with the month of March after a mere eight weeks, but this time Noel did not worry – he had turned the corner beyond 'promising' and his play was soon to be published, with the author receiving a handsome percentage of the subsidiary performance rights.

Now with casting almost complete – except for the male lead[2] – it would soon be time to begin rehearsals for *London Calling*. Noel, disappointed at first because this was not to be totally a one-man effort, supplied most of the music and lyrics (the balance was provided by Philip Braham, who also conducted the orchestra). Additionally he wrote the lion's share of the sketches, the remainder being supplied by Ronald Jeans. Charlot called in Fred Astaire to choreograph some of the dance numbers. With Noel supported by Gertrude

[1] *A to Z* was a smash hit in London, running for over four hundred performances. It featured Beatrice Lillie, Gertrude Lawrence and Jack Buchanan, and introduced the Braham-Furber hit 'Limehouse Blues', and Novello's comic 'And Her Mother Came Too'.

[2] When Charlot agreed in Switzerland to bring in *London Calling* under his aegis he offered Coward a mere £15 a week, a salary which the latter refused. Now, as time until the opening was running out, Noel cannily demanded and got £40, and an escape clause (should he tire of the revue) to boot.

Lawrence, Maisie Gay, Eileen Molyneux and Tubby Edlin there was no lack of talent. But it is one thing to entertain at parties, singing witty songs to one's own accompaniment, and another to stage a proper revue with a full company. Mounting *London Calling* would require choral parts, key changes, segues, and a proper musical score in manuscript – professional techniques Noel had merely heard about. Somehow Coward inveigled Fred Astaire (who, because like Noel he had gone on the stage at an early age, had never had any conservatory training) to enroll with him at the Guildhall School of Music in London. Noel signed on for the full course, Astaire only studied sight singing, but the former's experience was his first and last with 'proper' conservatory dogma. He recalls it in his preface to *The Noel Coward Songbook*.

> ... I was told by my instructor that I could not use consecutive fifths. He went on to explain that a gentleman called Ebenezer Prout had announced many years ago that consecutive fifths were wrong and must in no circumstances be employed. At that time Ebenezer Prout was merely a name to me (as a matter of fact he still is, and a very funny one at that), and I was unimpressed by his Victorian dicta. I argued back that Debussy and Ravel used consecutive fifths like mad. My instructor waved aside this triviality with a pudgy hand, and I left his presence for ever with the parting shot that what was good enough for Debussy and Ravel was good enough for me. This rugged outburst of individualism deprived me of much valuable knowledge, and I have never deeply regretted it for a moment.

Coward goes on to explain that his involvement in acting, writing, singing and dancing seemed more important in his early days than learning to write counterpoint. He admits he is often irritated by his inability to write down tunes and his complete ignorance of orchestration which forces him to rely on the skills of others, but rationalizes this by saying that he has never been unduly depressed that all his music has had to be dictated. In actuality he is right. This writer believes with Noel that 'there are many light composers who have never so much as put a crochet on paper'.

Because of his inability to write his songs down he needed to find someone musical enough to capture the melodic, harmonic and rather subtle rhythmic feeling embodied in them. Just such a one he found in Elsie April. Elsie, who had worked on countless Charlot revues, was to become his musical amanuensis and involved in all of his work from *London Calling* until the beginning of the Second World War, at which time Norman Hackforth took over. Elsie never ceased to mystify Coward, who remarked 'she could transfer melody and harmony onto paper with the swiftness of an expert shorthand stenographer'.

The first edition[3] of the revue which ran for 316 performances comprised twenty-six numbers. Noel was responsible as composer or lyricist for

[3] Programming for a Charlot revue was never rigid. Skits that were no longer newsworthy were deleted later in the run, songs that failed to elicit the required enthusiasm from performer or audience were dropped. New and topical skits and songs (in the tradition of current New York and London cabaret) were frequently added.

sixteen of them. His hand was evident everywhere, and the notices announced it as *his* revue, for he was on stage as creator or performer almost throughout.

The critics were enthusiastic although some threw a few brickbats, notably at Noel's singing and dancing of a number he had been coached in by Fred Astaire which he thought would be the hit of the show. Coward himself was not as much deceived as disappointed. Recalling that fiasco he was to write:

> The only complete and glorious failure was my performance of 'Sentiment'. I bounded on fully confident that I was going to bring the house down...Immaculately dressed in tails, with a silk hat and cane, I sang every witty couplet with perfect diction and a wealth of implication which sent them winging into the dark auditorium where they fell like wet pennies into mud...I executed an intricate dance...tapping, after-beating, whacking my cane on the stage, and finally exiting to a spatter of applause led, I suspected, by Mother...

Coward is much too hard on himself here. The real culprit is Philip Braham who sets Noel's passable lyric with a boringly jerky melody (Bar 1) replete with wrong accents (Bar 2) and then strangles the phrase before completion so that the words 'at all' (Bar 4) come out as a senseless hiccough.

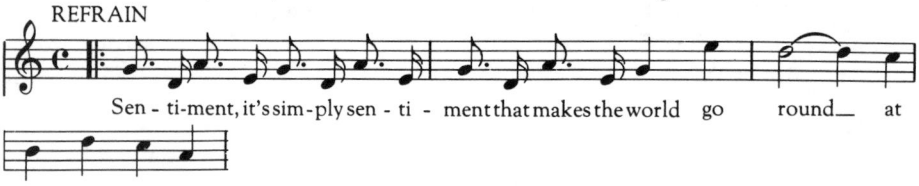

But, beyond that, there seemed to be nothing but praise for the show. Gertrude Lawrence, crooning the exotic 'Tamarisk Town' (much used by Noel for early auditions) and later wistfully singing 'Parisian Pierrot' in what the critics called a 'spectacular' Commedia del Arte scene, stole the hearts of all the gentlemen of the press. Miss Lawrence, who shared the comic songs with Maisie Gay was given one of the show's most arch numbers, 'Carrie', in which she portrayed a modern-day bad seed. Some of Coward's lyric is printed below.

Verse I
Carrie as a baby was a darling little pet
And everybody loved her, from the Vicar to
   the Vet.
Her manners when at school were most
   ingenuous and quaint,
She had the reputation of a little plaster saint...

Refrain 2
Carrie was a careful girl,
Such a very careful girl,
She stole out on the landing while the
others were at prayers,
And rubbed a lot of grease upon the
   dormitory stairs,
Carrie was a careful girl,
In her little cot she'd curl,
The teacher fell down half a flight and
   landed on her head,
And naturally to Carrie not a single word
   was said
'Cos they found a pat of butter in her little
   sister's bed,
Carrie was a careful girl.

In the succeeding verses and choruses, Carrie's nefarious exploits go far beyond tripping up the headmistress. Soon she blackmails her father, cheats at craps and traps a nobleman into marriage, thus qualifying as a fully-fleshed Cowardian character.

Maisie Gay, too, came in for her share of hilarity. As a tired actress in a delighful music hall number, 'There's Life in the Old Girl Yet', she had lines like 'They call me Flossie/Because I'm mossy/And because I always go the pace./I show traces of laces and silk underneath/I'm as old as my tongue but much older than my teeth/My goodness gracious,/I'm so vivacious/Always ready for a kiss or two/Tho' at one time people always called me "Gladstone's Pet",/Still there's life in the old girl yet.'

Coward's best songs were the spritely 'Other Girls', which he himself sang, and the haunting 'When My Ship Comes Home'[4] which presages the Ira Gershwin-Kurt Weill 'My Ship', from Lady in the Dark, by some twenty years.

Noel was indeed modest to share credit for the book with Ronald Jeans, for undoubtedly the best sketches of the evening were his own. His 'Rain Before Seven' was a hilarious caricature of a Platonic honeymoon, and 'Early Mourning' a satire on social mores. The latter concerns a wife who is awakened by a police report of her estranged husband's jump off Waterloo Bridge, and then arranges a luncheon to gossip about his death. Of course just before the black-out, we learn the suicide was not her husband.

Hilarious as this sketch was, and though it did give Gertrude Lawrence a chance to distinguish herself, its humour was dwarfed by a playlet that was to become a cause célèbre and contribute mightily to the longevity of London Calling. Called 'The Swiss Family Whittlebot', it was an obvious swipe at Osbert, Sacheverell and especially Edith Sitwell. Poets, memoirists, critics, these three well-born, to many insufferable siblings appointed themselves commandants of the avant garde in its perpetual battle with the philistines. For the purpose of his sketch Noel renamed them Gob, Sago and Hernia Whittlebot, dressed the brothers in Victorian outfits as designed by a dadaist, and gave them queer musical instruments to play. The recitation was done by Maisie Gay, superbly broad as Hernia.

After some nonsense verses, Noel has his protagonist declaim these lines which were to spark a ten-year feud with Edith Sitwell:

I will now recite my tone poem 'Passion' to which special music
has been set by my brother, Gob, on the Cophuitican.

    Passion's dregs are the salt of life   Drains and Sewers suppose the quest
    Spirits trodden beneath the heel of   Of eternal indulgence
Ingratitude.   Thank God for the Coldstream Guards.

---

[4] See Musical Analysis Appendix.

Hernia continues with her long poem, 'The Lower Classes', wherein she endeavours to portray the 'bottomless hostility of the Labour Party', and is eventually pushed off the stage still reciting:

... Freedom from all this shrieking vortex   Of local Aprophlegmatism
Chimneys and tramcars and blackened branches   Melody semi-spheroidal
Of superfluous antagonism   In all its innate rotundity
Oxford and Cambridge count for naught   Rhubarb for purposes unknown ...
Life is ephemeral before the majesty

The critics took sides on the propriety of the satire while the theatre-going public avidly soaked up the news. Osbert fanned the flames ignited after Noel had ostentatiously walked out of a poetry reading of his by announcing that he would have to miss the revue because he was called out of town for a few days. Noel's riposte was that he would put a stage box at Osbert's disposal to hold his sister, brother and all their followers and admirers whenever they wished to attend. Even well after the opening furore had quietened Noel kept the character he had created alive, and news of Hernia Whittlebot's activities (such as her latest book *Gilded Sluts and Garbage*) began appearing regularly on the BBC and in gossip columns.

The publicity did neither of them any harm, but although Edith grudgingly forgave Noel, after he wrote a public apology, in her heart of hearts she still harboured resentment. One can note her 'persecution complex' in an excerpt from a letter she wrote to John Lehmann as late as 1947:

> ... I am sick of being attacked by persons of no talent ... In 1923 Mr. Coward began on me in a 'sketch' of the utmost indecency – *really filthy*. I couldn't have him up, as I had no money and didn't know how to set about it. Nobody helped me, and I had to put up with having *filthy* verses about vice imputed to me and recited every night and three afternoons weekly for *nine months*.[5] They weren't just dirty, they were filthy. The woman who recited them went so far in her persecution of me as to have a photograph of me in her dressing room. These attacks...have gone on since then and I have always had to put up with them.

Edith Sitwell's imprecations notwithstanding, *London Calling* continued to sell out. Now Charlot, of course, was eager to bring his hot new property to New York. Leaving Maisie Gay, Tubby Edlin and Noel to hold the West End, he sent Gertrude Lawrence abroad and engaged Beatrice Lillie and Jack Buchanan (whose names were well known to the Americans) to ensure his success on Broadway. And he further scuttled the London company by sending the best of the chorus to New York.

Although he enjoyed seeing his name twinkling above the theatre and hearing his music played in restaurants, Noel, left floundering with the second cast, soon became bored with the revue. The decision to forgo his weekly £40

---

[5] *London Calling* actually ran a full year.

Tubby Edlin (left)
introducing 'The Swiss
Family Whittlebot':
Gob (Leonard Childs),
Hernia (Maisie Gay)
and Sago (William
Childs)

salary was not easy, but since he had ensonced Violet comfortably in a country cottage and his father was taking care of both Eric and the boarding house, and, perhaps most important of all, Noel had that all-powerful escape clause written into his contract, he decided to leave for America four months later. Besides, since the opening of *London Calling*, he had written two new plays, *Fallen Angels* and *The Vortex*, that he felt were worth peddling, and was ready to knock on the doors of these very producers who had been "out of town" to him two years ago.

In his ultimate determination he was not unlike Cole Porter, who, in his quest for an assignment, would come out of the doldrums and batter his knuckles on producers' doors three years later. For the time being, though, the differences between them were marked, Noel, in 1924, was practically penniless, and only at the beginning of his career. Cole, in the same year, became heir to a fortune, and forsook real talent for an endless round of drugs, alcohol and promiscuity. Soon they were to meet, devastate each other, and eventually become lifelong friends.

COLE
1924-1930

I T TOOK COLE PORTER until 1927 to learn belatedly what most of his thick-skinned contemporaries had known since the outset of their careers: if one chooses the 'profession' of songwriting one must be able to face rejection without being overwhelmed. Noel had been 'rising above' (his favourite phrase) since he was a child, and that gave him the somewhat smug sense of confidence that was to be his trademark, but Cole was unable to face the brush-off no matter how gentle the glove. Yet he was no longer able to convince himself that the few interpolations, occasional performances and flops he had been associated with so far gave him more than amateur standing.

Vain as he was, even his mirror must have told him that now, at thirty-six, he was well beyond the emergent artist stage. At last he realized that, with his timidity about putting his own work forward, he would have to hire somebody who could do it for him. Once he had come to this decision, he booked passage on the next liner to America for himself and Linda, moved into a suite at the Ritz in New York and invited the super-agent Louis Shurr to lunch. It was to be the most important career decision of his life.

Shurr looked after the careers of Irene Dunne, Jeanette MacDonald, Marilyn Miller, Bert Lahr, Victor Moore, Jack Pearl, William Gaxton and Clifton Webb, all of whom were then stars on Broadway and several of whom would soon achieve stardom in Hollywood. Since Shurr was familiar with and thought Cole's songs were far above what was being written at the time, he immediately proposed that his new client be given a chance to write the score for a forthcoming review under the aegis of Broadway's top producing team, Alex Aarons and Vinton Freedley.

Aarons and Freedley were producers of style and sophistication who had made their fortune with meticulous productions of the Gershwin shows. Starting with a very successful production of *Lady Be Good* in 1924 they had gone on to present *Tip-Toes* in 1925, and now the money was pouring in from their production of *Oh, Kay!*, starring Gertrude Lawrence, which had been running for a whole year.

In 1927 they were looking for a new musical, but were split on the suitability of Cole's songs. Freedley considered them too recherché, more like revue material (which they were), while Aarons felt they were old-fashioned compared to Gershwin's (which they weren't). In the end the producers decided to stick with George and Ira, commissioning them to do yet another show.[1]

But, before Cole could be too depressed by this further rejection, Shurr was approached by Ray Goetz, songwriter, playwright, producer and, more importantly, husband of Irene Bordoni, with a request that Shurr acquire the talents of Rodgers and Hart to write the score of the forthcoming show he intended to produce with Gilbert Miller. Of course, the show which would be called *Paris* would feature the fey Miss Bordoni, who had a reputation for singing amusingly suggestive songs. Shurr admitted that he thought Rodgers and Hart might do a creditable job, but he had to point out to Goetz that they were even now busily employed turning out the score of *A Connecticut Yankee* and suggested Cole instead. Goetz knew Cole's work, since they had collaborated on the gentle love song 'Washington Square' way back in 1920[2]. As an agent selling his client, Shurr was quick to point out Cole's unique way with suggestive material and to mention that his American and Parisian background suited him admirably for the job. Goetz agreed completely and, as soon as the contracts were signed, a jubilant Cole and Linda returned to Venice where Cole would begin work on the show.

For what would turn out to be their fifth and last summer there they again rented the Palazzo Rezzonico. In previous years the Porters had organized a whole series of charity balls and soirées. But this summer would be different. Now Cole invited only Goetz and Bordoni, and, although there were sun and sand in the afternoons and small entertainments in the evenings, the script and songs of *Paris* took precedence on Cole's agenda. Even Linda must have felt *de trop* for she went off to Switzerland claiming she was having another of her bronchial attacks.

Unfortunately, in the midst of this first summer of Cole's working in earnest, his father, Samuel Porter, with whom he had had scant contact in recent years, died, on August 18. A few days after the funeral, the weekly *Peru Republican* carried this story:

> Samuel F. Porter, age 69, prominent Peru business man for many years and father of Cole Porter, author of several musical comedies and the song 'An Old Fashioned Garden', died last Thursday ... of complications following a nervous breakdown[3]. He had been ill 38 days ... Cole Porter was to have left Paris Saturday and is expected to arrive in Peru the first of the week.

---

[1] The show they sponsored that year was the overwhelmingly successful *Funny Face*. Although the team of Aarons and Freedley was to face hard times and split up as the result of the Depression, Vinton Freedley was to bounce back alone and to shepherd Cole's masterpiece *Anything Goes* onto the stage.

[2] Goetz had the good taste to be able to spot talent. He collaborated (writing mostly lyrics) with Irving Berlin in 1913, Sigmund Romberg in 1915 and with George Gershwin in 1922 (this was before Ira became his brother's lyricist).

[3] The psychoanalyst Leonard Diamond, after reviewing the facts of Samuel Porter's demise, was of the opinion that the cause of death was probably suicide.

Cole had indeed rushed back to Paris, sailed on the *Berengaria* and hurried to Peru, not because of any filial affection – he often stated that his father never appreciated him – but because he wanted to comfort his mother. It was to be many years before Cole would grudgingly admit that, however ineffectual his father had been, it was from him that his son's early love of rhymes, poems and cadences had stemmed.

That autumn, while Cole was hard at work preparing the score of *Paris* for a February opening, he was approached by Edmond Sayag, the director of the Ambassadeurs nightclub, to write a revue. Located on the rue Gabriel, just off the Champs-Elysées, with its sumptuous auditorium, well-spaced tables and a fully professional stage, the Ambassadeurs was the French capital's most expensive show-spot – charging an unheard-of $70 for dinner and a revue. It was frequented almost exclusively by sovereign dignitaries, most of whom spoke English, and if they did not would be too snobbish to admit it.

For this edition of the show, Sayag signed Morton Downey, a well-known balladeer; Evelyn Hoey, an ingénue singer; Frances Gershwin, another ingénue singer and, the sister of George and Ira; Georgie Hale, a dancer; Buster West, the comedy star; and the Fred Waring orchestra to back them. These were tempting talents to write for and, since the revue was not scheduled to open until next May, by which time *Paris* would have been unveiled, Cole accepted eagerly.

What he created is an unknown and (except for 'Pilot Me', one of the show's weakest songs) an unrecorded gem. Because the audience he was writing for was to be so international, Cole was able to mine material he knew best: money, lechery, travel and snobbery. The twenty-four-song score he produced for what was simply called *La Revue des Ambassadeurs* marks a turning point in Cole's career and displays a hitherto unexplored musical experimentation and maturity especially in metre, rhythm, balance and variety. Cole was always at his best in revue or when he followed a mere wisp of a plot, for his songs never revealed his characters in the way they illuminated himself. In this score one can glimpse some of the European *weltschmerz* of Kurt Weill mixed with the bluesy sound of George Gershwin. A cursory look at the best of the songs follows:

The Lost Liberty Blues. Sung by Evelyn Hoey as the Statue of Liberty, this number is a diatribe against the loss of personal freedoms, especially the prohibition of alcohol which was then current in the United States. It uses typical blues chord changes (I to IV Dominant 7 to V) and the blues triplet. The lyric of its verse talks about how, when France gave the landmark to the US, she was supposed to be a symbol of freedom, but, she continues in the chorus, 'I've got those lost liberty blues/ With a pair of handcuffs on my wrist/ And padlocks on my shoes/ Can you expect me to be gay/ Or ask me to enthuse?/ While reformers lead 'em/ From the battle cry of freedom/ To the lost liberty blues.'

In a Moorish Garden. Sung by Morton Downey. A rather sentimental, exotic song, the kind that was all the rage in the Valentino-mad '20s. Written in the key of F and using A A B A form which would be preferred for the majority of songs in the '30s, there is a delicate modulation leading to G minor at the end of the second A. The bridge uses the circle of chords and much inner rhyme as well as the following melody and lyrics:

Almiro. Introduced by Basil Howes. This narrative song about the rise and fall of a Brazilian dancer is the kind of gigolo summation that Cole was to do devastatingly well. With lines like: 'Almiro/ Brought a step from Rio Janeiro/ People cheered whenever Almiro/ Started dancing it up and down./ And though Almiro,/ As a lover equalled a zero,/ All the ladies called him the hero/ Of Rio Janeiro Town.'

You and Me. A duet for Mary Leigh and Basil Howes. This is the kind of melody that Noel Coward was to write a decade later or Stephen Sondheim was to re-invent in a quarter of a century. The verse introduces some of the 'pseudo-Jewish' melodic line for which Porter would become famous in his later work. The lyric, though breaking no new ground, is simple, elemental, honest and easy to sing.

Fish. Sung by Carter Wardell. The most obvious thing about this song is its double entendre lyric. For, in the largest sense, the 'fish' referred to in the title of the first chorus is one a country girl would like to catch with lines like, 'Fish, fish,[4] don't be so capricious, sample my line. All the other fishes say it's delicious.' The second verse has the girl go off to 'Paree – where even the wise fish get caught'. Thus, when the same chorus lines are now sung jadedly, the song becomes a clear-cut one of solicitation. Interesting as the lyric is, one should not overlook the melody which alternates between a I and a IV dominant 9 as follows:

---

[4] The word 'fish' was used by Cole as well as Noel Coward as an ethnic slur on the French. Coward wrote 'There's Always Something Fishy about the French.' Both men were not immune to the prevailing fashion of denigration. One can find 'coon', 'nigger', 'kike', 'wop' and 'frog' in their lyrics.

Military Maids. Introduced by Evelyn Hoey and the chorus. As the title predicts these are Amazons, properly feral and aiming to battle until they get their men. With a bugle-like verse and a stirring chorus in minor, this is an irresistible number.

Blue Hours. This waltz sung by Morton Downey was originally intended for *Paris*, but since there were too many waltzes in that score it was used here. It presages the '30s in form and its use of the I and the IV minor 6. A glance at the theme will expose Porter's strong harmonic security.

Baby, Let's Dance. Introduced by Buster West. This is the most daring number Cole had created so far. Although written in 4/4, a two measure sample of the verse emerges as 3, 3, and 2 (thereby adding up to 8 beats in a manner nobody but Gershwin and Weill were writing into popular music). The blues-like chorus switches in and out of the modes. The lyric, with its references to 'baby' in both senses and 'bottle' holding either milk or gin, is often brutal and sadistic and is certainly one of Porter's best:

Verse

Come, Baby, wake up,
Put on your make-up,
It's time to take up
Your bottle, Baby.

So, dry your eyes up
And hush those cries up
Or Poppa'll rise up
And throttle baby.

Turn on the Victor
Please me to death,
Be a boa constrictor
Squeeze me to death.

Refrain

Take hold of my hand,
Baby, just listen to that band,
Baby, oh isn't it just grand?
Baby, let's dance.
I've got a new step,
Baby, so come on and get hep,
Baby we'll turn on the old pep,
Baby, let's dance.
Just put your head on my heart

And we'll start
Shakin' the shoes,
Wakin' the blues,
Breakin' the news.
Hang on and hold tight,
Baby, I feel like a big night
Baby, so give me a kick,
Out of a quick
Dance, Baby, let's dance.

Old Fashioned Girl and **Old Fashioned Boy**. The former was sung by Basil Howes and the latter by Mary Leigh. Perhaps this song was written because Cole's best-known song up to that point had been 'Old Fashioned Garden', but actually this tune which might have been written by Jerome Kern is more interesting and the lyric is unsentimentalized when the girl tells us what kind of old fashioned boy she's looking for. (There is a savoury and characteristically Kernlike harmonic change occurring from the 12th bar of the verse onward.)
Fountain of Youth. Sung by Buster West and the ensemble, this must have wowed the somewhat mature audiences who would have attended this show. The rather bluesy melody with a strong Charleston rhythm was coupled with lyrics that exhort the elderly to 'jump in the cool Fountain of Youth,/ Continue swimming about/ Till your grey has turned to gold/ And you'll come out/ Just a gay young two year old'.

The ten terrific songs mentioned above are only part of a score that contained 'Looking At You', added when Clifton Webb joined the company and later used in *Wake Up and Dream*; 'Alpine Rose', and an amusing yodel number, 'Hans', in which a frustrated Dutch housewife pleads, 'Hans, Hans, let's go to the dance/ The others all have gone./ The sweet summer breeze is/ So fragrant with cheeses/ There must be a party on./ Hans, Hans, One night of romance/ would fill my heart with joy,/ But a much longer wait'll/ Prove fatal/ to Gretel/ So hurry, Hans, my boy!'

Although this revue marked the end of a long period of creative stagnation, it was with the next show, *Paris*, that Cole would finally be accepted into the upper echelon of Broadway songwriters. While not a revue, the plot of *Paris* is so slight that the critics couldn't find it.

A young Bostonian is rescued from the clutches of a naughty Parisian showgirl (Miss Bordoni) by the arrival of his society-matron mother. Only in a '20s musical comedy could the mother then be transformed through drink into a flapper, foiling her son's romance and sending the showgirl back into the arms of her leading man. (The concept of the son ending up with his now-sexually-enticing mother sits perfectly with the events in Cole's real life.)

The reviewers found the librettist's greatest achievement of the evening was the introduction of an eleven-piece orchestra into Miss Bordoni's unit-set hotel room. But the musicians also served as an *ad hoc* chorus singing and dancing at times, giving the evening a freshness not previously seen on Broadway.

The show opened in Atlantic City in February 1928, a mere five weeks after the Kern-Hammerstein *Show Boat* in a season that set records for quality and variety boasting *Good News*, *My Maryland*, *A Connecticut Yankee*, *The Three Musketeers* and *Rosalie*. Goetz wisely kept *Paris* on the road for eight months, touring and polishing, while Cole shuttled back and forth, preparing *La Revue* for production, and adding and deleting songs to and from both shows.

Although Cole treated his involvement with the revue as a gigantic social event, he supervised rehearsals with his thoroughly seasoned cast and held to the highest professional standards. When *La Revue des Ambassadeurs* opened on May 10, 1928 it received excellent critical notices in the French press. The social pages of those same papers carried columns describing the lavish first night (and succeeding) parties at the club. Indeed this opening night was to become the prototype for every succeeding Porter show, and Cole was never to tire of the attendant excitement, the invitations that he and Linda would oversee, the pre-performance white tie dinners and post-theatre champagne buffets. In one of the rare departures from their opening night ritual, when *Paris* opened on Broadway, in October of that year, the Porters were so ensconced in the night-life of the French capital (and perhaps because Cole had come to expect so little at the hands of the New York critics) they did not attend.

The New York critics were extremely sympathetic this time and singled out Cole's songs for praise. Although Goetz and his ever-present collaborators had contributed heavily to the score, the *Herald Tribune* went so far as to call Cole 'the flaming star' while Charles Brackett, the critic of the *New Yorker*, described him as 'a rare and satisfactory talent', adding that 'no one else now writing words and music knows so exactly the delicate balance between sense, rhyme and rhythm'. Miss Bordoni sang 'I've Got Quelque Chose', 'Don't Look at Me That Way', and 'Let's Misbehave', but her greatest triumph occurred when it was decided to replace the negative aspects of 'Let's Misbehave' with what has become one of Cole's best known songs, 'Let's Do It'.[5] The censors insisted that the title be printed as 'Let's Do It, Let's Fall in Love' lest the 'it' be taken for what Cole had intended it to mean in the first place.[6]

---

[5] See Musical Analysis Appendix 2.
[6] When 'Let's Do It', a tremendous hit in the US, was added to the score of *Wake Up and Dream* and was performed in England, Cole was justifiably nervous that the lyrics might be too salty to be approved by the British censors. He was mightily relieved when the Lord Chamberlain congratulated him for the extensive animal, ethnic and insect research that had gone into his lists of creatures who 'do it'.

Irene Bordoni, star of *Paris*, with members of the Irving Aaronson orchestra

With two practically simultaneous successes to his credit, it was clear that Cole's career had suddenly shifted into high gear. Now everybody wanted him. And his work produced in 1929 was to be received with even louder hosannas.

La Revue, an undoubted success in Paris, and *Paris*, selling out nightly in New York, made it inevitable that the British impresario Charles B. Cochran would call on him. The previous year he had successfully produced Noel Coward's *This Year of Grace* which was still packing them in at the London Pavilion, now he wanted to try his talents on a lavish entertainment, a Ziegfeld-like extravaganza.

It would be called *Wake Up and Dream*[7] and would have 24 elaborate settings, 500 costumes and a thread of a book by John Hastings Turner. The large international cast would feature Jessie Matthews, her husband Sonnie Hale, the dancer Tilly Losch and George Metaxa, and Cole would provide the entire score, whose most memorable numbers would be 'The Banjo That Man

[7] This rather incongruous title only makes sense when one remembers Cole's lyric which begins: 'When you grumble and sigh/ And you ask yourself why/ You've the weight of the world on your mind,/ Did you ever reflect/ It's because you neglect/ The dreams you've left behind?/ They were gay, they were mad,/ Those dreams you had,/ And you welcomed them with open arms./ But in giving your life/ To the world and his wife/ You have fallen asleep to their charms.... Wake up and dream ... Things are really not what they seem ...'

Joe Plays', 'I Loved Him – But He Didn't Love Me', 'Looking At You' ('I'm filled with the essence of, the quintessence of joy. Looking at you I hear poets tellin' of lovely Helen of Troy'), the British première of 'Let's Do It – Let's Fall in Love', and what would become one of his most frequently performed songs, 'What Is This Thing Called Love?'

This last was given sensual choreography by Tilly Losch in an exotic setting before an enormous African idol. The orchestra whipped up a persistent tom-tom beat to which Miss Losch danced, while Elsie Carlisle, the

Tilli Losch (left) and Toni Birkmayer in front of idol William Cavenagh in *Wake Up and Dream*

show's languorous torch singer, leaned against the proscenium arch and intoned the refrain. The song, while far from one of Cole's best, created a palpable sexuality and became the hit of the show.

Totally overlooked by most critics, or worse yet listed as 'comic numbers', were 'I'm a Gigolo,' and 'The Extra Man', the kind of heartbreaking songs Cole Porter alone could write. The lyrics of the bridge of the former sum up Cole's keen observation of men whom he called 'undersexed', and who were always found 'next to some dowager who's wealthy rather than passionate':

I get stocks and bonds	Still I'm just a pet
From faded blondes	That men forget
Ev'ry twenty-fifth of December,	And only tailors remember.

In 'The Extra Man', Porter's empathy with the expendability of a human being in his rarefied social set is even more pathetic. He describes him thus: 'I'm handsome, I'm harmless, I'm helpful, I'm able,/ A perfect fourth at bridge or a fourteenth at table.' And of his projected death Cole's lyric goes: 'You will feel sad as the news you scan,/ For that means one less extra man.'

Although Cole was often thought of as being a cold, uncaring man, his feelings for the lonely, the ostracized members of society, in these and other songs like 'Love For Sale' or 'Down in the Depths', display a sensitivity rarely accorded him.

Wake Up and Dream received mixed reviews from London's critics but still was able to chalk up a run of 263 performances; this was enough for Cochran to decide to transfer the production and its stars to Broadway's Selwyn Theater, opening on December 30, 1929. With unenthusiastic reviews and the recent stock market crash cutting into its audiences, even an expensive extravaganza like this one was only able to eke out 136 performances. But, because Walter Winchell singled out 'What Is This Thing Called Love?' as an example of the newest breed of love song, Cole's personal success was assured.

Between the première of *Wake Up and Dream* in March and its transfer to Broadway at the year's end, Cole became involved in two projects that would further secure his reputation. The first, a movie assignment, was inevitable. Paramount Pictures, like all the movie studios, was trying to slake the public's newborn thirst for singing, dancing, talking pictures. (Ever since Al Jolson's *The Jazz Singer* only eighteen months before, all the studios had begun hiring well-known songwriters.)

Paramount's project seemed tailor-made for Cole. To star Gertrude Lawrence in her first celluloid appearance, and called *The Battle of Paris*[8], it

---

[8] At the time he contracted with Paramount, *Paris* was still running on Broadway.

looked at first like a certain success. Gene Markey, the prominent script-writer, undertook the screenplay but unfortunately what he turned out was a banal musical comedy into which even Robert Florey, brilliant director that he was, could not breathe life. When the movie was finally released, Miss Lawrence, who played a singing-pickpocket gamine replete with upper-class British accent and her perennial habit of singing off pitch, made this view of 'the lighter side of war' utterly ludicrous and fired the critics to coin the term 'floperetta'. To make matters worse, Cole's songs, which were decidely second-rate did not seem to fit into the score at all. 'Here Comes the Bandwagon' and 'They All Fall In Love' were written in New York and sent off to Hollywood; and, although the Porters would later rent a glamorous house in the cinema capital, and spend much time basking in the California sun, Cole habitually and noticeably wrote down for the movies.

The other project to occupy him in mid-1929 was a new show, *Fifty Million Frenchmen*, produced by Ray Goetz and with a libretto by Herbert Fields. The plot, rather a good one and not unlike what Frank Loesser would turn to a quarter of a century later when he wrote *Guys and Dolls*, concerns a young reprobate millionaire who bets his friend he can win the affections of Loulou, an American debutante who is visiting Paris with her parents. He takes a job as their tour guide which conveniently allows for songs by all the others on the tour. Helen Broderick, as a filthy-minded fur buyer who sends French postcards home to her children, stopped the show with 'Where Would You Get Your Coat?' ('If you modern wives led more domestic lives/ And started singing "Home Sweet Home"/ There'd be no more divorce in Paris and/ There'd be no more annulments in Rome ... / If the dear little rabbits weren't so bourgeois in their habits,/ Tell me where would you get your coat?') and 'The Tale of the Oyster'.[9] Of course, at the final curtain Loulou abandons the Grand Duke her parents have selected for her and the hero wins the bet (further borrowing, now from *Around the World in 80 Days*) just before time runs out.

The hits of the show were 'You Do Something To Me' ('Do do that voodoo that you do so well') and 'You've Got That Thing' ('Just what made Samson be for years/ Delilah's lord and keeper?/ She only had a pair of shears,/ But you, you've got a reaper'), but several numbers, some of which were dropped from this frankly over-long score, have since found their way onto cabaret stages or recordings, among them: 'Find Me a Primitive Man', 'The Happy Heaven of Harlem', 'Why Shouldn't I Have You', 'You Don't Know Paree',[10] 'I'm Unlucky at Gambling', 'Please Don't Make Me Be Good', 'The Queen Of Terra Haute', 'Why Don't We Try Staying Home', 'Let's Step Out'

[9] See Analytical Appendix 5.
[10] See Analytical appendix

and, a special favourite of Cole's which he would try to use in future shows, 'I Worship You'.

Fifty Million Frenchmen received mixed reviews. Gilbert Seldes led the cheers with 'the lyrics alone are enough to drive anyone but P. G. Wodehouse into retirement', and Gilbert Gabriel chimed in with 'the best thing in seven years!' but there were several objections. Among them were Brooks Atkinson and Richard Watts who respectively damned the show by calling it 'pleasant', and saying 'there's not an outstanding song hit in the show'. Since this was an expensive production ($254,000) and needed to gross $30,000 per week in order to keep running, the reviews it received condemned it to closing within three weeks.

Helen Broderick, who had received good personal notices, objected strongly to the reviews. She recalled the time she and Cole ran into one of the negative critics in the lobby of their hotel. In spite of Cole's objection she approached the journalist and shouted, 'You critics are like eunuchs, because you tell us how to do things you cannot do yourselves!'

Luckily, there was a *deus ex machina* waiting in the wings. This time it was Irving Berlin, long a staunch champion of Porter's work[11], who took out a paid advertisement proclaiming: 'The best musical comedy I have seen in years ... More laughs than I have heard in a long time. One of the best collections of song numbers I have ever listened to. It's worth the price of admission to hear Cole Porter's lyrics.'

Fifty Million Frenchmen weathered the storm, and eventually chalked up what was then a long run of 254 performances. (It was filmed in 1931, starring Helen Broderick and William Gaxton, but with a philosophy understood only in Hollywood the Porter score was heard merely as background music and there was no singing or dancing in the movie.)

Yet, at the time of *Fifty Million Frenchmen*'s opening, even though the American economy had been broken by the devastating stock market crash of October 29, the presence of two of Cole's shows and one of his movies running simultaneously announced to the world that Cole had indeed arrived as a major force in world musical theatre. There seemed to be a place for his kind of non-commercial, intellectual song. He had, of course, come down a bit from his elevated perch and had taken the convolutions out of his melodies and lyrics. Like an expert tightrope walker he had achieved this balance without the net of convention below him. Sticking to his ideals while refining his craft had brought him prominent professional standing.

As the decade ended, Cole's prospects were highly favourable. He could pick and choose whichever project it suited him to work on next – and

[11] The admiration was mutual. Several years later, in the score of *Anything Goes*, Cole would write, 'You're the top/ You're a Waldorf salad,/ You're the top/ You're a Berlin ballad.'

he could decide when and where he would commence work. Nor was his world terribly affected by the bleak economic climate around him since most of his holdings were in real estate and utilities. He and Linda kept their funds in foreign banks which unlike their American counterparts remained solvent. Best of all, never having had a penchant for gambling, he had not invested in the stock market whose collapse was to ruin so many in his social set.

Now he and Linda and an entourage of friends set off on New Year's Day, 1930, for a six-month tour of the Far East and Europe. Leading the pack, mixing hard work writing songs with playing practical jokes, spending reams of cash while earning pots of money from his shows, Cole would soon enlarge his reputation as a successful songwriter and as a wayward millionaire. It was to be *his* decade, his time of greatest triumph, for, in the last analysis, success came to him too late, and Cole Porter was not sufficiently roaring, perhaps his work was not vulgar enough to personify the 'Roaring '20s'. He could only *live* the decade. But as a craftsman he *was* the great iconoclast, the innovator, the perfect incarnation of the 'Naughty '30s'.

NOEL
1924-1929

IF COLE was not 'roaring' enough to personify the '20s, his British counterpart, Noel Coward, certainly was. Eager to get started, uncowed by rejection, he would merely shrug and say, 'They don't know what they missed.' Coward's flamboyance came to him naturally. Describing him, the novelist Stella Gibbons said he seemed 'to incarnate the *myth* of the '20s (gaiety, courage, pain concealed, and amusing malice)'. As for flamboyance, the one essential Gibbons omits, and which seems in retrospect to be the distillation of the decade, Noel had trouble holding his in check.

These very dashing ways, mixed with his ready sense of wit, if they were not to propel him into immediate theatrical success were to lead him into the most provocative weekends in the country and the grandest social circles. The Vanderbilts, and from the theatre the Hartley Manners, Laurette Taylor, Eva Le Gallienne, Ethel Barrymore, Alex Woollcott, the Kaufmans and the newly-married Lunts were to become even closer to him. Their shop-talk, social gossip and especially their subtext; as Noel himself was to write, 'small talk, with a lot of other thoughts going on behind', this was to become grist for his plays.

But the theatrical offering which Noel had travelled across the Atlantic to see and had assumed would be an American edition of *London Calling* was now called *Charlot's Revue*. He was disappointed to find it was quite different from the one he had quit in the West End. Opening on January 9, 1924 at the Times Square Theater, it was a compilation of all the impresario's past productions in this form with only a few Coward numbers. The best of his skits which were too British for New York had been deleted. Here on Broadway Noel's name was not up in twinkling lights; he was merely a contributor to a fairly successful show that starred Beatrice Lillie, Jack Buchanan and Gertie Lawrence. The latter stopped the action nightly with the show's hit song, Braham's 'Limehouse Blues'. It was not long before Coward realized he would have no more luck in America this time than last and, gritting his teeth, returned to England.

Once reconciled and settled, he wrote (amazingly, in three days) *Hay Fever* which he presented to Marie Tempest. After he had read it to her, she pronounced it charming but too slight, so the determined young playwright cogitated over his drawing board and turned out *Easy Virtue* – this one, as he was to confess later, took him somewhat more time. A week?

Meanwhile both *Fallen Angels* and *The Vortex* were 'voyaging disconsolately in and out of most of the London managers' offices'. With four excellent plays (our hindsight shows us) getting nibbles and offers, it was only a question of time before one was to be presented. That was to be *The Vortex*, and its production was to catapult its author and its leading man – he had written the juicy part for himself – to overnight acclaim in Britain as well as America.

The idea for the play, whose controversial theme was one of the main reasons for the queues at the box office, came to Noel when he was invited to a party by his friend Stewart Foster. Across the room he glimpsed Stewart's beautiful and seductive mother, Grace, sharing a banquette with a young admirer. As soon as the party was seated one of the young girls blurted out, '*Look* at that old hag over there with the young man in tow; she's old enough to be his mother.'

The Freudian Oedipus complex, the Hamlet-Gertrude relationship and perhaps Stewart Forster's own attentions to his seductive mother at the soirée immediately propelled Coward's dramaturgical mind into the concept of weaving the plot of a play wherein both a son and her young lover would vie for the love of the mother. The idea, already daring enough, became even more scandalous when Coward built drug addiction into the character of the son. And, almost going too far, he climaxed the third act with a tearful confession the son wrenched from his mother exposing her near nymphomania; that she had actually slept with many other young admirers as well. As the curtain descends on this bleak, melodramatic and hopeless scene, a repentant son buries his face in his humiliated mother's lap.

It was not easy to get backing for so controversial a play, but Norman Macdermott, manager of the tiny, hard-seated Everyman Theatre in Hampstead, agreed to take a chance. When Macdermott's resolve floundered and it looked as if the production would be scratched, Noel's old friend Michael Arlen who had just had a bestseller in *The Green Hat* was forthcoming with £200, enough to assure a short run. Gladys Calthrop contributed sets and costumes without pay and Lilian Braithwaite, one of London's finest actresses, saw the possibilities in the mother's role and accepted £10 for two weeks' work.

After that first night, Noel had arrived. He had moved from 'promising' in January of 1924 to 'delivered' by December of the same year. The events of those first heady successful weeks are best described in Cole Lesley's memoir:

No less than eight managements made bids for *The Vortex* and only two weeks after the Hampstead first night it opened at the Royalty Theatre in the West End. Lilian and Noel settled in for a long run which had from the beginning a gratifying glow of success about it. With the accompanying prosperity, Noel recklessly indulged in several suits, many silk shirts, pyjamas and a new car. Ebury Street also blossomed; the plumbing now gushed piping hot water and Noel's rooms were done over, his bedroom particularly striking with walls of scarlet further embellished with murals in Bakst-like colours by Gladys. Lorn was raised to the rank of Permanent Secretary for Noel's Affairs; she came into this riot of colour every morning and sat on the end of the bed armed with a shoebox called Shortly into which they piled all pending letters. They learned from experience that if Shortly was left undisturbed for a month or longer, most of the letters had answered themselves and consequently always employed this efficient and time-saving device.

Noel's élan and industry during this time seem almost uncanny. Besides playing the harrowing and exhausting part of Nicky Lancaster every night and being seen everywhere pre- and post-theatre, he managed to write songs, short stories, satire and even ideas for plays into his schedule. Somewhere along the line he accepted a call from Charles Cochran – an offer no one in the theatre could refuse, to become involved with a new revue, *On With The Dance*. Sensitive to the hottest new young talent after the phenomenal success of *The Vortex*, and wishing to jump on the Coward bandwagon, Cochran asked Noel

Coward, with Lilian Braithwaite in *The Vortex*, 1924

to write lyrics and sketches, but insisted the music be left to his staff composer, Philip Braham (who had contributed so heavily to Charlot's *London Calling*).[1]

But Coward who, in spite of a major contribution, had not received the credit due him on *London Calling*, cleverly worked his songs so that they grew out of the sketches, with the songs themselves being part of the black-out or punch line. Braham was left in the cold creating the melodies for only three songs. One of the best of this highly original form, the 'sketch-song', in *On With The Dance* is 'First Love'. Set in a schoolroom, it is basically a playlet for an adolescent boy, his sister, and their French teacher. The children bicker until the young man gets Mademoiselle alone with the following dialogue that leads inevitably into the song:

Mlle: Do you know your verbs?

Rupert: Only one.

Mlle: Which one?

Rupert: (looking up) Je t'aime.

Mlle: I thought that was it.

Rupert: You knew all the time?

Mlle: I guessed, silly boy.

Rupert: It's not silly; it's the most wonderful thing in the world ... love!

Mlle: First love.

[1] Once the show was mounted it was obvious to Cochran that Coward needed no collaborator – and that was the last time Noel ever allowed himself to be bullied into using one – for although the lyrics to the Braham contributions, 'Couldn't We Keep On Dancing?' and 'Come a Little Closer', were acceptable, even Cochran had to admit that their tunes were awkward, pretentious and instantly forgettable.

Lance Lister and Alice Delysia sing 'First Love' in *On With The Dance*, 1925

NUMBER

VERSE 1

He

If you could only realise
And knew how I idealised
The very slightest thing you say or do

She

I've guessed and felt a bit
Depressed because I know that it
Leads to complications
Think of your relations'
Point of view.

REFRAIN 1

He

First love,
Completely unrehearsed love,
Has all the spontaneity of youth.

She

Well, to tell the truth
I am quite unversed, love.
In treating suitably these adolescent scenes.
You're indisputably the victim of your
        teens.
New love
Must always seem the true love,
Experience will teach you as you go
Till you really know
Just the way to woo, love.

He

I wish you'd show me how my passion
        should be nursed.

She

Your Papa will have to raise my wages first,
        love.

VERSE 2

He

I've burned to kiss your darling hand,
And yearned to make you understand
That you're the only one in life for me.

She

I fear I can't reciprocate,
But, dear, I do appreciate
Having made you suffer,
Darling little duffer,
You'll soon see.

REFRAIN 2

She

First love
Is generally the worst love.

He

I'm trying to restrain it all the time
I've a feeling I'm
Really going to burst, love.

She

I fully realise your true romantic soul,
But you must utilise a little self-control.

He

Calf love is never half-and-half love;
To me you're just the fairest of your sex
How I love you –

She

Ex – Scuse me if I laugh, love,

He

Let's plunge in passion 'till we're totally
        immersed.

She

I shall have to ask my husband first,
        love[2]

On *With The Dance* had other remarkable songs: 'Cosmopolitan Lady', built on the daring concept that fidelity that slips now and then is more intriguing than the true-blue kind, 'So In Love', a charming soft-shoe, and the show's most popular skit-song, 'Poor Little Rich Girl'.[3] This last, a scene in which a

[2] Reading the lyric of 'First Love' gives no idea of the remarkable musical interest inherent in this song. Besides misplacing the beat in eager adolescent style through hemiola (this musical device which unfortunately sounds like a disease is explained fully in the Musical Terms appendix) and held notes alternating with short jumpy ones, the tune has a catchy youthful élan. In the lyric, one should also note that, although this is a love song, Coward never chooses to rhyme the word 'love' (which has only inappropriately awkward rhymes like 'above', 'shove', 'glove' and 'dove'. Notice, too how Noel has used the words 'first' and 'love' separately and as a phrase to maximum effect. And who cannot smile at the delicious rhyming in Refrain 2 of 'sex' and 'ex'?

[3] Rodgers and Hart had produced their successful musical, *Poor Little Ritz Girl*, in 1920. Coward, who admired this team tremendously, had obviously 'borrowed' the title. Titles fall outside copyright laws and are in the public domain.

maid (Hermione Baddeley) lectures her pale, tired mistress (Alice Delysia) to give up the debauched life she is leading, was to become Coward's first authentic hit.[4] Coward and Delysia (and the critics) thought it the high point of the evening, but it was almost thrown out of the show in the Manchester previews by Cochran in his attempt to cut down the evening's over-long running time.

While *On With The Dance* was being prepared it was possible for Noel to commute back and forth without missing any of the London performances of *The Vortex*, but when the time came for the revue to open in Manchester he was obliged to oversee the dress rehearsals and allow his understudy, John Gielgud, to fill his role. Coward always hated foisting understudies on the paying public and after he became successful would insist the management close any of his plays if a major player was taken ill. Even in this case he felt guilty but, when Gielgud did eventually become a star in his own right, Coward was heard to say what he had done was not so bad.

Having rehearsed the sketches and songs extensively before the previews Noel had a hunch the revue would be a success when it hit London. What he had not counted on were the three cumbersome Léonide Massine ballets, and Noel had no idea where Cochran was planning to put them. Somehow, Noel, taking complete charge at the eleventh hour, fitted the pieces of this massive jigsaw together, and, after a 23-hour dress rehearsal during which everything went wrong, the show opened the next night. With running time miraculously pared to the then ideal length of $2\frac{3}{4}$ hours *On With The Dance* was wildly applauded. A month later, on April 30, 1925, it transferred to the London Pavilion where it enjoyed a run of 229 performances.

Even while *On With The Dance* was getting into its stride in Manchester, Anthony Prinsep, who had bought Coward's early play, *Fallen Angels*, as a vehicle for Margaret Bannerman, put it into rehearsal with Edna Best playing the other starring part. Then, hardly a week before the first night, it became evident that Miss Bannerman's slipping memory would certainly sink the play.

Luckily, Tallulah Bankhead who had just been denied the leading part in *Rain* by its author Somerset Maugham, was available. 'In two days,' as Noel reports, 'she knew the whole part perfectly, and on the first night gave a brilliant and completely assured performance. It was a *tour de force* of vitality, magnetism and spontaneous combustion ...

'The press notices for *Fallen Angels* were vituperative to the point of incoherence. No epithet was spared. It was described as vulgar, disgusting,

---

[4] 'Poor Little Rich Girl' was later to become the subject of a furore that included threats of injunctions when Gertrude Lawrence wanted to sing it in the second Charlot revue in New York dressed as a prostitute lecturing an elegantly dressed Constance Carpenter. Noel objected strenuously, but Gertie had her way and, although far from the concept he intended, even Noel had to admit that her interpretation made the song a hit in America as well.

shocking, nauseating, vile, obscene, degenerate, etc., etc. The idea of two gently nurtured young women playing a drinking scene together was apparently too degrading a spectacle for even the most hardened and worldly critics. The *Daily Express* even went so far as to allude to these two wayward creatures as "sub-urban sluts".'

With *Fallen Angels, On With The Dance* and *The Vortex* running simultaneously 1925 looked like Coward's year. Less than two months later, Marie Tempest for whom Noel had written the juicy role of Judith Bliss in *Hay Fever* and who had rejected the play as being 'too light and plotless', decided that this comedy about an ex-actress and her two admirers (a light-hearted *Vortex*?) was a perfect vehicle. The play opened in June and she was to revel in the part for almost a year. With four successful plays to his credit in as many months, even Noel was to say, 'I was in a enviable position. Everyone but Somerset Maugham said I was a second Somerset Maugham.'

Coward's life as well as his works became the focus of social discussion. All over London young men were buying red satin dressing-gowns and young women were struggling with ivory cigarette-holders. Cynical, world-weary men with clean-cut profiles exchanged light-hearted badinage with thin, provocative companions. Reality merged with theatricality and a sense of drama hovered over everything as youths down from Oxford tried to speak in Cowardesque epigrams, young women dramatically applied lipstick, pencilled their eyebrows or casually threw fox furs round their shoulders in the manner of Best, Braithwaite or Bankhead. Suddenly the tournure of phrase, the theatrical gesture rather than content, became the centre of all élitist conversation.

It was inevitable that the Coward craze would spread across the ocean, and before long Noel was signed up by the American producers Charles Dillingham and Abe Erlanger to play the drug-addicted Nicky Lancaster on Broadway. By May, after six months of hurtling down *The Vortex* in London nightly, much of the glitter had understandably washed from his performance, and he was to admit that he was walking through the role waiting only for the New York opening. It was then that John Chapman Wilson, always known as 'Jack', the man who was to become his lover, producer, manager, companion and eventually bête noire entered his life. Jack, only four months older than Noel, was from a wealthy family and had graduated from Cole Porter's alma mater Yale (a decade later than Cole). Although he had trained to be a stockbroker like his father, he was passionately interested in the theatre, and had spent his holiday in London seeing everything the West End offered. Broad-shouldered, dark and strikingly handsome, Jack Wilson was impossible to overlook. Noel who would always remember this momentous turn in his fate was to recall all the details of their meeting in his autobiography.

One night in May a young man in the front row of the stalls caught our attention early in the first act. His rapt absorption in the play inspired Lilian and me to renewed efforts, and at the final curtain we both conceded him a gracious bow all for himself ... On that particular night, the young man responded nobly to our bow, by applauding even more loudly. I remember remarking to Lilian that he must be an American because he was wearing a turn-down collar with his dinner jacket. A few days later, a mutual friend told me he knew a young American who was very anxious to meet me, and could he bring him round to my dressing-room one night, and the next evening Jack Wilson walked nervously, and with slightly overdone truculence into my life.

Coward goes on to add that Jack extended a luncheon invitation in New York before *The Vortex* opened, but once Noel arrived there all social thoughts had to be put aside for he was embroiled in an unpleasant situation brought on by his small-minded American producers. Dillingham and Erlanger insisted the final scene in his play did not conform to their opinions of American morals – they could not countenance a son so vilely abusing the woman who gave him birth, and insisted he alter the ending. Of course, Coward was incensed, but rather than change the play he changed producers. Smelling a hit, Sam Harris and Irving Berlin readily took over from Dillingham and Erlanger. The latter's disapproval did much to undermine Noel's confidence in his play – for America had not been good to him so far – but to his surprise *The Vortex* opened to an ovation and glowing reviews, quite surpassing even the London ones. Now Noel was sure he had established his career on both sides of the Atlantic.

After the first matinée of *The Vortex* Jack appeared at the stage door and the relationship that was to last until Jack's death in 1961 was forged. As they became close friends, Noel realized he could no longer afford to be without someone with a knowledge of contract law, royalties, percentages and the like in his corner. Jack gladly offered to give up his incipient stockbroking career in order to manage Coward. Noel confessed, 'In which capacity he has bullied me firmly ever since.'

By the time *The Vortex* ended its New York run, early in 1926, Noel was a well-known celebrity. Richard Rodgers, two years younger than Coward, and at the beginning of his fame, recalled their amusing first meeting in his biography *Musical Stages*. 'I formed another valued and enduring friendship. I have already mentioned the three other major musicals that opened in the same week as *Dearest Enemy*. In addition, a drama that had its première on the very same night as *No, No, Nanette* – September 16, 1925 – was to serve as my introduction to one of the theatre's supreme talents.

'The play was *The Vortex* and the author in his first Broadway appearance was Noel Coward. A daring study of upper-class decadence, *The Vortex* was a resounding hit, and I was fortunate enough to get tickets to a Saturday matinée. Though I was impressed with the writing and acting, the high point for me, possibly because it was so unexpected, occurred in a party scene early in the second act. Urged on by friends, the character Noel was portraying sat down at the piano to play a dance number which turned out to be my own song, "April Fool", from *The Garrick Gaieties*. It was not then, nor has it ever been, well known, and since I was aware that Coward himself was a gifted songwriter, I took it as a tremendous compliment that he would choose "April Fool" over something better known or something that he himself had written.

'A couple of days later I went to Rudley's, a restaurant in the theatre district, for lunch. Rudley's was below street level, and as I walked down the steps I happened to notice a couple seated at a side table. The man's trim elegance and the slightly Oriental cast to his features could belong to no one else but Noel Coward. We had never met, but I knew that I had to speak to him. Although well aware of his reputation for cutting remarks and the fact that he could devastate my naive enthusiasm with no more than a raised eyebrow, I boldly walked over and introduced myself. "I'm Dick Rodgers, and —" I began. No sooner did I get the words out than Coward jumped up from his chair, threw his arms around me and proceeded to shower me with praise. Every time I tried to get in a word about how much I admired his play and his music, he would top me with a new expression of admiration for *my* music. When I finally left his table, I was so overcome that I simply walked back up the steps and out of the restaurant. It wasn't until I was halfway down the block that it dawned on me that I hadn't had any lunch.'

From the vantage point of senior composer, by the time his autobiography was published after Coward's death, Rodgers goes on to criticize the critics who disparaged Coward's eclecticism: 'This sort of enthusiasm for other people's work was typical of Noel Coward, just as his criticism was as outspoken as it was deft. Perhaps his outstanding quality was style. He wrote with style, sang with style, painted with style, and even smoked a cigarette with a style that belonged exclusively to him. Despite his ability to do so many things so superbly, he always had to endure the put-down that anyone so versatile could not possibly be a first-rate talent. What nonsense! Versatility on so high a level needs no excuse. Even one of his lesser-known operettas, *Conversation Piece*, contains more charm, skill and originality than fifty musical plays put together by men specializing in particular fields.'

If young Rodgers was impressed with Noel's talent, he was not the only American to be so. The distinguished actress Jane Cowl picked up *Easy Virtue*, the play he had written in 1924, and decided to give it a lavish production. It would be the first of his plays to have its première in the United States and gave a further indication of his bonding to Jack and things American.

By now Jack had taken charge of Coward's affairs. He had been given

Noel's total trust, down to power of attorney, a right that even Lorn did not possess. Returning on the *Olympic* with Noel and Mrs. Coward, the members of his close circle, although they were outwardly friendly, resented the handsome wisecracking American. For no one could overlook Jack's heavy drinking, the freedom with which he dispensed Noel's money, and, most of all, his absolute control of the man who was writing all those golden plays. Yet it was hard to remain immune to Wilson's good humour and wit, the intimate trio of Gladys Calthrop, Jeffery Amherst and Lorn Lorraine was soon expanded to a quartet. All of them were aware that Jack had 'become so much a part of their lives that scarcely any decision would be made without him'.

Noel's next play, *This Was a Man*, which he dedicated to Jack, was tepidly received. Eking out a few performances in New York and later in more liberal Berlin and Paris when it was denied the approval of London's Lord Chamberlain, it was considered indecent because in its last act a cuckolded husband bursts into gales of laughter because his wife has seduced his best friend.

Coward (centre) and Porter (right), with Jack Wilson at the Lido, Italy, 1926

Brooks Atkinson, criticizing the play in the *New York Times,* saw other reasons for its ban. On November 14, 1926 he was to write:

Last spring the Lord Chamberlain, solicitous of the morals of his countrymen, forbade the production of *This Was a Man* in London. Perhaps because the talk is frequently as loose as the characters; or perhaps because Carol Churt slips into the Major's bedchamber for a showy second act curtain. In a fit of temperament, Mr. Coward is reported to have said: 'I shall in the future concentrate on New York, where I am taken seriously as a serious writer, whereas in England people think I am out for salacious sensations. I shall from time to time write a pleasant little trifle for London.' The tone of *This Was a Man* is obviously serious. But the drama is trifling. Possibly Mr. Coward has confused his audiences.

Sonnie Hale (left) and Jessie Matthews sing 'A Room With a View' in *This Year of Grace,* 1928

Things were to get worse in the succeeding year. Ever after, Noel was to call 1927 his 'Disaster Year.' *The Marquise*, with a plum role that Marie Tempest acted to the hilt, failed as a drama, while *Home Chat*, agonizingly slow in performance and action because of a large cast of elderly actresses constantly forgetting their lines, hardly ran a month. Noel himself criticized the latter, saying, 'When I wrote it I naturally considered it good; so did she [the star, Madge Titheradge], and everybody concerned, but we were wrong. It was a little better than bad, but not good enough ...'

As can happen to any idol of the moment, Noel's reputation plunged drastically as soon as the reviewers found chinks in his armour brought on by productions of his less well made plays. They impaled him totally after the catastrophic opening of *Sirocco*.

Basil Dean had inveigled Ivor Novello into starring in this frankly juvenile play, which turned out to be a fiasco for all concerned. It was the only time in his career that Noel would be jeered on stage, offstage at the stage door and in the press.[5]

But the first rule of show business – that one needs only a single smash hit to turn the tide and drown the lemmings – applied in late February 1928 when he was to set all England humming with what would be one of his greatest revue scores, *This Year of Grace*. Containing such gems as 'Teach Me To Dance Like Grandma', 'Mary Make Believe', 'The Lorelei', and two enormous hits in 'Dance, Little Lady' and what has since become the quintessential Coward song, 'A Room With a View',[6] it would even outrun *On With The Dance*.

The morning after it opened, the critics were unanimous in their praise, with St John Ervine outdoing all the others in a glittering alphabetical list of superlatives. He called *This Year of Grace* 'the most amusing, the most brilliant, the cleverest, the daintiest, the most exquisite, the most fanciful, the most graceful, the happiest, the most ironical ... 'continuing the printed kudos until he arrived at the letter "x", adding, 'if any person comes to me and says that there has ever, anywhere in the world, been a better revue than this, I shall publicly tweak his nose.' Terence Rattigan was to call Ervine's critique 'the best notice ever written anywhere by anyone about anything'.

This Year of Grace broke new ground, even if it was not the milestone the press claimed. Whereas in his previous work he had taken swipes at particular people or groups, now that Coward had travelled so extensively his

---

[5] Hannen Swaffer writing in the *Sunday Express* gloated: 'At last the public seems to appreciate the truth ... Noel Coward has nothing whatever to say ... he has no wit, and his sneers at ordinary people are irritating to the point of painfulness.' Noel, with his usual *sang froid* rebutted the critics' opinion of *Sirocco*. 'The Press,' he announced, 'found it dull, unreal, immoral, stupid, over-produced, over-acted, under-produced and under-acted; the few kindly exceptions found it vital, significant, moral, dramatic, exquisitely produced and profoundly interesting. The Public,' he added, 'hardly found it at all.'
[6] See Musical Examples Appendix.

bead on society was much sharper. He could show audiences the sun-drenched permissive Lido in Venice and follow this with a sketch of a miserable British seashore resort complete with leaden sky which he called 'The English Lido'. In another sketch he deplored the British habit of hastening to stand 'in a queue, even if they didn't know what it was for'. And, in 'The Lorelei', he empathised with the poor sirens, choking in the smoke of the few tramp steamers they are able to seduce.

But it is 'Dance, Little Lady', confronting as it does audiences with the heartbreaking sight of an ingénue dancing mirthlessly and endlessly, which is probably one of the peak moments in the revue. Oliver Messel created unchanging masks, painting the faces with vacuous expressions. The startlingly cruel scene was brilliantly satirical. In its ten minutes it sums up the frenzy, the vapidity and restlessness of the Jazz Age as well as the entire oeuvre of Fitzgerald.

Yet one must not assume *This Year of Grace* was all heavy going. There was Maisie Gay's delightful clowning in 'It Doesn't Matter How Old You Are', whose lyric asserts 'if the joys of life are sweet,/ It doesn't matter how old you are,/ If you've still got central heat./ I've seen raddled wrecks/ With false pearls hung round their necks/ Get away with lots of sex appeal ... It doesn't matter how old you are/ It's just how young you feel'. Jessie Matthews had two solo hits, besides 'A Room With a View': the first act finale, 'Teach Me To Dance Like Grandma (Used to Dance Sixty Summers Ago)', and 'Try To Learn To Love,' with lines like 'though you're aesthetic, apathetic to all men but Bernard Shaw ... try to learn to love a little bit more'.[7]

Once Cochran knew he had an established hit in *This Year of Grace*, he thought of opening it in New York, with Noel starring alongside his good friend Beatrice Lillie. Having accepted the leading role in S.N. Behrman's play *The Second Man*, and once again having received brilliant notices, Coward had the enviable choice between staying in Britain where he was the toast of the country or augmenting his now considerable fame abroad. His royalties for *This Year of Grace* alone were totalling more than a thousand pounds a week, and for the first time he was given the opportunity to choose his next vehicle.

It was a hard decision to make and Noel postponed it while he went with Gladys Calthrop for a weekend with her family solicitor in Surrey. It was there, after the solicitor's wife played a new recording of *Die Fledermaus*, that he made up his mind. The operetta form was new to him, but he knew that the romantic side of his nature would allow him to pull off a colourful work containing the nervous '20s with *mittel-Europa* whipped cream. He would do the revue in New York, and give himself the time and the distance from England to put his ideas together.

[7] Coward's clipped speech and elided 'r's' permitted him (as well as many British lyricists) to rhyme 'Shaw' and 'more' with impunity. Cole Porter never allowed himself such latitude.

Coward and Sir Gerald du Maurier at a theatrical garden party, 1927

Many have said, and some still maintain, that Noel Coward's enormous success with *Bitter Sweet* parochialised the British musical for the next fifty years, while the American musical constantly broke new ground. Whatever the cost may have been to British theatre, it is certainly true that Coward rounded off the '20s with a brilliant throw-back and created one of the world's most popular works in that form.

This Year of Grace, with Coward and Lillie, was a considerable success in New York, while *Bitter Sweet* captivated London. But, after a long run, when the time came for *Bitter Sweet* to cross the ocean, the world had gone mad, the bottom had fallen out of the stock market. Nobody wanted the swirling musical or even the subtle ironies of a revue. In fact nobody could afford to go to the theatre. Thus, although his career was in high, Noel's world, like everybody else's was in low.

COLE
1930-1935

IF THE PORTERS and most of their travelling set remained solvent as the '30s dawned, the general public and that 'fabulous invalid', the theatre, did not. And, throughout the world, but somehow more especially in the United States, the greatest non-essential seemed to be the musical. So it was that, in the 1930–31 season, theatre closures, folding shows and bankruptcies among producers were rife. The theatrical empires of Charles Dillingham and Arthur Hammerstein collapsed, never to rise again, as did the great network of the Shubert brothers (although the latter was eventually able to retrieve most of its theatres and win back the lion's share of Broadway houses).

One who kept his resources, largely due to the success of Cole's *Paris* and *Fifty Million Frenchmen*, was Ray Goetz, and the Porters had hardly ended their tour of Japan when he wired them with an intriguing proposal. After writing two successful shows set in Paris, why not create one built around the other great metropolis Cole knew and loved? New York? Goetz finished the telegram by adding that he intended to hire the same team that had made *Frenchmen* such a smash, Herbert Fields would write the libretto and Monty Woolley, Cole's old friend, would direct. It was too tempting an offer to refuse and, even before Cole and Linda left Paris that April, Cole had set to work and turned out two songs that would become classics, 'Take Me Back to Manhattan' and 'I Happen to Like New York'. Once the Porters were ensconced in their Park Avenue apartment that summer, work on the show began in earnest.

The New Yorkers, which opened in December 1930, had been fashioned into a flashback musical which Brooks Atkinson – this time in Cole's corner – described glowingly, saying it managed 'to pack most of the madness, ribaldry, bounce and comic loose ends into a lively musical ... while keeping as far away from sociology as boisterous entertainment can'. Indeed that was Herbert Fields' aim for he had devised a plot long on irony and short on believability. It vaguely concerned an ingénue, her lover (a murdering bootlegger), her father and his mistress, her mother and her gigolo, and yet another gangster (this one played raucously by Jimmy Durante). Gangster one is arrested, not for murder, but for illegal parking and sent to Sing-Sing. When he is released he is elected President of the United States running on the Temperance ticket.[1] With such 'immoral' plotting, the only way in which these characters could get

---

[1] The gangster anti-hero, a frequent theme for Hollywood in the '30s, was to be used satirically by many of Cole's librettists not only here in *The New Yorkers* but in *Anything Goes*, *Red, Hot and Blue*, *Mexican Hayride* and *Kiss Me, Kate*.

past the censors would be for the entire show to be cast in that old chestnut device, the dream sequence.[2]

But, even so, the lyric to the best song of the evening, 'Love For Sale', was to become a cause célèbre for many decades to come. Considered too risqué by the guardians of morality, the Federal Communications Commission, it was banned from the airwaves and recordings – all to the delight of Cole. The song which combines elements Porter wrote of with especial honesty – money and sex – is the frank soliciting of a rather poetic prostitute. The FCC having no jurisdiction in the theatre had to permit the song to be sung on stage, and although Cole's tune when performed on the radio had to remain wordless the melody had such bounce and harmonic interest (written in Eb, its first two chords are Eb and an unexpected Bb *minor*) that it was recorded and danced to all over the world.

Yet Goetz, fearing the brouhaha might alienate the public and affect ticket sales, quickly changed the setting for the song from a Manhattan street where white Kathryn Crawford sang while lasciviously plying her wares to the stage of the Cotton Club in Harlem. Here Elizabeth Welch and three of her black girlfriends sang the number as part of their act. Of course, without its streetwalking aspect, the song had no punch or meaning, but such was the prevailing morality dictated by the white majority in the early '30s. It permitted a 'coloured girl' to *sing* about sex, while a caucasian was forbidden to do so. And the white girl could certainly not *sell* it.

'Love For Sale' bears much of the major-minor fluctuation (often in reverse) that is uniquely Porterian and which many musicologists regard as middle-Eastern or Jewish. Even Richard Rodgers, in his biography, *Musical Stages*, makes this connection when he recalls his and Cole's first meeting in Venice in 1926. At that time Cole had written three shows that had reached Broadway but had not been successful. Intimating that he had discovered the formula for success, Cole confided, 'I'll write Jewish tunes.' Rodgers goes on: 'I laughed at what I took to be a joke, but not only was Cole dead serious, he eventually did exactly that. Just hum the melody that goes with "Only you beneath the moon and under the sun", from "Night and Day", or any of "Begin the Beguine", or "Love For Sale", or "My Heart Belongs to Daddy", or "I Love Paris". These minor-key melodies are unmistakably eastern Mediterranean. It is surely one of the ironies of the musical theatre that, despite the abundance of Jewish composers, the one who has written the most enduring "Jewish" music should be an Episcopalian millionaire who was born on a farm in Peru, Indiana.'

---

[2] In defence of Herbert Fields' libretto one must say that musical comedy books of the period were *purposely* naive and unbelievable, to allow the public respite from the business of the evening: the singers, the dancers, the songs and the lyrics.

Like Rodgers, most chroniclers of Cole's life suggest that this was his way of joining the reigning Jewish hit-masters on Broadway, taking his place beside Irving Berlin, the only other predominant songwriter equally adept at both music and lyrics, but my ears tell me that some of this shifting from the major to minor mode more closely resembles the ambivalent French chansons popular around Pigalle than true Yiddish music. (None of Cole's tunes has the interval of a step-and-a-half, the augmented second, so much a trademark of Hebraic or Jewish song.) Cole's cadences which can go to either major or minor are often directed to the unexpected minor chosen for freshness or surprise.

Besides 'Love For Sale' and its hymns to New York, *The New Yorkers* boasted hits like 'Go Into Your Dance', 'Where Have You Been', 'The Great Indoors', 'The Poor Rich' and 'Just One Of Those Things' (not the famous one, which was to be written for *Jubilee*, five years later). With uniformly good

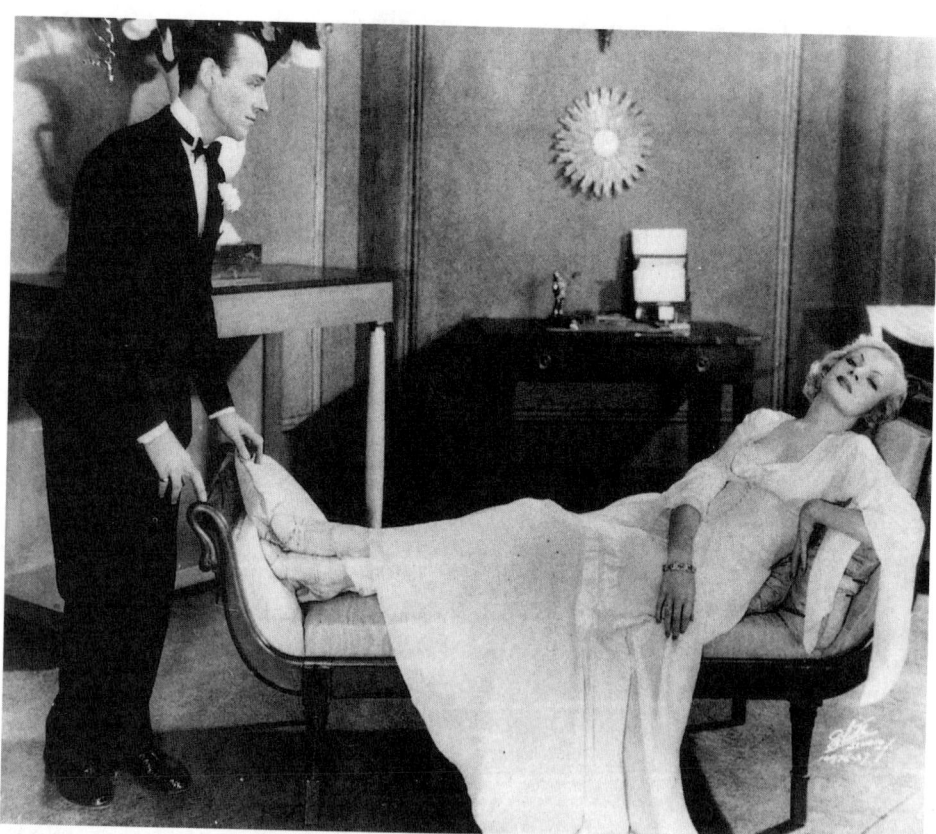

Fred Astaire and Claire Luce in *The Gay Divorce*

reviews, it should have run for years, but closed after only 168 performances. The reason: three days after it opened the Bank of the United States failed, closing its sixty branches and wiping out the life savings of some 400,000 families.

By 1932, the Depression was at its most drastic. Most of America had to settle for listening to the radio, which was free, or attending an occasional 15 cent movie. Only the rich could afford a night on the town at the theatre and even they could only be enticed by the promise of top-drawer talent or a number-one song hit. Luckily, with his next chow Cole had both. Fred Astaire, dancing for the first time without his sister Adele[3], starred in *The Gay Divorce*, which also boasted a song which was played and sung everywhere, a song with such an elemental name that one wonders why no one had juxtaposed those words before. It is perhaps the only song that immediately conjures up Porter's name and career for the public at large, for it was used as the title of his biographical movie – 'Night and Day'. From its inception, *The Gay Divorce* seems to have led a charmed life. It introduced Cole to the totally professional producing team of Dwight Deere Wiman[4] and Tom Weatherly[5] who brought with them the imaginative new director Howard Lindsay,[6] and the idea of securing Astaire as the star. Cole was so excited by the project that, contrary to his usual practice, he began writing the score before the contracts were signed.

Dwight Taylor's story was wonderfully brittle, slightly naughty and simple. Astaire, playing a writer, comes to interview lovely Clare Luce. She mistakes him for the co-respondent she has hired so that she can obtain her divorce. He, for his part, has met her before, been smitten and goes along with the game until their final love scene.

Astaire, urbane and suave, was a perfect choice for the role, and this glowing score gives him several remarkable songs, 'After You, Who?'[7], 'I've Got You On My Mind', 'Although I'm disinclined/ You're not so hot, you/ But I've got you on my mind), 'You're In Love,' 'A Weekend Affair' (cut before the opening) and 'Night and Day'.[8]

[3] Adele, who until that time had been considered the major partner in the act, had recently married the Duke of Devonshire's son and retired from the stage.
[4] Wiman, the more experienced of the pair, had produced a series of revues called the 'Little Shows', prior to his involvement in *The Gay Divorce*. After this, his only connection with a Cole Porter score, he would go on to produce the most successful shows of Rodgers and Hart.
[5] Ray Goetz, Cole's former producer, was no longer presenting shows because of his devastating and costly divorce from Irene Bordoni.
[6] Howard Lindsay was to direct and co-write two more Porter musicals, *Anything Goes* and *Red, Hot and Blue*, before he turned to writing librettoes exclusively. Teaming up with Russel Crouse he created long-running hits like *Call Me Madam* and *The Sound of Music*.
[7] On June 30, 1953, Cole wrote to his friend George Byron, 'I shall always be grateful to "After You", because I had been engaged by Dwight Wiman for *Gay Divorce*. Our great hope was to persuade Fred Astaire to play the lead. We were living in Paris at the time and I asked Fred over to the house to hear what I had written so far. Once I had played "After You", he decided to do the show.'
[8] See Musical Analysis appendix.

Many stories have arisen as to the birth of this famous song. When interviewed, Cole always said the melody was inspired by the Mohammedan call to prayer, although I hear little of Middle Eastern influence in the tune. George Eells' biography of Cole recounts that the 'drip, drip, drip, of the raindrops' line was proclaimed by Porter's hostess in consternation at a noisy broken eaves-spout during a luncheon in Newport, Rhode Island.

But, regardless of its origin, the song bears the hallmark of Porter's best work. Constructed with a long verse, which unlike that of the Gershwins or Rodgers and Hart is essential, it leads implacably to the refrain built in A A B A form. This opening A or primary strain is repeated slightly differently in typical Porter fashion – 'one should never be bored' at its second announcement. And then comes the bridge.

Alan Jay Lerner singled out Porter's bridges as unique when he mentioned their 'growing intensity'. The bridge section of a song, called by most music analysts the release (sometimes laughingly called 'relief'), is usually a time for the melodist and lyricist to turn to fresh or opposite ideas. Thus, if the A melody has been a descending one, the release is generally ascending; if the A lyric dwells on the joy that comes when the loved one is near, the release talks of the sadness of separation. Porter's bridges are an exception to this pattern, for they are *not* a release but more of the same. One could make an analogy with the development of the second theme on the same materials, as in the music of Bach, and contrast that with Mozart's second themes which are in such direct divergence that the terms 'masculine theme' and 'feminine theme' were coined to describe them. Porter's are always fresh yet developing a generic element that has appeared in the A. They are not so much a departure as a continuation. One has only to think of 'Let's Do It', or 'What Is This Thing Called Love' to be aware of this. And this technique is nowhere more apparent than in 'Night and Day'.

Back in his Yale days, long before he wrote *The Gay Divorce*, Cole had learned to tailor his songs to the particular singing or non-singing talents of his fraternity brothers. Now, as he was to tell the press in every future interview, he wrote 'Night and Day' for Fred Astaire's particular singing abilities. Astaire had a vocal timbre which would eventually make him equally popular in song or dance, but at that time was known primarily for his dancing, so Cole wrote his melody to remain throughout in mid-range with hardly any vocal leaps to betray a breathless dancer.

It certainly brought out what was best in his star's voice. Astaire, who had never studied singing seriously, and had been given only short, non-sustaining phrases in former shows, felt 'Night and Day' with its long-held notes (especially on the word 'day') might point up the weakness in his voice. And he objected to its octave-and-a-fourth range, fearing his voice might crack.

He wanted the song dropped and went so far as to enlist the co-producer Tom Weatherly, who did not care for the song either, to plead his cause.

Cole, who long before had gone on record to say that if a star didn't like any of his songs he would throw it out and write another, for once remained adamant. He believed in the song and went so far as to have a full verse and chorus of 'Night and Day' played at the start of the overture; and after a potpourri of other music the band plugged the song *again* before the curtain rose. His faith was rewarded within two months when Leo Reisman's and Eddie Duchin's recordings of 'Night and Day' became bestsellers. And Astaire's singing of the song became its prototype.

Although *The Gay Divorce* was received tepidly by the critics (some of them refused to accept Astaire without his sister), it chalked up a healthy 248 performances and was optioned for a film[9] by RKO. Released in 1934, it would provide Astaire with the first of his successful screen roles paired with a consummate dancing partner, Ginger Rogers. Although the rest of Cole's score was dropped, 'Night and Day', accepted by then as a standard, was retained. In spite of being outvoted by Con Conrad's 'The Continental', which won the first Academy Award bestowed on a motion picture song, it became the most lasting song in the score of the movie. ASCAP rates it as one of the top money-earners of all time, and almost sixty years after it was written it still earns a phenomenal $10,000 a year.

A month after the Broadway opening of *The Gay Divorce* Cole and Linda took off for an extended tour; this time they would stay in Vienna and Carlsbad. Once the touring and the baths were behind them, they settled back in 13 rue Monsieur and were again caught up in a swirling social round. But it was not long before they were contacted by Charles Cochran who always came up with themes that combined revue – irresistible to Cole – with a book musical. Cochran came over from London to talk about his idea for a new musical based on James Laver's frankly scandalous book, *Nymph Errant*. He was planning to star the reigning British musical comedy star, Gertrude Lawrence, in the project.

What Cochran did not tell Porter was that the idea had originated with Gertrude herself, who with Cochran had already been to see Noel Coward. He had turned them down saying, 'though he would soon be writing for his old friend, this would be something of his own devising; he was not, he added, some kind of hired hack who could simply be summoned to the piano whenever Miss Lawrence needed a vehicle for her talents'.

---

[9] Called *The Gay Divorcée* because the censorious Hays Office with their curious sense of morality decreed the whole question of divorce should never be light-hearted, yet a woman freed of her marital obligations could be.

Yet Cole, who appreciated Gertrude Lawrence's charisma (she had done a valiant job singing his songs in the dreadful movie, *The Battle Of Paris*, but had never sung his music on stage), read the book in a single evening and eagerly agreed to do the songs.

The plot by Romney Brent, as adapted to Cole's proposed score, concerns the picaresque adventures of a beautiful young English girl with the unsullied name of Evangeline in her quest to lose her virginity, travelling to a sheik's desert tent, Neauville-sur-Mer (a take-off on Deauville), a nudist camp, a Turkish harem, a Parisian follies stage, a Venetian palazzo, before returning to England with her hymen still miraculously intact. The plot proved, as one critic wryly put it, to be pure fantasy *indeed*.

Although it was never produced on Broadway, over the years *Nymph Errant* has developed a kind of cult following because of the worldliness and sexual sophistication of its score which Cole himself always considered his best. Excerpts from some of this author's favourites are printed below.[10]

EXPERIMENT. This is perhaps the best known song in the score, sung in the show by Gertrude Lawrence.
... Experiment,
Make it your motto day and night,
Experiment,
And it will lead you to the light.

IT'S BAD FOR ME. Sung by Gertrude Lawrence.
... Oh, it's sweet for me, it's swell for me
To know that you're going through hell for me,
Yet no matter however appealing
I still have a feeling
It's bad for me.

NEAUVILLE-SUR-MER. Sung by the ensemble.
... Just what could be glummer than summer at
Neauville-sur-Mer?
For here when the rain comes and drives you indoors,
It pours and it pours and it pours and it pours.
...And yet though aware
The place is nothing but a washout,
Each August with care
We get the little mackintosh out
And come back to swear
At Neauville-sur-Mer.

THE COCOTTE. Sung by Queenie Leonard.
... Since only dames with their names on their checks appeal
To modern men, instead of sex, I now have ex-appeal.

HOW COULD WE BE WRONG? The show had only two ballads (the other being 'You're Too Far Away'). This one was by far the better. It was sung by Gertrude Lawrence.
... How could we be wrong?
When we both are so set on it
How could we be wrong?

THEY'RE ALWAYS ENTERTAIN-ING. Sung by a sextet of servants in the employ of Americans who had (like the Porters) rented a Venetian palazzo.
... They're always entertaining
These Americans who come to town
Forever entertaining,
It's no wonder we're a bit run down.
Ev'ry day they ask a bunch
Of celebrities for lunch,
If you think that is all
Ev'ry night they give a ball.
So excuse us for complaining,
But these Americans are always entertaining.

[10] A small and delightful Equity Library production was well-received in 1982. This was the first time the entire score was heard in New York. In 1989 an all-star complete concert version was mounted (and recorded) in London.

GEORGIA SAND. This take-off on George Sand's penchant for dressing in trousers was sung by Doris Carson. A bit too sophisticated for general audiences, it was replaced early in the run by Casanova. The chorus is supposedly sung by Georgia's lover, Alfred de Musset
... Georgia Sand, dressed up like a gent,
Georgia Sand, what do you represent?
Where are your frills
That gave me such thrills?
Where are those undies
That made my Saturday-to-Mondays? ...

THE PHYSICIAN. Sung by Gertrude Lawrence.
... He said my maxilaries were marvels,
And found my sternum stunning to see,
He did a double hurdle
When I shook my pelvic girdle,
But he never said he loved me.
He seemed amused
When he first made a test of me
To further his medical art ...
Yet he refused
When he'd fixed up the rest of me
To cure that ache in my heart.
I know he thought my pancreas perfect,
And for my spleen was keen as could be,
He said of all his sweeties,
I'd the sweetest diabetes,
But he never said he loved me.

SOLOMON. Sung by Elizabeth Welch in the original recording in 1933 as well as in the concert version recorded in 1989.

... Solomon had a thousand wives,
And being mighty good, he wanted all of them
To lead contented lives;
So he bought each mam a plat'num piano
A gold lined kimono and a diamond studded Hispano,
Solomon had a thousand wives.

SWEET NUDITY. Sung by the ensemble, but cut before the opening when Cochran, in a clever deal, agreed to drop the nude scene from the musical if the censor permitted all the other racy songs to be heard.
... *Girls*: No hats to choose, no frocks to tear.
Boys: No studs to lose and no stiff shirts to wear.
Girls: No ladders running up and down our hose
Boys: No drawers to open and no drawers to close.
Girls: No powder puffs, no further frills,
Boys: No fights with laundries and no tailor bills.
All: So nudity, sweet nudity,
No wonder in return we sing to thee.

SI VOUS AIMEZ LES POITRINES. Sung by busty Iris Ashby.
... Ces belles poitrines sau-vages
May be very fair perchance,
But why should one voy-age
When the best of them are made in France?

The excerpts above, while offering a clue to the wit and humour (admittedly some of it adolescent) of *Nymph Errant*'s lyrics, give no clue to the intricacy of the musical line. 'Experiment', 'The Physician', 'Weren't We Fools' and 'Solomon' may be short on rhythmic daring, but they each go into harmonic and melodic areas where Cole had never ventured before. ('Solomon', with its melismatic[11] passages and violent ending, especially, gives a foretaste of a melodic line that was to prevail in 'soul' and the literary mayhem that could often be found in rock in the late '80s.)

Miss Lawrence's charm, the animated choreography by Agnes de Mille (her first), Romney Brent's lively book and direction, and Cochran's lavish production were not wasted, but even the most generous English critics could

[11] See Musical terms appendix.

Gertrude Lawrence (second from right) in *Nymph Errant*

not remain blind to the fact that the peregrinations of Evangeline in her quest for sex had to pale eventually. As for the public, once the parade of gala audiences and glittering celebrities had dried up, they were faced with a musical that had *no* leading man, and *no* love interest – all of which added up to *no* long run.

Three days after *Nymph Errant* closed in London, Cole's former sponsors Alex Aarons and Vinton Freedley opened the last show they would produce together. Titled *Pardon My English*, and with a scintillating Gershwin score, a winner but, because this musical had a German setting and Hitler had recently assumed power, the public dismissed *Pardon My English* after forty-six performances. Deeply in debt, both Aarons and Freedley left the country to escape their creditors. Aarons was never to recover but Freedley, while relaxing in the Pearl Islands during this enforced vacation, rethought his whole approach to the musical. Instead of commissioning a book and score, then searching for a director and cast, hoping ultimately for acceptance in the theatre, he would imagine an ideal property with stars and writers the public would clamour for.

Ethel Merman, the clarion-voiced ex-secretary who had made history in the 1930 smash hit *Girl Crazy*, would be featured. William Gaxton, the personification of the musical leading man, would be her co-star, and for comic relief Freedley would engage Victor Moore who had recently scored a personal triumph as Throttlebottom in the Gershwins' Pulitzer Prize-winning *Of Thee I Sing*. He would hire P. G. Wodehouse and Guy Bolton, who had scripted his biggest hit *Oh, Kay* a few years back, to write the show, which he conceived as sheer escapism from the Depression. The theme would avoid any political or international problems – an ocean liner, a shipwreck, a peaceful desert island would be idyllic and ideal. He contemplated hiring Rodgers and Hart to write the score but knew they were involved with Billy Rose and his circus musical, *Jumbo*. He next considered Gershwin but realized he too was busy, with *Porgy and Bess*. Then his thoughts turned to Cole.

Although he did not have the money to back the production of his idea, Freedley's record as a producer was sound enough to get the project off the ground. He returned to the United States and began enlisting investors, writers and cast. Telling Bolton and Wodehouse he had already signed Merman, he was able to work out a contract with the writers. Then he came to Gaxton and Moore, and lastly to Merman, with these writers in his pocket.

His plan began its charmed life. Originally titled *Hard to Get*, then *Bon Voyage*, the show we now know as *Anything Goes* shares the honours with *Kiss Me, Kate* as Cole Porter's chef d'oeuvre. No less than five of its songs became outstanding hits. 'Blow, Gabriel, Blow', 'I Get a Kick Out of You', and 'You're the Top' were written before the show went into rehearsal. Still to come were 'All Through the Night' and the title song, 'Anything Goes'.

But if Cole's score was inspired, the script that Bolton and Wodehouse turned in to Freedley was not. The producer found their treatment of the desert island shipwreck heavy-handed, too romantic and short on jokes. To make matters worse, when the show was in rehearsal during September 1934, the *Morro Castle*, a super-luxury liner, ran aground and burned off the coast of Asbury Park, New Jersey, with the loss of over a hundred lives. The director, Howard Lindsay, and Freedley immediately decided the book had to be rewritten – and in a hurry because Freedley had a high-priced cast and very little money. He could not afford a postponement.

Worse still was to come when Freedley discovered both Wodehouse and Bolton were involved in new projects and could not be cajoled into rewriting. Scheduled to open at the Alvin, the theatre he had built and named after his former partner and himself (Alex Aarons and Vinton Freedley) and which ironically had been taken from him with the collapse of *Pardon My English*, on November 21, the show was in desperate trouble until Howard Lindsay magnanimously offered to rewrite at night while he was directing by day *if* he could have a collaborator. He chose Russel Crouse who was then employed in the public relations department of the Theater Guild. Writing what turned out to be practically a new script, they retained only part of the first act of the Bolton-Wodehouse original. When they were well into rehearsals they admitted they still had no idea what was going to happen in Act II.

Lindsay and Crouse decided to follow Freedley's design and build their story around the suitability of their stars. Ethel Merman became a former evangelist (so that she could sing 'Blow, Gabriel, Blow' – which had already been written) turned night-club hostess. Victor Moore would be Public Enemy Number 13 disguised as a clergyman; William Gaxton could play the perennial playboy who hops the liner *sans* ticket or passport in pursuit of lovely Bettina Hall. Each of these principals was told that his or hers would be the 'star' role.

Working almost round the clock, at last the collaborators completed and rehearsed the first act. As Crouse says:

> Finally, one night, we telephoned Mr. Porter and told him there wasn't going to be any second act unless he could find a way to get it started musically. He came in the next morning with 'Hymn to the Public Enemy', one of the finest bits of satire, both musically and lyrically, I've ever heard.

But an opening does not an act make, so there was still much to be written, and according to Ethel Merman the last scenes of *Anything Goes* were completed at the half-past-eleventh hour. Lindsay and Crouse emerged from the men's smoking room on the train from New York to Boston, where the first try-outs would be held, with the final pages in their hands.

However hurried and tentative the writing might have been, the show had 'hit' written all over it. Word had got round Broadway that the opening night of *Anything Goes* was going to be the greatest gala since the start of the Depression, and tickets were going for $50 apiece. Cole and Linda, immaculately dressed, sat near the front surrounded by their fashionable friends. As usual on first nights Cole applauded enthusiastically. Waving at someone during the intermission, he said, 'Good, isn't it?' Russel Crouse's subsequent comment was that 'Cole's opening-night behaviour is as indecent as that of a bridegroom who has a good time at his own wedding'.

But good it was. And all the reviewers said so. The *New York Times* called the 'humour by Guy Bolton and P. G. Wodehouse completely unhackneyed' (understandably misplacing the credit since all four writers were listed in the programme), and the *New Yorker* said that 'Mr. Porter is in a class by himself'. Cole himself was aware of his achievement. Late in life he said, '*Anything Goes* was the first of my two "perfect" shows – musicals that had no tinkering whatever on them after opening night. The other, *Kiss Me, Kate*, was a tribute to the assembled stagecraft of those associated with me.'

When *Anything Goes* catapulted Cole into the front rank of Broadway composers with his 'perfect' show he was generous enough to share the praise with Lindsay and Crouse who had written the sparkling book and Vinton

Freedley who had masterminded the whole project. Freedley in turn was flying high and intending to repeat the process that had produced this super-hit. He signed Cole, Gaxton, Merman and Lindsay and Crouse without delay. Looking for his funny man, he went to Hollywood, hoping to add Eddie Cantor's name to the list. But Cantor was unavailable, and it was to take Freedley almost two years to find the right man, during which time he was unsuccessful with Jack Benny, Sid Silvers, Bert Lahr, Jack Haley and the Howard Brothers. At last Jimmy Durante was put under contract and Freedley could go about producing *But Millions*, which became *But Millions $*, then *Wait For Baby*, and finally *Red, Hot and Blue*. *Anything Goes*[12] was Cole's longest-running show up to that point, chalking up 420 performances at the Alvin on Broadway and 261

[12] According to Russel Crouse, the eventual title came when the show was well into its rehearsal period. William Gaxton was asked if he would mind making his entrance several minutes after the curtain had gone up. Gaxton, realizing the plot was still being constructed, replied, 'In this kind of a spot, anything goes.' Crouse continues: 'We all leaped on the last two words ... Mr. Porter dashed off to write a title song. He came in with it the next day.'

Anything Goes, 1934

at the Palace Theatre in London. It has twice been filmed, starring Bing Crosby and Ethel Merman in 1936, and again twenty years later also starring Bing Crosby, this time paired with Mitzi Gaynor. There have been innumerable revivals, including a handsome off-Broadway production in 1962[13] and one at the Lincoln Center in 1988.

It is easy to see why *Anything Goes*, in spite of a truncated story line that is almost dismissible, refuses to date. This is partly because it encapsulates the 1930s when anything actually went, as the title song proclaims: four-letter words, nude parties, or 'If saying your pr'yers you like/ If green pears you like/ If old chairs you like/ If backstairs you like/ If love affairs you like/ With young bears you like/ Why, nobody will oppose'. Not only here, but throughout the score, Cole does not pull his punches; in 'I Get a Kick Out of You', besides holding the record for internal rhymes ('*flying* too *high* with some *guy* in the *sky* is *my* idea of nothing to do')[14] Porter is the first to mention sniffing cocaine; in 'All Through the Night', with his line 'you and your love bring me ecstasy', he is talking about lovers *sleeping* together, not simply dreaming of each other. The girls singing 'Where Are the Men?' threaten to jump overboard if the sailors ignore their wishes. In short, Cole Porter's idea of freedom in the '30s is timeless.

'You're the Top' is one of Porter's two most popular list songs the other being 'Let's Do It'. 'In this one song', the critic for the *New Yorker* wrote, 'he has summarized American civilization better than any symposium of national thinkers has ever been able to do.' Its construction, which allows the 'you' to be exceptional, while the 'I' is always the 'bottom', gives the song a masterly contrast. The songwriter maintains freshness, unusually for Cole, by avoiding all sexual innuendoes and concentrating on the current and the greatest; but even here his choice is supremely iconoclastic – juxtaposing accepted superlatives like a 'summer night in Spain, the National Gallery, Garbo's salary' with everyday products like 'cellophane'.

With the opening of *Anything Goes*, Cole and Linda were not only the toast of New York but irresistible fodder for the media. Magazine articles about how and where they lived proliferated and news about their lavish lifestyle was eagerly devoured by anyone even remotely connected with the theatre. Cole even began to perpetuate the old myths concerning his war record. Anyone emerging from such bleak financial times doted on glamour,

---

[13] This particular revival began the practice of adding hit songs from the composer's other works and eliminating from the score the ones that are not well-known. 'Friendship' (from *Dubarry Was a Lady*, 1939) 'It's De-lovely' (*Red, Hot and Blue*, 1936), and 'Easy to Love' (*Born to Dance*, 1936), among others, have generally been interpolated into subsequent productions.

[14] The original line with far fewer internal rhymes – 'I shouldn't care for those nights in the air/ That the fair Mrs. Lindbergh goes through' – had to be scrapped when the show went into rehearsal because of the kidnapping and murder of the Lindbergh baby.

and the French Foreign Legion had rather more cachet than the Army Relief Corps. Cole and Linda spelled high adventure.

It came then as no surprise when the *New York Herald Tribune* of January 12, 1935 proclaimed: 'Balladeer, With Moss Hart, to Pass Five Months Seeking New Musical Comedy.' Cole, Linda, Monty Woolley, Howard Sturges and young Moss Hart, who had already written *Merrily We Roll Along* and created the sketches for Irving Berlin's blockbuster musical *As Thousands Cheer*, would be doing the very thing the public expected of them. Cruising the world in search of material for songs and stimulation for a script, working in their cabins every day, five months later when the *Franconia* docked in New York harbour Cole and Moss were ready to take the train to Hollywood where they planned to set up shop and begin casting and rehearsals for their new musical: *Jubilee*.

NOEL
1929-1932

COLE's EXPERIENCE on the *Franconia* was new to him: writing. He could have taken a lesson in industry from Noel Coward who six years before had composed the whole first act of *Bitter Sweet* in the six days it took to cross the Atlantic on the *Berengaria*.

Cochran was so intrigued with what he heard as Noel read the opening to him that he promised to produce it as soon as it was complete. But, although the plot of Coward's masterly excursion into the *derrière garde* was quickly conceived, it would take an arduous six months before the final two acts were written. These days, half a year is a very short time in the conceptual life of a musical, but one must remember that Noel, besides being prolific, was a very fast worker who grew bored or abandoned a project if ideas refused to come to him.

In the genesis of *Bitter Sweet*, the main stumbling block was the song of regret that the music teacher Carl Linden sings to his beloved pupil Sarah Millick, a song on which the whole plot pivots. Its concept, lyric and melody eluded Coward for many months; finally it was created in a taxi while Noel was appearing in the New York production of *This Year of Grace*. "'I'll See You Again'", he says, 'dropped into my mind, whole and complete, during a twenty minutes' traffic block. After that everything went smoothly, and I cabled Cockie in London suggesting that he start making preliminary arrangements regarding theatre, opening date, etc.'

The move from his accustomed revue, where skits and tunes are all that need be created, to full-blown operetta, which demands songs that develop character, concerted numbers with a certain amount of set dialogue, would terrify anyone but the young or the supremely gifted. Fortunately Noel was both. And fortunately he was not an egomaniac, and could allow himself to take advice from accomplished professionals like Elsie April (to whom he dedicated the score), who could write down what he played and sang and arranged the chorus numbers as well. He put the considerable task of orchestrating the score for large orchestra into the experienced hands of Orellana. Noel was to write four more operettas (*Conversation Piece*, *Operette*, *Pacific 1860* and *After the Ball* but none rivals the heart-wrenching inspiration he lavished on the story of Sarah and Carl. (The title – a masterstroke that describes an audience's feelings after witnessing a performance – was suggested by Alfred Lunt after the nameless operetta was well into rehearsal.)

Bitter Sweet had more than its share of casting problems. Critical were the two leading parts. Evelyn Laye who was Noel's first choice was not available for the role; it went to the American, Peggy Wood. (Miss Laye would star in the New York performances.) For the leading male role, both Noel and Cochran auditioned endless British tenors without success. Finally they travelled to Vienna, and there found an ideally handsome leading man with a brilliant voice whom Noel wanted to engage at once. His name unfortunately was Hans Unterfucker, and Cochran, purple with laughter, said, 'I don't care *how* it's pronounced in German – imagine it written on the side of a British bus!' George Metaxa, an operetta stalwart, was given the part.

Once the casting was completed, Noel, Cochran and Gladys Calthrop could concentrate on the look of the piece. For the second act, which evokes 1880 Vienna, they brought in the eminent Austrian set-designer, Ernst Stern. The exquisite choreography was by Tilly Losch.

Although *Bitter Sweet* was indeed beautiful to behold, what makes it a perennial, revivable work is its outstanding score, which mixes Charleston and ragtime with *alt Wien*. However, at the time it was written, it had additional shock-value because of its plot which concerns a young lady abandoning her fiancé to run away with her penniless immigrant music teacher.[1]

---

[1] Perhaps part of *Bitter Sweet*'s failure on Broadway can be attributed to the lack of caste consciousness in America where it is not uncommon for well-born young ladies to run away with their handsome music teachers.

Austin Trevor, Peggy Wood and George Metaxa in *Bitter Sweet*, 1929

The score deserves an almost-complete list of its treasures.

The Call of Life. This is the first big number in the show and it explains the seventy-year-old Marchioness of Shane's approval of youth seeking love rather than arranged marriages. The refrain divides itself into two parts, the first utilising 4 bar phrases (See Fig. 1) and the second built more thrillingly on 2 bar ones (See Fig. 2). Andrew Lloyd Webber used a similar construction in 'This Is All I Ask Of You,' his main love theme in *The Phantom of the Opera*.

Fig. 1

There   is   a   call_____ that ech - oes   sweet - ly_____

Fig. 2

Fling   far   be - hind   you_____ The chains that   bind   you_____

If You Could Only Come With Me. This, Carl's only solo, is closer to the art songs of Reynaldo Hahn and Gabriel Fauré than to the operettas of Lehar or even Gilbert and Sullivan, the lyric full of yearning and poetry. It was the song Coward was proudest of in the entire score.

Though there may be beauty in this land of yours,
Skies are very often dull and grey.
If I could but take that little hand of yours
Just to lead you secretly away.
We would watch the Danube as it gently flows
Like a silver ribbon winding free.

Even as I speak of it my longing grows
Once again my own dear land to see –
If you could only come with me,
If you could only come with me.

The motif of longing is beautifully expressed in a chordal phrase built upon a D major 9th and given to the flute (See Fig. 3).

Fig. 3

I'll See You Again. See Musical Analysis Appendix.

Footmen Quartet. Injecting a spot of ironic humour into a very romantic situation, the servants' lyric indicates another breakdown of the classes:

Now the party's really ended
All our betters have ascended
All with throbbing heads
To their welcome beds.
Pity us who have to be up
Sadly clearing the debris up,

Getting for our pains
Most of the remains.
Though we all disguise our feelings pretty well
What we mean by 'Very good' is 'Go to Hell' ...

Opening Chorus – Act II. This is a rather intense counterpointed number for the waitresses, waiters and cleaners in a Viennese café. It leads directly into **Ladies of the Town.** Written for four soubrettes.

If Love Were All. This song, which almost became Coward's signature tune, is sung by Manon, a French *diseuse* somehow misplaced in the Austrian capital. Manon, in love with Carl in the old days, dominates the whole act – being given three show-stopping numbers. The lyric of the refrain incorporates the well-known line 'a talent to amuse', which has served as title for countless Coward revues, books and concerts – thereby unjustly pigeonholing him as a light entertainer. The melodic line with its *parlando* verse and four-square credo refrain is brilliantly conceived, employing the difficult rhyme scheme of A, B, C, D, E, F without the slightest hint of forcing (see lyric analysis below) in its primary sections; contrasting this with an A, B, A, B for the release. The entire melody is poignant indeed but it is the brilliant lyric, seeming to express the plight of entertainers since antiquity, that has touched the world and made the song a standard.

Verse 1
Life is often rough and tumble
For a humble *diseuse*;
One can forget one's troubles never
Whatever occurs.
Night after night,
Have to look bright
Whether you're well or ill,
People must laugh their fill,
You mustn't sleep – till dawn comes
    creeping.
Though I never really grumble,
Life's a jumble indeed.
And in my efforts to succeed
I've had to formulate a creed.

Chorus
I believe in doing what I can   A
In crying when I must,   B
In laughing when I choose,   C
Heigh – o,   D
If love were all,   E
I should be lonely.   F

I believe the more you love a man   A
The more you give your trust,   B
The more you're bound to lose: C
Although,   D
When shadows fall   E
I think if only –   F
Somebody splendid really needed me
Someone affectionate and dear,
Cares would be ended if I knew that he
Wanted to have me near.
But I believe that since my life began
The most I've had is just
A talent to amuse.
Heigh – o,
If love were all.

Verse 2
Tho' life buffets me obscenely   A
It serenely goes on   B
Although I question its conclusion   C
Illusion is gone.   D
Frequently I put a bit by   E
Safe for a rainy day.   F

Nobody here can say
To what indeed, the years are leading.
Fate may often treat me meanly
But I keenly pursue

A little mirage in the blue,
Determination helps me through.
(Repeat Refrain)

Dear Little Café. This duet is a bid for another 'A Room With a View,' and succeeds almost as well. The last eight bars are delightful in both words and music. (See Fig. 4)

Fig. 4

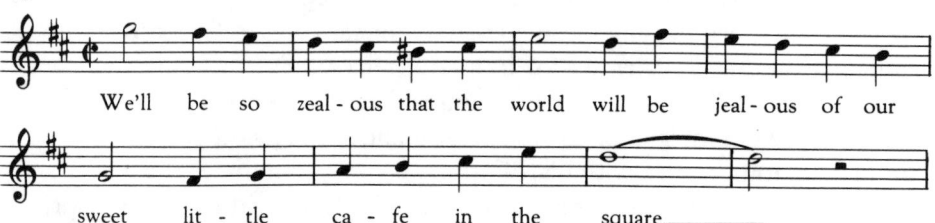

We'll be so zeal-ous that the world will be jeal-ous of our sweet lit-tle ca-fe in the square_____

Tokay. This would fill any operetta's requirement for a lusty drinking song suitable to a male chorus. The duple time and the long-held opening note are typical of Romberg and even of Rodgers' *Oklahoma*, which would be written more than a decade later.

Bonne Nuit and **Kiss Me.** The former, a naughty boulevard song *à la* Yvette Guilbert, is Noel showing off his knowledge of French. The latter is an English waltz similar to (but not quite so good as) others in the score.

Green Carnation. The last act has two superb numbers: this one and the ever-popular 'Zigeuner'. 'Green Carnation' is a jab at the effete; Coward poking fun at Oscar Wilde's famous *boutonnière*, and perhaps himself? I have printed the best lines below:

Blasé boys are we.
Exquisitely free
From the dreary and quite absurd
Moral views of the common herd.
We like porphyry bowls
Chandeliers and stoles,
We're most spirited, carefully filleted souls!

Refrain I
Pretty boys, witty boys, too, too, too,
Lazy to fight stagnation.
Haughty boys, naughty boys, all we do
Is to pursue sensation.
The portals of society are always
    open'd wide,
The world our eccentricity condones,
A lot of quaint variety we're certain to
    provide
We dress in very decorative tones.
Faded boys, jaded boys, womankind's

Gift to a bulldog nation.
In order to distinguish us from less
    enlightened minds
We all wear a green carnation.

Refrain 2
Pretty boys, witty boys, you may sneer
At our disintegration.
Haughty boys, naughty boys, dear,
    dear, dear,
Swooning with affectation.
Our figures sleek and willowy,
Our lips incarnadine
May worry the majority a bit.
But matrons rich and billowy
Invite us out to dine
And revel in our phosphorescent wit.
Faded boys, jaded boys, come what may
Art is our inspiration.

And as we are the reason for the
   'nineties' being gay,
We all wear a green carnation.

Zigeuner like 'Tokay' is perhaps more Hungarian than Viennese, but it is Coward's attempt at a party-scene entertainment, an old operetta tradition carried on from the ballroom scene at Prince Orlofsky's in *Die Fledermaus* to the song 'Vilia' in *The Merry Widow*. Its quasi-improvised melodic line is a study in lower neighbours and appoggiaturas (see Fig. 5), while its harmonic richness (especially the lowered VI chord going to the V) is obvious.

Fig. 5

bird on the wing___Your mel-o-dies a - dor - ing___ soar - ing.

Although *Bitter Sweet* received tepid reviews, most critics chiding Coward for being over-sentimental, the British public took the operetta to its heart. In England alone, nearly a million people saw it during its 769 performances. It went on, as *Au Temps des Valses*, to conquer Paris, and was twice filmed, once in Britain in 1933 with Anna Neagle and Ferdinand Gravet, and again in 1941 with Jeanette MacDonald and Nelson Eddy, this time in Hollywood.

Coward was justifiably proud of his accomplishment and sought all his life to recapture, in other operettas, the inspiration he achieved here. Some years later he entered in his diary 'of all the shows I have ever done *Bitter Sweet* gave me the greatest personal pleasure', but it was left to Max Beerbohm to put his finger on the underlying reasons for its great success. He wrote, 'Sentiment is out of fashion, yet *Bitter Sweet*, which is nothing if not sentimental, has not been a failure. Thus we see the things that are out of fashion do not cease to exist. Sentiment goes on unaffrighted by the roarings of the young lions and lionesses of Bloomsbury.'

Launching the American version of the operetta proved to be one of the true ordeals Noel was to suffer in his career. Again, the key but unreward-ing role of Carl seemed impossible to fill until a tenor appeared with an introductory letter from Princess Jane San Faustino.[2] 'He had a good voice,' writes Noel, 'long eyelashes, short legs, no stage experience and a violin, and although at the moment he couldn't speak a word of English, he swore with fervour that he would learn it in two months if we would only give him the part. We all felt a little dubious, but he seemed the likeliest possibility so far and so, after a certain amount of weary discussion, we engaged him.'

By the time of the Boston opening, all concerned realized that their Roman tenor could never appear without doing incalculable harm to the operetta. He did not seem able to project his voice over the orchestra so that he was inaudible beyond the third row, and his English had not improved enough to make what little came across of his lyrics intelligible. Certainly he would

---

[2] Princess Jane, a rich and influential Roman, an intimate friend of Cole Porter's from his Venice days, was the protagonist in his classic song 'The Tale of the Oyster,' which he originally wrote as 'The Scampi'. (For an outline of this musical gem see the Musical Analysis Appendix.)

never be able to be heard in New York's mammoth Ziegfeld Theatre where *Bitter Sweet* was scheduled to open in a mere three weeks. At the last moment Gerald Nodin, who had played a bit part, and was quite the wrong type for the sensitive role of Carl, was engaged, and it was left to Evelyn Laye to carry the whole show on her slender shoulders. Succeed she did, yet, in spite of splendid reviews and even more glowing personal ones for Miss Laye, the crashing stock market called a halt after a short but respectable run of 160 performances.

Wise enough to know that he would burn himself out without a holiday from his arduous recent schedule (appearing in *This Year of Grace* while writing, casting and directing *Bitter Sweet*), Noel now decided to take six months off, making his way slowly by train and tramp steamer to the Far East, the first leg of a journey round the world. He intended to travel by way of New York to Hollywood; thence to Hawaii and on to Tokyo where he would meet up with Jeffery Amhurst. But for the most part he would be alone, hoping to renew his energies.

When Coward originally conceived *Bitter Sweet* he had meant the leading part for Gertrude Lawrence, but soon realized her voice was too small for the demands of the role. Foolishly, he had told Gertie of his intentions, whereupon, to mollify his favourite acting partner, he added that he would soon write something in which both of them could play.

As a *bon voyage* token Gertie had given Noel a gold book from Cartier, which, when opened, disclosed a clock and a pensive picture of herself. Unable to come up with any ideas for their play, one sleepless night in his cabin, he later wrote in his diary, 'I finally gave up. This was a holiday after all, and I refused to allow my writer's conscience to agitate it any further. I also resolved never again to make any promises that implicated my creative ability … I would write whatever the spirit moved me to write.'

Then he closed Gertie's gift and read a book.

But a few evenings later, hoping to greet Jeffery's seven o'clock in the morning arrival in Tokyo as brightly as possible, Noel retired early. No sooner had he switched off the light when 'Gertie appeared in a white Molyneux dress on a terrace in the South of France, and refused to go away again until four AM, by which time *Private Lives*, title and all had constructed itself'.

Noel did not leap from his bed and write the play in a fever heat as he might have done a decade earlier, but mulled over his ideas for a month until he and Jeffery arrived in Shanghai; there, laid low by a bout of influenza, he got them down on paper in his normal four days. A month later, after fussing with a final draft, he sent copies of the script to Jack and to Gertie, requesting they wire back their opinion of the play. His obligation to his acting partner discharged, he could move on with impunity to enjoy his Far Eastern holiday.

Laurence Olivier and Adrianne Allen (standing), with
Coward and Gertrude Lawrence in *Private Lives*, 1930

But it was not to turn out as he dreamt. Now it was Jeffery's turn to fall
seriously ill, almost succumbing to amoebic dysentery. Noel spent most of the
spring of 1930 marking time in a series of hot cities, visiting his friend in
hospital and sitting out the sweltering nights in pavement cafés.

Although *Private Lives* is played by a cast of five, it is basically a tour de force
for two actors. Noel lavished his attention on every nuance of its production
and Gladys Calthrop designed a ravishing set for what has been called the
second greatest balcony scene ever written. Care was taken to cast two brilliant
actors, Adrianne Allen and Laurence Olivier, as the new spouses of the
divorced protagonists, Elyot and Amanda Chase. They are, in Noel's own
words, 'little better than ninepins, lightly wooden, only there at all in order to
be repeatedly knocked down'. As Amanda and Elyot, Gertie and Noel were to
give quintessential, by now legendary, performances, revealing the catastrophe
of two hot-tempered people deeply in love but unable to live together.

We know that, after the third act curtain descends, Amanda and Elyot, afflicted with the well-known twentieth-century malady of the struggle for supremacy, will claw at each other for the rest of their days. Perhaps that is why *Private Lives* brings a lump to the throat in the midst of our laughter – and why it refuses to date.

The extraordinary first act was helped by the addition of a seemingly prophetic song played repeatedly by the hotel orchestra. The words Amanda finally sings, 'someday I'll find you – again', are the whole theme of the play, and, canny showman that he was, Coward used the song as a writer of musicals would use underscoring. With dialogue above, he plugs it over and over again, going so far as to reprise it in the second act. Finally he even italicizes its use with Elyot's line, 'Strange how potent cheap music is.'[3] No wonder the published and recorded version of 'Someday I'll Find You' became one of Coward's big money-makers.

After the opening night there were happily some reviewers who appreciated what they saw on stage, and Noel noted in his diary that the press described his play as 'tenuous, thin, brittle, gossamer, iridescent, and delightfully daring. All of which connote to the public mind cocktails, evening dress, repartee and irreverent allusions to copulation thereby causing a gratifying number of respectable people to queue up at the box office.'

Noel knew his fellow countrymen. *Private Lives* was an unqualified hit. Now it was just a question of time – for Noel stuck to his vow of not appearing in even his most successful role for more than three months – before he and Gertie and Olivier (with the latter's new wife, Jill Esmond, playing Sybil[4]) would take the play to Broadway. There, like *The Vortex*, it was even more successful than in the West End.

Before leaving England, however, Noel contributed five numbers to Cochran's short-lived next revue. This entertainment which the showman called by the egotistical title of *Cochran's 1931 Revue* was hastily put together and well deserved its quick demise. Three of the songs Coward wrote for it, if not his best, are worth noting for various reasons.

'City' is the kind of agit-prop production number that was in vogue throughout the early '30s. Marc Blitzstein, Brecht-Weill and the Gershwins were all writing mini-operas for revues about the oppressiveness of life in the modern metropolis; all of their works, so fervent then, have dated until they are impossible to revive. Noel's is probably the worst of the lot, replete with crashing diminished seventh chords and containing lyrics like: 'City,/ Why are

[3] That is how the line was spoken by Noel on stage and in the recording, although the playscript substitutes 'extraordinary' for 'strange'.
[4] Adrianne Allen, who was pregnant, was forced to stay in England. The baby, Daniel Massey, who was to become Noel's godson, would be cast as his godfather in the filmed version of Gertrude Lawrence's biography, *Star!*, in 1964.

you casting this spell on me?/ City/ What if you crumbled and fell on me?/ Ev'ry weary prisoner/ Someday must be free/ City/ Please have pity on me.'

The individual trapped from birth is also apparent in another rather arty song, 'Half Caste Woman'. Its mystical lyric contains lines like 'Half caste woman,/ What are your slanting eyes/ Waiting and hoping to see?/ Scanning the far horizon/ Wondering what the end will be'. Musically, here instead of bombast we are given the whole tone scale, exotic, but certainly not Eurasian – yet it piques the ear and creates the desired alien sound. The song was to become one of Coward's most durable cabaret numbers.

Noel wrote of 'Any Little Fish' that, 'when sung with sufficient grimaces and innuendoes [it] is tolerably suggestive', and it is difficult not to agree. Its melody, bright and catchy, was responsible for whatever little success *Cochran's 1931 Revue* had. Certainly if Cole Porter had not written 'Let's Do It' two years earlier, this song's somewhat raunchy lyric, amusingly listing the *non*-amorous activities of the denizens of the animal world, might have been more effective.

Perhaps one can attribute the lacklustre nature of these songs to the fact that they were all written in a week in late 1930. Noel was spending the Christmas holiday with Jack at Goldenhurst, an extensive farmhouse with land he had bought in 1926, and his mind was certainly not on being another contributor to Mr. Cochran's hotch-potch.

What did occupy him was his next work. With the eclecticism of genius, he longed for it to be in direct contrast to his usual one-set, four-character play. Not yet recognizing the screen as a legitimate art form, he wished to compete with the then-lavish productions imported from Hollywood and showing in British cinemas. Many had casts of thousands who could talk *and* sing. He got the idea for a generational story while browsing through copies of the *Illustrated London News*. His would be a quasi-pageant, beginning in 1899 (the year of his own birth), while the Boer War was already in progress, encompassing Queen Victoria's death, the First World War and ending in the present. It would contain music but would not *be* a musical. And his cast, if it was not to number in thousands, would at least be in the hundreds.

Cochran could not wait to produce it. Packing all his research material, Noel set off early in 1931 to do his stint in *Private Lives* on Broadway. He relished the kudos he received in New York, the parties, the publicity, but his mind was in the new project.

By the time he had finished the outline of the new play, he knew he would need a theatre with a large revolving stage, and asked Cochran to secure the Coliseum, whereupon the producer wired back that it was unavailable and that he could take out an option on Drury Lane if Noel could give him an opening date. Always hating to be pinned down, Noel reluctantly targeted late

September to begin rehearsals. Now, instead of a revolving stage, Coward would content himself with six hydraulic lifts for *Cavalcade*.

Noel and Gladys worked frenziedly that summer of 1931; he on the book and she on the extravagant production which called for twenty-two scene changes and literally thousands of costumes (by actual count 3,700) that needed to be designed. The sheer logistics of a production that size involving such pageantry are staggering, for, in addition to a large cast of actors, four hundred extras were to be hired for the crowd scenes.

Directing such a huge ensemble was to be an awesome experience but Noel came up with a solution that would have made even Cecil B. De Mille smile. He had a set of twenty large plaques made in different colours and had them numbered from one to twenty. 'Number one,' he writes, 'in each group was the captain and was virtually in charge of the other nineteen ... This scheme, after a little preliminary confusion, worked splendidly. I could direct, through my microphone in the dress circle, without the strain of trying to memorise people's names, entirely by numbers and colours: "Would number seven red kindly go over and shake hands with number fifteen yellow-and-black stripe?"'

In a burst of inspiration he described a scene, cautioned the extras not to overact and allowed the enormous forces on stage to improvise. 'Little bits

The troop departure in *Cavalcade*, 1931

of excellent business crept in,' he noted, 'a child burst its balloon and screamed and its mother smacked it; an old lady collapsed in a deck-chair, and one young woman shut herself up in her parasol when she heard the noise of an aeroplane.'

As for the musical numbers, Coward mixed familiar patriotic songs like 'Rule Britannia' and 'Land of Hope and Glory' with songs of the period, and, for a theatre scene and a cabaret finale, threw in some of his own creation. Chief among them were 'The Mirabelle Waltz' (its first eight bars unfortunately an exact replica of 'My Buddy') and 'Twentieth Century Blues', which, as the excerpt reproduced here indicates, is not a blues at all but a contemporary-sounding copy of a torch song with a walking bass.

Of the other original songs, only 'The Girls of the C. I. V.', with lines like '... for our bravery is such/ That the Boers won't like it much,/ When we chase 'em across the Veldt/ And teach 'em double Dutch', had much originality. But musical or lyrical invention was not the keynote here. Pageantry, production, humanity, sentiment – all the capabilities of an evening in the theatre – were the goals. Raw emotions were highlighted – losing sons in the wars, the breakdown of caste, the aimless jazz age. Coward was not writing a musical, he was creating an epic.

The finale was especially moving for it came out of a chaotic nightclub scene with 'Twentieth Century Blues' used as music for 'dancing without any particular enjoyment'. In this respect it was not unlike the chilling masked number in 'Dance, Little Lady'. But here, as the scene faded, one saw the Union Jack glowing softly in the background, and now the entire company came on stage to sing 'God Save the King'.

The audience gave the play a standing ovation. They refused to leave until a smiling Noel Coward came on stage. He was to regret his curtain speech which closed with the line, 'In spite of the troublous times we are living in, it is still pretty exciting to be English.'

Although *Cavalcade* succeeded notably, running for 405 performances and chalking up a profit in spite of its enormous running costs, Coward was roundly criticised by critics, especially those with leftist leanings, for his jingoism. Certainly in preparing and rehearsing his play he could not have known that Britain would come off the gold standard shortly before opening night or that, hardly a week before the pageant's opening, a General Election would throw out the ruling Labour government.

Declining to answer the critics of his play and of his curtain speech, certain that in this time of national crisis they would not even listen to his explanation – simply that he had not written a patriotic tract, but rather a paean to courage and an ironic diatribe against the uselessness of war – Noel left the country for an eight-month trip through South America with his ideal travelling companion, Jeffery Amherst.

Noel was not running away, but once again felt the need for a chance to rest, and a time to consolidate his thoughts. He hoped he could now honour a promise made many years before to his friends, Alfred Lunt and Lynn Fontanne; a pledge that when they were all successful he would create a comedy for the three of them. No ideas came until his journey was almost over. Then in ten days (writing only in the mornings) he turned out *Design For Living*, a non-shocking play, if such a thing can be, about a ménage à trois.

While waiting for the Lunts to be free of commitments, Noel approached Cochran with an idea for another revue. Determined that it would have none of the usual skits and special material that had to be included with stars of the calibre of Lillie, Buchanan or Lawrence, this time he intended to construct the work as he would a play. There would be no juggling of scenes to accommodate a costume change, no songs 'in one'[5], no lavish ballets set in sunny Mexico or romantic Heidelberg, no scantily clad chorus line thrown in to please the public, and no slapstick comedy.

When Coward showed Cochran the early sketches for skits encompassing attacks on the press, songs about the rich feeling the crunch of worldwide depression, a take-off of the serious drama, *Journey's End*, and another admonishment to the 'younger generation', he was justifiably alarmed. Not only would this be 'Coward's Revue' instead of 'Cochran's', but, with little dancing and without stars, the master showman felt Coward was being egotistical in substituting intellect for entertainment, and was not afraid to tell Noel he felt the work would find little favour with the public. Yet he was in no position to argue. Coward was not only persuasive, he was pre-eminent. With *Cavalcade* selling out nightly, the film of *Private Lives* having just opened to rave reviews in Leicester Square, and wirelesses all over Britain constantly playing tunes from *Bitter Sweet* it was obvious Cowardmania had swept the country. Noel was a star of the first magnitude, and Cochran, now merely a producer, was forced to acquiesce.

As it turned out, in the business sense, Cochran was right and *Words and Music*, as the revue was eventually called, found its audiences dwindling after a few months. It was the first Cochran-Coward production to lose money.

But, in the artistic sense, Coward's vision was correct, for this is a highly estimable creation in the revue form. Its highlights are outlined below:

Opening Chorus. A view into the dressing room backstage. 'Mr. Cochran's Young Ladies' complaining to the costume mistress Maggie (played by Ivy St. Helier but certainly modelled on Gladys Calthrop) about all they have to do, the costumes not suiting them or being ill-fitting. With lines like

'Maggie!
Have you a scissors handy?
Maggie! We want a port and brandy.

Maggie answers:

'Freda dear, you must,
Do something with your bust
You'd best tie a knot
You can't show them all you've got ...'

[5] In front of the curtain, usually while a set change is going on behind.

At last the girls go out on stage and sing:

'... We're Mr. Cochran's young invincibles,
He much prefers us to the principals.
For ev'ry scene he cuts out
He says, 'just send the sluts out.'
And that's the reason why we have to work our guts out ...
    while we break our necks we feel
That so much animation wrecks appeal
Sex appeal
Never can show when there's too much
    endeavour ...'

Noel was later to admit that *Words and Music* was 'too clever by half'. Certainly he put his finger on the trouble with the opening number.

Let's Live Dangerously. The song's apologetic and somewhat polite tone blunts its message. With succeeding phrases espousing a turbulent or boisterous life, the first refrain ends:

'We'll be spectacular
In the vernacular
And so, until we break beneath the strain,
In various ways, we're going to be raising Cain.'

The final time the lines are changed to

'Where we'll end up, nobody can tell,
So pardon the phrase,
We mean to be raising Hell!'

Children of the Ritz. This is a true downer, but nevertheless a real gem. I quote

Joyce Barbour and chorus sing 'Children of the Ritz' in
Words and Music

the end of the first refrain. The lines are as devastating as Cole Porter's
Depression lyrics.

'In the lovely gay
Years before the crash
Mister Cartier
Never asked for cash,
Now shops we patronised are serving us with writs,
What's going to happen to the Children of the Ritz?'

Mad Dogs and Englishmen. This famous standard was written the previous
year while Noel was on his Far Eastern jaunt. In the show it is sung by a wise
clergyman who understands the natives and deplores the implacable and
unyielding attitude of his countrymen. The lyrics are too well known to be set
down here, but who could help reminding his reader of the three perfect
rhymes that end the first half of each refrain?

'... But Englishmen detest a
Siesta.'

'... They put their Scotch or Rye down
And lie down.'

'... To reprimand each inmate
Who's in late.'

Let's Say Goodbye. With the divorce rate rising and the transience of love
affairs an established fact, this song of parting without rancour, when an affair
is over, was one of the timeliest in the show:

'Let's look on love as a plaything,
All these sweet moments we've known,
Mustn't be degraded,
When the thrill of them has faded,
Let's say "Goodbye" and leave it alone.'

The Hall of Fame. This was a clever piece about advertising the ordinary;
making news out of the commonplace. Some of the people interviewed were:
the man who caught the biggest shrimp, the man who rowed across Lake
Windermere in an India-rubber bath, a mermaid, a clergyman who's never
been to London and a chorine who became a celebrity by marrying a Lord.

The Oldest Postmistress. This is my particular favourite.

'I'm the very oldest Postmistress in England,
And probably the oldest on the earth.
I've been asked by all the papers for a statement,
So I give you these few facts for what they're worth.
My appetite is absolutely splendid,
There's nothing in the world I can't digest,
I seldom feel uneasy or distended,
And I'm never disagreeable or depressed.
I still deliver all the letters daily.

Tho' my memory is just as good as new,
I've a hazy recollection of Disraeli,
And I lived in Bray in eighteen-forty-two.
I think the modern girl is very pretty.
I've never smoked a single cigarette.
I think all this divorcing is a pity,
And I'm sorry that the nation is upset.
I well recall in eighteen-thirty-seven
My parents lived in Weston Super Mare
I'm actually one hundred and eleven,
But I cannot see why anyone should care.'

Mad About the Boy. See Musical Analysis Appendix.

Three White Feathers. The breakdown of the classes again, this time done with great panache.

'We had a pawnshop on the corner of the street
And father did a roaring trade.
I used to think those rings and necklaces were sweet,
Now I wouldn't give them to my maid
... Today it may be three white feathers, but yesterday it was three brass balls.'

Something To Do With Spring. This number, one of the hits of the show, strikes this writer as trying too hard for cleverness in both its music and lyrics. This is unfortunate, for the lilting tune *almost* succeeds. The musical line, which begins attractively, gets subverted from its inevitable minor conclusion (Fig. 1) the last time it appears (Fig. 2). The lyric in the second chorus – with lines like 'they say that rabbits have minds like sinks', and 'but why should the cows behave with *no* restraint?' – is not even amusing.

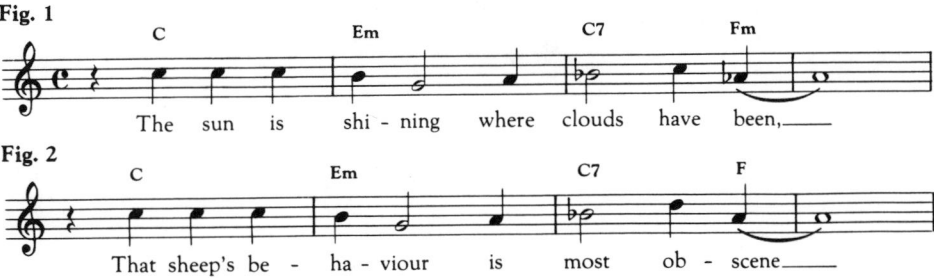

Fig. 1

The sun is shi-ning where clouds have been,____

Fig. 2

That sheep's be-ha-viour is most ob-scene____

The Wife of the Acrobat. One of Coward's funniest numbers, all but hidden in the middle of the second act. The awkward, knobbly-kneed wife who states,

'Apart from waving my hand about
When he's finished a trick
I do nothing but stand about
Feeling slightly sick,'

uttering 'Allez Oop' with great embarrassment, makes a hilarious picture. The comic words are wedded to a real show-biz, almost acrobatic melody. Just look at the tune for 'Allez Oop'.

giv - ingshows in Hea - ven, three per - for - man-ces a day,_____ I'll

say what all the An - gels are ex - pect - ing me to say 'Al - lez

Oop, Al - lez Oop, Al - lez Oop!'

I defy anyone listening to the third refrain not to laugh aloud.

'I'm the wife of an Acrobat,
When my old man don't feel well,
To hold each prop
And wonder if he'll drop
Is my idea of Hell.
What a life for an Acrobat
When I watch him loop the loop,
I wonder what he's thinking upside down on the trapeze,
And if he's really happy with his head between his knees,
And then his face goes crimson and I know he's going to sneeze,
Allez Oop, Allez Oop, Allez Oop!'

The Party's Over Now. This song, written to close the show, would serve Coward all his life as a perfect signing-off number for his cabaret acts. The first section has such a memorable and lilting melody that one often overlooks the marvellous bridge (see below), built on the fresh harmonies of E minor and A followed by D minor and G.

If Noel was suddenly shaken by the reality that not everything he wrote must be an immediate hit, he could comfort himself in the autumn of 1932 that though *Words and Music* was playing only to half-empty houses at least it *was* playing. Not so with his friend Cole Porter, whom he saw whenever he was in New York. A year earlier Cole had written the entire score for *Star Dust* as a vehicle for Peggy Wood when she closed in *Bitter Sweet*. But, such are the vicissitudes of Broadway, the cigarette manufacturer who was to underwrite the production backed out when the US government, fighting its way out of the Depression imposed a large tax on their product.

The show was never produced, but Cole, not one to discard good material, used the words and music for 'But He Never Says He Loves Me' as 'The Physician' (see p. 107) in *Nymph Errant*, and 'I've Got You On My Mind', 'Mister and Missus Fitch' and 'I Still Love the Red, White and Blue' in *The Gay Divorcée*. One of his greatest hits, 'I Get A Kick Out of You', did not die along with *Star Dust*; he was to use it in *Anything Goes*.

Yet, even after the American success of *The Gay Divorcée* and the British production of *Nymph Errant*, Cole was to face more disappointment. *Ever Yours*, another score which Cole completed in 1934, had a libretto by Guy Bolton, but this show, too, was never produced. Of the fifteen numbers, most of which were never published, a few – 'When Love Comes Your Way', 'Once Upon a Time', 'Yours' and 'When We Waltz Down the Aisle' among them – have become favourites of cabaret performers.

Cole seems to have taken these disappointments with his usual equanimity, and his career was certainly rising. But, as 1933 dawned, the songwriter of the hour was certainly Noel Coward.

Things were to change after *Anything Goes*. Noel's fame was not to diminish but, in a mere matter of six months, Cole's star was to experience a meteoric rise.

COLE
1935-1937

ALTHOUGH HIS NEXT TWO SHOWS were to be indifferently received, Cole Porter, the name and the image he projected through his songs, had by now become a resounding success. In 1935, if you were to ask the knowledgeable man-in-the-street to name the world's top song-writers his list would certainly have included Cole Porter along with Irving Berlin, Rodgers and Hart, Jerome Kern and the Gershwin brothers.

With *Jubilee*, which opened in October 1935, and *Red, Hot and Blue*, presented a year later, Cole now settled into the habit of presenting a new show every year or so. The shows would be expendable, their books so cliché-ridden as to be laughable, but Cole's songs would be remembered, even though critics were perpetually to proclaim something to the effect of 'not top-drawer Cole Porter'. This pattern was to remain unbroken until *Kiss Me, Kate* opened in 1948.

The habit of presenting an annual show was due to the fact that it had taken Cole so long, almost forty-five years, to arrive at his success, that he wanted to remind the world of his present pre-eminence. The expendability of the shows he worked on was not of Cole's making but was prevalent in musicals the world over. The stories that made up the libretti of the average musical comedy, created to escape the Depression blues, were deliberately unbelievable. Almost all these shows – with the exception of *Show Boat* and *Anything Goes* are mere museum pieces today.

What was it that kept the public flocking to these hits? What was it audiences found in them then that they do not find today? The answer is simple. Contrivance could be overlooked as long as a musical was lush, opulent, colourful, amused its audience and was witty. The wit need not be appropriate to the character on stage, it could very well be the author's, but since no one *believed* the character on stage it did not matter. Since the theatre, and the musical as well, was tailored for an affluent, intellectual audience the wit had to be wide-spread, topical, and satirical. All these qualities have disappeared from today's musical theatre. Only the lavishness, alas, has remained.

Cole Porter and Moss Hart, touring the globe in search of inspiration for the musical the papers had already announced, must first have decided that their show had to be heavy on wit and satire. Both being men of the theatre with the knowledge that extravaganzas were ringing the cash registers at box-offices everywhere, they must have decided to make their musical, *Jubilee*, inspired by the silver one King George V and Queen Mary were celebrating that May, as lavish as possible.

The plot is a simple cut-out into which eight principals – with their attendant songs – could be fitted. A king and queen, prince and princess are advised to go into hiding because of a possible overthrow of their monarchy. Taking on the alias of 'the Smith family', they pretend to be commoners until the trouble blows over. The queen succumbs to the brawn of (here comes the satire) Charles Rausmiller, a thinly disguised copy of the movies' Tarzan, Johnny Weissmuller; the princess falls for Eric Dare, a playwright-director-actor à la Noel Coward (Dare – Coward). The king is in the best tradition of the elderly musical comedy lecher and the prince, of course, pursues a showgirl, which allows for tap and elaborate production numbers.

In spite of *Jubilee*'s simple story, or perhaps because of it, Cole's score contains some of his most daring, and best-known, songs. 'Begin the Beguine' was written to be the central dance number of the show. Yet, though well received by the critics, the song did not catch on with the public until Artie Shaw made a hit recording of the tune some three years after *Jubilee* closed. But, ever since, its enormous popularity has ensured that the mere mention of the beguine conjures up Cole Porter's name. Not only did he single-handedly add that term to musical language, but throughout his career he was to write many more similar, languorous melodies that were invariably performed in 'tempo di Beguine'. Of its origin Cole wrote:

> I was living in Paris at the time and somebody suggested that I go see the Black Martiniquois do their dance, the beguine, in a remote nightclub on the Left Bank ... I was very much taken by the rhythm ... practically that of the already popular rhumba but much faster[1] ... I thought of 'Begin the Beguine' as a good title for a song and put it away in a notebook, adding a memorandum as to its rhythm and tempo. About ten years later, while going around the world we stopped at a place called Kalabahi ... a native dance was started for us, of which the melody of the first four bars would become the melody of my song ... I looked through my notebook, and found again, after ten years, my old title, 'Begin the Beguine'. For some reason, the melody that I heard and the phrase I had written down seemed to marry. I developed the whole song from that.

Porter, always the parodist, was the first to make fun of his own work. In *Seven Lively Arts* (1944), he wrote 'Let's End the Beguine' for Beatrice Lillie. These are a few of its lines.

When I left my home in Bali	Some orchestra guy
For a show in N.Y.C.	Begins the Beguine
Some cheroot in Tin Pan Alley	Accompanied by
Wrote this song espeshly for me.	Drums
So wherever I'm seen	Those jungle drums!

[1] Although 'Begin the Beguine' derives its rhythmic origin from French Martinique, and its melodic one from an Indonesian island, it is generally danced by specialists in rhumba, cha-cha and other South American steps.

| Due to that beguine, I detest those songs, | Due to that beguine I resent each tune |
| Where the groaners go for calico sarongs | That involves an actor with an actor-oon. |

The beguine is so obvious and became such a rage that others jumped in to parody this embodiment of the sensual torrid dance. Because of their friendship Noel Coward, parodist par excellence, could throw the gentlest barbs. His 'Nina' from *Sigh No More*, in 1945, tells the story of an Argentine Miss who refused to become a cliché and balked at dancing to any of those South American rhythms.

Coward reports

She declined to begin the Beguine when they requested it
And she made an embarrassing scene if anyone suggested it,
For she detested it.

In the next verse Noel goes further:

She refused to begin the Beguine when they besought her to
And in language profane and obscene she cursed the man who taught her to.
She cursed Cole Porter, too.

'Begin the Beguine' was not the only slow starter in *Jubilee* to become a standard. 'Just One Of Those Things,' whose message is considered by many to be the epitome of Porterian insouciance and style, and whose melodic refrain with its minor opening, tantalizing modulatory bridge and offbeat rhythmic design was to make it a favourite of critics and cabaret performers everywhere, was the big number in the second act. Like 'Begin the Beguine' it did not catch on until years after it was introduced.

One would assume that a show with those two hits, and additional numbers like 'The Kling-Kling Bird in the Divi-Divi Tree,' 'Why Shouldn't I?'[2], 'When Love Comes Your Way', 'A Picture of Me Without You' and 'Mr. and Mrs. Smith', could not possibly fail but *Jubilee* seems to have been jinxed from the start.

The timing, one of the most important attributes of the theatre, was against the show. A depressed Broadway mounted fifty fewer productions in the season *Jubilee* opened than in the previous year, and most of those were losing money. Then, while the show was still in rehearsal, various cast members received threatening letters saying they would be shot at if they went onstage. Mysterious fires (probably set by a disgruntled actor-arsonist) broke out back-stage. All this understandably upset the show's superstitious star, Mary Boland, formerly an important stage performer now turned Hollywood headliner. Miss Boland, who played the key role of the queen, took too many nips from the bottle to ease her terrified mind, and when the show was only four months into its run she was 'released' from her contract. Laura Hope Crews (who became better known as Scarlett's hysterical Aunt Pitty-Pat in

---

[2] See Musical Analysis Appendix.

Gone with the Wind) tried to fill her shoes, but her talent and image were not big enough to keep the show running.

Jubilee, as its title implies, was a lavish and costly production and in many ways it was not unlike a light-hearted version of Coward's Cavalcade. The critic Gilbert Gabriel writing in the New York American said, 'It is the ultimate of the post-Ziegfeld period ... an extravaganza extraordinary ... almost fabulous.' On paper it had looked so certain to succeed that MGM gladly put up most of the $150,000 pre-production money. The prospect of recouping his money in a matter of a few weeks tempted even a non-gambler like Cole to invest. With his loss of $18,000, he made a vow – and kept it – never again to put money into one of his own shows.

Since the critiques were good, and Jubilee seemed neatly tucked into a long run (it actually ran for 169 performances), Cole and Linda set out for Hollywood in December 1935. Cole's contract to turn out the music and lyrics for a motion picture which did not even boast an outline paid him the handsome fee of $75,000 for this, his first original score. It was planned as a romantic comedy for Clark Gable and Jean Harlow but, when it was discovered that neither Gable nor Harlow could sing, in typical '30s Hollywood fashion the story was quickly transformed into an ice skating epic starring Sonja Henie. Finally it emerged as a battleship romance starring Eleanor Powell as a lonely-hearts club hostess who meets and instantly falls in love with sailor Jimmy Stewart.[3] The heavy in this concoction is Virginia Bruce who plays a Broadway musical comedy star. Predictably, in the last reel Eleanor wrests Jimmy from the clutches of the actress.

Cole kept voluminous notes of his experiences during the five months it took to make the film called Born to Dance, which was released in November 1936. Reading between the lines, one feels that, although Hollywood adored him, he looked down his nose at this group of ex-glove and car salesmen so recently turned impresarios.

Although Linda put up with the garrulous social world of Hollywood with difficulty, Cole loved the sun-filled life of a much-sought-after composer. He had rented Richard Barthelmess's lavish estate, and enjoyed the pool and the telephone by the pool, the tennis courts, the lounging, drinking, tanning, and even the social obligations. He had truly 'gone Hollywood', as he told the New York gossip columnist, Dorothy Killgallen. 'When I first came here they told me, "You'll be so bored you'll die. Nobody talks about anything but pictures." After I was here a week, I discovered I didn't want to talk about anything else myself.'

[3] Jimmy Stewart could sing no better than Clark Gable, but he semi-talked-sang 'Easy To Love' with charm and honesty. The song was originally written for William Gaxton to sing in Anything Goes. Gaxton complained that the opening notes of the song were too low for his voice, at which point Cole wrote 'All Through the Night' for him.

Because of plot delays filming *Born To Dance* took longer than Cole and especially Linda, who was eager to get back to New York, anticipated, but when it was released Cole had at least one more hit to his credit: 'I've Got You Under My Skin.' The unusual title is a direct translation from the opening line of a French song Cole admired, a ballad so identified with Fanny Brice as to become her signature. The song 'My Man' ('Mon Homme') by Maurice Yvain, begins and is, in fact, subtitled 'Je l'ai tellement dans le peau', (I've got him so much in my skin).

Well sung in the film by the beauteous Virginia Bruce, 'I've Got You Under My Skin' caught on almost immediately. The fifty-six bar song with a repeated 16-bar A section followed by an extended bolero-like bridge and a foreshortened A3 reminded most listeners of the beguine, by now a Cole Porter trademark.[4]

Once he had seen the rushes of the film, Louis B. Mayer realized that Cole's score was the best thing about *Born to Dance*. MGM's chief gushed over the songwriter and offered him the enormous sum of $100,000 to return next year and write the score for *Rosalie*. It was an offer tempting to Cole's ego. Then Mayer called Cole's Hollywood agent, Arthur Lyons to work out the details, and before they left California – and over Linda's strong objection – Cole signed the contract.

So it was with work in view and money in hand, Cole and Linda left Hollywood in early summer to return to New York and their apartment in the Waldorf Towers[5] where Cole would immediately begin work on his next Vinton Freedley production.

Red, Hot and Blue was not jinxed in the way *Jubilee* had been. But it was fraught with personality clashes because everyone concerned (almost the entire *Anything Goes* group), Cole included, was now successful, pig-headed and 'a star'. Cole leisurely motored east from Hollywood, which considerably delayed the start of rehearsals. When he returned to Broadway, he was to find a disgruntled Freedley and an irate Gaxton. Gaxton had overheard the show's librettists telling Ethel Merman that hers would really be the starring part; shortly after that he quit. Freedley quickly signed Bob Hope[6] and, consistent with his axiom that 'the stars bring the customers', he looked to build up the

---

[4] In 1990, 'I've Got You Under My Skin' was to become the lead song in a best-selling pop album called *Red, Hot and Blue*, (having no relationship to the show) and have a new life as a rap song pleading for the use of preventive measures to stop the spread of AIDS. Repeated lines were 'under my skin' referring to the injection of needles and 'use your mentality, wake up to reality,' pleading for those infected to seek medical help.

[5] Elsa Maxwell, always accustomed to having things given her in the name of publicity, had talked the management of the Waldorf-Astoria into renting a fourteen room apartment in the Waldorf Towers to the Porters for $35 a day. She had convinced the rentors (and rightly so) that having these famous tenants in the building would attract those who were merely rich, and who could be cajoled into signing long leases at extravagant yearly rentals.

[6] *Red, Hot and Blue* was to be Hope's last featured Broadway role before he headed west to star in movies. A serviceable second lead and a good singer and dancer, he had first attracted notice in *Roberta* (1933) and *The Ziegfeld Follies* (1936). Although Broadway producers (including Freedley) made the mistake of casting him in a romantic role, Hollywood immediately realized his enormous potential for comedy.

Ethel Merman and Jimmy Durante both demanded top billing; Cole solved the problem by swapping the position of their names every two weeks

comedy role and signed Jimmy Durante. Because of these cast changes he also demanded a great deal of rewriting from his librettists and Cole.

By the time the show was in rehearsal there was another fracas. Both Merman's and Durante's agents insisted that their clients' name should be above the title. Fortunately Cole came up with a solution that crossed the names left to right and reversed them on the marquee, alternating every six weeks. Although none of the stars liked each other, an armed truce was declared so rehearsals could proceed. Cole was happy that his song 'It's De-Lovely',[7] which had been written on the round-the-world tour and rejected from both *Jubilee* and *Born to Dance*, would be included. The casting of Jimmy Durante as comic-in-chief gave him the opportunity to write one of his most daring transvestite songs which could only appear harmless and hilarious when sung by a diminutive womanizer like Durante: 'A Little Skipper From Heaven Above'.

Verse
The raging sou'wester was over,
It was calm, and the heavens had cleared,
The sails were gently flapping,
The sailors all were napping,
When the hero, Captain Cosgrove,
    appeared.
It was obvious he had been crying,
And he seemed to have lost all his poise,
As he stood there so stark
And was heard to remark,
'I have something to say to you, boys' —

Chorus
I'm about to become a mother,
I'm only a girl, not a boy.
Years ago I disguised as my brother,
And went rolling down to Rio, ship ahoy.
Though it hurts me to leave ye, me hearties,
Still you must understand, it was love.
And I'm about to give birth
To the sweetest thing on earth,
A little skipper from heaven above.

In the next refrain (although the language sounds to this writer suspiciously like Durante's) Cole writes his only slur on homosexuality when he explains to the assembled sailors how all this came about: 'Years ago I discovers my brother was a nance,/ So I gives him my petticoats and puts on his pants,/ Then I finds me a sailor who's looking for romance.'

If Cole enjoyed writing low-down comic bits for Durante, he felt passionate about the sound of Merman's delivery, her professionalism, her ability to memorize lyric changes quickly and even her shorthand.[8] He declared in print that 'her voice is thrilling', and added, 'She has the finest enunciation of any American singer I know. She has a sense of rhythm which few can equal and her feeling for comedy is so intuitive that she can get every value out of a line without over-stressing.'

Ethel Merman, who returned the compliment by saying unequivocally, 'I'd rather sing his songs than those by any other writer,' sang some of Cole's best songs in *Red, Hot and Blue*. Besides 'It's De-Lovely', which quickly became the hit of the show, he wrote 'The Ozarks Are Calling Me Home', 'You're A Bad Influence on Me', the title song, 'Red, Hot and Blue', 'Down in the Depths (On the Ninetieth Floor)', and another of his standards, 'Ridin' High', all with La Merman's (as he called her) clarion voice in mind.

In spite of the energy evinced in the Merman songs and the obvious tenderness of ballads like 'Ours', and 'Who, But You?', Cole's songs in *Red, Hot and Blue* were so criticized by the press that the show only achieved a limited run. Now, after two failures in a row, Cole was able to take a dispassionate look at his own work and say to a reporter that his scores had been written 'for the understanding and enjoyment of about eighteen other people, all of whom are first nighters anyway. Polished, urbane and adult playwriting in the musical field is strictly a creative luxury.'

Taking his own criticism to heart, *Red, Hot and Blue* became a turning point in his career. He announced that he had decided to write songs, as he put

---

[7] See Musical Analysis Appendix.
[8] Ethel Zimmermann (hence Merman) had been a secretary-stenographer before going into show business.

it, 'with wider appeal for the common people and less of the brittle, bright poesy with which I've been associated'.

That winter, when he began work on *Rosalie*,[9] the Hollywood remake of a Wodehouse-Romberg-Gershwin 1928 hit, Cole remembered this promise. He held back the bright, sophisticated rhymes, the syncopated or swinging rhythmic lines and intricate harmonic changes. Now he replaced them with obvious operatic pretentiousness, romantic soupiness, and melodies patently written to please the public-at-large. In a way he was pulling the legs of his Hollywood employers and much of what he turned out for this picture was in the minor key, what Cole himself referred to as 'Jewish-type songs'. They did not fail to hit the mark. 'In the Still of the Night', for example, written for and rejected by Nelson Eddy as unsuited to his operatic voice, was taken to L.B. Mayer for a final decision. The high tessitura and sentimental intensity of its bridge ('Do you love me/ As I love you?/ Are you my life to be,/ My dream come true?') were enough to bring tears to the eyes of the notoriously stone-hearted head of MGM. Eddy was overruled.

Rosalie's title song was to give Cole much trouble. He himself said he wrote seven versions (although I have been unable to locate more than four), and that he was fondest of 'Rosalie' number six. Mayer, perhaps because he had made things easy for his employee on 'In the Still of the Night', sent the frustrated songwriter back again and yet again to his keyboard, with the advice to 'forget that you're writing for Nelson Eddy', and in the hope that Cole could simplify his ideas. Finally Porter is reputed to have scribbled the approved version as a parody, never dreaming it would become so successful. Cole often stated that he wrote the song in hate, and that it was his least favourite composition, but mitigated his stand when Irving Berlin wrote to him, 'Listen, kid, never hate a song that has sold half a million copies.'[10]

During that particular winter in Hollywood, the gulf between Cole and Linda, who never had been very happy in the movie environment, widened. Deeply in love with Cole though she was and always the dutiful wife, Linda was unable to countenance his frequent homosexual encounters as she had the year before. Linda had always known and accepted Cole's sexual preferences but it was impossible for her to witness daily the more flamboyant side of his homosexuality which life in California brought out. Perhaps it was the assemblage of so many chorus boys at their pool each afternoon, or because

[9] *Rosalie*, the Ziegfeld extravaganza starring Marilyn Miller, was a big romantic operetta with splendid bright songs like 'Oh Gee! Oh Joy!' and 'How Long Has This Been Going On' from the Gershwins and operatic gems like 'The Hussar March' and 'The King Can Do No Wrong,' by the master of the genre, Sigmund Romberg. In typical Hollywood fashion, the tired plot about a princess from a mythical European country named Romanza travelling incognito and falling for an American flier was retained; the Gershwin and Romberg treasures were discarded and a new score was commissioned from Cole.
[10] 'Wunderbar', the quasi-German waltz Cole wrote as a parody for *Kiss Me, Kate*, was to share the same fate – great unbidden success.

Cole who had never been 'in the closet' was now so patently out of it that made her fear he might be a target for adverse publicity, especially now that he was a world-famous celebrity. Rather than risk a blow-up, Linda quietly returned to their house in Paris.

Once filming was completed, Cole hurried to join her, hoping to effect a reconciliation, but Linda was cool towards him. So Cole joined his long-time homosexual friend Howard Sturges and the latter's young friend, the architect Ed Tauch, on a walking tour of central Europe and Scandinavia. Looking at the vast number of photographs the three men took during this lengthy trek, one sees no indication of tension in Cole's face, nothing that betrays any malaise caused by Linda's aloofness.

Porter, at Elsinore, shortly before the accident

The press was kind – or uninformed. If this enchanted couple were drifting apart, the world knew little of it. Because Cole's work called for him to spend time in Paris, London, New York or Hollywood, even in Greece (Vinton Freedley had just announced that Cole was working on a new show *Greek to You*), no gossip columnist even hinted at an estrangement.

Throughout the autumn of 1937, Linda was seen at all the Paris openings and couturiers' shows, while Cole who had just returned from Europe to start work on his new revue called *You Never Know*, starring Libby Holman and Clifton Webb, frequently had his photograph in the papers looking the picture of health and energy.

It was then that Cole accepted an invitation from the former Edith Mortimer, now Countess de Zoppola, to spend the weekend at her estate in Oyster Bay, Long Island.

Always trying to escape boredom, Cole spent several hours on the telephone arranging a riding party at the nearby Piping Rock Country Club. At the stable he chose an especially skittish horse and insisted on riding it in spite of the groom's advice. Soon after the party set out, and as they came up over a small rise, Cole's horse was frightened by a clump of bushes in his path. It was later said that Cole did not pull in the reins fast enough, but Cole, although an excellent horseman, had never been faced with such an emergency. The frightened animal, not knowing whether it should jump the bushes or go around them, simply reared up so high it fell backwards. Caught unawares, Cole was unable to kick the stirrups free and, as the horse attempted to get up, it fell on its side, rolling and shattering the bones in Cole's right leg. Then, as it partially regained its footing, it fell back a second time on the opposite side, this time crushing Cole's left leg.

When the horse finally got to its feet and ran off, Benjamin Moore, the first member of the party to reach him, saw that Cole was badly hurt and hurried to call the North County Hospital for an ambulance. None was immediately available. Luckily, Moore had the presence of mind to telephone the Locust Valley Fire Department which quickly sent an ambulance to speed Cole to hospital. He went immediately into shock and remained unconscious for two days. Meanwhile Linda was contacted in Paris while Kate hurried eastwards from Indiana.

When he finally regained consciousness, Cole was visited by Elsa Maxwell who reported later in *Harper's* that Cole had lost none of his wit. Upon seeing her he is said to have remarked, 'It just goes to show that fifty million Frenchmen can't be wrong. They eat horses instead of riding them.'

Cole's doctors gave out little information to the press that might indicate the gravity of the situation. The *New York Times* reported merely, 'Cole Porter is hurt in fall from horse'. But Linda, in a frank telephone conversation with Dr. Joseph Connolly, the orthopaedic surgeon who was treating Cole, was told the whole truth. Seeing how badly shattered the leg was, and fearing that gangrene might set in, he recommended amputation of the right leg and possibly of the left leg as well.

Linda knew this would kill Cole; that because of his tremendous vanity he could suffer excruciating pain, but would not survive any maiming of his body. An amputation was out of the question. She put Cole's well-being to the forefront and asked the doctor to postpone any surgery until her return to New York.

As soon as she arrived in Manhattan she brought in a distinguished bone specialist, Dr. John J. Moorhead, to discuss the possibility of reconstructive surgery on Cole's legs. Moorhead warned her (and Kate, who with Linda made these vital decisions that were to affect the rest of Cole's life) that pinning Cole's bones together would be a long and difficult process. They could expect, he told them, Cole to be in the hospital for months after the operation because torn nerve and muscle tissue heals so slowly. He advised them that Cole would need painful daily therapy during that time. Did they think the patient would agree to this?

Knowing as they did the importance Cole placed on personal appearance, there was little question that he would, especially since the only alternative was amputation. After the operation, doctors and nurses could not believe how brave and stoical Cole was as he faced the reconstructive process.

At the moment the prognosis held a reasonable glow of optimism. An operation, seven months in the hospital, some therapy and all would be as it was before. Cole and Linda, the enchanted couple, were together again and they were looking forward to the day perhaps a year in the future when they could book a table at the Waldolf Astoria's Starlight Roof and dance all night.

NOEL
1933 - 1937

FOR COLE PORTER 1937 was a tragic year. Matters were equally catastrophic in the outside world: Spain was embroiled in civil war; German aggression was mounting. The economic depression was beginning to recede but Broadway and the West End were in a sorry state. There was no place for the wit of Coward or the sophistication of Porter. Most of the successful British shows were American imports done on the cheap, the few home-grown products, many by Ivor Novello, being either hopelessly *old-fashioned* or having scores (like *Me and My Girl*) which the man-in-the-street could sing or might even compose. That summer, the world of music suffered a crushing blow when George Gershwin died at the age of thirty-nine.

Noel Coward had his own problems. The first volume of his autobiography, *Present Indicative*, had not been well received. Cyril Connolly, in the

Louis Hayward (left), Yvonne Printemps, Coward and
Irene Brown in *Conversation Piece*

New Statesman, called Coward 'a person of infinite charm and adaptability whose very adaptability however makes him inferior to a more compact and worldly competitor in his own sphere like Cole Porter'. Connolly equated Noel's career with the quest for money, announcing that his 'book reveals a terrible predicament, that of a young man with the Midas touch, with a gift that does not creep and branch and flower, but which turns everything it touches into immediate gold. And gold melts too,' he concluded.

As Noel was then thirty-seven he stated publicly that he was not at all bothered by the criticism, and especially relished being called a 'young man'. In the past few years he had been experienced illness, accidents and the tragic death of his young brother, Eric. He had also had his share of success mitigated by a somewhat larger portion of failures. But the publication of one's autobiography leads to stock-taking.

In the success column he could list *Design For Living*, with which he and the Lunts captivated Broadway. He had even bent his rule of not playing for more than three months in anything, adding an additional eight weeks in response to a clamouring American public.

His next work, *Conversation Piece*, was a true labour of love, for Noel, captivated by the diminutive Parisian star, Yvonne Printemps, was hoping to write something that would display her remarkable vocal range and talent. While he was on a Caribbean cruise he picked up a copy of *The Regent and His Daughter* by Dormer Creston. Set in coastal Brighton, the book sparked a fresh idea, the combination of a French courtesan, a penniless French aristocrat and Regency Brighton. He would cast a youthful Romney Brent in the leading male role, but he must, subliminally, have been thinking of the part for himself for, when Brent objected to playing a fifty-four-year-old high-class procurer, Noel stepped in and filled the part perfectly.

On his return from Trinidad with nothing more than vague sketches and few musical ideas, he told Cochran of his proposed new project, his plans to star Mlle Printemps, and swore him to secrecy. Cochran, eager to produce the new operetta, made an immediate announcement to the press, and Yvonne Printemps – although it was the first she had heard of it – wired from Paris that she would be delighted to star in M. Coward's new work.

As with *Bitter Sweet*, Noel could not plunge deeply into the composition of his play without a haunting melodic theme, a *leitmotif*, a concept, a key song that would act as the turning-point on which the entire action would depend. And again, as in his earlier work, it eluded him. He spent ten days (the time it usually took him to write an entire play) cursing Cochran for the premature announcement. Coward was, he writes, determined to cable Cochran and Printemps the very next morning, saying he was resolved to postpone the entire project for another six months.

I felt fairly wretched but at least relieved that I had had the sense to admit failure while there was still time. I poured myself a large whisky and soda, dined in grey solitude, poured myself another, even larger, whisky and soda, and sat gloomily envisaging everybody's disappointment and facing the fact that my talent had withered and that I should never write any more music until the day I died. The whisky did little to banish my gloom, but there was no more work to be done and I decided to go to bed. I switched off the lights at the door and noticed that there was one lone lamp left on by the piano. I walked automatically to turn it off, sat down and played 'I'll Follow My Secret Heart', straight through in G flat,[1] a key I had never played in before.

'I'll Follow My Secret Heart' has become one of Coward's most loved waltzes, often being compared to *Bitter Sweet*'s 'I'll See You Again'. This writer finds the latter infinitely more moving and original, though there is a memorable first phrase with its big skip on the word 'follow' coupled with a magnetic augmented chord (see *) and a moving appogiatura on the word 'life' (see**) that ends the phrase.

Noel was right. The play could not go further without the song, for this scene, occurring early in the action, tells the audience that Melanie (Yvonne Printemps) is being forced into an affluent marriage by her 'guardian' Paul (Noel Coward), an improverished French duke. Coward plays lightly with the plot and the audience does not know, when Melanie sings about following her secret heart, if it will lead her to a love match with the young Marquess of Sheere (Louis Hayward), his father or Paul himself. After a ballroom scene, Melanie has another waltz to sing, 'Nevermore' one of the best Coward ever wrote. Its first theme, built on II and V chords is given here.

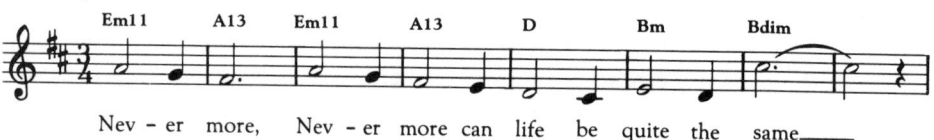

[1] G Flat, a key with six flats, is almost never used in printed sheet copies. The song was published a half-tone higher in G – only one sharp for the amateur accompanist to contend with. Mlle Printemps sang the song on stage in the key that was eventually chosen for her by Coward (and published in the score), a full tone higher in A flat.

The rest of the score strikes me as heavy-handed. 'Regency Rakes', instead of poking gentle fun, again uses a heavy $\frac{3}{4}$ beat. A quartet of British noblemen declaim:

Regency Rakes,
And each of us takes
A personal pride
In the thickness of our hide,

Which prevents us from seeing
How vulgar we're being
Without making us wince ...

Later, in an effort to make this a true historical operetta, Coward takes a swipe at the notorious womanizing of George IV when he says:

... we follow the Prince.
Ev'ry orgy
With our Georgie
Lasts till dawn without a lull;

We can venture
Without censure
To be noisy, drunk and dull ...

Slightly more amusing is another supposedly comic number sung by two British courtesans:

English gentlemen,
Spanish noblemen,
Indian merchantmen, too,
Always play the game,
Never cause us shame, But

Refrain
There's always something fishy about
    the French,
Whether prince or politician
We've a sinister suspicion
That behind their savoir faire

They share
A common contempt for ev'ry
    mother's son of us.
Though they smile and smirk
We know they're out for dirty work.
We're most polite,
But don't put out the night light.
Ev'ry wise and thoroughly worldly
    wench
Knows there's always something fishy
    about the French.

Yet, in spite of an undistinguished score, *Conversation Piece* played to standing room only for five months and, even though audiences were unable to understand most of her lines, London, ravished by Yvonne Printemps's voice and charm, took her to its heart. Unfortunately Mlle Printemps, indeed a star who could burst into tears when taking a curtain-call, came replete with a star's penchant for tantrums. As she refused to learn English, it was to her credit that by the end of the run the entire cast was speaking French. But Noel, for the first time in his life, in a role for which he was ill-suited, was to admit that his performance, mannered with a fake French accent, was wooden. He also recognized that the plot of *Conversation Piece* rambled and contained more than its share of anachronisms. After playing the role of the Duc de Chaucigny-Varennes for only two months, Noel's usual boredom set in and Printemps's fiancé, Pierre Fresnay, filled the part more than adequately.

When the play closed the company went to Broadway. But New York was not seduced by its charm and *Conversation Piece* succumbed after a few performances.

By mid-1934, Noel's trust and belief in Jack Wilson was supreme, though the heat of the long love affair had somewhat cooled partly because of the latter's heavy drinking. But Jack, the only member of the Coward troupe who had been trained in contracts and finance, pointed out that there was no reason for Cochran to take the lion's share of the proceeds from what was essentially totally Coward's work. He was not implying that Cochran was devious – merely that he was a businessman. Wilson originated a plan to organise a limited group – consisting of himself, Noel, and the Lunts[2] who would thenceforth produce and direct their plays. And they would not be obliged to share the proceeds with anyone. Noel wrote to his old friend Cochran what must have been a fiendishly awkward letter – rupturing their strong, nine-year business relationship without impinging on their strong friendship:

> My dear Cocky,
>   If you were a less understanding or generous person this letter would be very difficult to write; as it is, however, I feel you will appreciate my motives completely and without prejudice.
>   I have decided after mature consideration to present my own and other people's plays in the future in partnership with Jack. This actually has been brewing up in my mind over a period of a year and I am writing to you first in confidence because I want you to understand that there would be no question of forsaking you or breaking our tremendously happy and successful association for any other reason except that I feel this is an inevitable development of my career in the theatre.

The letter went on to thank Cochran for all past help, saying that he, Noel, would never have reached the position in the theatre he had achieved without Cochran's assistance, and ended by hoping that Cochran would continue to give him 'the benefit of [his] invaluable friendship'.

Cochran, ostensibly wounded by Noel's decision, chose not to answer. At last, when Noel demanded a reply, the producer said that his dog had a habit of chewing up letters left on the doormat and Noel's must have suffered this fate. But he gave Noel, as a parting souvenir, a Georgian silver snuffbox inscribed rather snidely: 'For Noël, in memory of a not altogether unsuccessful association.'

Even though he would no longer be producing Noel's work, the

[2] The Lunts were never as enthusiastic about the partnership. Hardly a year later Noel received a cable from Alfred saying that, rather than be a partner in the John C. Wilson management, he had decided to accept an offer to become director of the board of the Theater Guild. Noel's return cable congratulated him, asking him to 'read every script carefully and send us all the ones the Guild turn down. They are usually the best.'

producer's career was hardly devastated by the break. Cochran continued to produce hits until his death in 1951. He had brought most of Kern's and Porter's works to London, and some months after *Conversation Piece* closed and his negotiations with Coward were dissolved he masterminded the British production of Cole's biggest hit, *Anything Goes*. Later he was to produce such notable home-grown products as *Home and Beauty*, the long-running *Bless the Bride* and *Big Ben*.

As luck would have it, Noel's and Jack's company was off to a depressing start with its first presentation, S. N. Behrman's *Biography*. The play starred Ina Claire and Laurence Olivier and was directed by Coward, but even these glittering names failed to draw the British public to what was a Broadway comedy. The fledgling production company had yet to learn, as many impresarios have never learned, that although Britain and America share the same language they differ greatly in their sense of comedy.[3] Fortunately it was able to turn its fortunes around with its next effort, *Theatre Royal*.[4]

Then, what little they amassed was lost again in *Point Valaine*, a play written for the Lunts which opened and closed rapidly on Broadway. Only Noel's reputation saved the play from total dismissal as Brooks Atkinson's critique in the *New York Times* attests:

> If there is any Coward manner discernible among all his talents, Mr. Coward had departed from it in *Point Valaine* which was acted at the Ethel Barrymore Theater last evening. He has written the drama of a lurid episode of lust in the semi-tropics, and Lynne Fontanne, Alfred Lunt and Osgood Perkins appear in it. Although it contains only a trace of the darting banter and neurotic theatricalism that have been the hallmarks of the Coward drama, it is unmistakably the work of a master of the stage ...

Noel was even blunter when he said, 'The fundamental weakness of the play was its basic theme. It was neither big enough for tragedy nor light enough for comedy. The characters were well drawn but not one of them was either interesting or kind ...'

With two failures out of three tries, it was obvious that the new production company was in desperate need of a hit to survive. It was then that Noel conceived the idea of a series of short plays starring himself and his most successful co-star, Gertrude Lawrence. Noel's name had not been linked with Gertie's since their enormous success in *Private Lives* and each was aware how the cash register at the box-office would react to their reunion. Gertie's name had made headlines in the tabloids recently when she declared herself bank-

---

[3] Neil Simon's comedies are never successful in the West End while Alan Ayckbourn's plays invariably fail on Broadway. Each has something to say that is only appreciated by his fellow countrymen.
[4] *Theatre Royal* was the title chosen for the Kaufman-Ferber play, a take-off of the over-acting Barrymores (now renamed the Cavendishes), and originally called *The Royal Family*. The latter title could never have been acceptable in Britain.

rupt. Noel knew that this state of affairs would make her only more popular with the public and also allow him to get her signature on a contract more easily.

Preliminaries arranged, he booked a long sea voyage – New York to Hollywood, to Honolulu, and thence as far as China and Singapore in the hope of encouraging his writing muse.

It worked. By the time he returned to Britain he had written *Fumed Oak*, *Hands Across the Sea*, and sketched other plays for what would be not one evening but a pair of evenings of theatre. He called the ensemble *Tonight at Eight-Thirty*[5]

Eventually, ten plays were written, and nine selections from this output were presented in three succeeding performances. Audiences were of course obliged to pay for two, and then three, admissions in order to be able to witness or discuss the entire group of plays.

Taken together these ten plays form a remarkable tour de force, displaying Coward's ability to write honestly not only of the glamorous upper classes, but of ordinary people, sometimes descending as far as the sleazy. Additionally, each programme included a play with music – a further drawing card, since both Noel and Gertie were internationally known musical comedy stars. The variety of roles they had to play, besides representing a challenge, staved off boredom – for which both of them were famous. And, if a play did not find favour with its audience, it could be dropped.

In *Tonight at 8.30* it seemed there was no style Coward could not master, no character he could not write or portray. One theatre-goer who had seen six plays in succeeding matinée and evening performances wondered 'what Noel was like on a tightrope'.

The first series, which had its première in London on January 9, 1936, introduced *Family Album*, *The Astonished Heart* and *Red Peppers*, this last the simplest and by far the most successful of the lot. *Family Album* is a curious mini-operetta whose main thrust comes from the toast a bereaved family head proposes when he and his siblings and assorted wives and in-laws return to the family home after a funeral. They have just buried their father, and gradually, with tongues loosened by glass after glass of his best Madeira, their respect for the patriarch crumbles. We learn of his lechery and self-importance and then are treated to a happy ending shortly before the curtain when we discover that the delightful servant has burned the latest will of the old curmudgeon which would have disinherited the family and left most of the estate to pay for a statue to himself to be erected.

---

[5] When the play was previewed in Manchester it was given the provincial title of *Tonight at Seven-Thirty* and on matinée days was advertised as *Today at Two-Thirty*.

The musical device introducing the family is somewhat naive and the play itself is rather preachy, but there is one duet (which Noel wrote for himself and Gertie) that has an interesting melodic and harmonic style. Its first phrase is quoted below:

The second play in the initial programme, *The Astonished Heart*, was built on a melodramatic theme that Coward was to use often in his work: a strong sexual obsession, too passionate to last; while the last of the group, *Red Peppers*, Coward himself termed 'a vaudeville sketch sandwiched in between two parodies of music-hall songs'.

Lily and George Pepper, whom Coward portrays with sensitivity and affection, are third-rate Cockney vaudeville entertainers, long married and constantly squabbling throughout the play. George castigates Lily for dropping her telescope in their nautical skit, whereupon she retorts by accusing him of 'sucking up to the top liners' and the leader of the pitiful orchestra who drinks. At the end, when the tipsy conductor takes the tempo of their number so fast that George slips and falls, Lily throws her hat at the conductor, screaming, 'You great drunken fool.' The interlude ends in a mêlée. Lily's defensive loyalty to George warms the audience's hearts as the curtain descends. As in much of Coward's best work a tremendous sadness and sympathy for the untalented Peppers comes through, and as we leave the theatre we feel in our heart of hearts that it won't be long before George and Lily get the sack from even the most dilapidated music-halls and are replaced by movies. Swept along with the Peppers, laughing all the way, one hardly realizes the built-in tragedy of their obsolescence, but it hits home later. In *Tonight at 8.30's* initial run *Red Peppers* was the audience's favourite out of all the plays.

Two parodies of typical music-hall numbers are woven into the play. The first is 'Has Anybody See Our Ship?' with its jaunty melodic line and irreverent lyrics full of innuendo. Some of my favourite lines are quoted below:

Has anybody seen our ship
The H. M. S Peculiar?
We've been on shore for a month or more,

Coward with Gertrude Lawrence in *Red Peppers*, one of the nine one-act plays in *Tonight at 8.30*, 1936

And when we see the captain we shall get what for.
Heave Ho! me Hearties,
Sing Glory Hallelujah.
A lady bold as she could be
Pinched our whistles at the 'Golden Key'
Now we're in between the devil and the deep blue sea,
Has anybody seen our ship? ...
We had a binge last Christmas year,
Nice plum pudding and a round of beer
But the captain pulled his cracker and we cried, oh, dear! ...

The other, 'Men About Town', is practically a pub-song.

The second London programme which opened four days later, on January 13, comprised *Hands Across the Sea*, *Fumed Oak* and *Shadow Play*. Of the first, which Coward called 'a gay, unpretentious little play ... acted by Gertie with incomparable brilliance', Ivor Brown wrote in the *Observer*:

> *Hands Across the Sea* suggests the sequel to one of those reckless invitations issued in return for hospitality overseas. 'Come up and see us.' Of course they will not. But they may. And here they are ... bravely butting into the kind of smart house where the telephone never stops.'

The second play, *Fumed Oak*, might have been subtitled 'Rebellion in Clapham', for it concerns a middle-aged salesman who has saved £500, which gives him the freedom to break away from his bleak surroundings and family and to leave the country. Chilled by the cold supper he is offered, his courage warmed by downing a couple of whiskies, he revolts, leaving his nagging wife, shrewish mother-in-law and snivelling adenoidal daughter.

Audiences and critics alike appreciated the play. They were not alone – for Coward wrote: 'I loved Henry Gow from the moment I started writing him, and I loved playing him more, I think, than anything else in the repertoire.'

Shadow Play, the longest of the evening's offerings, demonstrated how easily Coward could bring up to date a well-worn theme – that of a jealous wife who takes a heavy dose of sleeping pills because she feels divorce is her only recourse since her marriage is cracking up. In her drugged state she goes back to the beginning of her relationship with her husband, before waking to find the crack-up was all in her imagination.

The play contained three first-rate songs: 'Then', which sums up the concept of the play in a nutshell with lines like 'Then, we knew the best of it,/ Then our hearts stood the test of it./ Now the magic has flown/ We face the unknown/ Apart and alone'; 'Play, Orchestra, Play', a lively, rather raucous tune, with a mundane lyric; and 'You Were There', one of Coward's most enchanting creations.[6]

6 See Musical Analysis Appendix.

On January 29, *We Were Dancing* replaced *Family Album* in the first programme. Though he called it a comedy it was Coward's way of pinpointing the tragedy of temporary relationships. A couple fall desperately in love while dancing. She is married; he is divorced. Again, Coward puts the concept into the form of song – 'We were dancing,/ And the music and lights were entrancing/ Our desire/ When the world caught on fire ...' Faced with his wife's decision to leave with her dancing partner, her buttoned-up husband acquiesces. When they have all talked the matter through until dawn, the wife is no longer interested.

The third programme[7] was not finally assembled until mid-May, by which time *Ways and Means* had been written. It is a farce about a young couple who have lost all their money gambling and, in a Maugham-like finale, set about recouping it. The other play, somewhat longer and with more substance, called *Still Life*, is perhaps better known as the scenario for the film *Brief Encounter*. The critic for the *Sunday Times* called the play 'a tiny masterpiece of economical writing [which] is beautifully acted by Mr. Coward and Miss Gertrude Lawrence'. *Still Life* (or *Brief Encounter* – there is very little change, only expansion, in the cinema) is a heart-wrenching story of duty triumphing over love, a hollow victory that perhaps could only take place in the '30s and among the middle classes in England.

Of all the plays, the public drew this last one closest to its heart. But each of the segments of *Tonight At 8.30* had its own raison d'être. The ultimate imperishability[8] of the series can perhaps best be summed up in a quote from Ivor Brown:

> Mr. Coward describes the reinstatement of the short play on the professional stage as one of the his more sentimental ambitions. It is also, on his part, a generous exercise; the man who used to write very slight, long plays has now composed very full, brief ones, which really means that as actor, author, composer and producer he had to put in three times as much work as before. There has been no scamping; and, if anybody regards the short play as short measure and a casual offering, he is mistaken here. When Mr. Coward brings his three little pigs to market he is his own exhibitor – diligent, alert and giving them every chance to be approved. They turn out to be considerable animals.

Once *Tonight at 8.30* had achieved a respectable run in the West End, Noel and Gertie decided to launch it in America. It was less enthusiastically received there, perhaps because Americans like a full evening of theatre rather than short plays, no matter how intriguing.

---

[7] A fiasco entitled *Star Chamber*, which concerned elderly thespians conducting a meeting to raise funds for a home for destitute actresses, was given one performance in March and quickly withdrawn. Although the play has never been published, some of the characters in it were to become the prototypes for one of Coward's last plays, *Waiting in the Wings*.
[8] A cinema version of *Red Peppers*, *Fumed Oak* and *Ways and Means* was made in Britain and released under the title of *Meet Me Tonight*. *We Were Dancing*, *The Astonished Heart*, and of course *Brief Encounter*, were also filmed. A series of eight teleplays starring Joan Collins was released in 1991.

But it did make money and could easily have enjoyed a longer run except that after four months an exhausted Noel decided to call a halt. It had been eighteen gruelling, albeit varied, months from the first previews in Manchester to the closing on Broadway in the spring of 1937.

After near-collapse in May, Noel suffered an uneasy summer, with two losses. The first, the death of his father, he would take with equanimity. Just as with Cole Porter and his father, theirs had never been an intimate relationship. Arthur Coward succumbed peacefully in England while Noel was directing a play in America. The other would be a shattering blow, for, on September 1, Jack Wilson married the beautiful Princess Natasha Paley.

Natasha's claim to royal status rested on her conviction that she was descended from Grand Duke Paul of Russia. But Natasha (or Natalie as she

Coward with
Gertrude Lawrence
in *Shadow Play*,
from *Tonight at
8.30*, 1936

Americanized her name), even if not a *bona fide* princess, was certainly an expert on the Russian upper class, for some years later Alexander Korda would employ her technical expertise in his film, *Anna Karenina*. The new Mrs. Wilson was not only on very friendly terms with Noel, but was a confidante of Linda Porter's. She had had a very brief career in films, appearing the year before her marriage with Katharine Hepburn in *Sylvia Scarlett*. Tall, patrician, with dark eyes, like Linda she would often follow extreme and faddish régimes for health or beauty. And both were heavy smokers.

Porter, of course, had much in common with Jack. Both were from wealthy families, heavy smokers who hit the Scotch bottle heavily, now they would both be married to beautiful, stimulating women who could ignore their reputedly enormous sexual appetites and openly homosexual peccadilloes. Lesbianism would often be whispered in connection with their wives.

Noel, not only an ex-lover but Jack's business partner, attended the wedding at Jack's family estate in Fairfield, Connecticut in early September. He and Baron de Gunzburg wrote ribald verses to celebrate the occasion, while Lorne Lorraine cabled: 'IN EVERY PAPER OF THE ENGLISH PRESS/ ARE PHOTO-GRAPHS OF DAB[9] AND HIS PRINCESS/ ALTHOUGH A DEEP DYED SECRET LATTERLY/ ALL LONDON SENDS ITS LOVE TO YOU AND NATALIE.'

For the following two months Coward worked on his next project, first in the bucolic surroundings of his friend Alexander Woollcott's lodge in Vermont and then later on the Lunts' dairy farm in Wisconsin. At last he cabled Lorn, 'I CAN'T WORK OUT HERE AND AM LONGING TO GET ON WITH IT', the 'it' referring to his next musical, *Operette*.

Noel's involvement with this tuneful work set in the Edwardian era had begun some months before when he went for a short holiday to stay with Eleanora von Mendelssohn in her castle in Upper Austria. There he became friendly with Fritzi Massary, a former opera star now retired for five years. He fell immediately under the spell of Fritzi's delicate soprano which floated atop an accented English, just as he had been entranced by Yvonne Printemps.

Knowing that Fritzi, a Jewess, was a prime target for the Nazis, he resolved to star her in an operetta. The humanitarian gesture aside, Noel was hoping to duplicate *Bitter Sweet's* success. It was only incidental that Fritzi could be imported to Britain and after the run of the operetta would be able to make her way from England to America where her daughter resided.

Operette, which tried to be *Bitter Sweet* moved on one generation, was doomed from the start to be one of Coward's least successful works. By the late '30s theatre-goers had turned their backs on the cumbersome operettas of the past. The only connection with a sentimental era was provided by Ivor

[9] Dab was Jack's nickname.

Novello whose *Careless Rapture* and *Crest of the Wave* had pre-empted Noel's romantic allure. Now London was eager to laugh again. *Me and My Girl*, billed as the 'Lambeth Walk' musical, was the success of the 1937 season and lovers of the musical who had already been exposed to Cole Porter's *Anything Goes* and Rodgers and Hart's *On Your Toes* were eager for quicker, peppier entertainment.

The convoluted play within a play that Coward created, with its many digressive, long, dry quasi-arias, was almost impossible to follow and the lack of dancing or sprightliness made for an interminable evening. Coward himself admitted that 'it was overwritten and undercomposed', but neglected to add that, worst of all, *Operette* had no one to advertise it – only a retired Viennese opera star in Fritzi Massary and an ageing Peggy Wood, the American soprano who had charmed London in *Bitter Sweet* a decade ago.

Operette begins amateurishly on an apologetic note with the chorus thanking the audience for 'keeping still', and ends by plugging the hit songs reprised again and again. Most of the music is competent, very much like the '20s operettas of Kern. Much of the score is tedious and repetitive. A look at the lyrics of the heroine Mitzi's first song, which are repeated five times throughout the evening, will show why:

They call me Countess Mitzi	**Chorus**
But I can't imagine why,	We can perfectly well see why,
For my name is really	That to alter it people try;
Lodovika, Anastasie,	For they'd rather say Countess Mitzi
Frederika, Isabel,	Just a teensy weensy bitsy,
Rosa, Mariposa	Than a string of names like
Nikinikolay ...	Lodovika, Anastasie,
	Frederika, Isabel,
	Rosa, Mariposa
	Nikinikolay ...

But there are a few gems scattered in the score. It is hard to overlook the haunting waltz 'Dearest Love', which is the theme song of the play, the truly funny 'Stately Homes of England',[10] and the almost unknown, rather Porterian 'Island of Bollamazoo', charming though admittedly male-chauvinistic.

On the Island of Bollamazoo	**Second Refrain**
Life is almost too good to be true.	On the Island of Bollamazoo
You can fish on the reef	Life is almost too good to be true.
Wearing pearls and a leaf	You don't have to care what your
Which at Brighton you never would do.	neighbours might think
For a few coloured beads from the Penny	If a charming young lady should give
Bazaar	you a wink
You can buy luscious oysters wherever you are,	You can buy her outright for the price
And you don't have to wait for a month	of a drink
with an 'R',	On the Island of Bollamazoo.
On the Island of Bollamazoo.	

[10] See Musical Analysis Appendix.

Third Refrain
On the Island of Bollamazoo
Life is almost too good to be true.
No one ever gets warm
Over Tariff reform
And the thought of Home Rule is taboo.
Unlike Campbell Bannerman's dignified
    pose,
The local Prime Minister welcomes his foes
With a club in one hand and a ring through
    his nose,
On the Island of Bollamazoo

Fourth Refrain
On the Island of Bollamazoo
Life is almost too good to be true.
The ladies are dusky, domestic and fair
For the suffragette movement they
    wouldn't much care.
And they'd think 'Votes for Women' were
    something to wear!
On the Island of Bollamazoo.

Noel, never a coward, himself took the blame for the failure of *Operette*, stating that 'neither the part and the songs [he had written for Fritzi Massary] were worthy of her'. As for the libretto:

> Another aspect of *Operette* was the triumphant confusion it established in the minds of the audience. This was cunningly achieved by the switching of the action back and forth between the stage play and the real play. I remember peering from my box in the Opera House, Manchester, and watching bewildered playgoers rustling their programmes and furtively striking matches in a frantic effort to discover where they were and what was going on.

Always the first to poke fun at himself, Coward adds:

> If the reader ... is interested in how *not* to write a musical play, in how to overload a light, insignificant story with long stretches of accurate but uninspired dialogue, and in how to reduce an audience of average intelligence to a state of frustrated confusion, he will probably enjoy [*Operette*] immensely.

Operette was not Coward's swan song in the operetta form but it would be the last of this 'art' music to be presented under Jack's aegis. The marriage had separated Noel from Jack yet, strangely, had brought him close to Natasha. However, with Jack's continuing presence in America, now that he was producing the works of other playwrights and composers, their professional relationship disappeared. Jack and Natasha, however, remained good friends of his and Coward frequently sought their counsel, although he invariably disregarded any advice.

As war with Germany reared, Noel was relegated to the sidelines. He might easily have attempted to write another *Bitter Sweet* or, in such times, another jingoistic *Calvacade*, but the whole experience of *Operette* had left so sour a taste in his mouth that, except for occasional individual songs, he would not have the temerity to touch the musical form again for seven years. And even then he would revert to revue.

COLE
1937-1939

NO ONE BUT COLE PORTER, with his stoicism and his ironic, almost masochistic sense of humour, could have had such a sense of the fantastic as to personify his injured legs. Early in his recuperative period he did precisely that. He called his right leg, the one whose bones had been crushed in the fall, thereby severing the nerves, by a name appropriate to a Southern belle: Geraldine. For the left one he chose a name suitable for an empress: Josephine.

Linda, always deeply indulgent of her husband, went along with the jest and immediately ordered a gold cigarette case encrusted with sapphires. She had 'Merry Christmas and Happy New Year to Jo and Geraldine' inscribed on the inside cover.

Cole's humour went even deeper than that. When Dr. Moorhead suggested that under heavy sedation it would be therapeutic to 'write out' the pain he was experiencing, Cole, so passionately wanting to get well and ever the model patient, composed almost a dozen fanciful paragraphs that he dubbed 'A Few Illusions Caused by an Injured Anterior Popliteal Nerve'.

Although the notes were written after injections of morphine, one can sense the fantasy and theatricality with which Cole imbued them. The first illustrates a feeling familiar to anyone who has had an arm or leg set tightly into an unyielding plaster cast:

> I'm a toe dancer, but a toe dancer who dances only on the toes of his right foot. The music in the orchestra pit is charming and it's very pleasant hopping around and around to that gay tinkling strain. But after a while I realize that my toes are tired and, risking the reprimand of the ballet master, I decide to drop to the ball of my foot and give them a rest. But, lo and behold, try as I may, I cannot do it, for my ballet-slipper has been made in such a way that I must stay always on the tips of my toes. So, long after the curtain has gone down and I'm alone in the theatre, I watch the sad shadow I make as I go on and on, doomed forever to hop around on those poor tilted toes.

Cole described the considerable drawing pain that accompanied the healing process from the ankle to the knee:

> My right leg stretches, slanting upwards before me, like the side of a hill, the summit of which is my toes. From the ankle down – and approaching me – any number of small, finely-, and sharply-toothed rakes are at work. Each one has about the same routine. For instance the rake that has been allotted to the inside of the leg begins at the ankle, proceeding slowly toward the knee, and digs as deeply as it can into the skin, at times much deeper than at others, and, consequently, varying in its painfulness. It goes slowly on in this manner until it reaches a point just a little short of the knee, then retraces its tracks until it finds the spot where it

is able to penetrate the most, at which point it settles down to dig to its heart's delight. The same procedure takes place over the entire leg and continues until I yell for a hypo.

Besides the 'rakes' in his chronicle of pain, Cole wrote imaginatively of other torturous instruments: 'a jagged glass shoehorn' inserted inside his cast, 'a rough stone one', 'a very unusual sock made of finely woven wire mesh, highly charged with electricity', 'long-handled knives with heart-shaped blades and a rough-surfaced cord drawn between the toes'. Then Cole imagined 'little men with picks' who were digging a deep hole on the inner side of his right instep. Cole's diary may have rivalled the Marquis de Sade's, but through it all it is reported that he was a model patient.

He seldom complained and eventually, after several months, when the pain reached more reasonable dimensions, he was allowed to go back to his apartment at the Waldorf Towers.

It was fortunate that Dr. Moorhead knew and greatly admired Cole's work. He suggested that Cole should use his strongest medical asset, his ability to write songs, for Moorhead believed firmly that, with withdrawal from drugs, and a positive frame of mind occupied with work and manipulative therapy, his patient would eventually regain the use of his legs. Cole desperately wanting mobility, agreed to follow his doctor's plan and happily discovered that concentration on his music was as effective as sedation. To this first end his grand piano was raised on blocks so that Cole could work from his wheel-chair,[1] and a physiotherapist visited him daily.

What he was working on would eventually be called *You Never Know*. Based on the mildly successful 1929 Viennese romantic comedy, *By Candlelight*, which had starred Gertrude Lawrence and Leslie Howard, the creaky and simplistic plot involves a butler who impersonates his master and a maid who passes herself off as her mistress. Of course the butler believes the maid is the duchess while the maid assumes the butler is the duke. What could be more routine?

The show was to be produced by the Shubert brothers – new to a Porter collaboration – and had been rushed so as to begin out-of-town try-outs in March 1938. It was to star Cole's old friend Clifton Webb,[2] 'Mexican Spitfire' Lupe Velez and the blues specialist, Libby Holman. Unusually, Cole's publishers, Chappell, would not allow the songs to be performed on the radio, for they wanted to keep them fresh for the New York première.

Since Cole was unable to leave his apartment to attend rehearsals, J.J. Shubert, in an uncharacteristically magnanimous gesture, brought the cast and

[1] In 1937 wheelchairs were high wooden contraptions, quite different from today's variety.
[2] This was be Webb's last Broadway venture before becoming one of Hollywood's most engaging performers. From his début as the malevolent Waldo Lydecker in *Laura* to his creation of the acid know-it-all servant Mr. Belvedere, he had a long and distinguished movie career.

eighteen musicians to the Waldorf to play, sing and rehearse the work for him. At the time, *You Never Know* sounded like delightful middle-European music and lyrics, but Porter was later to admit it was an inferior score and the worst production with which he was ever associated.

The critics agreed with Cole. Except for 'At Long Last Love', 'From Alpha to Omega' and 'For No Rhyme or Reason', all conceived before his accident, the score is third-rate Porter. No standards emerged from the show except 'At Long Last Love'. Again, as in 'You're the Top', Cole had created a list song aimed at contrast. This time it was real love contrasted with infatuation and the examples he chose were even more urbane than in earlier list songs. But the missing element here – and throughout the show – was Cole's apparent loss of melodic invention. The song seems to have survived, however, perhaps on its words alone.

Verse

I'm so in love,
And though it gives me joy intense,
I can't decipher,
If I'm a lifer,
Or if it's just a first offence.
I'm so in love,
I've no sense of values left at all.
Is this a playtime,
Affair of Maytime,
Or is it a windfall?

Refrain I

Is it an earthquake or simply a shock?
Is it the good turtle soup or merely the
    mock?
Is it a cocktail – this feeling of joy,
Or is what I feel the real McCoy?
Have I the right hunch or have I the wrong?
Will it be Bach I shall hear or just a Cole
    Porter song?
Is it a fancy not worth thinking of
Or is it at long last love?

Refrain 2

Is it the rainbow or just a mirage?
Will it be tender and sweet or merely
    massage?
Is it a brainstorm in one of its quirks?
Or is it the best, the crest, the works?

Is it for all time or simply a lark?
Is it the Lido I see or only Asbury Park?
Should I say 'Thumbs down', and give it a
    shove?
Or is it at long last love?

Refrain 3

Is it a breakdown or is it a break?
Is it the real Porterhouse or only a steak?
What can account for these strange
    pitter-pats
Could this be the dream, the cream, the
    cat's?
Is it to rescue or is it to wreck?
Is it an ache in the heart or just a pain in
    the neck?
Is it the ivy you touch with a glove,
Or is it at long last love?

Refrain 4 (Unfinished)

Is it in marble or is it in clay?
Is what I thought a new Rolls, a used
    Chevrolet?
Is it a sapphire or simply a charm?
Is it—— or just a shot in the arm?
Is it today's thrill or really romance?
Is it a kiss on the lips or just a kick in
    the pants?
Is it the gay gods cavorting above?
Or is it at long last love?

Besides this song, *You Never Know* contained some other true Porter touches, such as a prescient song (long antedating the *West Side Story* one) whose theme is the beauty of the sound of the name 'Maria', and a charmer called 'I'm Back in Circulation Now'. Incomprehensibly, Cole was subjected to the indignity of having his sensitive title ballad, 'By Candlelight', replaced by the old-hat waltz

– a left-over from the original play *By Candlelight* – written by the adaptor-director Rowland Leigh and Robert Katscher.

The show had a long and arduous tour, and gained much publicity – most of it unfavourable – by the in-fighting of its leading ladies. Libby Holman and Lupe Velez took an instant dislike to each other, a situation which climaxed in a New Haven performance, during which they engaged in a tussle between curtain calls that ended with Lupe blacking one of Libby's eyes.

Not only did this feud help to sink the show, there seemed to be no agreement between the director and J.J. Shubert[3] who, seeing failure in the cards, decided to replace the intimate quality of the show with the big *Blossom Time* operetta style for which he and his brothers were famous. Now, what could have been a saving intimacy was discarded in favour of a lavish production. Finally, George Abbott was called in, but even that considerable musical doctor could not cure *You Never Know*'s maladies. It should be added that Broadway was still in the grip of the Depression, a time when only smash hits survived.

But at last the show opened, not surprisingly to the most devastating reviews Cole had received since his Yale days. John Mason Brown reported, 'It snuffs out whatever gleamed in *By Candlelight*. Mr. Porter's invention is missing ... his lyrics strain and strain for glib rhythms which they achieve without humour.' Other critics joined the chorus, calling it 'prodigiously dull', 'disappointing'. *Variety* was succinct: 'A limited stay is indicated.'

The next morning J.J. assembled the cast, reduced the size of the chorus and the number of dancers and persuaded the principals to agree to a pay cut which would mean lower box-office prices and perhaps guarantee a run, but nothing could breathe life into *You Never Know* and it closed after ten weeks.

Cole had no time to be depressed while *You Never Know* was going through its death throes, for he was busy creating a new show. *Leave it to Me* would open to rave reviews a month before *You Never Know* closed.

This time his collaborators were mostly old friends. The producer was the sensitive Vinton Freedley – the antithesis of J.J. Shubert – who had always been on Cole's wave-length and piloted him through *Anything Goes* and *Red, Hot and Blue*. Both Victor Moore and William Gaxton who had starred in several previous Porter hits were cast in the leading men's parts. The librettists, however, were new to Cole, for the book had been specially adapted from their play *Clear All Wires* by Sam and Bella Spewack, famous for the comedy hit *Boy*

---

[3] Although J.J. Shubert was insensitive to the intimate spirit of *By Candlelight-You Never Know* Cole was grateful for the rest of his life to these theatrical landlords for having helped him back to work after the accident, and thereafter insisted all his shows be booked into Shubert brothers theatres. However, he was not above taking a swipe at the kind of 'girlie shows' they presented when he wrote a decade later in *Kiss Me, Kate*, 'Since I reached the charming age of puberty, /And began to finger feminine curls, /Like a show that's typically Shuberty/ I have always had a multitude of girls.'

Meets Girl. Sam Spewack would direct, and Sophie Tucker, Merman's near rival in the voice-of-brass department, would play the lead. Even the story, a broad international satire, was set in an area in which Cole operated smoothly.

It was a delightful plot. Both Spewacks had served as foreign correspondents in the '20s and drawn upon their experiences which, in their play, made the diplomatic corps and politics in general the target of their humour. Playing a wealthy Kansas businessman who has been appointed ambassador to the Soviet Union because of the sizeable campaign contributions of his wife (Sophie Tucker), though he would much rather stay at home casting horseshoes, the self-effacing, bumbling and rotund Victor Moore had a role that might have been tailored for him. Ambassador Moore, hoping to be recalled, kicks the German ambassador, a Nazi, in the stomach and then takes a potshot at a Russian commissar (who turns out to be a counter-revolutionary). Instead of being recalled in disgrace for these actions he is wildly acclaimed until late in the second act when he takes his job too seriously and advocates the interchange of troops and a United States of Europe. Only then do his superiors bring him back to Kansas and his beloved horseshoes.

In order to counteract Moore's lethargic character, the plot introduced William Gaxton as a fast-talking newspaperman. And for romantic interest there was Gaxton's girl, Tamara. To further brighten the proceedings Sophie Tucker was given two brassy hits, 'Tomorrow', a kind of gospel shout that almost recaptured the success of 'Blow, Gabriel, Blow', from *Anything Goes*, and an I've-been-through-it confessional, 'Most Gentlemen Don't Like Love'. Nor was William Gaxton short-changed, for Cole wrote two fine numbers, 'From Now On' and 'Far Away', with his voice in mind.

Even the sultry-voiced Tamara was not overlooked. She was given another imaginative song, 'Get Out of Town', whose lyric displays a fresh love-hate relationship ('Get out of town, Before it's too late, my love ... just disappear, I care for you too much/ And when you are near, close to me dear, /We touch too much ...'). Hardly six months after his last operation, Cole's melodic inspiration seemed to have returned full-blown.

Creativity is something one takes for granted in the musical theatre, but the discovery of a major new star is unfortunately a rarity. The most exhilarating

Sophie Tucker in *Leave it to Me*, 1938

moment in *Leave it to Me* happened when, in her Broadway début, Mary Martin is discovered wrapped only in furs, sitting on a trunk at a Siberian railway station. As she sings 'My Heart Belongs to Daddy', the song with which ever after she would be identified, she gradually does a strip-tease.[4]

The minor melody and melismatic incantations of 'My Heart Belongs to Daddy' have always been held up as subtle evidence of Cole's anti-semitism. Many have written that the 'daddy' referred to in the song's 'dah-dah-dah' refrain is a rich and powerful Jew who is financially supporting a defenceless WASP. But, aware that Cole mined mostly minor keys which he believed held the secret of success ('Get Out of Town', 'I Love Paris', 'Ace in the Hole', 'So In Love', 'Easy To Love', to name a few), I would maintain that he needed an accessible hit after the débâcle of *You Never Know*. Additionally, he (and his critics) may have confounded 'Jewishness' with 'Russianness' or 'Frenchness'.

When *Leave it to Me* opened in New York Cole was well enough to attend a pre-performance dinner at home, but chose to stay in his apartment rather than suffer the indignity of being carried into the crowded theatre for the première. Linda went in his place and telephoned him excitedly immediately after the curtain had gone down to tell him he had a hit. 'The greatest hand of the evening was *not* gotten by Sophie Tucker with the "Tomorrow" number, as you supposed,' she announced, 'it was little Mary Martin. She stopped the show cold!'

But almost everything about *Leave it to Me* achieved critical raves. Richard Watts, usually a tough reviewer to please, wrote, 'The local musical comedy stage is in proper shape again,' and went on to laud the performances of each of the principals. Cole was back in the good graces of the critics again, for Watts ended his critique with 'one of Cole Porter's choicest scores', and the *New Yorker's* Robert Benchley slyly added that he felt 'his lyrics are in his best, which means his most you-know-what vein'.

Cole felt that he had regained his professional stride and was creating lyrics *and especially* music as well as he ever had. Because of the crippling of his legs, certainly much had changed in his sexual life, but Cole was unwilling to admit to the world that anything had altered in his private life.

Dr. Moorhead did not pull his punches and, waiting until Cole had the emotional reinforcement of a hit show, informed his patient (although Cole must have suspected something from the repeated breaking of his bones) that he had developed osteomyelitis, a rarely curable disease of the bone marrow which would make the total recovery he had foreseen impossible.

---

[4] Mary Martin's singing this suggestive song was used as ammunition by Noel when she refused to sing his 'Alice Is At It Again' in *Pacific 1860*. She dismissed the parallels in the two concepts with a wave of her hand, adding, 'That's a different kind of show.'

Instead of staying in New York within range of medical treatment, Cole booked for himself and Linda an extended Christmas trip to Cartagena, Colombia. Early in 1939, he spent a month in Havana, then in April, as if in a final test of endurance, accompanied by his valet Paul Sylvain and his male nurse Ray Kelly, Cole set out to explore the ruins of Machu Picchu, the Lost City of the Incas, 8,000 feet up in the Peruvian Andes. The trip had the approval of Dr. Moorhead, who must have had little knowledge of how arduous it would be. With his legs still in braces, Cole had to be lifted on to the back of a horse in order to make his way up the steep rocky paths. Every morning Cole set off, usually alone and supported on two sticks, to explore the ancient ruins.

This assurance that he was still able to satisfy his curiosity as to how the world had lived or was living, to indulge his passion for visiting the exotic, had the desired effect on his ego – the one that Dr. Moorhead had hoped for. Cole was now ready to take on any new project.

While her husband was exploring the Andes, Linda, aware of the deteriorating political situation in Paris and realising that the time had long gone when they would be giving lavish soirées, closed her beloved house at 13 rue Monsieur. She sensed too that Cole would want more and more time to bake his legs in the sun, and had most everything they both loved shipped to their house in Hollywood. In addition, she rented a small beach house-cum-office in Malibu, a retreat where Cole could write his scores while taking in the sun and sea air. And, if he wished to indulge in any of the peccadilloes that had made their relationship unbearable to her, at least they would not be happening directly under her nose.

After their return, comfortable in these surroundings and his new-found relationship with Linda, Cole began work on *Broadway Melody of 1939* (so delayed that it had to be retitled *Broadway Melody of 1940*). For it he wrote one of his enduring classics, 'I Concentrate On You' (which the critic Fred Lounsberry termed Cole's greatest song), the charming 'Please Don't Monkey With Broadway', and 'I've Got My Eyes on You'. But the most thrilling moment in the movie came when Fred Astaire and Eleanor Powell danced an exotic and extended treatment of what had by now become Cole's classic, 'Begin the Beguine'. With his fame now at its zenith, his mobility – albeit on sticks – restored, whatever Cole's private feelings may have been, to the public and to his highly social friends he was still the smiling, talented bon vivant, with a carnation always in his button-hole.

NOEL
1938-1945

H IS MUSICAL FINGERS BURNED with the collapse of *Operette*, Noel Coward turned towards comedy and drama, the area in which he felt confident and knew he was still respected. Although the imminent outbreak of war made production of his next works impossible, in the space of a few months he would pen three of his biggest stage successes, after which he would have regained the self-assurance to write more music. But first he took his usual recuperative holiday. This time he went on board a ship of the Royal Navy, travelling at the request of his friend, Lord Louis Mountbatten, to Palestine, Cyprus and Albania. He was to talk to regular officers and enlisted men alike to find out what kinds of films they were interested in seeing off duty.

Noel not only found out about the top brass's cinematic preferences, but enthusiastically enjoyed his discussions about current British foreign policy. Seeing the storm clouds of totalitarianism gather, he lectured practically anyone who would listen about rearmament and preparedness. He was to speak out even more strongly when, a few months later, Neville Chamberlain came back from Munich waving his scrap of paper. He feared for Britain's future and felt his country had been severely compromised by its Prime Minister's 'peace in our time' appeasement manifesto.

Although war was brewing in Europe, America chose to remain strongly isolationist for three more years. Theatre in the States was hungrily looking for escapist entertainment to counteract the depressing news from abroad, and Jack Wilson decided to jump aboard the bury-your-head-in-the-sand bandwagon on Broadway. Noel's *Words and Music*, now edited and renamed *Set To Music*, was a perfect choice. It opened at the intimate Music Box Theater under Noel's direction. Wilson was a canny enough producer to know that a small revue such as this needed some big names and starred Beatrice Lillie, Richard Haydn, Moya Nugent and Gladys Henson – but the critics had eyes and words for no one but Miss Lillie. Brooks Atkinson writing in *The New York Times* termed it the 'Lillie revue'. He went on to say:

> Whenever they are not changing the scenery, the radiant lady turns up in a whole bag of tricks, from schoolgirl admiration of a movie star, to the ironic abandon of a secret service burlesque in a railroad station. She is the world weary actress disdainfully clutching at the treasures her admirers bring ... the condescending manager of a charity ball, and the mistress of society revels in an English colony in Europe. And whatever she is, she is always the miracle woman of mockery – keeping high comedy just a bit on the vulgar side and rescuing low comedy from common excesses.

Coward was partly responsible for the show resting so heavily on Miss Lillie's bony shoulders, for, although *Set To Music* borrowed 'The Stately Homes of England' from *Operette* (which Noel knew would never be mounted in America), he had given her all the comedy songs. Beatrice Lillie (who abhorred using her title, Lady Peel) was a genius in performance but a pain in the neck at rehearsal. The bane of directors, she never repeated a performance in the same way. She breezed through rehearsals not even trying for laughs for she realised full well that the cast could not be expected to go into paroxysms at lines they had heard scores of times before, and she chose not to expend the effort. Yet, put in front of any audience, she would bring forth a stunning range of unexpected tricks from her arsenal of zaniness.

Noel had written a parody of a successful singer's lament, especially for Lillie. It also contains a sly reference to Cole Porter's 'My Heart Belongs to Daddy', which was packing them in at the gigantic Imperial Theatre immediately next-door. In 'Rug of Persia', Miss Lillie is discovered lamenting while weaving an oriental arras. The song ends:

Here on the right	Object on my left
Is the moon of my delight.	Is the Star of the East, of course.
This is a Persian horse.	Though you may think I am far too faddy
This little deft	My heart belongs to my old Bag-Daddy.

Noel gave Lillie another show-stopper towards the end of the evening in 'I Went To a Marvellous Party', (Later, for some reason I have never been able to comprehend, the solo lyric was published as *'I've Been* To a Marvellous Party' which makes the refrain sound as though it is in the wrong tense. See below.) 'Party', which was to become one of Noel's best-known numbers, a staple of superannuated actresses who pretend – or actually succeed – in getting progressively drunker while singing it, was inspired a year earlier by an invitation from Elsa Maxwell to attend a 'come-as-you-are-when-you-receive-this-invitation' beach party. The second verse supplies the raison d'être for the entire piece, but my favourites are the second and fourth refrains.

Refrain 2

I've been to a marvellous party
I must say the fun was intense,
We all had to do
What the people we knew
Would be doing a hundred years hence.
Dear Cecil arrived wearing armour,
Some shells and a black feather boa,
Poor Millicent wore a surrealist comb,
Made of bits of mosaic from St. Peter's in
        Rome
But the weight was so great that she had to
        go home.
I couldn't have liked it more!

Verse 2

People's behaviour
Away from Belgravia
Would make you aghast.
So much variety
Watching Society
Scampering past.
If you have any mind at all
Gibbon's divine *Decline and Fall*
Seems pretty flimsy
No more than whimsy.
By way of contrast
On Saturday last ...

Refrain 4
I've been to a marvellous party,
Elise made an entrance with May,
You'd never have guessed
From her fisherman's vest
That her bust had been whittled away.

Poor Lulu got fried on Chianti
And talked about esprit de corps.
Maurice made a couple of passes at Gus,
And Freddie, who hates any kind of a fuss,
Did half the Big Apple and twisted his truss.
I couldn't have liked it more!

Set To Music received mostly good reviews and business to begin with was excellent. But, in the spring of 1939, when ticket sales began to fall off, and Noel happened to be passing through New York, Jack asked him to join the show opposite Bea Lillie. The two stars might have given *Set To Music* the shot in the arm it needed to turn the tide of Broadway's spring doldrums, but Coward, who had just published a book of short stories, to excellent reviews, preferred to listen to the call of his writing muse. In addition, fears for his now widowed mother coupled with his own sense of loyalty to his country, threatened with war, sent him home. Without new blood to spark it *Set To Music* limped to a close after four months.

Back in England at Goldenhurst, where he could work undisturbed, Noel resumed his accustomed routine. His valet, Cole Lesley, woke him each morning at 6.30. Coward sprang eagerly from bed, bathed and shaved while Leslie lit a fire in the library, in front of which he ate a trencherman's breakfast. He was at work at his big scrubbed oak table-desk by 7.30. All calls and messages were held until 2 p.m. and Coward was only disturbed by the arrival of a large pot of steaming coffee at 11.

What he wrote during that fecund period were two plays, initiated, perhaps, by recollections of his success and joy during the run of *Tonight at 8.30* when he could stave off his habitual boredom by playing nine different roles in three nights. Planning to direct and star in the West End he wrote two contrasting evenings, each with a major part for himself: one a comedy, *Present Laughter* (originally lugubriously called *Sweet Sorrow*), the other a drama, *This Happy Breed*. Each play dealt with a subject Coward knew intimately: *Present Laughter* takes a conceited actor-playwright as its protagonist and has consequently been called Coward's most self-revelatory play; while *This Happy Breed* concerns the middle-class (from which Noel never forgot he sprang), their fears, their sense of honour and their courage.

During the writing of these plays in tandem Noel noted in his diary that because of the impending war 'in all probability they will never be produced', and indeed they were not to be seen in England until 1942.[1] Once they were written and polished, Noel learned there was to be a six-week wait before they could be put into rehearsal. Anxious to visit a world he might never see again, he set forth on a flying trip to Warsaw, Danzig, Moscow, Leningrad, Helsinki, Stockholm and Copenhagen.

[1] They toured Britain during that year and did not arrive in London's West End until April 1943.

Coward's reminiscences of these days before England declared war on Germany are amusingly and straightforwardly recounted in his second auto-biography, *Future Indefinite*, but even a Coward with his inborn sense of the ridiculous could never have contrived the cloak-and-dagger events in which he would soon be caught up.

He had hardly returned from his tour of Scandinavia and Russia to begin rehearsals of *This Happy Breed* and *Present Laughter* when he received a summons to a midnight secret rendez-vous. There Noel met Sir Campbell Stuart, then in charge of British propaganda, and was entreated by him to set up a Bureau of Propaganda in Paris immediately – if and when war broke out.

Coward's bureau, which would work in conjunction with the French Ministry of Information then run by Jean Giraudoux with the help of André Maurois, was to be top secret. Noel was to receive no salary but his expenses would be paid by the British government. Sir Campbell went on to explain that Coward had been chosen for the job because it was felt the British should provide someone of equal eminence to their French counterparts.

Sir Campbell warned Noel that he must continue his theatrical activi-ties as though none of this was happening. Even Noel's closest friends and his mother knew nothing of this fresh assignment, for the playwright-actor nonchalantly directed his cast by day while being briefed concerning his military duties each evening. Then, when at last Germany did invade Poland on September 1 and war was only a few hours away, he assembled his company and told the actors that he had agreed to serve his country and leave the stage for the duration of the conflict. The plays were to be put into mothballs hoping to be unwrapped at a later date. There was no question of carrying on with an understudy since he had written the parts to star himself.

A few days after a state of war was announced between Britain and Germany, Noel was in the French capital. Accustomed to the Paris of his friend Cole Porter, he moved into a suite at the Ritz until proper accommoda-tion for the Bureau of Propaganda could be found. He was soon given an office near the place de la Madeleine, a staff of five and a charming flat in the place Vendôme[2].

Throughout 1939 Noel and his staff were not exactly clear what their duties were supposed to be besides discussing methods of propagandizing the Allies' cause and reading a great many boring dispatches. The Maginot Line seemed impregnable, the Germans were beyond the horizon, and it seemed war had been moved offstage, or at least into the wings. Coward was even able to leave his duties in charge of his staff to take a holiday in London every month.

[2] After the war, Noel was able to rent this flat and it was to be his Parisian home for many years.

At last, in March 1940, by which time the most he could boast of having accomplished was closing a small headstrong radio station broadcasting in violation of Franco-English policy, he appealed to Sir Campbell Stuart, claiming he was but a figurehead and his office could be run equally well by his aides. Stuart gave him leave to go off for six weeks but suggested it would be to the advantage of the Bureau if he would holiday in America – which was exactly where Noel hoped he would be allowed to go. Before he left Stuart extracted a promise from Noel to return and re-man the Bureau no later than June.

During the next weeks Noel accomplished little propagandizing even though he travelled to Washington to dine and discuss the war with President and Mrs. Roosevelt. While he was there he was asked by the Australian Minister, Richard Casey, to visit his country and entertain the troops. Noel agreed to go once he was released from his Paris position.

For the present he was trying to husband his energies, and to make the most of what was left of his six-week holiday. But, even though he could put the war clouds out of his mind in the hot Pacific sun, he realized that he must return to Europe. By now Germany had invaded Holland, and Campbell Stuart had been replaced as Minister of Information by Noel's old friend Duff Cooper.

Eager to serve his country, Noel now cabled Cooper asking whether he should return to London or Paris. Cooper responded by requesting Coward to stay in America, which Coward had often avowed was his second home. But Noel's eagerness to find his place in the war machinery and his ardour for his country were not to be put aside, as he noted in *Future Indefinite*:

> My fears for my personal friends, the people I loved were easy to understand; also my irrational, but quite natural, desire to be with them in time of trouble rather than comfortably ensconced on the other side of the Atlantic. But England itself? That damp, weather-sodden little island from which for many years I had escaped at the first opportunity? ... I actually wasted a great deal of time, because all that finally emerged from [my self-analysis] was that I had no cynical detachment where my emotions were concerned, and that I was a flagrant, unabashed sentimentalist and likely to remain so until the end of my days. I did love England and all it stood for. I loved its follies and apathies and curious streaks of genius; I loved standing to attention for 'God Save the King'; I loved the justice, efficiency and even the dullness of British Colonial Administration. I loved the people – the ordinary, the extraordinary, the good, the bad, the indifferent, and what is more I belonged to that exasperating, weather-sodden little island with its uninspired cooking, its muddled thinking and its unregenerate pride, and it belonged to me whether it liked it or not.

Brushing aside Duff Cooper's advice, and deftly pulling strings so that he might at least return to close down the Paris office before the Germans arrived Noel was able to wangle a passage on a flight to Lisbon. From there he booked passage on the train to Paris the next afternoon. But he received a telephone call from the British Embassy and was told that Sir Walford Selby wished to breakfast with him before his departure. The Ambassador explained that travelling overland was entirely against his official advice, and that he would arrange air passage to get Noel to London (from there he could go to Paris if and when that was possible).

Coward recalled that he was 'impressed by the urgency of his tone and the common sense of his words ... The Sud-Express left that morning without me and arrived, presumably, in Paris on the morning of the 13th, twenty-four hours before Hitler. Had I been on it I should have only discovered my flat empty and the office evacuated and abandoned: I should also have discovered that every avenue of escape was closed and, in due course, been arrested, imprisoned and possibly shot. I owe indeed a great debt of gratitude to Sir Walford Selby.'

What Noel did not learn until 1945 was that he and a great many other dissenters, intellectuals, patriots, spies, homosexuals and Jews were targeted for immediate execution once the Germans reached Paris. Noel was all of these except for being Jewish and would have stood no chance of survival. His name was high on Hitler's black list of those to be immediately 'exterminated'. At the end, under 'w', came the name of Noel's friend Rebecca West. After V. E. Day, when the list was published, she wired: 'MY DEAR THE PEOPLE WE SHOULD HAVE BEEN SEEN DEAD WITH!'

With the closing of the Paris Office of Information, Noel was free to fulfil his promise to Richard Casey and set out to do benefit concerts in Australia as well as to entertain the troops. But it was not always easy to amuse a foreign group of young men most of whom had never heard of this urbane, middle-aged, balding Englishman with very little voice who was singing sentimental songs most of them had never heard. Often, because they would much rather have had a curvaceous female to entertain them, they were rowdy. But Coward was a veteran of many bad plays, and his years in the provinces had given him the ability to cope with the disorder, lack of interest and bad manners.

'I let them get on with their whistling and catcalls for a little,' he stated, 'and then announced with some firmness through the microphone, that I intended to sing steadily for three quarters of an hour whether they liked it or not. This dreadful threat silenced them for a moment and gave me a chance to bawl out "Don't Put Your Daughter on the Stage, Mrs. Worthington" which drew from them a few grudging titters, after which I was allowed to get on with the rest of the programme. At the end they applauded and cheered vociferously, and carried me ... on their shoulders, which was uncomfortable, but gratifying.'

Conquering his audiences may have been the easiest part of that South-Eastern Pacific jaunt. For the ensuing nine months he combined a gruelling schedule of singing for the troops with fund-raising events. Because of Noel's charity concerts alone, the Australian Red Cross made a profit of more than twelve thousand pounds.

Once he had toured Australia and New Zealand, Coward wanted to move on to more important war work. With his sense of the dramatic and fondness for disguise, he actually believed he could be an undercover agent – and, curiously, so did his friend Sir William Stephenson[3]. 'Open and above board,' was the way Sir William put it, 'no need for dark glasses.' But Noel was shattered when he received a note from Stephenson which read, 'A greater power than we could contradict has thwarted our intents.' Noel always believed the 'greater power' was Winston Churchill who had announced at the very beginning of the war that Coward's most valuable contribution would be to 'go out and sing "Mad Dogs and Englishmen"[4] while the guns are firing'. The statement had always nettled Coward who wondered how the troops could possibly hear his song with guns booming in the background. His relationship with Churchill, though each man respected the other, was strained ever after, and Churchill's assessment of Noel's 'most valuable contribution to the war' continued to rankle. So he decided that his offering might not necessarily be in the entertainment field, but in the *creative*. In the next four months, Coward was to contribute strongly to Britain's morale – with propaganda at its best. He would write an escapist masterpiece, four wartime songs, and begin a film that would illustrate the heroism the British in all walks of life were displaying. It would bring him a special Academy Award, international fame, and almost win him a knighthood.

The first result of this creative spurt occurred in early May 1941 when he and the actress Joyce Carey went on holiday in North Wales. Noel set down the whole of *Blithe Spirit* in six days – thereafter he changed only a few lines. For some time, as Noel says, 'the idea for a light comedy had been rattling at the door of my mind and I thought the time had come to let it in'.

Coward's total recall of the sequence of events in Portmeirion gives the reader a rare glimpse into the creative process that produced his longest-running play and one of the finest comedies of the mid-twentieth century:

> By lunch time the title had emerged together with the names of the characters, and a rough, very rough, outline of the plot. At seven-thirty the next morning I sat, with the usual nervous palpitations, at my typewriter ... There was a pile of virgin paper on my left and a box of carbons on my right. The table wobbled and I had to

---

[3] Stephenson was head of British Intelligence in the United States.
[4] This song, Churchill's favourite among Coward's *oeuvre*, was often bellowed by him. Its lyric had also been committed to memory by Franklin Roosevelt. The two men disagreed over a line and made a wager. When Roosevelt won, Churchill told Coward defensively, 'England can take it.'

put a wedge under one of its legs. I smoked several cigarettes in rapid succession, staring gloomily out the window at the tide running out. I fixed the paper in the machine and started: *Blithe Spirit. A Light Comedy*[5] in Three Acts.

For six days I worked from eight to one each morning and from two to seven every afternoon. The play was finished and, disdaining archness and false modesty, I will admit that I knew it was witty. I knew it was well constructed and I also knew it would be a success.

However much Noel might have believed in his new-born play, he would be hard put to imagine his enduring achievement. *Blithe Spirit* opened in Manchester six weeks after its completion and proceeded to London two weeks later where it continued to run for four and a half years. It has been filmed, televised, made the subject of a ballet, and a musical (*High Spirits*). The script has been published in fourteen languages and performed on stages throughout the world. It is even likely that the idea for 1990's cinematic hit, *Ghost*, which concerns a medium communicating with loved ones 'beyond' came from *Blithe Spirit*.

Its plot, concerning a séance during which a playwright's former wife is materialised by a clumsy medium and is visible only to him, has some of the macabre humour of *The Invisible Man*. But of course Coward is writing a comedy, so he deftly twists his characters to include a mistaken offstage murder of the first wife – always in the realm of farce – and the materialisation of the playwright's present wife by the time the second interval rolls around. This shift in the plot leads to hilarious rows and misunderstandings by the wives who try to get the writer to join them in ghostdom. By the final curtain these spirits have been dispatched, à la Shakespeare's *Midsummer Night's Dream* whence they came. With the war's losses and destruction all around them, *Blithe Spirit* afforded the British audiences a chance to laugh at death.

Even while rehearsals of *Blithe Spirit* were being held, Noel's creative energies, bolstered by the success of his play, spilled over into his song-writing. Of the four songs he published in these few months, three were splendid contributions to alleviate the gloom brought about by the Blitz. Only 'There Have Been Songs in England', which Noel termed 'pleasant but a little pretentious ... heavy and soggy', does not succeed. With lines like 'since our island arose from the sea ... very soon the birds appear'd, Later, lyric words appear'd' and a very sentimental melody, it had little chance.

'Imagine the Duchess's Feelings', another propaganda song Coward wrote that July, put into words and music his blatant antagonism towards the Russians. Although they were now allies of the British, he never forgave them for the treaty they had signed with Germany a few years before, and when any of his friends mentioned their wartime privations he overruled them vocifer-

---

[5] Noel substituted 'An Improbable Farce' for 'A Light Comedy' as the published sub-title.

ously, adding that the Russians were only saving their own necks. The duchess of the title quite condones the weakness of her first son and the stupidity of her second. The refrain ends with: 'her eldest son when in trouble went white,/ Her second son looked blue and hung his head,/ But imagine the Duchess's feelings/ When her youngest son went Red!'

'Could You Please Oblige Us with a Bren Gun?' is another story entirely. Its excessively polite complaint, a letter from a colonel who had served in the Boer War pointing out that the Home Guard has only outmoded and ineffectual weapons, is a typical Coward swipe at the ineptitude of the British Quartermaster-General's department – and thereby all bureaucracy. Although Coward himself predicted it was 'too topical to outlive the immediate moment', its continuing popularity proves otherwise. It is still funny, and its message viable. The jaunty tune, the lyric to one verse, and the first and last refrains are printed below.[6]

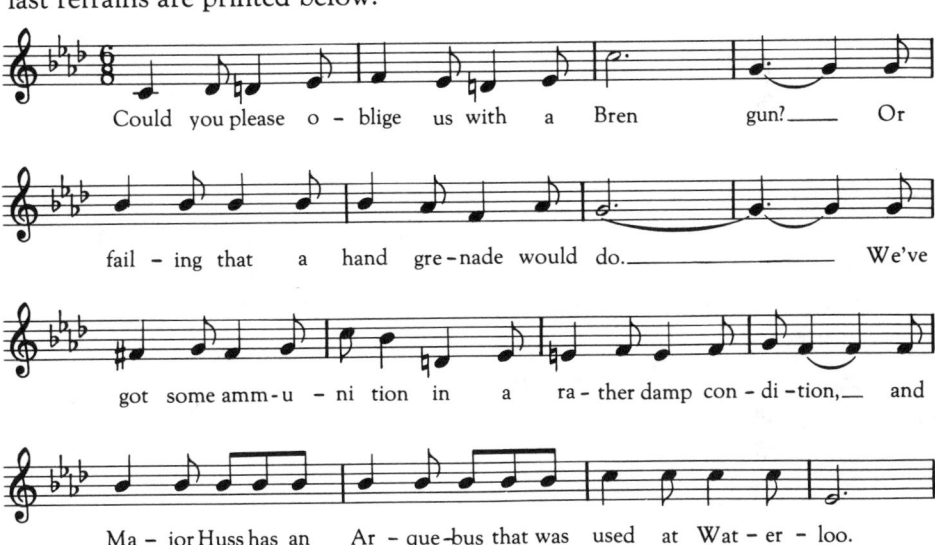

Verse I
Colonel Montmorency who
Was in Calcutta in ninety-two
Emerged from his retirement for the war.
He wasn't very pleased with what he heard
    and what he saw.
Whatever he felt
He tightened his belt
And organised the corps.
Poor Colonel Montmorency thought
Considering all the wars he'd fought
The Home Guard was his job to do or die;
But after days and weeks and years,

Bravely drying his manly tears
He wrote the following letter to the
Minister of Supply.

Refrain I
Could you please oblige us with a Bren gun?
Or failing that, a hand grenade would do.
We've got some ammunition
In a rather damp condition,
Major Huss has an Arquebus
That was used at Waterloo.
With the Vicar's stirrup pump, a pitchfork
    and a spade

---

[6] Coward's repressed 'r's make acceptable rhymes (in the verse) of 'war', 'saw' and 'corps'.

It's rather hard to guard an aerodrome.
So if you can't oblige us with a Bren gun,
The Home Guard might as well go home.

Refrain 4

Could you please oblige us with a Bren gun?
The lack of one is wounding to our pride.
Last night we found the cutest
    little German parachutist

Who looked at our kit then giggled a bit
    and laughed until he cried.
We'll have to hide that armoured car when
    marching to Berlin.
We'd almost be ashamed of it in Rome,
So if you can't oblige us with a Bren gun,
The Home Guard might as well come home.

The last of the quartet of songs Coward turned out in the summer of 1941 was 'London Pride'. Noel wrote that the idea for this came to him one morning while standing on the platform of a railway station after a bad blitz. Observing the determined Londoners scurrying about amid the broken glass, acrid fumes and dust in the air, he was overwhelmed by a wave of sentimental pride. 'The song started in my head then and there,' he wrote, 'and was finished in a couple of days. The tune is based on the old traditional lavender-seller's song, "Won't You Buy My Sweet Blooming Lavender."' Coward mentions that 'this age-old melody was appropriated by the Germans and used as a foundation for "Deutschland über Alles", and [that he] considered that the time had come for us to have it back in London where it belonged'.[7]

Indeed, the first phrase of the anthem of the Third Reich does bear a great similarity to the old British folk-song, 'Who'll buy my violets?' (see below), but as in every fine work of art, it's never the idea, it's the execution that makes the difference. Coward's exquisite extension and development of this simple melodic line – never overdone – make it one of his finest songs.

Shortly after *Blithe Spirit* opened to general enthusiasm, Noel was offered carte blanche by Filippo del Giudice and Anthony Havelock-Allan whose Two Cities film company had produced Olivier's *Henry V*. They would underwrite any picture on any subject he liked. And, further, he could dictate the cast and director – as long as he starred in the film. That approach, coupled with a dinner at the Mountbattens a few nights later, during which Lord Louis related

---

[7] See Musical Analysis Appendix for the complete lyric and further melodic excerpts.

the whole story of the sinking of the battleship *Kelly*, which was under his command, was the genesis of one of the finest films of the war, *In Which We Serve*.

Filming the sinking of a battleship, and the flashback memories of its survivors, was to take a full year. There were the expected delays while they awaited approval from the naval propaganda department who felt at first that showing a British ship actually being sunk was unpatriotic. And there was the unexpected interruption of work on the film when police officers bearing summonses appeared on the set. They informed Noel that he was liable for a heavy fine because he had spent money from his American royalties, earnings Jack had deposited in his account without telling him that they could not be touched without first obtaining permission from the Treasury.

His lawyers told him to plead guilty to the charge, and he was about to take their advice when he received a note from his old friend George Bernard Shaw which stated, 'There can be no guilt without intention.' The letter ended with: 'therefore let nothing induce you to plead Guilty.'

Coward took Shaw's advice and was let off with a small fine. The papers made as much as they could of the court hearing and almost succeeded in scuttling the continuation of filming *In Which We Serve*, but most of Noel's friends stood by him. Rebecca West, knowing Noel's ardent patriotism, wrote: 'I can't quite see what more you could do for your country, except strip yourself of all your clothes and sell them for the War Weapons Week, after which your country would step in and prosecute you for indecent exposure.' Now everything was over between Jack and Noel. Coward wrote to tell Wilson that he must never meddle in his financial affairs and cancelled the contracts that bound them.

When America entered the war in December 1941, Noel was still hammering out the script of *In Which We Serve*. The scenario was not to be finished for a further three months and it was not until June 1942 that the film would be in the can. When it was finally released and received with such tremendous enthusiasm Noel had the opportunity to return to live theatre and spent the autumn and winter of that year touring in a repertoire of three plays, *Blithe Spirit*, *Present Laughter* and *This Happy Breed*. Eventually he brought the trio into London for an eight-week season.

Noel was still not satisfied that he had done his utmost to help his country, and arranged to tour South Africa, Burma, India and Ceylon, performing for British and colonial troops, raising money for the Red Cross, throughout the next year and a half. Shortly before he left on this long trek in 1943, he introduced a new song called 'Don't Let's Be Beastly to the Germans' during a radio broadcast to the troops. It seems incomprehensible that anyone could mistake its ironic tone, and assume that when peace came Coward

Coward with Norman Hackforth, entertaining the troops, 1944

would propose forgiving the Nazis, but letters from people who had misunder-
stood poured in. The *Daily Herald* accused him of 'appalling taste and
mischievous disregard for public feeling', and the B.B.C. banned the song from
the airwaves.

> We must be kind,
> And with an open mind
> We must endeavour to find a way
> To let the Germans know that when the war is over
> They are not the ones who'll have to pay ...
> We must be just,
> And win their love and trust
> And in addition we must be wise,
> And ask the conquered lands to join our
>   hands to aid them
> That would be a wonderful surprise.
> For many years
> They've been in floods of tears

Because the poor little dears
Have been so wronged,
And only long'd
To cheat the world,
Deplete the world,
And beat the world to blazes.
This is the moment when we ought to sing their praises ...
Don't let's be beastly to the Germans
When we've definitely got them on the run.
Let us treat them very kindly as we would a valued friend,
We might send them out some Bishops as a form of lease and lend.
Let's be sweet to them
And day by day repeat to them
That sterilization simply isn't done.
Let's help the dirty swine again
To occupy the Rhine again,
But don't let's be beastly to the Hun.

When Noel Coward returned to England in late 1944, he began thinking of a new creative work for the stage. The idea of an operetta appealed to him, for by now, having lived down the failure of *Operette*, he was once again able to think of the success he had known with *Bitter Sweet*. He rejected it in favour of a revue. His successful war songs had given him courage to plunge once more into the short form of the topical revue, and he had matured enough to have a less sentimental view of love. As he plunged into creating words and music for his new revue *Sigh No More*, there was not a single sigh in sight.

COLE
1939-1944

WITH *Leave It to Me* settled in for an assured long run, Cole Porter embarked upon an unbroken string of five more hits.[1] *Du Barry Was a Lady, Panama Hattie, Let's Face It, Something for the Boys* and *Mexican Hayride* each ran for over 400 performances. *Panama Hattie* even broke a record and became the first non-revue show since the '20s to be seen over 500 times, while *Let's Face It* chalked up runs of 547 in New York and 348 in London.

In addition to this incredibly successful commercial output in the five years between 1939 and 1944, Cole turned out three complete movie scores. For Columbia films he wrote two classic musicals: *You'll Never Get Rich* and *Something to Shout About*. He also somehow got himself trapped in the Warners' film *Mississippi Belle* for which he wrote seventeen songs, the equivalent of a full theatre score. It was never produced.

It was as though, once the pain from the accident reached bearable proportions, Cole felt he had to drive himself on; plunge ever deeper into his work. Indeed, it was about this time that his friends began to mention his rudeness. He would suddenly break off a conversation, leaving a room or a dinner party, abandoning Linda to struggle on with the conversation alone. Few attributed this to his preoccupation with his work until much later.

This enormous spurt of creative energy coincided with the years of the Second World War, and Cole, like so many of his contemporaries, wanted to contribute songs for the U. S. Armed Forces. Unlike Coward, he was not naturally gifted with irony, so what he created was based on formula and cliché. 'Glide, Glider, Glide' was presented to the newly-formed Glider Corps and 'Sailors of the Sky' was written for the Navy.[2] He also found time to write some individual songs: his ballad 'So Long, Samoa' would be rewritten in 1940, then retitled 'So Long Samantha' would find a place in the film *Adam's Rib* a decade later. To celebrate his close friend Monty Woolley's role of a lifetime as *The Man Who Came to Dinner*, Cole wrote 'What Am I To Do', a ballad to be sung by a Cowardesque character in the play. He signed his manuscript as having been written by Noel Porter – although the royalties came directly to Cole.

---

[1] Even Cole's competitors, Rodgers and Hammerstein, who had enormous hits in *Oklahoma!, Carousel, South Pacific, The King and I,* and *The Sound of Music,* had their successes interspersed with flops and near-flops like *Me and Juliet, Pipe Dream,* and *Allegro.*

[2] The U. S. Navy was reluctant to print the song in their official songbook because, as they put it bureaucratically, 'the only factor preventing the exploitation of the song is Washington's frown on reference to girls in the lyric'. Cole's lyric ends: 'With the girls we rank first-raters,/ And they all cheer when we sail by,/ So our foes overseas/ Are the only enemies/ of the sailors of the sky.'

By now Cole had so mastered technique that he seemed able to write fluently in any style and the Coward-like melody and lyric were not only a tribute to his old friend but a genuine tour de force. Cole was equally able to capture the spirit of eighteenth-century France in the gavottes and minuets he created for *Du Barry Was a Lady*. Songs like 'Do I Love You'. 'Friendship', 'But In the Morning, No', 'It Ain't Etiquette' and 'Give Him the Ooh-La-La' were entirely appropriate to his two superstars: leather-lunged showstoppers for Ethel Merman (their third collaboration), and low comedy for Bert Lahr.

Cole's involvement in the war was tangential at most, but perhaps in 'Well, Did You Evah?' one can sense an effort to make his audience, even the fashionable social set he travelled with – who rarely sensed his message – aware that the world was about to explode in another war. The song (which was also interpolated into the film *High Society*) has four inventive refrains. Two of my favourites are printed below.

She: Have you heard the coast of Maine
Just got hit by a hurricane?

He: Well, did you evah!
What a swell party this is.

She: Have you heard that poor, dear Blanche
Got run down by an avalanche?

He: Well, did you evah!
What a swell party this is.
It's great, it's grand,
It's Wonderland!
It's tops, it's first,
It's DuPont, it's Hearst!
What soup, what fish,
What meat, what a dish!
What salad, what cheese!
She: Pardon me one moment, please,
Have you heard that Uncle Newt
Forgot to open his parachute?

He: Well, did you evah?
What a swell party this is.

She: Old Miss Pringle just came back
With her child and the child is black.

He: Well, did you evah?
What a swell party this is.

He: Have you heard it's in the stars
Next July we collide with Mars?

She: Well, did you evah!
What a swell party this is.

He: Have you heard that grandma Doyle
Thought the Flit was her mineral oil?

She: Well, did you evah!
What a swell party this is.
What daiquiris!
What sherry! Please!
What Burgundy!
What great Pommery!
What brandy! Wow!
What whisky! Here's how!
What gin and what beer!

He: Will you sober up, my dear?
Have you heard Professor Munch
Ate his wife and divorced his lunch?

She: Well, did you evah?
What a swell party this is.

He: Have you heard that Mimsie Starr
Just got pinched in the Astor Bar?
Well, did you evah?
What a swell party this is.

In *Du Barry*, Bert Lahr plays a small-time gambling washroom attendant in a nightclub. He has a crush on one of the girl singers and, when he wins the sweepstake, he finds himself transported (through a misplaced 'mickey finn') into the elegant court of Louis XV. Of course, Ethel Merman is the singer and in his dream she becomes his mistress, Mme du Barry.

The recruitment of Lahr, who had come up through the ranks of raunchy burlesque, coupled with the notorious permissiveness of the eighteenth-century French court led Porter to write some of his most ribald lyrics. On tour, the show was banned in Minneapolis as 'an affront to womanhood and marriage', while in Boston a group of schoolchildren who had come to see *The Wizard of Oz's* Cowardly Lion were summarily ushered out of the theatre by their shocked schoolmarm in midperformance.

But, if Lahr stated that 'nothing I sang in burlesque was as risqué as his lyrics', it was more *mal y pense* than actual smut. Although the show was built around 'that sly biological urge', in songs like 'Give Him the Oo-La-La', 'Katie Went to Haiti', and especially 'But In the Morning, No', which, like 'Love for Sale', was banned from the airwaves, and which the *New Yorker* critic termed 'dirt without wit', the actual dirtiness must have been supplied by the mind of the audience. All Cole supplied was the innuendo.

As a lyricist he was fond of lines like 'Katie knew her Haiti, and practically all Haiti knew Katie'.[3] In 'But In the Morning, No', which is categorized list song, Cole uses mountain-climbing, swimming, travelling, football, accounting, the stock market and so on. The refrains concerning these last two subjects with their perfectly harmless lyrics seem to have caused the fracas.

She: Are you good at figures, dear?
Kindly tell me if so.

He: Yes, I'm good at figures, dear.
But in the morning, no.

She: D'you do double entry, dear?
Kindly tell me if so.

He: I do double entry, dear,
But in the morning, no.
When the sun on the rise
Shows the bags beneath my eyes,
That's the time
When I'm
In low.

She: Are you fond of business, dear?
Kindly tell me if so.

He: Yes, I'm fond of business, dear,
But in the morning, no, no ... no, no
No, no, no, no, no!

He: Are you in the market, dear?
Kindly tell me if so.

She: Yes, I'm in the market, dear,
But in the morning, no.

He: Are you fond of bulls and bears?
Kindly tell me if so.

She: Yes, I'm fond of bulls and bears,
But in the morning, no.
When I'm waked by my fat
Old canary singing flat,
That's the time
When I'm
In low.

He: Would you ever sell your seat?
Kindly answer if so.

She: Yes, I'd gladly sell my seat,
But in the morning, no, no ... no, no
No, no, no, no, no!

But it was not only in the risqué lyric department of this show where Cole's technique shone, but in the composition. He had not had an opportunity to

---

[3] In succeeding refrains the biblical 'knew' is replaced by 'had' and Cole's special favourite two-way word which he used in many of his lyrics – 'made.'

write Frenchified music since *Fifty Million Frenchmen*, a decade before, and *Du Barry* which bounced between the twentieth century and the eighteenth, suited his musical talents eminently well. Cole's fanciful anachronisms added to the brilliance of the score. In 'Mesdames and Messieurs' he was able to use the French language and snatches of French folksongs; in 'Give Him the Oo-La-La' he even quoted from the 'Marseillaise'. 'When Love Beckoned on 52nd Street' displayed a jazz beat and 'Katie Went to Haiti' was redolent of a Caribbean samba.

After the rave reviews *Du Barry Was a Lady* received, Porter's ASCAP rating shot up to AA – which meant his royalties moved him to the very top income bracket of over $100,000 that year. Only Kern, Berlin and Gershwin were in that category. It was just a question of time before the property was bought by Hollywood, and indeed the movie was released in 1943 (Merman and Lahr were replaced by a posturing Lucille Ball and a clownish Red Skelton).

Although Cole's next show, *Panama Hattie*, starring Ethel Merman – for once receiving solo billing – was to break all previous Porter records for a libretto show, its score was not nearly of the same calibre as that of *Du Barry Was a Lady*. Perhaps the replacement of France by the Caribbean or Central America, which was not really Cole's forte, made him write less inventive music. Certainly he had no experience with such a sentimental plot.

The story, inspired by a song in *Du Barry*, 'Katie Went to Haiti', centres around Miss Merman who runs a nightclub in Panama ('I'm Throwing A Ball Tonight') and falls in love with a government official from Philadelphia ('My Mother Would Love You'). She foils a plot to blow up the Canal, is ridiculed for overdressing by the official's eight-year-old daughter and tries to drown her sorrows in booze ('Make It Another Old Fashioned, Please'). Gradually, she and the child come to an understanding ('Let's Be Buddies'), and in the end, of course, she gets her man.

The public and most of the critics loved the show and gave Miss Merman and her supporting cast, Betty Hutton, Rags Ragland and Arthur Treacher (Hollywood's perennial butler) nightly ovations. Some of the press, among them the acerbic John O'Hara, realized, however, that this was nowhere near top-drawer Porter. O'Hara wrote, 'Who'd have thought we'd live to see the day when Cole Porter, – *Cole Porter!* – would write a score in which the two outstanding songs are called "My Mother Would Love You" and "Let's Be Buddies?" ... Ah, well, he had a bad riding accident a year or two ago. This ought to teach him to stay in his Brewster-Ford and away from horses.'

Actually Cole would have nothing to do with a middle-class Brewster–Ford, for he always travelled first-class. Nor would he let pass the distinguished novelist's appraisal of his score. 'I took a tip from Buddy De Sylva's instinct for sentiment,' he wrote, 'and agreed with him that a composition to diddle the public into tears would be useful at the box-office ... "Let's Be Buddies", sung by Merman to a rather annoying brat ... was hogwash, but it made the box-office dizzy for a year.'

Even before most of the songs for *Panama Hattie* had been written, Linda began to drag Cole – by limousine – to the Berkshires where she had fallen in love with a 200-acre estate outside the college town of Amherst, Massachussetts. She had investigated the property originally merely as a place to store all the furniture, crystal and household items she had sent over when she closed the house in Paris; but, before Cole knew it, she made an offer and bought it, with her own money.

The estate, called Buxton Hill, had a largish gatekeeper's cottage which Linda turned into working accommodation for Cole. (So that he might work there undisturbed, he put up a sign lettered 'No Trespassing', and the cottage – even today – is known as 'No Trespassing'.)

For the first months Cole, who had never known country living, found the large stone edifice remote and depressing. Nor did he appreciate the three-and-a-half-hour motor trip needed to get there. But after some months he began to look forward to weekends out of New York, and in his later years he came to love the place and enjoy the parties, the large number of guests an estate of this size could comfortably accommodate.

The Porters next turned their attention to Beverly Hills. Cole began the score of *You'll Never Get Rich* which was to star Fred Astaire and Rita Hayworth. Produced by Columbia on a much more stringent budget than his other Hollywood efforts, Cole's involvement with this film was both frustrating and unpleasant. In his previous Hollywood films, *Born To Dance* and *Broadway Melody of 1940*, although they had little social contact, MGM's chairman Louis B. Mayer had shown a deferential respect for Cole's talent. But now, the Columbia Pictures chief, Harry Cohn, who had a notorious reputation for shady dealings and taking sexual advantage of the female stars he had under contract, subjected Cole's songs to the indignity of being 'tried out' on the office staff.

In spite of his unpleasant relationship with the boorish 'King Cohn', Cole enjoyed working in Hollywood so much that he wrote to his musical arranger Dr. Albert Sirmay wondering why 'people are willing to stay in New York when it is so simple to come to California'. As for the film, he added, 'I'm working very hard and I believe I have some good new numbers. In any case it's a most interesting job.'

Although none of the songs, which included 'Since I Kissed My Baby Good-bye', 'Dream Dancing', 'Shooting the Works For Uncle Sam', and 'So

Porter being carried into the theatre for one of
his opening nights

Porter map for prospective weekend guests
once he had moved to Buxton Hill

Entering Williamstown ignore sign which says
"GO RIGHT" and turn left

GO RIGHT

turn left

turn left

cemetery

brook

houses

caretaker's
cottage

guest cottage

main house

7

route 7 to
Williamstown

turn left

route 43

turn right

route 22 for about 55 miles

Amenia
turn left

11 miles

route 44

Millbrook

11 miles

route 82

turn right

40 miles

Eastern State
Parkway

Hawthorne traffic
circle

Sawmill River
Parkway

Hendrick Hudson Bridge

HUDSON RIVER

BEST TRAIN SERVICE "GREEN MOUNTAIN FLYER"
lv. GRAND CENT. TER. 10:15 A.M.
lv. NORTH BENNINGTON 4:27 P.M.

DINING CAR SERVICE

daylight saving time
ar. NORTH BENNINGTON 2:20 P.M.
ar. GRAND CENT. TER. 8:40 P.M.

BOTH WAYS BETWEEN N.Y.C. & TROY

LONG ISLAND
SOUND

Near and Yet So Far', reached hit status, the score is far above those of Hollywood musicals of that period. *You'll Never Get Rich* never made Cole or the studio rich, but, although Cole was later to admit that it was 'a bad score', he was always to qualify his criticism by saying his songs came from an even 'worse picture'.

Cole adored the Hollywood sunshine, but he sorely missed working on shows in New York and was eager to get back to New York and the madhouse world of the Broadway musical. Yet now, in the time that it had taken him to finish *You'll Never Get Rich*, Buddy De Sylva, the producer of his last two hits, had moved to Hollywood to head Paramount Pictures.

Even though Cole and De Sylva enjoyed a pleasant working relationship they had never been on the same wavelength, never had the same passion for vignettes or revue which Vinton Freedley possessed. Happily, De Sylva's new position left Cole free to return, without obligation, and to write a musical under the aegis of his favourite producer. Freedley, with whom Cole had not worked since *Leave It To Me*, told Cole that he would engineer this show just as he had *Anything Goes*. He planned to sign up the best young talent he could find and then would hire the writers to figure out the story.

Porter would not, however, be adrift in a sea of new faces, for, although the star of his show was to be the inimitable Danny Kaye[4] for whom Cole had never written, his librettists would be Herbert and Dorothy Fields, old friends who had penned his last two hits.

The story they came up with, an updated version of the 1925 farce, *The Cradle Snatchers*, concerned three young wives (Eve Arden, Vivian Vance, Edith Meiser), convinced their husbands are cheating on them, who take up with three soldiers (Danny Kaye, Benny Baker, Jack Williams). By the *very* long arm of coincidence, the husbands have taken up with the soldiers' girls (Mary Jane Walsh, Sunny O'Day, Nanette Fabray). At the end the soldiers end up with their girls and the wives are reconciled to their husbands.

This twelvesome plot was so loose and the talent Freedley signed so abundant that almost any song concept could be fitted into it – and was. The score contained such diverse gems as 'Farming' and 'Everything I Love', which have since become standards. 'Ace in the Hole'[5], 'You Irritate Me So', 'Let's Not Talk About Love', 'I Hate You, Darling' and 'Pets' went on to become great favourites of cabaret entertainers, but there are other interesting songs, many of which were dropped from the 21-song score: 'Make a Date With a

[4] Cole did not write all of Danny Kaye's songs in *Let's Face It*. Sylvia Fine, Kaye's wife, who had previously created his most successful material, wrote several including the evening's show-stopper, 'Melody in 4F', which concerns a rejected recruit.
[5] See Musical Analysis Appendix.

Great Psychiatrist', 'What Are Little Husbands Made Of?'. 'Revenge', and 'A Little Rumba Numba'.

No one has ever called *Let's Face It* a great musical. Nor did anyone expect it to be the smash hit it was, least of all its producer. Freedley was not deceived into complacency when in the *New Yorker* Wolcott Gibbs called it 'brilliant foolishness', or *Life Magazine* dubbed it the season's 'smash' and declared, 'Porter has come out of his slump.' He knew it was the stars, especially Danny Kaye's brilliant double-talk routines, and the wartime escape atmosphere that filled the theatre nightly.[6]

Perhaps it was the lack of Kaye and the other young members of the cast in the London production that caused *Punch*'s critic to write, 'Until we saw *Let's Face It* at the Hippodrome we fondly imagined that *Du Barry Was a Lady* at His Majesty's was as low as wartime entertainment was likely to reach. But not ... what repels in both these shows is not so much their shrieking vulgarity as their arrant witlessness.' The respected critic, James Agate, went one step further when he wrote that 'this piece has no wit, no spectacle. One would have given anything for a conjurer or a couple of acrobats.' One has to attribute *Let's Face It* settling down for a long run in London to wartime hullabaloo and the desire for pure amusement. Yet Cole was not deceived; he always counted the score of *Let's Face It* among his lesser efforts.

Things were not to improve when he returned to Hollywood in the spring of 1942 to fulfil his commitment for a second Columbia picture. This time 'King Cohn' kept his distance, but in his place Cole had to contend with Gregory Ratoff, Russian-born actor who had somehow been assigned as producer *and* director. Ratoff himself had chosen the title *Something to Shout About* which he felt had a strong ring of success and from their first meeting begged Cole to turn out a 'stunning, lively title song that will become the anthem of the entire picture'. Cole obliged moderately well and in addition to the title song wrote a routine rhumba, 'Hasta Luego', a war-rationing song, 'I Can Do Without Tea in My Teapot,' and the only number that registered with audiences, 'You'd Be So Nice To Come Home To'. Although Ratoff gushed over everything Cole turned out, and went so far as to write that 'the entire Columbia studio, front office and back lot, are of the opinion that *Something To Shout About* is not only the best musical Columbia has ever made, but one of the best musicals that was ever produced by any studio', Cole was not mollified. His own criticism of the film sounded very much like one of his lyrics: '*Something to Shout About* is nothing to rave about!'

---

[6] When *Let's Face It*, having exhausted its Broadway audience, opened in Chicago without Kaye and its other stars it flopped badly.

Soon Vinton Freedley, who had just signed up Ethel Merman for their next collaboration, brought Herbert and Dorothy Fields to discuss the plot of another light show, contemporary, but not truly topical – it bore a vague connection to the World War. This was to be called *Jenny Get Your Gun*.

The unbelievable plot had Ethel Merman saving the security of the Army, by receiving code messages through *the carborundum fillings in her teeth*. Even Freedley, who had always cared little for plot but insisted on talent and believability, could not convince the Fieldses to create a more sensible story and so bowed out. Vincent Freedley never again produced a Porter show.

When Freedley stepped out Mike Todd, who had clawed his way to the top by lavish productions of *The Hot Mikado* and *Star and Garter*, eagerly stepped in. He got on well with Cole for he was impressed not only with Cole's record in the hit-tune department, but with his urbanity; while Cole respected Todd's macho pugnacity and showmanship.

In spite of the presence of Ethel Merman (singing Cole's least interesting score), some clever direction by Hassard Short, mountains of costumes and tons of scenery and a couple of deadpan comedians in Paula Lawrence and Alan Jenkins, it is amazing that *Jenny Get Your Gun* which Todd retitled *Something For the Boys* did not fold its wings immediately.

The critics did not pull their punches. Louis Kronenberger writing in *PM* tolled the death knell: 'Mr. Porter isn't the composer he once was.' While George Freedley in the *Morning Telegraph* lamented: 'Cole Porter's last few shows have been disappointing, and this one perhaps most of all.' The rest of the reviewers were no kinder; several pointing to the fact that there was not a single hit tune in the show – and they were right. Yet, in spite of all this, Todd's lavish production coupled with enormous hullabaloo and advertising pulled the rabbit of success out of the hat and *Something For The Boys* chalked up 422 performances.

Todd repeated the same feat a year later when he produced an even more lavish and more tasteless show, *Mexican Hayride*. This reunited Cole with the Fieldses and the lighting man-director, Hassard Short, but the star this time was the low comic, Bobby Clark. Cole's score was little improved from *Something For the Boys* although he did produce one hit, 'I Love You', and a fairly successful ballad called 'Sing to Me, Guitar'.

The popularity of 'I Love You' was due to Cole's eagerness to win a bet he had made with his old friend Monty Woolley. Woolley had declared that Cole would be unable to write a song with the banal words 'I love you' repeated again and again. To prove him wrong, Cole, who hated to lose, turned out one of his most felicitous and memorable melodies. 'I Love You' starts with an A section melodic motif that descends a major seventh which is followed by an inspired appassionata bridge on the uninspiring words:

It's spring again
And birds on the wing again
Start to sing again
The old melodies.

Cole won $25 from Monty.

The show had the most lavish and expensive mounting Broadway had seen in years – but *Mexican Hayride* was Mike Todd's show, not Cole Porter's. With Todd collecting all the kudos and placing his name above the title one could easily overlook the score. Almost everybody did.

'Aladdin Todd rubbed his wonderful lamp and lifted us into a dream-world of splendor, mirth, melody and enchantment,' gushed Burton Roscoe in the *World Telegram*. 'Yes, yes, yes, indeed,' seconded Robert Garland in the

A rare picture of Porter's leg brace, Brentwood, California, 1944

Journal-American, 'the fabulous Todd produced a musical comedy so funny, so tuneful, so beautiful that you could hardly believe your eyes.'

With reviews like that it was a forgone conclusion that *Mexican Hayride* would have a long run. Opening in January 1944, its mindlessness and lavishness, and the fact that it had to do with gangsters – Mexican ones – far away from the European and Japanese war theatres, made it the perfect escapist show. It played to packed houses for almost 500 performances and except for *Panama Hattie* became the longest running Porter show to date.

Although 1944 began auspiciously, there was trouble ahead. Every project Cole tried seemed to go awry. His first disappointment came when Warner Brothers abandoned *Mississippi Belle*, the film Cole had been working on for over a year and for which he had written a complete and handsome score. Then there was his involvement with another showman, even more egotistical than Mike Todd, this time the diminutive Billy Rose. Rose owned nightclubs and theatres and had already displayed his tremendous showmanship by giving Broadway opulent productions of *Jumbo* and *Carmen Jones*. Rose had wanted to produce a 'high class' revue for some time and wooed Cole with the promise that he could do as many or as few songs as he liked. To one whose last film score had been shelved, Rose's offer was a tremendous ego boost.

The project was to be called *Seven Lively Arts* and on paper it looked like the kind of lavish revue that would please both critics and intellectual theatre goers who seemed to have very little choice on wartime Broadway. So intriguing did the show look that it built up the then tremendous advance of $350,000. Besides Cole's score, the evening included Igor Stravinsky's twenty-minute divertissement called *Scènes de Ballet*.[7] Moss Hart, Ben Hecht and George S. Kaufman had contributed the sketches, Salvador Dali had done the paintings, and Norman Bel Geddes had designed the sets. The glittering cast included Beatrice Lillie, Bert Lahr, Doc Rockwell, Dolores Gray and the ballet stars Alicia Markova and Anton Dolin; and besides the full orchestra in the pit there was Benny Goodman and his combo on stage.

But the entertainment fell somewhere between the consciously arty and the *déjà-vu*, and as soon as the public found out how dull and laconic the material in *Seven Lively Arts* was the advance soon dissipated and the show closed after twenty weeks.

---

[7] When Billy Rose heard Stravinsky's score in the composer's uniquely angular orchestration, at the Philadelphia try-out, he immediately wired the following telegram: YOUR MUSIC GREAT SUCCESS STOP COULD BE SENSATIONAL SUCCESS IF YOU WOULD AUTHORIZE ROBERT RUSSELL BENNETT TO RETOUCH ORCHESTRATION STOP BENNETT ORCHESTRATES EVEN THE WORKS OF COLE PORTER. Stravinsky immediately wired back: SATISFIED WITH GREAT SUCCESS. (Anton Dolin, who choreographed the ballet tells the story with more self involvement, probably with greater accuracy but far less amusingly. According to Dolin, it was he who simply wired that the ballet was *greatly successful* and could be even more so if the maestro would allow him to cut two minutes from an already overlong score. Stravinsky's return wire was the same as quoted above.)

The critics were hard on everyone involved but they seem to have been harsher with Cole than necessary, throwing barbs like 'Cole Porter seems to have lost his inspiration', and 'the score is serviceable without being distinguished'. Over-looked in Cole's score was one of his most haunting ballads, 'Ev'ry Time We Say Goodbye', but the intimacy this song requires to be effective was quite lost in the cavernous Ziegfeld Theatre. As for the amusing sketch-like songs he had written for Beatrice Lillie ('When I Was a Little Cuckoo' and 'Let's End the Beguine') and Bert Lahr ('Drink'), they simply went on too long or their humour was too cerebral to appeal to a large audience.

Humour is hard to coax into being at any time, but all during the rehearsals for *Seven Lively Arts* Cole had been suffering tremendous pain, now in both legs. Yet, professional that he was, he waited until the show opened before he checked himself into Doctor's Hospital for more surgery. Even before the fiasco of what was later to be called 'Billy Rose's Folly', Cole's belief in himself could be shaken by critical personal reviews. For this last six-year period almost every critic had written that he had gone steadily downhill since *Anything Goes*, and although he seemed to shrug the criticism off, often in print, in his heart of hearts he actually began to believe it. It was little comfort that his shows were sell-outs at the box-office, for he felt this was due to wartime hysteria, his stars or the glorious productions his songs had received. His own gifts, he felt, especially after an out and out flop like *Seven Lively Arts*, were slipping away from him. He was frequently plagued by fits of depression and began worrying unnecessarily about money. He could frequently be found sitting in a darkened room – and when at last he emerged he talked to no one.

He would not heed Linda's advice that they take an immediate holiday. He, who loved so to travel, chose to stay close to New York; nor would he seek the help of a psychiatrist. Perhaps these bouts with his psyche were forerunners of a later mental deterioration that would oblige him totally to give up song-writing in the last decade of his life.

For the moment, the worst – and then the most glorious best – was yet to come.

NOEL
1945-1950

SAMUEL GOLDWYN'S REMARK to Richard Rodgers after the movie mogul had attended the opening night of *Oklahoma!* shows how terrifying it can be to follow a smash hit. He cornered Rodgers in the foyer of the St. James Theatre and congratulated him, adding, 'Do you know what you ought to do next, Dick?' When Rodgers shook his head, Goldwyn supplied the answer. 'Shoot yourself.'

But for the professional, assured of his technique, the abyss into which he must occasionally tumble does possess a safety net. It is generally called a *succès d'estime*, an ego-massaging term that equals the kiss of death at the box office. Cole's *Seven Lively Arts* was one of those.

Hardly six months later, Noel was to experience his own débâcle in *Sigh No More*. The coup de grâce would come a year later with his next work, yet another operetta, *Pacific 1860*.

Sigh No More and *Seven Lively Arts* suffered from the same malady: catering to a specialized audience and artiness. By now, Noel and Cole were masters of technique and knew exactly what *they* wanted to write. In these two revues, they pleased themselves instead of their war-weary patrons looking for a good time. Both men had enough prestige to live down their fiascoes and each work had some extremely beautiful songs.

While he was finishing *Sigh No More* during the spring of 1945, Coward's mood was joyous and confident. He was supported by efficient professionals, especially his new musical secretary, Robb Stewart, who was able to notate music quickly and set keys for the singers. Additionally, he had the help of his wartime touring accompanist, Norman Hackforth, who arranged some of the numbers (and even wrote some) and of Mantovani, who would be conducting.

Remembering that *Operette* was said to have closed because of its lack of stars, this time Noel engaged Joyce Grenfell, a well-known comedienne who had in the past performed in partnership with Richard Addinsell – equally well known as the composer of the *Warsaw Concerto*. Addinsell would write a ballet based on *Blithe Spirit*, and some of the songs he had tailored for Miss Grenfell would be included.

Graham Payn was given all the romantic songs. Born in South Africa, he came originally to Noel's attention when he was auditioning youngsters for *Words and Music* back in 1932. The fourteen-year-old Graham sang 'Nearer My God To Thee' while doing a tap dance, and this combined effect so startled Coward that he hired him on the spot. In time they were to become increasingly intimate friends and Coward was to offer his protégé many important roles, even permitting Graham, who was almost two decades younger, to take over his roles in *Tonight at 8.30* when he himself moved on to other things. Graham, whom Coward nicknamed 'Little Lad', moved in with Noel in the early '40s. Payn, a competent actor, was an ideal Coward juvenile, for the image he projected was of the sensitive, artistic, often elegant chap, a perfect foil for Noel's perpetual strong, wilful heroine. Additionally, there was something in Payn's strong baritone voice that was very attractive to Coward and which inspired him to write some of his most moving music.

For comedy, the show boasted Cyril Ritchard and his wife, Madge Elliott. Ritchard, who had starred in many musicals, was noted for his bossiness and broad, almost pantomimic acting style – the antithesis of the Coward manner of the clenched jaw and throw-away line. Cyril, of course, had a strong ally in Madge, who adored everything her husband did, and the two of them would often join forces against Noel. The couple's heavy over-acting would later prove to be a distinct millstone to the production, which Coward himself was directing.

During previews in Manchester Noel wrote that he was 'depressed because Cyril and Madge ... are spoiling the show ... Cyril did the "Indian Army" song with such raucous vulgarity that I nearly stopped him from the stalls ... For nine weeks,' he was to add, 'I have been bored and irritated at their stupidity.'

Stage matters aside, nothing could dampen Noel's jubilant mood as the war ended. Just a week before *Sigh No More* opened in London the Japanese surrendered and all hostilities ceased. Even the critics were in a benevolent mood, and although Noel, who was fair game to the gentlemen of the press, received less than enthusiastic notices for his music, lyrics and direction, Grenfell and especially Payn, about whose career Noel felt justly proud, enjoyed considerable kudos.

Perhaps the show was not original enough or lavish enough for sustained success. There was very little dancing – merely the arty *Blithe Spirit* ballet at the end. Certainly it was too romantic and definitely not funny enough. But the half-dozen songs quoted below contain some of Coward's best ever work. One of Coward's most memorable songs, 'Sigh No More', is analyzed in the Musical Appendix. 'Matelot' whose musical analysis is also to be found in that section originated because Graham Payn refused to sing the song Coward had written for him. One could hardly blame him, for Coward had earmarked 'It Couldn't Matter Less' as Graham's big solo in the second act.

After having diligently rehearsed the song, Payn announced to the assembled cast that he could not make it work, and that 'the song just isn't good enough'.

Graham Payn sings
'Matelot' in *Sigh No More*,
1945

'Of course it is,' Noel retorted.

'Well, get up and do it then,' Payn shot back.

Graham recalls that Noel indeed had several tries to make something of that mediocre song with its unfortunate title, until at last he gave up and said, 'No. You're right. It isn't very good. I'll write you another.'

Coward had often promised to write songs that never got written, and, sensing he would have no shining moment in the show, Graham was deeply disappointed. But, this time he was lucky, for when Noel was confined to bed with a pulled muscle in his leg the idea for the French sailor song came to him. 'Matelot' and Graham Payn were a perfect combination and this song has been bound to his career.

Another *Sigh No More* gem, 'I Wonder What Happened to Him', was subtitled 'Indian Army Officer' and sung by Cyril Ritchard. It pokes fun at the colonials, Noel's favourite target, with their foggy memories, and hits home perhaps a little more strongly than 'Mad Dogs and Englishmen'. It has a wonderful tune but, because of its hilarious and somewhat shocking words, it is generally recited, not sung, over a piano accompaniment. Its first two refrains are the best:

Whatever became of old Bagot?
I haven't seen him for a year.
Is it true that old Briggs had to marry that
    faggot
He met in the Vale of Kashmir?
Have you had any news of that chap in the
    'Blues'
Was it Prosser or Pycroft or Pym?
He was stationed at Simla, or was it Bengal?
I know he got tight at a ball in Nepal
And wrote sev'ral four letter words on the
    wall.
I wonder what happened to him?

Whatever became of old Shelley?
Is it true that young Forbes was cashiered
For riding quite nude on a push bike
    through Delhi
The day the new Viceroy appeared?
Has anyone heard of that bloke in the 'Third'
Was it Southerby, Sedgewick or Sym?
They had him thrown out of a club in
    Bombay
For, apart from his mess bill exceeding his
    pay,
He took to pig sticking in quite the wrong
    way.
I wonder what happened to him.

Joyce Grenfell, with her droll delivery, made 'That is the End of the News', a song that lambasts the British 'stiff upper lip policy', especially in wartime, one of the show's highlights. Incomprehensibly, the song flopped when sung as a trio during previews in Manchester. Noel, however, believed firmly in its potential and gave it to Joyce.

'I couldn't sing that,' she said, 'because of my reputation on the radio.'

Never brooking insubordination Coward snapped back, 'Just learn the words and music and we'll do it here.' Disgruntled, Joyce had no choice but to follow what Noel (not for nothing called The Master) demanded and learn the song. She was the most surprised of all when 'That Is the End of the News' became another show-stopper. Its frankly boring rhythm and innocuous sing-songy melody only seem to add to its hilarity. My favourite excerpts are printed below:

Verse 2
We are told that it's dismal and dreary
To air our despairs.
We are told to be gallant and cheery
And banish our cares.
So, when fortune gives us a cup of hemlock
    to quaff,
We just give a slight hiccup and laugh, laugh,
    laugh.

Refrain 2
Heigho, everything's fearful,
We do wish that Vi was a little more
    cheerful,
The only result of her last operation
Has been gales of wind at the least
    provocation.
Now, don't laugh, poor Mrs. Mason
Was washing some smalls in the lavatory
    basin

When that old corroded
Gas heater exploded
And blew her smack into the mews.
We're in clover,
Uncle George is in clink
For refusing to work for the war.

Now it's over
Auntie Maud seems to think
He'll be far better placed than before.
What fun – dear little Sidney
Produced a spectacular stone in his kidney,
He's had eleven, so God's in his heaven,
And that is the end of the news.

There were other funny moments: the brilliant 'Nina' which satisfied Cole Porter's penchant for the beguine (see p.137.), and 'The Burchells of Battersea Rise', a riposte from the middle class Noel had called 'this happy breed'.

Then there were the ballads. Besides the exquisite 'Sigh No More', the moving 'Matelot,' the world-weary 'Parting of the Ways', and the tender 'Wait a bit, Joe', this revue introduced 'Never Again'[1] to British audiences. Originally written for *Set To Music*, it has since become a standard, with lines like 'Time changes the tune/ Changes the pale unwinking stars,/ Even the moon./ Let me be soon/ Strong enough to flout romance/ And say "You're out romance"/ Never again.'

Although Coward was to remark that the best thing about *Sigh No More* was its title, one has to feel his self-denigration was self-protective. Certainly, he must have kept a soft spot in his heart for its songs. When preparing his *Essential Noel Coward Song Book* in 1953 he included six songs from this revue, far more than he had culled from any of his other works.

But, shortly after the show opened, and in spite of its mixed reviews, Coward could not be totally depressed. *Brief Encounter* was about to receive raves. 'Not only the most mature work Mr. Coward has yet prepared for the cinema, but one of the most emotionally honest and deeply satisfying films ever made in this country,' was the way C. A. Lejeune, the critic for the *Observer*, put it. History has borne out Miss Lejeune's opinion, for after almost fifty years *Brief Encounter* holds up as an honest and moving film. Its carefully controlled emotional writing was to change the public's – especially the American public's (misguided) – viewpoint of Coward as capable only of flippant, acerbic dialogue that had little to do with the average human heart.

Noel's own heart had been in good condition while he was writing the screenplay for, in mid-summer that year, he bought the leasehold on a house by the sea. He would not have abandoned his beloved country house, Goldenhurst, but it had been requisitioned by the army, and though now vacated was badly in need of repair. Totally unable to do any creative writing in London, and knowing it would take a great deal of money and at least five years, with the difficulty of getting permits and materials, to repair his home, he looked for another temporary retreat. At last he found a house overlooking the Channel,

---

[1] Perhaps this song flopped in the US because Americans felt uncomfortable with the refrain's frequently rhyming 'again' with 'pain'. In New York 'again' rhymes properly with 'pen'.

and so close to the sea that, when the tide was high and the weather stormy, the waves broke over the sea-facing wall – a sensation Noel, with his sense of the dramatic, adored. White Cliffs, as he called his new retreat, was at St. Margaret's Bay, near Dover, and helped by his secretary, Cole Lesley, Noel moved in immediately. Graham Payn would drive down for weekends after the Saturday performances of *Sigh No More*. Then, as the box office for the revue became less than profitable, Noel began work on another operetta or, as he always Frenchified the term, operette.

By now he had eased himself back into the comfortable creative routine that worked so well for him before the war. Soon after he had finished converting White Cliffs, Gladys Calthrop bought a house directly above his, and with Joyce Carey and Clemence Dane coming down there were enough weekend distractions to stave off Noel's perennial boredom. But Monday to Saturday midday was devoted to solitary work. There, often with a clear view of France from his window he outlined *Somolo*, later to be called *Scarlet Lady*, and eventually produced as *Pacific 1860*, in five days.

He had Irene Dunne in mind to star in this story of a mature opera star who finds and loses her young love. The original plot had Kerry, the younger son of an important colonial, meeting Elena, the ostracised scarlet lady, while she is recuperating on the tropical island of Somolo[2]. Kerry is engaged to be married to his childhood sweetheart, but at first sight falls in love with Elena, and she with him. Because of contracts arranged by her crafty manager, at the close of the second act she must leave at once to appear in a series of opera houses all over the world. She writes to Kerry to come to the boat, but he misses the sailing. When she returns, a full year and an act later, it is only to learn that Kerry has just been married and is going off on his honeymoon. The saddened, wiser Elena has a tearful aria while the crowd sing happy songs offstage.

Unfortunately this plot, although resembling that of *Der Rosenkavalier*, time-worn and with a sentimental operetta quality, was changed greatly. As it was conceived, it might have recaptured some of the rueful quality Noel achieved in *Bitter Sweet*. Certainly the final scene is any actress-singer's dream, alone on stage with the counterpoint of the background chorus. But the whole play had to be adjusted because Irene Dunne could not obtain a release from her film commitments. Yvonne Printemps, enchanting in *Conversation Piece*, was considered, but her English was too poor. Finally Mary Martin, trapped in her own succès d'estime, the lavish but dull *Lute Song*, was asked, and wired from Broadway that she would be delighted to appear in Coward's operette.

---

[2] Somolo, a sort of never-never land, was an island Noel invented for *We Were Dancing*, one of the plays in *Tonight at 8.30*. He and Cole Leslie minutely pinpointed its location, topography, history, etc. in a full-page insert in *Pacific 1860*'s programme. Coward's inspiration seems to have come from his great love of sun-drenched islands in general and of Jamaica in particular.

Noel cast her unthinkingly in the role of Elena. Miss Martin was a star of the first magnitude, then in her early thirties and looking far younger. She would be playing opposite Graham Payn, who appeared to be the same age but was actually five years younger. This coupled with the fact that Mary Martin was a 'belter', which means she had a chest voice, not the traditional soprano of operetta, was enough to set *Pacific 1860* on a clear course for disaster.

The biggest hurdle now would be adjusting the love-him-and-lose-him plot, for it was obvious that, with a young star like Mary Martin, the lovers would have to be reunited at the finale. But how? Coward changed the story so that Elena returns in the last act amid the cheering – as before – and we learn that the cheering is because of a wedding. The newly-weds are Kerry's *brother* and *his* betrothed. All ends as expected: Kerry has waited for his true love's return and the curtain can descend – minus the sad solo – on a happy throng.

Pacific 1860 had originally been scheduled to open at His Majesty's Theatre but, when that medium-size stage was unavailable, Prince Littler placed it in the cavernous Theatre Royal, Drury Lane, then undergoing repairs from bomb damage during the war. At first Noel was delighted because he had kept a soft spot for 'The Lane' since it had brought him such good luck when

Mary Martin and Graham Payn (on steps) in *Pacific 1860*

he mounted *Cavalcade* there. He did not anticipate a permit for repairs that were supposed to be completed before the production went on stage in the beginning of November, being denied. This meant that construction would be going on simultaneously with rehearsals. Not only were the auditorium seats being hammered into place shortly before the opening, but the stage floor was being replaced and, worst of all, there was no heating. As if the fates had ganged up against the production, it turned out to be the coldest winter of the decade, and of course the cast was dressed in skimpy costumes suitable to the South Pacific island of Somolo.

To fill Drury Lane's enormous stage the cast had now to expand to over a hundred, and the production was too unwieldy to mark time out of London for there was no theatre available large enough to accommodate the set. Rehearsals, rushed as they were, had to be held there in that frigid barn, most of the cast singing through chattering teeth.

Fully a month before the opening in mid-December, Noel knew there were many things wrong with his operetta. Chiefly, it was his star who was hopelessly miscast. Not only did her strong Texas accent jar with the broad British sound of the others, but her drawl made her words incomprehensible. Much more critical was the score's unsuitability to her voice. In a mad scramble to lighten the operetta quality and hoping to turn the work into an acceptable musical comedy, he pressed. 'Alice Is at It Again', a song with a light-hearted view of prostitution, on Mary Martin. The number was totally wrong for Elena's character in the play or for Mary's own stage image. After a few rehearsals she chose to drop the song. Noel was predictably piqued.

There were other stumbling blocks between star and management, not the least of which was a running feud between Mary and Gladys Calthrop. As related by Graham Payn, it seems Mary told Gladys that in the costume design she was 'allergic to bows, and Calthrop's design for the all-important ball gown was covered with bows'. Noel, of course, was forced to take sides and as director could only stand with his designer against the star. Nor would she wear a wig or arrange her hair in the manner of the 1860s until Guthrie McClintic, the American director, persuaded her. Further pique.

But the failure of *Pacific 1860* all boils down to the inadequacy of the work. It seems incredible that a brilliant man of the theatre like Coward could be unaware of the changes that had moved musical libretti from unreality to believability since *Oklahoma!*, which had been written almost four years before.[3] *Pacific 1860* was a throwback to a much earlier, more naive period. Among the more laughable inconsistencies of the evening was the gobbledy-

[3] Ironically, Rodgers and Hammerstein's landmark musical, which would chalk up a run of 1,548 performances, was to be Drury Lane's next tenant. Mary Martin would captivate that theatre's audience in 1951 in the same team's *South Pacific*, which would run well into 1953.

gook sung by the natives of this mythical island, followed almost immediately by a Cowardesque waltz and a primitive hymn that tries to imitate a volcano erupting.

The newspapers uniformly attacked the show. They heaped further insult on Coward's head by comparing him to Ivor Novello. Noel was to write: 'The blackest and beastliest day of the year. To begin with a blast of abuse from the Press. Not one good notice, the majority being frankly vile.'

At first Noel thought of restructuring the show, especially its first act, but decided 'if the critics and the public don't like the show, that's their affair but I won't muck about with it and alter something that I consider charming and accurate and risk pleasing nobody, even myself'. Later, he changed his mind and, in a frantic attempt to add lightness to the evening, cleaned up another smutty cabaret number, 'Uncle Harry', which he had written two years before in Jamaica and added it to the score, although it was in a totally different genre.

But no amount of tinkering could breathe life into *Pacific 1860*. Unlike *Sigh No More*, the show had no fresh or even amusing songs Coward could be proud of; this operetta boasted only tired waltzes and polkas, a gypsy song that was not half so good as *Bitter Sweet*'s 'Zigeuner', a finger-wagging 'This is a Changing World', and two predictable numbers doomed to fall flat because their titles gave away their punch lines: 'I Wish I Wasn't Quite Such a Big Girl' and 'We're Sick of Being Pretty Little Bridesmaids (Instead of Being Pretty Little Brides)'. *Pacific 1860* staggered on for four frigid months. It was kept alive by Coward's and Martin's prestige, playing to half-empty houses most of whose patrons were frozen blue by the time the long evening ended. At its closing it had lost the then tremendous sum of £28,000 and severely damaged Noel's reputation in the musical theatre. But Coward followed the advice he so often gave others: 'Rise above it.'

No fool he, Coward knew the easiest way to rise above a failure is to follow it immediately with a guaranteed success. The last waltzes of *Pacific 1860* had hardly stopped swirling before Noel opened in *Present Laughter*, the play London had seen briefly – and adored – in 1943. The role of Garry Essendine, a romantic actor, came to him naturally[4] and had the relaxing dividend of allowing him to show off at the piano. The play recreates the drawing room comedy for which he was so famous, and it was no surprise to anyone (although he left the cast almost as soon as the play was on its feet) that the production ran for 520 performances.

---

[4] The glib phrases falling so easily off his tongue, Noel never realized the role was so long or complicated until a year later when he decided to play it in French – and succeeded. On the continent it was called *Joyeux Chagrins*, a direct translation from his original title *Sweet Sorrow*.

It was while he was playing Essendine that Coward's head turned towards a play he had started to write the year before – based on the daring idea of what might have happened had the Germans successfully invaded and occupied Britain. Called *Peace In Our Time*, it was particularly vitriolic towards Coward's bête noire, Neville Chamberlain, and his folly of appeasement. It was also far out of step with the quest for post-war escapism. Couched as it was in the *expected* Coward style of dialogue, Noel's melodramatic fantasy could not possibly have succeeded, especially after having received almost unanimously dreadful notices. The play did boast some splendid performances and made a valiant try, lasting for 167 performances in the West End. Writing from America, after he had heard about *Peace In Our Time*'s critical reception, he penned a rare diatribe against his country:

> ... if that play turns out to be a flop, I shall be forced to the reluctant and pompous conclusion that England does not deserve my work. That is a good play, written with care and heart and guts and it is beautifully acted and directed ... I have a sick at heart feeling about England anyhow. We are so idiotic and apathetic and it is nothing to do with the 'after the war' because we were the same at Munich.

It seemed that Coward's time for producing new works had passed. But his name and personality were larger than life, and revivals first of *Tonight at 8:30* and later of both *Private Lives* and *Fallen Angels* played on. As the 1940s petered out Noel busied himself with building a house in Jamaica, painting, writing short stories and working on his autobiography. He even found time to expand one of the successful segments of *Tonight at 8:30*, *The Astonished Heart*, for the cinema. He not only wrote the script and acted the leading role but wrote the quite appropriate background music. Then, once the picture was released, he adapted his score into a suite for piano. Its four movements, *Maestoso moderato*, *Espressivo*, *Vivo*, and *Tempo di Valse* (which concludes with a return of the *Maestoso* for a fortissimo finale), sound a bit like salon music that is trying to infiltrate the concert hall. Coward's transparent piano writing is heavily coated with bombast, making the suite slightly pretentious, although competently written.

Now it was time to write another musical, but not an operetta or a revue – he intended to modernize his output and create 'an authentic musical comedy'. Agreed, when one looks at the work, called by the disarming title of *Ace of Clubs*, the name of the *boîte* in Soho where the action takes place, one sees instead 'an authentic musical comedy' of the '30s, but that mattered very little to Coward's audience who relished their idol being a couple of decades behind.

Fortunately, Noel did not altogether leave his experience with revue behind. The unit set Gladys Calthrop designed, with a stage-within-the-stage, could be used for incidental numbers as in a revue, and the toughs, streetwalkers, chorus dancers, bar-girls and sailors necessary to his (somewhat convoluted) plot lent flexibility.

This was to be Noel's first real musical. Determined to make it up to date, for the first time he poured a plotted musical play into two acts. Because of his frequent hops across the Atlantic to see the latest on Broadway he was familiar with all the elements that went into other musicals, and not averse to raiding them. From his friend Cole Porter he borrowed the theme – involvement with gangsters, apparent in Cole's every hit including his latest blockbuster, *Kiss Me, Kate*; from Rodgers and Hart, the night club setting of *Pal Joey* and *On Your Toes*, and from Bernstein, Comden and Green, the gallant sailor on leave, protector of womanhood, as personified in *On the Town*. But *Ace of Clubs* had its closest similarity to the Gershwin-Bolton-Wodehouse *Oh, Kay* with its gangsterism, elegance and clever heroine.[5]

To give Coward his due, he did create some prototypes for Broadway to emulate: 'Three Juvenile Delinquents' was the forerunner of the Bernstein-Sondheim 'Gee, Officer Krupke' from *West Side Story*, and the *Ace of Clubs* chorine-heroine, Pinkie, always strikes me as the basis for Frank Loesser's Miss Adelaide in *Guys and Dolls*, which opened less than a year later.

The score of *Ace of Clubs* has an equal share of hits and misses. As with so much of Coward's (and Cole's) later work, there seems to be no middle course, his songs seem to be either inventive, moving and fresh; or derivative and forced.

The story involves a sailor, Harry Hornby, who knocks down the thug who tries to kiss Pinkie while she passes through the audience singing her song, an unquenchable torch, 'My Kind of Man'. (With its opening melodic line strait-jacketed into a tired diminished chord, we can see that this song would only work as travesty.)

As Pinkie and Harry rush from the club, inadvertently taking the thugs' stolen diamond bracelet, they find a Soho bench and sing a fine love song. Noel gives little thought to the first axiom of musical construction: that action should be moved along further with each song, when he ends 'This Could Be True' with a static: 'This could be sweet/ Gay and discreet/ If you will give me your hand/

5 Gertrude Lawrence was Kay, and she played and sang unforgettably.

The future's at our feet./This is the most incredible, magical moment we ever knew,/So to hell with rules and regulations, Darling/ This must be true.'

The proprietress of the *Ace of Clubs* is the kind of wise, mature soprano Coward placed on the pedestal of all his operettas. Now she comes on again as Rita, the second lead, and the woman who is in love with the semi-bad secondary thug. Rita's song starts as an up-dated beguine (Fig. 1) but in its refrain shifts into a lovely bitter-sweet *valse lente*. (Fig. 2)

Fig. 1

Fig. 2

The nightclub setting works for the next numbers, a sailor's shanty and a real love song. Called 'I'd Never, Never Know', its lyric, sung by Pinkie, contains prosaic stuff like: 'Why is the summer giving/London this lovely glow?/ What is the joy of living?/ Without him I'd never never know.' But Coward proves he has not lost his touch when, in the release, he writes simply, 'He won't please the highbrows/ Or drive Alan Ladd from the screen,/ But when he lifts his eyebrows/ I blush like a girl of fifteen.'

    Towards the end of the act after the lovers have had a minor quarrel, Noel brings on one of his finest songs, 'Sail Away'. So little of the emotional power of this song was tapped in *Ace of Clubs* that Coward wisely used it as the title song and indeed the emotional pivot of his 1961 musical of the same title.[6]

Now Pinkie gets her big number. Dressed in a Directoire-style white silk dress with a long blue velvet cloak and a glittering tiara, she comes on as the Empress Josephine. I have quoted only sixteen bars of the melody, but the lyric (although it could perhaps benefit from a final punch) is too good to let pass.

Jo - se - phine,___ Jo - se - phine___ from the first was ra - ther chic,___

As   a   tot___ she would trot___ thru the Is - land of Mar - ti - nique___

The lady was beautiful,	On volumes of history
The lady was dark,	And thousands of cheques
She wasn't too dutiful	And all through the mystery
But still left her mark	Of 'Ole Debbil Sex.

[6] 'Sail Away', both with its verse as originally written for *Ace of Clubs* and totally rewritten for *Sail Away*, is analysed in the Musical Appendix.

Ace of Clubs

Refrain 1

Josephine, Josephine
From the first was rather chic.
As a tot she would trot
Through the island of Martinique.
Her fortune was told by an aged old crone
Who prophesied fame and romance
And who hissed in her ear
The outrageous idea
That she'd also be empress of France.
Josephine, Josephine
Had with men a set routine,
And the people who thought
Her technique was self-taught
Didn't know
Josephine

Verse 2

Whatever she nearly did
From five to fifteen
We know that she really did
Begin the Beguine.
On first meeting Bonaparte
She murmured, 'Hell's Bells!
You let down the tone apart
From everything else.'

Refrain 2

Josephine, Josephine
Very seldom lost control
Though her wit was a bit

Overseasoned with 'Sauce Créole'.
She very soon married
This short young man
Who talked about soldiers all day,
But who wasn't above
Making passionate love
In a very coarse Corsican way.
Josephine wasn't keen
And Napoleon made a scene.
He said 'Dear, your unwilling
Behaviour is killing
The show, Josephine.'

Refrain 3

Josephine, Josephine
As a queen remained at home,
While her lord
Was abroad
Sending postcards in code from Rome.
He often appeared with a three-day beard
From Austria, Poland or Spain.
And one dreadful night
He arrived rather tight
Having messed up the Russian campaign.
Josephine, turning green,
Cried, 'Whatever does this mean?'
Then Napoeon said, 'Whoops
'I have lost all my troops
In the snow, Josie—
Oh, Josie,
Snow, Josephine.'

Borrowing a page from Cole, Coward has the chorus girls parade through the audience singing the first act finale, the single entendre 'Would You Like To Stick a Pin in My Balloon?'[7], but the curtain has no sooner risen on act two than we are off again with more cabaret numbers: a pastoral in front of an olio, 'In a Boat on a Lake with My Darling,' and 'I Like America', which Coward was to use a decade later with great success in his Las Vegas cabaret appearances.

As the second act winds down, surprise is non-existent. The missing diamonds and the chief gangster will be turned over to the police, Rita's Benny will be let off with a stiff warning, and Pinkie and her Harry will 'Sail Away'. En route to that happy ending we hear 'Chase Me, Charlie'.

Chase   me,   Char - lie,   Chase me,   Char - lie   o - ver the   gar - den

[7] This song's message couched in child-porn is the same as Cole's 'Jimmy Won't Gimmie his Yo-Yo'. Both numbers were denied publication.

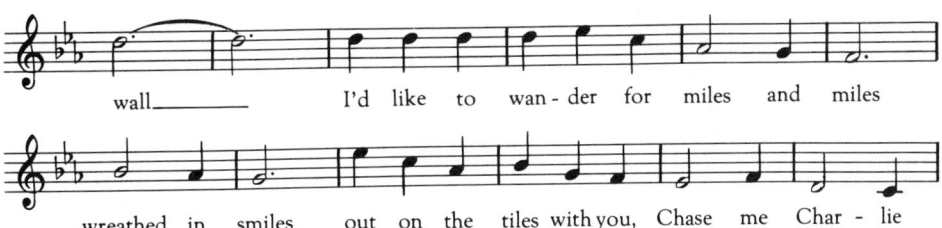

wall_____   I'd like to wan-der for miles and miles

wreathed in   smiles   out on the tiles with you, Chase me Char - lie

Coward subtitled *Ace of Clubs* 'A New Musical Play', and in light of his previous productions it might have been the 'New Musical Coward'. Most of the critics gave it faint praise, enjoying a field day with card-game metaphors: 'Not the ace of trumps, but it will serve to take the trick', 'Just a jack, not an ace', etc.

At first the box-office fared far better than the reviews would indicate and Noel went off for to New York to do some recordings feeling he had a hit in his pocket. His euphoria was short-lived for he soon received word that business was down to half-capacity. This prompted him to record in his journal, 'Oh Christ! It seems as though it is a flop after all. I really am very, very angry. If the public don't want to see that easy entertainment and listen to those lyrics and that music and if they do want to pack out [Ivor Novello's] *King's Rhapsody*, then they can get on with it.'

Yet there were many still who remembered Coward's pre-eminence in all forms of theatre and who knew that his name translated in to big dollars at the box-office. In September he was entreated by Richard Rodgers to direct and star in *The King and I* opposite Gertrude Lawrence. 'All this is very soothing to a bruised ego,' he wrote, adding that it might be an excellent thing 'as I get two percent of the gross which would amount to $1,000 a week for years if it were a hit, also $5,000 down and all expenses. It would entail three months' work.' His friends begged him to accept, but after giving the matter intense thought he entered in his diary:

> (a) Although probably some arrangement could be made with the Treasury, I should not by any means really get all that money.[8]
> (b) In three months I could either write a new play for myself or a novel or both or neither. But at least I'd be carrying out my own plan of relaxing for a year.
> In fact, tempting and exciting as it sounds, it would actually be a waste of time. I know that this is a moment in my life when I must really be careful. I have earned time to think and I am going to have it.

Rodgers sent over the script for Noel to read and he had to admit it was a splendid one. Then, over a high-powered lunch attended by many of those who would be involved in the new production, Noel told Rodgers he could not possibly do it because he was planning to go to Jamaica to write a new play

---

[8] Meaning that the Inland Revenue would take a huge bite.

for the Lunts by the end of March. Rodgers 'urged and pleaded, and offered to advance the production' so that Noel could get to Jamaica in March.

Noel dined that very night with his old and close friend, the novelist Edna Ferber, and of course talked to her about Rodgers's offer. 'Nonsense,' she said, 'why should you do a thing like that when there is no "food" in it for you?' 'I could have kissed her,' Noel wrote. When he arrived at his Manhattan apartment that evening he found a cable from London. Business at *Ace of Clubs* was up £500 for the week.

Soon he would be back in London, where the show would chalk up a respectable run of 250 performances. And, as his fiftieth birthday approached, he wasted few hours glancing back over his shoulder. He was looking for new ideas, new plays, experiences that might give him, as Edna Ferber had put it, 'food'.

COLE
1945 - 1951

A S FAR BACK AS 1934, Warner Brothers had offered Cole vast sums of money for the rights to film a story of his life. At his every refusal the studio countered by increasing the advance, but still Porter would not hear of it. It was generally thought that he did not need the money, but only a few people suspected that Cole was perhaps reluctant to allow the studio to research the past, his suspect war record, his and Linda's true ages, their marriage of convenience, and his and possibly Linda's homosexuality.

Cole might have continued to deny Hollywood the opportunity to peer into his most private world had his most revered colleague, Irving Berlin, not telephoned him in early 1942 (long before the *Seven Lively Arts* fiasco) to say that a great idea which might help America's war effort had given him a sleepless night. He was certain Cole's record of accomplishment, the string of hits he had just had, all coming after his accident, would be an inspiration to US servicemen and women wounded in action. Cole was persuaded but Linda thought it an abominable idea. She was not mollified until Cole assured her that they both would have approval of the actors who portrayed them and of the entire script. When she finally agreed, he called Warners and told them to go ahead and develop a screenplay.

His acceptance of the movie offer was not as altruistic as it sounds, for at the time Cole was what most businesspeople would call mildly but, with his passion for order and paying bills when they were presented, deeply in debt. The previous year he had added a new swimming pool to Buxton Hill and that spring he surprised Linda by enclosing her large sun-porch. Although Cole's royalties were high and the income from his holdings substantial, the Porters' lifestyle was even more substantial. Not only were they responsible for the upkeep of the Paris house (Linda had not sold it, merely closed it down), but since their reconciliation they had taken two separate residences in the expensive Waldorf Towers. And there were the Malibu houses and the two-hundred-acre estate at Buxton Hill, each requiring staff. Additionally, the Porter ménage in New York alone included six full-time salaried employees: chauffeur, valet, cook, secretary, a maid-of-all-work and a personal maid for Linda. Cole's twenty-odd operations had taken most of their ready cash and they had recently had a copyright infringement suit slapped on them, on top of which the US internal revenue department was demanding immediate payment of a $90,000 tax bill. The $300,000 Warners offered Cole for the right to film his life was a windfall.

Night and Day, as the picture was to be called, had trouble finding a plot, but in this respect it was not so different from the romantic rubbish Hollywood had long been fostering on a gullible public as the true stories of song-writers' lives. Kern, Rodgers and Hart, even Chopin, had had their lives turned into near-fiction.

Cole would be an even harder subject. Orson Welles, decrying the lack of story-line in his life, said, 'The only suspense will be – will he or will he not accumulate ten million dollars?' Finally, the director, Michael Curtiz, came to Cole's apartment and presented him with a script hammered out by Charles Hoffman, Leo Townsend, and William Bowers. Porter said, 'It was the strangest feeling – as if reading about someone I knew slightly.' Then he added, 'It ought to make a good film – none of it is true.'

Even more ludicrous would be the casting: Cole insisted that Cary Grant should impersonate him, while Linda chose Alexis Smith as her alter ego. Monty Woolley, brought into the film at his friend's request, was cast, not as Cole's contemporary, but as a Yale professor who prefers the stage to the classroom.

From the scenes of the fortyish Grant walking the New Haven campus, to his outlandish composing of 'Night and Day' during the drip, drip, drip of a tropical rainstorm, the picture is pure hokum. Among the outright fabrications in the plot, Cole's war record is magnified and he is portrayed as a soldier-hero, badly wounded by an exploding bomb. Nurse Alexis Smith (Linda who, in reality, hardly knew how to apply a Band-Aid) ministers with Tender Loving Care, which later leads to their passionate love affair.

As if this were not enough, Hollywood seemed to have got its geography muddled and added to the incongruity by having the Porter Indiana mansion staffed with black servants from the Deep South. Typically celluloid was the anachronism of portraying all the songs out of the time frame in which they were written.

But one cannot blame Curtiz and the Warners, for Cole and Linda clearly wanted to see themselves idealized in the picture. Porter actually insisted that the one honest episode, the reading of his grandfather's will, be cut because it might be embarrassing to his cousins, who felt (and rightly so) that his mother and Cole had been given the lion's share.

Night and Day's budget originally allowed for all the stars who had appeared in Porter productions to come on and do cameos of his songs. Arthur Schwartz, the movie's producer, had even prevailed upon Cole to write and ask them to contribute, but during the shooting, as costs spiralled, it was decided that Ginny Simms – Hollywood's all-purpose singer – could sing the songs made famous by Irene Bordoni, Ethel Merman, Virginia Bruce, Sophie Tucker – even William Gaxton. The only star who sang the song she had introduced was Mary Martin who came west to repeat 'My Heart Belongs to Daddy'.

Because of these false economies which Cole felt could only cheapen the final film and because of continuing friction between Cole and the film's producer, Arthur Schwartz, Cole and Linda left Hollywood during the making of *Night and Day* to return to New York. Schwartz, a first-rate composer, who had collaborated with Howard Dietz, coincidentally now head of production at Paramount (together they had written 'Dancing in the Dark', 'By Myself', 'I Guess I'll Have to Change My Plan', etc.), had antagonized Cole before when he insisted that many of the songs from the unproduced *Mississippi Belle* be re-written. Cole, who preferred creating a totally new song to re-writing, had no patience with critical producers – he wanted them to concentrate on adulation. When he signed his contract for *Mexican Hayride*, Cole had promised Mike Todd another show, and now seemed the perfect time to honour the commitment. Todd had taken an option on Jules Verne's 1897 novel, *Around the World in 80 Days*, and asked Orson Welles to adapt and direct it.

Once the rehearsals began, it soon became clear that Welles would not be content to wear merely two hats. He evidently wanted to adapt, write, direct, star and even produce the project, as he had done with great éclat with *The War of the Worlds* and *Citizen Kane*. Todd soon bowed out. But not Cole, who was always intrigued by gargantuan theatrical personalities like Billy Rose, Todd or Welles. Unfortunately, Welles's desire to be a theatrical superman was the undoing of *Around the World*, whose title he shortened as his first directorial act.

When they began working together Cole was fascinated by Welles's energy and wrote to a friend, 'Even if the show flops, I shall at least have had the experience of working with a wonderful guy,' but as they got closer to opening night, and Welles began to cut song after song, Cole became disenchanted with his producer's enormous ego and left for Hollywood, telling Welles that his early departure was to fulfil his commitment to write the score for an MGM film called *The Pirate*. But, as he left New York on the very day before *Around the World* opened, Welles interpreted such action coming from Cole who so loved opening nights as a stinging slap.

Around the World, which Welles himself described as 'an extravaganza in two acts and thirty-four scenes', opened the next night, a sweltering May 31, 1946, in the non-air-conditioned Adelphi Theater. Never one to do things by halves, the production included silent movies, *Hellzapoppin'*-like skits, exotic dances, a two-ton mechanical elephant and, when things became bogged down, an extended magic show with Welles as the chief prestidigitator. Cole's score, which by now had been cut to 'book-songs', seemed no more than serviceable. So much was happening nightly on stage, in the balcony, in the aisles, that any score would be lost in the mêlée. All the critics decried the evening as one of excess without art, but Howard Barnes excoriated Welles's production by calling it 'more exhibitionistic than entertaining', thus dooming it to closure before the summer was over.

Ironically, after the demise of Welles's production, Mike Todd waltzed back in and re-acquired the rights to the property. His Todd AO film adaptation, now called *Around the World in 80 Days*, starring David Niven, Shirley MacLaine and Cantinflas, became one of the major motion pictures of 1956. The score and title song, which won the Academy Award, were the work of Victor Young. None of Cole's music was used.

But that summer, with the release of *Night and Day*, Cole's star was once again in the ascendant. That the film was a huge box-office success was a tribute to the magic in Cole Porter's songs. Every critic laughed at the ridiculous casting of Grant and Smith, the ludicrous story, and the economy of having a colourless actress strive valiantly to play all the singing parts, but to a man they wrote that Cole's classy and now classic songs provided whatever entertainment value *Night and Day* had. The picture's release also gave new impetus to his oeuvre. 'What Is This Thing Called Love', 'Night and Day', 'I Get Kick Out of You', 'Begin the Beguine' and 'Just One of Those Things' were now ranked among the top forty all-time US song favourites.

With his return to Hollywood and the beginning of work on *The Pirate*, Cole was once more in his element. Writing romantic songs for the substantial voice of Judy Garland and for the lighter, but eminently musical one of Gene Kelly was its own reward. Adapted by S.N. Behrman from a swashbuckling romance which had starred the Lunts, *The Pirate* was produced by MGM musicals' Freed unit and directed by Vincente Minnelli who was at the time Judy Garland's husband. Judy sang 'Mack the Black', 'Love of My Life', and 'You Can Do No Wrong', Gene Kelly the romantic 'Nina' (no relation to Noel's cantankerous 'Nina' from *Sigh No More*) to her. As Kelly came to know Cole better he confided that he thought the score lacked a knock-down, drag-out, song and dance number. Always quick to oblige, Cole presented him with the best number in the score, 'Be a Clown', the next morning. Minnelli then turned it into a duet over Judy Garland's objections. Judy said she could not see the humour in the lyrics, but a summary of some of the lines shows she was searching in the wrong places.

> If you become a doctor, folks 'll face you with dread,
> If you become a dentist, they'll be glad when you're dead,
> You'll get a bigger hand if you can stand on your head,
> Be a clown, be a clown, be a clown.
> A butcher or a baker ladies never embrace,
> A barber for a beau would be a social disgrace,

They all'll come to call if you can fall on your face,
Be a clown, be a clown, be a clown.
A college education I should never propose,
A bachelor's degree won't even keep you in clo'es,
But millions you will win if you can spin on your nose,
Be a clown, be a clown, be a clown.
If you become a farmer, you've the weather to buck,
If you become a gambler, you'll be stuck with your luck,
But jack you'll never lack if you can quack like a duck,
Be a clown, be a clown, be a clown.

In its final release the film of *The Pirate* used only five Porter songs out of the eight he turned in. But they were good ones, helping the film achieve some of the cult status it has enjoyed in recent years and almost erasing the stigma of the unenthusiastic notices it received when it first came out.

But, for Cole, this period seemed to be his nadir. With two gigantic Broadway flops and a tepid movie score, the word on the street was that the Porter well had run dry. To make matters worse, for the last two years, Broadway had enjoyed its best seasons in a decade. While all around him others were turning out flourishing hits (Rodgers and Hammerstein with the long-running *Oklahoma!* and *Carousel*, Irving Berlin scoring a bull's-eye with his phenomenal *Annie Get Your Gun*, and younger teams like Lerner and Loewe and Harburg and Lane impressing both critics and public with *Brigadoon* and *Finian's Rainbow*), producers and librettists seemed to be avoiding Cole and no new project beckoned. Even the biographical *Night and Day* worked against him, stamping him with the image of a song-writer from the past.

Cole had even gone so far afield from the accepted Broadway community as to approach Elaine Carrington, a well-known writer of sentimental soap-operas, to collaborate with him on a musical about a beauty contest. Carrington had submitted the libretto for the first act when Cole was approached by the agent for Arnold Saint Subber who had been stage manager for the Lunts. Hearing the famous couple bicker offstage during a performance of *The Taming of the Shrew*, he conceived the idea of a back-biting play within a play. Saint Subber (he was soon to drop the 'Arnold') had enlisted Lemuel Ayres, costume- and set-designer,[1] as his co-producer, and as their first creative act had approached Burton Lane to write the music. Rejected by Lane who had been deluged with offers since the smash success of *Finian's Rainbow*, the inexperienced team abandoned their quest for a song-writer – but not before commissioning Sam and Bella Spewack, who had fashioned the excellent book for Porter's *Leave It to Me*, to shape the libretto.

Just as Bella was later to have difficulty convincing Cole to abandon his beauty contest musical so did these producers have difficulty in convincing the

---

[1] Ayres had won rave notices for his atmospheric sets for 'Oklahoma!' and 'Bloomer Girl'.

Spewacks that *The Taming of the Shrew* might be turned into an amusing musical.

'It's a lousy play,' Bella had said at first. 'One of the worst Shakespeare ever wrote; I read it in high school.'

But, after she had thought about it for a few weeks, she came up with an almost perfect musical comedy idea – how the players off-stage could be transformed in the way Shakespeare's characters on-stage are. She herself approached Cole. He refused – saying that Shakespeare always had a limited run on Broadway, and reminding her that his work in *Seven Lively Arts* and *Around the World* had been severely criticised for being too high-brow. No, he would work on something that the common man could relate to, simple emotions, postcard settings, plentiful cheese-cake – the beauty contest was it.

Bella would not be put off. She pointed out that the story was not Elizabethan at all but that Shakespeare had borrowed it from a common Orthodox Jewish tale. In her religion, the younger daughter is not allowed to marry until her older sister is safely wed and tucked away. *The Taming of the Shrew* was merely an amplification of that. She browbeat and flattered Cole alternately.

Still he was not sure, and was about to follow Dr. Moorhead's advice to bake his right leg in the California sun, until he found out that the US Department of Internal Revenue were insisting he pay a higher tax if he spent more than six months and one day in California. Frugal millionaire that he was, he decided to remain in New York. Beginning treatment which was so painful that he frequently lost consciousness, he realized that the only way to get through this difficult time was to plunge himself deeply into work. And, although Oscar Hammerstein had advised him to continue work on the beauty contest libretto, he discarded it and immersed himself instead in Bella's Shakespearean imbroglio.

Using Saint Subber's idea of the argumentative stars as a point of departure, Bella had developed a plot concerning the newly-divorced Fred Graham and Lilli Vanessi, musical comedy luminaries who are constantly feuding while trying out a musical version of *The Shrew* in Baltimore (Fred is Petruchio and Lilli is Kate). In the company are Lois Lane and Bill Calhoun who constantly have to postpone their wedding plans because of Bill's compulsive gambling and Lois's unstable fidelity. (They play Bianca and Lucentio.)

The story, which begins a few hours before opening night ('Another Op'nin', Another Show') progresses through the love song ('So In Love'[2]) Lilli sings when she receives flowers from Fred that he intended for Lois. Although basically in love with Fred, Lilli, for her part, is engaged to the stuffed shirt,

[2] See Musical Analysis Appendix.

Harrison Howell. Now, due to go on stage, she buries the card with its note to Lois in her bosom, and it is only after Fred as Petruchio sings his emotional ballad ('Were Thine That Special Face') that she has a chance to read it. As Kate, she has just sung 'I Hate Men!' but as Lilli she is moved by Fred's ardour – that is until she reads the note. Then she becomes Shakespeare's hellcat.

By way of sub-plot, early in the first act, two gangsters are sent to collect an IOU Bill has passed and to which he has signed Fred's name. After they have impounded the show until they get their money, Fred calls on Lilli for help. She, in turn, telephones her suitor, rich Harrison, to bail the company out so that the show can go on. He rushes to the theatre, but on his way to Lilli's backstage dressing room runs into Lois who reminds him that they have met before when he told her his name was Harold. 'Don't you remember,' she insists, 'we met in front of the Harvard Club. I had something in my eye, and you took me to Atlantic City to take it out?'

The gangsters have been holding the principals of the company at gunpoint but in the final scenes, as Lois promises Bill that she will give up all her extra-curricular activities and Lilli and Fred decide to sneak off and get remarried, they announce that their boss has been 'rubbed out', and sing a show-stopping number ('Brush Up Your Shakespeare') as the play within the play winds up with Kate-Lilli confessing, 'I Am Ashamed That Women Are So Simple.'[3]

Although its sounds somewhat involved on paper, so convoluted indeed that Cole claimed he could not follow it even after three readings, the elements of this plot fit together remarkably well. Once Porter had fleshed out the story with music and lyrics that always advance the action, the evening became a tour de force of intrigue, literate dialogue, songs that reflected a great love affair like Lilli's and Fred's; light-heartedly sexy ones like 'Tom, Dick and Harry' or 'Always True To You In My Fashion' for Lois, and songs that *might* have been written for a splendid musical version of *The Taming of the Shrew*. Perhaps it is the brilliant anachronistic quality of these quasi-canzonettas that makes *Kiss Me, Kate* work on so many levels. With its dazzling settings and costumes, one believes this is no second-rate touring company giving audiences confidence that what they are witnessing is as close as they will ever come to eavesdropping on real backstage life.

Just as the action of the book moves in and out from *The Shrew* to back-stage intrigue, so Cole's score alternates deftly between the on-stage play and the showbiz songs for Fred, Lilli, et al. 'Another Op'nin, Another Show', 'Wunderbar' and 'So In Love' have since become twentieth-century classics while 'I've Come To Wive it Wealthily in Padua'' (in which Cole rhymes

[3] The lyric to this number comes directly from Shakespeare's closing lines to *The Taming of the Shrew*.

'Padua' with 'what a cad you are'), 'We Open In Venice', 'Where Is the Life That Late I Led'[4] and 'Were Thine That Special Face' smack musically of an earlier century. In all of these the lyrics are Porterian, mixing metaphor and anachronism deftly while clearly helping to define the characters who are singing, not – as Lorenz Hart and Ira Gershwin always seem to this writer to do – rhyming dizzily to show the lyricist's erudition.

As for the music, happily Cole avoided the angular polyphony of seventeenth-century Elizabethan and chose the warm, Italianate nineteenth. So we are treated to *saltarellas*, *ricercares* and especially lively *tarantellas*. Orchestrated with strumming mandolins and pizzicato violins, the sound from the pit is more suggestive of Calabria or Sorrento than Stratford-upon-Avon.

Cole was to call *Kiss Me, Kate* 'my second perfect show' (the other being *Anything Goes*), and while he was writing it sensed that he was mining a vein of pure gold. Naturally he was reluctant to stop and, long after Spewack and the director Jack Wilson[5] called a halt with the fourteen glorious songs in the score, he continued to add new songs.

'Bianca'[6] was added for Bill (played by the Ballet Theater dancer Harold Lang, as the part was originally intended as pure dance); 'Always True To You (In My Fashion)' was added for Bianca because Lisa Kirk with her belting chest voice contrasted well with Patricia Morrison's soprano; and 'Brush Up Your Shakespeare' which is sung by the two uneducated hoods (originally intended purely as comic speaking parts), fitting deftly into their characters and replete with malapropisms and some of Cole's most risqué lines: 'When your baby is pleading for pleasure/ Let her sample your Measure for Measure/ If she says she won't buy it or tike it/ Make her tike it, what's more "As You Like It"/ If she says your behaviour is heinous/ Kick her right in the Coriolanus.'

If the creation of *Kiss Me, Kate* was a smooth affair, getting the production on stage was not. Although the show was capitalized for only $180,000, not a huge sum of money then, and far less than for Rodgers and Hammerstein's *South Pacific* or Irving Berlin's *Miss Liberty*,[7] which were even

---

[4] See Musical Analysis Appendix.
[5] Jack had first been bitten by the bug to be a producer-director in 1943 and directed a successful revival of Rodgers and Hart's *A Connecticut Yankee*. Now, since his business relationship with Noel Coward had been terminated, he was interested not only in producing but combining the two talents.
[6] The lyrics of the verses for 'Bianca' which ridiculed Cole's song-writing rivals were justifiably deleted from the score. They are printed here for the first time.

In the street called 'Tin Pan Alley'	For all of you,	I shall now repeat my ballad,
I have suffered endless wrongs.	Then take it away, Berlin – – –	Then I'll rush to Irving quick.
For I'm the dog	Are you list'nin'?	And if he thinks
Who writes incog	Ev'ry night I write for Irving	My ballad stinks,
All of Irving Berlin's great songs.	Till I nearly bust my bean.	He'll sell it to Oscar and Dick.
Here's a new one dedicated	Cause Irving fears	Are you list'nin'?
To my fav'rite heroine.	Two rival peers	
I'll sing it through	Known as Rodgers and Hammerstein.	Bianca, Bianca,
		Oh, baby, will you be mine?...

now being prepared for production, investors were actually turned off by the Porter name being connected with the show in view of his recent flops. Since Subber and Ayres, with no track record as producers, were unlikely to inspire confidence, Jack Wilson, who had recently had a hit with *Bloomer Girl*, was called in as co-producer and director.

Over forty auditions were necessary to raise the money. With the show practically completely written, the cast waiting to go into rehearsal, the situation was a nightmare. All the 'angels' with experience and pedigrees avoided the project. At last, thousand by thousand, the money was squeezed out of seventy-two investors – none of them a member of the usual Broadway crowd.

But, of course, once the word got round from cities where the show was being tried out the advance began to build and, by the time the production opened on Broadway, there was absolute truth in the last sentence of Robert Garland's rave review printed on the last day of 1948 in the *Journal-American*.

> If *Kiss Me, Kate* isn't the best musical comedy I ever saw, I don't remember what the best musical-comedy I ever saw was called. It has everything. A show of shows that is literate without being highbrow, sophisticated without being smarty, seasoned without being soiled, and funny without being vulgar. When I left the Century, the excited congregation was crying 'Bravo' for Cole Porter and Lee Shubert was in the box-office selling seats for next year's Christmas holidays.

All the other papers concurred. Ward Morehouse, writing in the *Sun*, observed that '*Kiss Me, Kate* struck gold last night. This new and festive musical comedy is the best song-and-dance show of the season and one of the best Broadway has had in ten years.' Richard Watts, critic for the *Post*, wrote 'From the opening number it was obvious to everybody that the first-nighters were seeing a smash hit of epic proportions, and nothing occurred throughout the evening to let them down.' The critics were unanimous.

Cole won his first Tony, Broadway's most coveted prize, for his remarkable score, and *Kiss Me, Kate* was adjudged Best Musical, beating *South Pacific*. The show, far and away Porter's most successful, would chalk up 1,077 performances in New York; 400 at London's Coliseum.

If Cole's producers had difficulty raising the cash for *Kiss Me, Kate* they experienced the happy opposite with their next project. It was based originally on Giraudoux's hit play *Amphitryon 38* but, in order to save money, the producers did their own adaptation of the Amphitryon legend, called *Heaven on Earth*, *Cloud-burst*, and eventually *Out of This World*. Subber and Ayres wanted $220,000 As Cole said: 'They could easily have raised two million!'

---

[7] Both productions, which would open the following season, were obliged to turn away backers eager to invest in a sure thing. As it turned out *South Pacific* was indeed a bonanza, while *Miss Liberty* was a resounding flop.

But the confidence of 'angels' does not necessarily spell a hit, and, although the score of *Out of This World* contains some fine songs,[8] among them four imaginative ballads – 'I Am Loved', whose title says it all; 'Where, Oh Where' ('Where, oh where/ Is that combination so rare,/ A youth who is able/ To wrap me in sable/ Who'd still be a millionaire?'); 'No Lover' ('No lover/ No lover for me./ My husband/ Suits me to a T.'), and 'Use Your Imagination' ('Use your Imagination,/ You'll see such wonders if you do./ Around you there lies,/ Pure enchantment in disguise,/ And endless joys you never knew') – and a fistful of songs with amusing lyrics, the whole project was swamped by a tedious adaptation of the sexual adventures of the Greek gods and mortals.

When he began to work on it, Cole was to admit that he was a push over for lavishness or magic in the theatre, and to add, 'That's why I love this new show. There are so many tricks in it.'

But, if *Out of This World* was replete with tricks, it contained very little else. Dwight Taylor, who wrote the effervescent libretto for *The Gay Divorce* in 1932, had no sparkle left by this time. Realizing he had lost his light touch, the light comedy writers Comden and Green, the serious playwright Reginald Lawrence, and eventually the farceur F. Hugh Herbert were called in one after another – all to no avail. Agnes de Mille's direction was revamped by George Abbott but by now the show was in questionable taste and beyond repair. Cole's score could never become more than an adjunct to the leering lines of the story, pleasant costumes and remarkable scenic effects.

Perhaps the reason the score never rose above a basic level was because *Out of This World* was so deeply immersed in homosexuality. Giraudoux's original wit was shunted aside and what was finally presented on the Broadway stage, in the writing, production, acting and dancing, was largely a gay romp.

With Linda away in an Arizona spa, Cole reverted to his college-type show – and in the end there seemed to be no one to call a halt to the pubescent and mostly genital humour. Worse, with all these different frantic creators tinkering and putting his or her imprint on the show, the original concept disappeared. What remained was only a great deal of sex, camp, and beefcake.[9] Unfortunately *Out of This World* had very little more.

The strong accent on potency and the erotic is evident from Jupiter's opening lines which are:

---

[8] One of Porter's most exciting and enduring songs, 'From This Moment On', was deleted from the show in Philadelphia by George Abbott. Abbott confesses: 'Yes, I take responsibility for dropping "From This Moment On", in order to tighten the show.' But Cole believed so strongly in the song he insisted it be included in the movie version of *Kiss Me, Kate* which was released in 1953. The song caught on at once.

[9] Forced by the Boston censors to clothe the chorus boys more fully and to remove references to 'god' and some bawdy lines like 'nobody's goosing me', and 'quieting my urgins for sev'ral vestal virgins', the producers profited by Boston's puritanism and announced in the press that, when the show opened on Broadway, all the excised lines would be restored and the production would be seen in its original pristine smuttiness.

I, Jupiter,
I, Rex,
Am positively teeming with sex.
Brek, ek, co-ek, co-ex,
Brek, ek, co-ek, co-ex,
    Brek, ek, co-ek, co-ek, co-ek, co-ek, co-ek, co-ek,[10]

The rest of the libretto was not much more subtle. It was built on the single joke of Jupiter descending to earth to pursue the mortal, newly-wed Helen who lives in contemporary Athens, a tired concept which wore thin before the curtain went down on act one. He is followed by his furious, bitchy wife, Juno, portrayed by Charlotte Greenwood, famous for her loose-jointed, high kicking dancing.[11] Of course, in the final scenes, Juno and Jupiter are returned to Mount Olympus hurling thunderbolts and verbal barbs at each other while Helen and her spouse revel in married bliss. Miss Greenwood had all the best and funniest songs which she delivered with her customary steely brightness.

Opening at the Century Theatre *Out of This World* was naturally measured beside *Kiss Me, Kate* which, now transferred to the Booth Theatre, some fourteen blocks downtown, was still running strong. The critics had a hard time forgetting that, in the two intervening years between these two shows, Broadway had seen *South Pacific*, *Gentlemen Prefer Blondes*, *Lost In the Stars*, *Call Me Madam* and *Guys and Dolls*, all of which had believable books and considerable entertainment value. Compared to these, *Out of This World* was juvenile stuff indeed; as Brooks Atkinson proclaimed in the *New York Times*, the show was destroyed by its passé 'sex pranks that used to set the customers to giggling nervously many long years ago'.

Although the box-office had a healthy advance, with merely middling reviews and playing in a theatre far uptown, one to which audiences would only travel to see a smash hit, *Out of This World* soon swallowed up its advance and closed after 157 performances.

As the 1950s opened, then, Cole, who had been crowned with accolades for *Kate* and damned with the usual 'not up to Mr. Porter's standard' for *Out of This World*, ignored the hit and saw only the flop. He was not mollified by the fact that he had come out of his song-writing doldrums, far from it. Suffering from constant depression, and pessimist that he was, he saw his glass as half-empty rather than half-full. Jumpy, insomniac and plagued with frequent headaches, he was rude even to friends and would fly into unprovoked rages. He considered *Kiss Me, Kate* a fluke, something he could never repeat, and swore that he had lost his creative flair. In spite of assurances from those who handled his financial affairs he was also convinced he was going broke.

[10] The 'Brek-ek' cheer was one of Yale's most popular football yells. It derives from Aristophanes's *The Frogs*.
[11] She was delighted to be offered the role which had previously been rejected by both Mary Martin and Carol Channing. Coming out of a ten-year retirement, she accepted without hesitation. Rejection by two of the musical theatre's biggest stars should have made Cole suspect he might be in for a flop.

Linda tried to cope with his lack of realism but her own fragile health had been failing for the last two years. Thinking that a change of scene would pull her husband out of his melancholia, she booked a few weeks' holiday in the Mexican sun for them and their old friend Howard Sturges. Cole was only sightly less paranoid upon their return.

Linda's emphysema stopped her from accompanying Cole to the only place she was certain would cheer him up: Paris. Even so, she booked him into the Ritz (with his chauffeur to look after him) for a six-week holiday. Unfortunately the lights of the Ville Lumière seemed to have gone out for him and he cancelled his plans abruptly and returned to New York after only a week. The glow of Paris would not be rekindled for him again until two years later, when he created his radiant hymn to his beloved city – *Can-Can*.

NOEL
1950-1959

COLE PORTER WAS NOT ALONE as the 1950s rolled in: feeling like a bystander, attending a game he did not understand. His confusion was shared by many, for it was a time of great upheaval, and those like himself and Coward who had made their reputations several decades before were at a loss as to how to fit in.

Matters should have been slightly easier for Porter, for since he wrote only songs he could ally himself with the best theatrical minds who took care of the libretti or, as it was now fashionable to call it, the book. But rhythm and blues had taken a stranglehold on popular music and the old A A B A and A B A C forms that Cole worked in were being replaced by more varied constructions. The novelty song and the country song would soon be cutting into the musical's share of the entertainment dollar. Rock was about to enter the mainstream of music, and, though it would never violate the protective walls of the musical theatre, some part of its influence and form would be adopted by Cole's contemporaries, leaving Porter, with his beguines and innuendo, far behind.

Noel was even farther out of the mainstream.

Much as he protested that he was finished with operetta, in his inner heart Coward still clung to the hope of creating one more successful one. Luckily, he put the dream aside to work on a comedy, *Relative Values*, because he came to understand that it would be an impossible one to fulfil. In the long theatrical tradition he sprang from, his barometer of success, 'the song that stopped the show', was anathema now and forever. Since *Oklahoma!* and *Carousel*, song was required to 'carry the show forward'. Noel realized that to be the case, but his ego would not permit him to believe it. His long training in revue had made him a miniaturist. As far as the stage was concerned, even his best operetta characters were one-dimensional and epigrammatic. They, like Oscar Wilde's creations, always spoke in Noel's own distinctive voice. As far back as *Bitter Sweet* his heroine Sarah was merely an upper-class young woman in love; Carl, simply a music teacher. When the audience left the theatre, they knew little more about the protagonists than their caste or profession.

He had passed the age of fifty but, until both Charles Cochran and Ivor Novello died within a few days of each other, he did not think of retirement. Then he wrote that 'the worst thing about growing old is watching your friends die off', adding some rueful lines applicable to his own career; luckily 'Ivor died at the height of his triumphant career and will never know ... the sadness of decline'.

One of his contemporaries who was very much alive, however, was Beatrice Lillie. During the summer of 1951 she brought her zany brand of humour to a month-long engagement at the Café de Paris in London. Noel, who was then in the midst of rehearsing *Relative Values*, went to see her and her long-time accompanist, Norman Hackforth. Coward had toured with Hackforth during the war and they had complete musical accord as they went slogging through the South Pacific, entertaining the troops. Over a drink with the management, Norman offered to play for Coward, whereupon the manager of the Café jumped in with an offer of £750 per week if Coward would agree to a month's run. Before he left they had fixed a date for Noel's début in late October, shortly after the out-of-town opening of *Relative Values*.

So it was that, by the end of the year, Coward's career had turned around. His long period of decline in the theatre ceased and he found a new facet of entertainment he had never realized existed before, that of cabaret artist.

On October 29, the Café de Paris was packed to the rafters and glittering with celebrities. Princess Margaret and Princess Marina headed the impressive list, that included stars from London, Paris and even Broadway. None of them knew that Noel had lost his voice from over-work and nerves and that a throat specialist had treated him for laryngitis that very afternoon. In spite of all this Noel's mood was jubilant. The word was that the Master had reassumed his mastery and *Relative Values* was vintage Coward. Everyone felt it was due to be Gladys Cooper's biggest success since *The Shining Hour*, twenty years before.

Cole Lesley gave the following account of Noel's personal triumph:

Anyone who ever saw Mistinguette make one of her celebrated entrances down those long flight of stairs at the Folies Bergère – and Noel saw her many times – knows that she looked straight out front as though the stairs didn't exist. Noel descended the stairs that night, smiling as though he hadn't a care in the world, and, like Mistinguette, never once looked down. Once he saw he was *bien descendu*, he opened wide his arms as though welcoming the audience to a marvellous party, bowed low and then, with a graciously modest gesture, silenced the applause. [The throat specialist's] treatment, or some other magic, had done the trick. From the moment he opened his trap, as he liked to put it, the sounds that issued when he went into the medley of his most famous sentimental songs were surprising mellifluous ... He had to be seen to be believed. Sometimes exuberant, slapping his thigh with glee as he prophesied 'There Are Bad Times Just Around the Corner', he more often used complete repose, so that only the slightest gesture, a sideways glance or a raised eyebrow, was needed to produce a devastatingly funny effect. He had immense variety: the unbelievable speed of 'Mad Dogs', the wistful melancholy of 'World Weary', and the terrible vehemence with which, in the last refrain, he forbade Mrs Worthington to put her daughter on the stage. He had learned years ago never to go on too long; thirty-five minutes and, with seeming reluctance, he left us, giving us a benign wave as he walked up the stairs. Of course, he had to come back ... to acknowledge the continuing applause and yells of bravo. And then, once more having induced silence, he sang gently and really rather movingly:

The party's over now
The day is drawing very nigh,
The candles gutter
The starlight leaves the sky ...

And that was that, forty-five minutes in all.

Noel was singing better than ever, 'cooing like a baritone dove', as Kenneth Tynan accurately described it. Less percipient reviewers did not know what to make of it; one paper called it 'a shocking voice', but was obliged to add that it held the audience spellbound. Noel himself crowed about his 'really triumphant success', adding that he 'tore the place up'. Immediately after the first few packed nights at the Café, the management offered to boost his salary to £1,000 if only he would play an additional two weeks. Noel agreed, but took a charming little Boudin he had long admired in a Bond Street gallery in exchange for the windfall.

During the six weeks he appeared at the Café, *Relative Values* opened at the Savoy Theatre to wide acclaim, as had been predicted. Anthony Cookman in the *Tatler* called it a 'flawless piece of work,' and J. C. Trewin wrote, 'Once the comedy has fairly begun ... Coward is away, flicking out the lines as in vanished years,' ending by calling the play 'a happy return journey to an earlier Coward'.

But there was more to come. Noel had decided to turn his entire life back to the way it had been in his heyday. That meant giving up White Cliffs and moving back to Goldenhurst.[1] The idea had been needling him for several months.

> I decided that I am going to give this up and go back to Goldenhurst. It is my own land and so much quieter. I shall miss the sea and the ships but I shall have the Marsh and the trees, the pleasure ... [here] there is something distracting; someone crunches by on the beach or a big ship passes and one's concentration snaps.

Back in the peaceful setting of Goldenhurst, Noel quickly put the finishing touches on a play he had long wanted to write for the Lunts. It was called *Quadrille* and, as the name implied, turned out to be a four-character romp, not unlike the mix and match set-up of *Private Lives*.

The reviewers were not enthusiastic, but the public flocked to see the flawless Lunts play their hand-in-glove brand of high comedy. It was not only the stars who made the public disregard the notices, it was Coward's name. With *Relative Values* selling out nightly, *Quadrille's* London engagement

---

[1] Ian Fleming, who was yet to write his *James Bond* series, and his bride Anne Rothermere, both close friends of Coward's, took over the lease on White Cliffs.

already pre-sold and Noel's name still resounding because of a promised return engagement at the Café de Paris, Coward was enjoying the same golden success Cole had after *Kiss Me, Kate*. *Quadrille* eventually ran some 300 performances.

At the height of his joy, shortly before the opening of *Quadrille*, Noel learned of Gertrude Lawrence's death. She had been his loving and beloved friend in and out of the theatre for almost forty years. He had last seen her only a few months before in New York in *The King and I*. They had lunched together and he had told her about a new play he had written for her, *Island Fling*.

Unable to come to the charity preview of *Quadrille* (she was in hospital, ostensibly suffering from jaundice, but actually dying of cancer), she had sent a cheque and a note that ended, 'Nothing to worry about, I just struck a bad patch and you came and sat in it. Oh dear – and it's always you I want to please more than ANYONE.'

Noel went off to Jamaica to write that winter of 1953 and returned to London in the spring for his second engagement at the Café de Paris and another excursion into the past: the role of King Magnus in Shaw's *The Apple Cart*. This and the cameo roles he was soon to portray in many movies seemed to fill any vacant corner of his life. It was as though he were trying to juggle all the arts – even painting in oils – so that there would be no diminution of his powers, or that nothing he had not yet explored to his satisfaction would go untried.

But he was still obsessed with operetta. While he was in Jamaica, Cole Lesley turned Oscar Wilde's *Lady Windermere's Fan* into a libretto, Coward retitled it *After the Ball*, and immediately began to develop it by adding a flowingly artistic score to Wilde's tightly constructed story. Robert Helpman would direct, and the prize role of Mr. Hopper, half aborigine, half British, was reserved for Graham Payn.

The combination of Coward and Wilde should have produced an ideal operetta, but epigrams do not sing well, and Coward, in an effort not to violate the text, stuck closely to Wilde's plot line. Yet where Wilde could look benignly at the Edwardians, Coward only seemed to burlesque them. Again, the times were against him; by 1954 people did not go to the musical theatre to spend three hours sneering at propriety. As *My Fair Lady* was to prove, only two years later, a single number, the 'Ascot Gavotte', would suffice. For the rest of the evening audiences wanted to empathise with the characters.

Coward was interested in the plot (his first adaptation of someone else's story), hoping the collaboration with Lesley and Wilde would keep him from making the musical too convoluted. He well remembered the bewildered audiences at *Operette* searching with matches to find out where, according to their programmes, they were supposed to be. But here he only succeeded in slowing Oscar Wilde's pace to a near-standstill.

Musically, it is an excellent score. Much closer to opéra-comique than it is to operetta, it shows a freedom and sensitivity that is audible in no other of his works. Coward obviously was happy writing these arias and quartettes and felt completely at home in the period. 'I can scarcely go to the piano without a melody seeping from my fingers,' he was to note in his diary, 'usually in keys that I am not used to and can't play in.'

Even though the songs themselves have an assurance not seen in Coward's work before, his compositional penchant is misdirected. True to his spots, the leopard constantly gave his best, most moving, music to the mother figure, Mrs. Erlynne, rather than to Lady Windermere.

Mary Ellis, who was chosen to play Mrs. Erlynne, and who had made her début at the Metropolitan Opera when she was eighteen, was in her mid-fifties when *After the Ball* opened, and she had lost her voice years before. It is incomprehensible that Noel did not get her out of the company at the first rehearsal for after the preview in Bristol he was to write, 'Mary Ellis acted well but sang so badly that I could hardly bear it.' A month later she was still the

After the Ball, 1954

company's millstone and Coward noted that 'the whole project has been sabotaged by Mary not being able to sing it'.

Coward was no sentimentalist. Even his friend Norman Hackforth, whom Noel described as conducting the orchestra 'like a stick of wet asparagus' was sacked and replaced by Philip Martel. Robert Helpman too came in for his share of criticism though, since the whole idea of the operetta originated with him, he stayed on (Noel noted that he is 'not yet, I fear, a good enough director; being a dancer and choreographer he has a dread of repose'). But Mary Ellis was not replaced. Noel's training in revue was once again to do him down. Take, for instance, the excellent 'Something on a Tray', which is sung by four ageing aristocrats near the end of the operetta. In the song they express relief that the Season is over. No longer does one longer have to be *comme il faut* and be seen dining at the best homes. One can simply relax in bed. The lyric goes:

Advancing years may bring about
A rather sweet nostalgia
In spite of rheumatism and gout
And certainly neuralgia.
And so, when we have churned our way
Through luncheon and a matinée,
We gratefully to bed retire
Obsessed with an acute desire
To rest our aching, creaking vertebrae
And have a little something on a tray.

Some ageing ladies with a groan
Renounce all beauty lotions
They dab their brows with eau-de-Cologne
And turn to their devotions
We face the process of decay,

Attired in a négligé
And with hot water bottles at our toes
We cosily in bed repose
Enjoying, in a rather languid way,
A little 'eggy' something on a tray.

Advancing years that many dread
Still have their compensations
We turn when youth and passion have fled
To more sedate sensations.
And when we've fought our weary way
Through some exhausting social day
We thankfully to bed retire
With pleasant book and crackling fire
And, like Salome in a bygone day,
Enjoy a little something on a tray ...

The words are amusing and the rather madrigalish tune appeals, but Coward seems to spoil the effect with his line about Salome. However big a laugh he may get from his audience, such words could not possibly come from the mouths of such thoroughbred ladies.

Here, perhaps, is the reason why Coward – and his repertoire – was so successful in cabaret. His songs are best when they are *divorced* from the play, for they only help to amplify Coward's own character rather than those who are carrying the story along.

As the production moved closer to London, more and more solecisms crept in. Irene Brown, playing the Duchess of Berwick, was given an increasing amount of comedy. But, as everyone else's role was built up, poor Lady Windermere, nicely played by Vanessa Lee, looked more and more like a colourless ninny.

When *After the Ball* opened in June, Noel predicted it would run for six months and he was right, though the critics were kind. But it was to be a bitter

Coward's mother, Violet, in New York, 1942

time for him. Before the month was out, Violet Coward died. No one could write more movingly of life, love or death than Noel who was to inscribe the next day in his private diary some of his more personal thoughts:

> ... I sat by the bed and held her hand until she gave a pathetic little final gasp and died. I have no complaints and no regrets. It was, as I always hoped it would be. She was ninety-one years old and I was with her close, close, close until her last breath. Over and above this sensible, wise philosophy I know it to be the saddest moment of my life. Owing to my inability to accept any of the comforting religious fantasies about the hereafter, I have no spurious hopes that we shall meet again on some distant Elysian shore. I know that it is over. Fifty-four years of love and tenderness and crossness and devotion and unswerving loyalty. Without her I

could only have achieved a quarter of what I have achieved ... She was gay, even to the last I believe, gallant certainly. There was no fear in her except for me. She was a great woman to whom I owe the whole of my life. I shall never be without her in my mind but I shall never see her again. Goodbye, my darling.

But Violet Coward's passing, no matter however painful, was to set him free. He may never have seen any connection, but the leading ladies of his musicals from then on for the rest of his life would all be vital young women.

'Work, blessed work' was, as Noel often said, 'his saviour in troubled times', and the loss of his beloved mother was to be somewhat eased by preparation for his by-now annual act at the Café de Paris. To spruce up his performance he added a parody of Cole Porter's 'Let's Do It'. Cole, although he never sanctioned any alterations to, or parodies of any of his work, wholeheartedly approved of Noel's lines and sent his blessing.

Then taking death, which had occupied his thoughts so recently, as a point of departure, he lightened the concept by chronicling the demise of a well-to-do English gentleman and wrote one of his most amusing works. He put his irreverent words into the mouth of the widow, a Mrs. Wentworth-Brewster, who is certainly first cousin to Mrs. Worthington of the ungainly daughter. 'A Bar on the Piccola Marina' has a catchy little theme, a few bars of which are printed below, but what put a smile on the faces of Café de Paris audiences was its lyric extolling the delicious incongruity of a straitlaced British matron in her first encounter with Italian sexuality.

In   a   bar   on   the Pic - co - la   Ma - ri - na   Life   called   to Mis - sus

Went - worth Brew - ster.

Verse

In a 'bijou' abode
In St. Barnabas Road
Not far from the Esher by-pass
Lived a mother and wife
Who, most of her life,
Let every adventure fly past.
She had two strapping daughters and a
    rather dull son
And a much duller husband who at
    sixty-one
Elected to retire
And later on expire.
Sing Hallelujah, Hey nonny-no,

Hey nonny-no, Hey nonny-no!
He joined the feathered choir.
On a wet afternoon in the middle of June
They all of them came home soaking
Having laid him to rest by special request
In the family vault at Woking,
And then in the middle of the funeral wake
With her mouth full of excellent Madeira
    cake
His widow cried, 'That's done,
My life's at last begun,
Sing Hallelujah, Hey nonny-no,
Hey nonny-no, Hey nonny-no!
It's time I had some fun.

Today, thought hardly a jolly day
At least has set me free,
We'll all have a lovely holiday
On the Island of Capri!'

Refrain I
In a bar on the Piccola Marina
Life called to Mrs Wentworth-Brewster,
Fate beckoned her and introduced her
Into a rather queer unfamiliar atmosphere.
She'd just sit there propping up the bar
Beside a fisherman who sang to his guitar.
When accused of having gone too far
She merely cried 'Funiculi!
Just fancy me!
Funicula!'
When he bellowed 'Che Bella Signorina!'
Sheer ecstasy at once produced a
Wild shriek from Mrs
      Wentworth-Brewster.
Changing her whole demeanour.
When both her daughters and her son said,
'Please come home, Mama,'
She murmured rather bibulously,
'Who d'you think you are?'
Nobody can afford to be so lahdy-bloody-da
In a bar on the Piccola Marina.

Interlude
Every fisherman cried
'Viva, viva', and 'Che Ragazza'
When she sat on the gran piazza
Everybody would rise.
Every fisherman sighed,
'Viva, viva che bell'Inglesi,'
Someone even said 'Whoops-adaisy!'

Which was quite a surprise.
Each night she'd make some gay excuse
And brimming with good will
She'd just slip into something loose
And totter down the hill ...

Refrain 2
To the bar on the Piccola Marina
Where love came to Mrs
      Wentworth-Brewster
Hot flushes of delight suffused her,
Right round the bend she went,
Picture her astonishment.
Day in, day out, she would gad about
Because she felt she was no longer on the
      shelf.
Night out, night in, knocking back the gin
She'd cry, 'Hurrah!
Funicula, Funiculi,
Funic yourself!'
Just for fun, three young sailors from
      Messina
Bowed low to Mrs Wentworth-Brewster
Said 'Scusi,' and politely goosed her.
Then there was quite a scena.
Her family in floods of tears, cried
'Leave these men, Mama.'
She said, 'They're just high-spirited,
Like all Italians are,
And most of them have a great deal more to
      offer than Papa
In a bar on the Piccola Marina.'

Coward's appearances at the Café de Paris were outstandingly polished and, because they were attended by so many old friends, were always peppered with new materials like the 'Piccola Marina'. Noel was certainly in top form when the American agent, Joe Glaser, came to hear him and offered him the then-unheard-of sum of $40,000 for four weeks at the Desert Inn in Las Vegas, Nevada.

While Noel was waiting for the American contract, he went back to Blue Harbour, his house in Jamaica, where he seemed able to write in comparative tranquillity. Years before, he had fallen in love with a property called Look Out high above Blue Harbour. Eventually he bought it, changing its name to Firefly (because the land around teemed with them in the evenings). Now he dreamt of designing and building a house and pool there, selling Blue Harbour, and making this his mountain retreat.

His fifty-fifth birthday had come and gone, and he often wrote privately of his financial worries. 'I am £15,000 pounds overdrawn ... and I fully intend to end my curious days in as much comfort, peace and luxury as I can get,' he confided to his diary. Ambition had seized him, and he wanted desperately to have the money to complete his dream.

In a burst of inspiration that winter in Jamaica he wrote half a novel. As if that were not enough he completed two comedies, *Nude With Violin* and *South Sea Bubble* (a complete re-write of his unsuccessful play of 1949 which had had a few performances in Westport, Connecticut starring Claudette Colbert).

In spring 1955 the big Las Vegas contract came along. Eventually it was to solve Coward's financial dilemma, for he was paid $15,000 a week, subject to tax, and an extra $60,000 listed as a tax-free capital gain – more than enough to serve as a down-payment on his dream house (Coward deferred his dream and used the Las Vegas bonanza to satisfy his outstanding British income tax bill). This engagement with its huge rewards was the first in a chain of triumphs which would make Coward realize that more money was to be made outside of England than at home. At a time when his plays, his songs and even his voice had been written off by the British critics this unforeseen success greatly influenced Coward.

'I have had screaming rave notices and the news has flashed round the world,' he was to say, and to add, 'I am told continually, verbally and in print, that I am the greatest performei in the world.' The American papers concurred heartily, *Variety*, screaming: 'LAS VEGAS FLIPPING ... COWARD WOWS 'EM IN CAFÉ TURN.'

But it was gruelling work: two shows nightly for a solid four weeks including Sundays, interviews and appearances during the day. The final four performances climaxed with a Columbia recording, for the sleeve design of which Noel was driven out into the Nevada desert and photographed in his dinner jacket sipping a cup of tea. The temperature was 118°. Cole Porter attended the show that night and Noel crowed that he gave a 'sensational performance, because I so wanted Cole to see me at my best – and he certainly did'.

With the engagement completed, the money banked and a well-deserved rest in view, Coward noted:

> I am really proud and pleased that I succeeded in doing what no one suspected I could, and that is to please the *ordinary* audiences. Obviously on certain nights crammed with movie stars and chums I had no difficulties and every number went wonderfully, but the dinner shows, filled with people from Kansas, Nebraska, Utah, Illinois, etc., were what really counted and their response was usually splendid ... It has been a triumphant adventure and I feel very happy.

Coward in Las Vegas

Now, in theatrical terms, Coward was a 'hot property'. As he said, 'All the studios are vying for my services and all the agents are tying themselves in knots ... Twentieth-Century-Fox are sitting with their fingers crossed. Paramount want me to do a picture with Danny Kaye and/or anything I bloody well like on my own terms.'

What he liked was to become a Ford television spectacular, the first ever broadcast in colour, starring himself and Mary Martin with whom, after their feud during *Pacific 1860*, he had buried the hatchet. The show, one of three that he was to write for the motor company – the others being his TV adaptations of *Blithe Spirit* and *This Happy Breed* – set Ford back half a million dollars, one fifth of which was paid to Coward for this particular show. Alone on camera, live for an hour and a half, the two entertainers sang through songs by Gershwin, Porter, Kern and Rodgers and Hammerstein as well as a good part of the Coward oeuvre.

It was called *Together With Music*, and Noel wrote a song using this title, as well as one that might be viewed as an honest musical appraisal of the show, 'Ninety Minutes is a Long, Long Time'. It was an evening of nostalgia and impeccable performances – Coward had insisted on an unprecedented forty-one rehearsals – but short on inspiration. Yet, now that he was the darling of the critics, the *New York Times* gushed that 'Coward can write off this occasion as one of the triumphs of his career'.

As the money rolled in, and now that he was finally out of debt, after conferences with his lawyers and accountants Coward realized that it was 'ridiculous to spend eight weeks in England ... and to pay for that privilege,

With Mary Martin in the first CBS-TV coast-to-coast colour broadcast, *Together with Music*

roughly £20,000 in income tax! My brains, my talent, and my industry, and the exchequer walks away with twice as much as I do,' he commented bitterly. He decided to sell Goldenhurst and his large house and studio in London, and to establish residence in Bermuda where there was no income tax at all.

It was heart-wrenching to have to resign from all his London clubs and to sell his collection of Impressionist and Fauvist paintings (including the charming Bonnard he had earned for one day's work in Mike Todd's *Around the World in 80 Days*). What was more distressing was the obligation to give up his presidency of the Actors' Orphanage, a position he had held since 1934 and a large part of whose budget he personally assured through benefit performances and funding drives.

'I must not set foot in England on any pretext between now and April 1957,' he wrote from his newly-acquired home on Bermuda at the beginning of 1956, and for the next sixteen months he commuted between New York, Paris, Hollywood and Jamaica. During that time, although *South Sea Bubble*, the comedy he had originally written for Gertrude Lawrence, opened successfully in London, starring Vivien Leigh, he resolutely stuck to his guns and stayed away from his homeland. 'It is maddening that I shall not pop over and see it, but I can't have my cake and lie on it,' he wrote. Yet he did mistakenly go to Dublin four months later for the pre-London engagement of *Nude With Violin*, the play he had written two years earlier in Jamaica, and which was directed by and starred John Gielgud. Coward sensed the play needed cutting and revising, and since Ireland was a tax free state he felt his position was not in jeopardy there.

It was a colossal miscalculation. He had taken the *Queen Mary* and, while the liner was lying offshore, early in the morning before departure for Le Havre, reporters swarmed around him in his stateroom. He told them that to go ashore would cost him £25,000. They interpreted this to mean he had not paid his taxes for the current year, whereas he owed the Inland Revenue not a penny. What he was too proud to tell them was that *all* the money he had earned in Las Vegas had gone to pay his tax bill of £27,000 the year before. In Dublin he was met with yet another barrage of reporters.

Very soon world headlines screamed that Coward had kicked the country that nurtured him. They ignored the truth – that he was leaving England to avoid future taxation rather than past due taxes – and overlooked what Winston Churchill, coming to Coward's defence, proclaimed has always been every Briton's inalienable right: to make his home, career and fortune where he chooses. Since Coward was the first of the scores of actors, singers and sports figures who would seek tax havens abroad he was also the first to be pilloried. His two new plays – indeed, his choice of themes, his very style of play-writing and acting – in short his élitism and escapism, were roundly criticised. Noel's detractors were helped by the fact that John Osborne's *Look Back In Anger* opened shortly after *South Sea Bubble*.

Aware of the turmoil his name and works were causing in Britain, yet separated from it by the tranquility of Spithead Lodge, for the next few months Coward buried his head in a new novel, cooking and verse – as distinct from lyrics. He was eventually to return to England on the *Queen Elizabeth* in June 1957 and write about his mixed feelings on coming home: 'It will be sweet to see my loved ones but otherwise I feel fairly dreary about it. Even this ship reflects subtly the insidious influence of the welfare state.'

By the autumn, he was off to star in *Nude With Violin*. It was twenty-one years since he last played New York and he opened to glowing personal notices and contemptuous ones for his play. Contrary to the West End where it had run for almost a year and a half, the comedy eked out a four-month run. Coward wrote an analysis of why successful British plays can fail in New York that has never been surpassed.

> ... in England the public is more prone to think for itself. In America they are resolutely told by the press what to enjoy and what to avoid, not only in the theatre but in every phase of life. They are told by television and radio what to eat, drink and smoke, what cars to buy and what laxatives and sanitary towels to use. They are told, in no uncertain terms, what movies to go to and what stars to admire ... The power of individual thought has been atrophied in them by the incessant onslaughts of commercialism.

That summer, while staying with friends on the Côte d'Azur, he honoured a promise he had made to his lifelong friends, Laurence Olivier and Vivien Leigh, to adapt Feydeau's farce *Occupe-toi d'Amélie* into a stage piece for Vivien. In this transformation, which they called *Look After Lulu*, Coward received assistance from Cole Lesley who had by now become more of a collaborator than a secretary. Although Lesley's name does not appear on the playscript, Noel made no attempt to hide his contribution and wrote in his diary: 'Coley arrived last Monday and by slogging away for two or three hours every morning, with him typing in the afternoon we have managed to inject some wit and tempo into the first act.'

A month later he was to note: 'Coley and I, by drudging away for three hours a day, managed to finish *Look After Lulu* and, to my surprise, it's very funny indeed and Vivien is mad about it.'

But Noel could keep himself away from music for only so long, and that autumn, when Anton Dolin, director of the London Festival Ballet, gave him carte blanche for scenario and music in a field he had never tried, he eagerly agreed. The score poured out of him, and, since the arrival of the tape recorder, it was no longer necessary for Noel to have a musical amanuensis standing nearby to take down his ideas. Peter Matz who had been his brilliant arranger and pianist in Las Vegas helped him refine his harmonies and set Noel's mind at ease when he signed a contract to orchestrate the score in the next few months.

The scene of the ballet, which Coward appropriately called *London Morning*, is before the gates of Buckingham Palace. There are dances for the sentries, policemen, sailors and their girls, a group of schoolgirls and nun, a lovers' pas de deux, a family ensemble, an *allegro con brio* dance for juvenile delinquents, with the whole company coming on for the bombastic finale – of course, the Changing of the Guard – using Coward's 'London Pride'. Generally, though, his music, which tried to be 'arty', fell between the two stools of popular song and serious ballet music and ended up pleasing no one.

But creating a ballet had opened the musical floodgates.

For some time Noel had been pondering a new musical. Called *The Young Idea*, it would be set on a cruise ship. Now, with so many tunes flowing out of him, he expanded the theme; intended to star Ethel Merman, it became somewhat like a sequel to Cole Porter's ocean liner musical, *Anything Goes*. Because of Merman's maturity, Coward shifted the story to the further adventures of Mrs. Wentworth-Brewster, the one who discovered love in a bar on the Piccola Marina. This necessitated changing the title to *Later Than Spring*. Then Ethel Merman flatly refused the part.

Not one to be put off easily, Noel contacted Rosalind Russell, who had made such a hit in Leonard Bernstein's *Wonderful Town*. She greeted his performance of the score with stony silence. Coward was even prepared to get in touch with Irene Dunne when fate intervened in the person of Cyril Ritchard, who announced that he was going to direct *Look After Lulu*. Because the stars were available, ready and eager, Ritchard planned to put it into rehearsal *immediately*. Roger Stevens, the impresario, had no trouble raising the necessary capital and the play, starring Tammy Grimes, Roddy McDowell, Ellis Rabb, Jack Gilford and Kurt Kaznar, opened early in 1959. That this delightful farce was a failure on Broadway is still an incomprehensible mystery – although some blamed Ritchard's directorial touch. *Look After Lulu* went on to become a huge success in London, starring Vivien Leigh, and later Elizabeth Sellars. When *Later Than Spring* re-emerged fully two years later it would be called *Sail Away*, star Elaine Stritch, become the first Coward musical to open on Broadway, and contain some of Coward's happiest and most youthful words and music in years.

But, more importantly, it would not be operetta or revue or a bastardization of either. *Sail Away* was to become a good-time show; a fully-fledged, fully-choreographed, swinging, singing Broadway musical comedy – the kind Noel always hoped he could write.

COLE
1952-1964

FOR ALMOST TWO YEARS, in 1951 and 1952, Cole's depression increased. He worried that no producer had appeared after *Out of This World* to offer him another show and felt certain that no one ever would again. Seeing himself as relatively poor, he fretted that he would be forced to give up the lease on his California house. When his tax advisers told him that the contrary was the case, that it would be monetarily advantageous for him to spend six months in the California sunshine and the rest of the time at his Waldorf Towers apartment, as the rents on both of these were tax deductible, he brooded that he would now be forced to give up the Williamstown estate, and tearfully announced, 'It's my only extravagance.'

Although his fears were unrealistic, his loss of weight, headaches and insomnia were not. Linda insisted, and at last, realizing he was on the point of a nervous breakdown, he went into hospital. Fearing the headaches were symptoms of a brain tumour, Cole was relieved when they were diagnosed as acute sinusitis. Yet what relieved him most was to be able to work, and at last, in spring 1952, Cy Feuer and Ernest Martin, hard-headed former businessmen, who had successfully produced Frank Loesser's *Where's Charley?* and *Guys and Dolls*, came to him with an idea for a belle époque musical that would reunite him with the Spewacks. Cole, delighted to be writing about Paris again, began to write songs almost before he had heard from his librettists.

Although Cole's and Bella Spewack's personalities clashed, he was professional enough to set these personality clashes aside and eager to work with them again. Because Sam and Bella were involved in a new play, it was not to be. Rather than postpone the project for another year, Cole, ever anxious to collaborate with success, agreed to work with Abe Burroughs, who had tailored the award-winning book for *Guys and Dolls*. Burroughs was much in demand as the most irreverent and brightest of the current crop of book writers (he would never let himself be referred to as a librettist).

Burroughs (*né* Abram Solman Borowitz) was a workaholic and by mid-June had come up with a believable plot and sub-plot that would take place in the Paris of Toulouse-Lautrec. The new show would be a hymn to the joie de vivre of Paris – and to love. The main story concerns a handsome young judge who is sent to investigate the scandalous dancing at a Montmartre café. At the end he falls in love with both the dance and the spirited café owner. Musically, the show would climax with a gigantic can-can.

Cole shut himself away and, hardly a month later, after daily telephone calls during which Burroughs would read him his latest dialogue, and Cole would respond by tapping and singing a sketch for the appropriate song, a great part of *Can-Can* had been completed.

Work was interrupted in early July when Cole rushed back to Westleigh Farms because his mother, now ninety, had suffered a cerebral haemorrhage. There was little he could do but be near her; she was in a deep coma from which she would never awake. As before, he found solace in his songwriting and remained at the Indiana homestead, working on the score of *Can-Can*. Sadly, he recalled sitting on the back porch, writing the rousing, raucous and ultimately joyous finale. 'It was,' he said, 'one of the strangest experiences of my life, but the number had to be done.'

Kate Porter died on August 3, 1952. In death as in life her son was paramount in her thoughts and, aside from a few personal bequests, she left everything to Cole including her securities and the Westleigh Farms house. Linda, her own health precarious, was unable to fly to Peru for the funeral. In the months ahead her lungs would become more and more congested and she would not recover sufficiently to be able to attend the première of *Can-Can*. Having lost one of the women whose advice acted as a rudder for his life, her fragile state was an added source of worry to Cole. It is amazing that, surrounded by death and the illness that was to kill his beloved Linda less than two years later, he was able to turn out one of his sunniest scores in *Can-Can*.

Although it was tepidly reviewed, most of Cole's music caught on at once. Chief among the hits was 'I Love Paris,'[1] its dark, ultra-minor opening ruminating through the seasons – especially the summer 'when it sizzles' and the winter 'when it drizzles' – when Paris is at her most fetching. Other successes which were to receive a giant share of sheet music and record sales were 'C'est Magnifique', a swinging fox-trot, 'Allez-vous en', a heart-breaking waltz, and 'I Am In Love', a typically Porterian beguine. And one should not overlook 'It's All Right With Me',[2] one of his most moving and loved songs.

Even the book songs had a certain lilt, charm and wit: 'Maidens Typical of France', 'Never Give Anything Away', 'Come Along With Me', 'Live and Let Live'. It seems that Cole was riding a melodic and lyric juggernaut that would not be stopped. There are two songs for every situation in the book, and a number of first-rate songs – 'What A Fair Thing is a Woman,' 'I Do,'[3] 'When Love Comes To Call,' and the very moving 'Who Said Gay Paree' – were all dropped from the show. The title song has lilt and syncopation in its tune, but

[1] Cole was forever embittered (and would say so to anyone who would listen) that the French government never acknowledged the most memorable hymn to that city written in the English language. In the ensuing years, all over the world, the theme of 'I Love Paris' has conjured up for millions a romantic image of Cole's beloved city. His anger turned to bemused astonishment when, two years later, he learned that 'C'est Magnifique' was the number one song in France. 'It's rather nice,' he wrote to a friend, 'to find that when I tried to write a typical French popular song, that was dismissed by the critics, it has at last become a *typical French popular song*.'
[2] See Musical Analysis Appendix.
[3] With a new lyric, the infectious melody of this one became 'Who Wants To Be a Millionaire', in *High Society*, the film whose score Cole wrote next in 1956.

Gwen Verdon, who stole
the show; *Can-Can*, 1953

Lilo, the star of *Can-Can*, 1953

what is best about it is its amusing lyric that sets the most unlikely pairs of humans and animals a-can-canning.

Verse
Ev'rybody
Chic or shoddy,
Ev'rybody loves to dance,
Since that big dance,
Infra-dig dance
Called the can-can captivated France.
Why does it kill ev'ry care?
Why is it done ev'rywhere?

Refrain 1
There is no trick to a can-can,
It is so simple to do.
When you once kick to a can-can
'Twill be so easy for you.
If a lady in Iran can,
If a shady African can,
If a Jap with a slap of her fan can,
Baby you can can-can too.
If an English Dapper Dan can,
If an Irish Calahan can,
If an Afghan in Afghanistan can,
Baby you can can-can too.

Refrain 2
If in Deauville ev'ry swell can,
It is so simple to do.
If Debussy and Ravel can,
'Twill be so easy for you.
If the Louvre custodian can
If the Gard Republican can,
If Van Gogh and Matisse and Cézanne can,
Baby, you can can-can too.
If a chief in the Sudan can,
If the hefty Aga Kahn can,
If the camels in his caravan can,
Baby, you can can-can too.

Refrain 3
Takes no art to do a can-can,
It is so simple to do.
When you start to do a can-can,
'Twill be so easy for you.
If a slow Mohammedan can,
If a kilted Scottish clan can,
If in Wagner a Valkyrian can,
Baby you can can-can too.
If a lass in Michigan can,
If an ass in Astrakhan can,
If a bass in Saskatchewan can,
Baby you can can-can too.

Refrain 4
If the waltz king, Johann Strauss, can,
It is so simple to do,
If his gals in *Fledermaus* can,
'Twill be so easy for you.
Lovely Duse in Milan can,
Lucien Guitry and Réjane can,
Sarah Bernhardt upon a divan can,
Baby, you can can-can too.
If a holy Hindu man can,
If a gangly Anglican can,
If in Lesbos a pure Lesbian can,
Baby, you can can-can too.

Refrain 5
If an ape gargantuan can,
It is so simple to do.
If a clumsy pelican can,
'Twill be so easy for you.
If a dachshund in Berlin can,
If a tomcat in Pekin can,
If a crowded sardine in a tin can,
Baby you can can-can too.
If a rhino with a crash can,
If a hippo with a splash can,
If an elm and an oak and an ash can,
Baby you can can-can too.

As was the case with *Out of This World*, the leading role in *Can-Can* was first offered to Carol Channing who had captivated Broadway in *Gentlemen Prefer Blondes*. This time she accepted. However, now that she had become a star, she demanded the right of approval of both songs and script – conditions unacceptable to both Cole and Burroughs. A search abroad uncovered a starlet called Lilo, who was imported from Paris and belted out Cole's score adequately enough. But, as the critics acidly noted, she went into the production in a starring role and came out a supporting player. The real star of *Can-Can* was the red-headed dancer, Gwen Verdon, in her first major role. She over-whelmed the hardened first-night audience with an Adam and Eve ballet and then her outrageous can-can.

In spite of the *New York Times* declaring there was 'nothing original in the show' and that Porter's score was 'not half so bright as the score Kay Swift wrote last season for *Paris 90*', by mid-spring there was a six-week wait for tickets. *Variety* listed five songs from the show as the top hits of the year, and there was little doubt that *Can-Can* was indeed a resounding hit. It went on to become Porter's second longest running show (surpassed only by *Kiss Me, Kate*), playing for nearly two and a half years on Broadway. London, too, received it with unenthusiastic notices, but it ended up running a full year.

Two months after the opening of *Can-Can*, while Cole was in Holly-wood overseeing the filming of *Kiss Me, Kate*, he was called urgently back to New York and Linda's bedside. Never before had she allowed her illnesses to interfere with Cole's smallest career obligation, but this time it was out of her hands. Linda's doctors had summoned him home, knowing their patient's condition was terminal.

The emphysema which for so long had placed a tremendous strain on her heart and lungs had at last depleted her reserve strength. Although she was kept in an iron lung to facilitate her breathing, as the days passed it was clear she was suffering the agonies of slow suffocation. George Eells reports that she 'clutched at her husband's hand and, in a gesture that was designed to comfort him, whispered that death held no terror. "I want to die, I'm in so much pain."' Then she added that she wanted to be buried high on Buxton Hill, overlooking the Berkshire Mountains; the estate in Williamstown that she single-handedly had discovered, bought with her own funds, repaired, and decorated with such exquisite taste.

From a place he had at first been reluctant to visit Buxton Hill[4] had by now become an idyllic retreat where Cole repaired to his studio at the foot of the hill from Friday night until Monday morning and felt at his most creative. Evenings would be spent with guests at the main house. It was a special place for the 'Coleporteurs', one that was discussed affectionately and frequently during that last week of Linda's life. Then, although Cole never left her bedside, his urging and their reminiscing could no longer keep Linda alive. Death came to her early on the morning of May 20.

Cole decided to disobey Linda's last wish and have her remains interred in the family plot in Peru – where he left a grave for himself. (Curiously, he is buried with his father to his right and Linda to his left.) One can only guess at his reasons for over-riding Linda's final request (especially in view of the fact

[4] So important was Buxton Hill to Cole, that early in the 1940s he named his music publishing firm after it. Buxton Hill Publications was subsequently taken over by Harms, Inc. but many of Cole's scores still bear the former imprint.

Linda, 1954

that the final six years of his life were spent as a recluse at Buxton Hill) but it may have been that the presence of her grave on the Massachusetts property would have been overwhelmingly depressing to him, or that he only saw his *own* final place in Peru, Indiana, the plains he had sprung from, and in the self-centred manner that was part of his nature, visualized himself resting among those who had given their utmost for him and whose love he cherished.

As for Linda's bequests, except for a few gifts of jewellery to some of her long-standing friends, Cole inherited everything. Chided by her social set in the last two years of her life for curbing her extravagant tastes and not ordering, as she used to, a dozen gowns or elaborate jewellery, Linda countered that she wanted to leave Cole an even two million dollars. She nearly succeeded; her estate was valued at $1,939,671. As a memorial to Linda who so loved flowers, especially roses, shortly after her death Cole hired horticulturalists to develop an exquisite pink rose which was called the 'Linda Porter Rose'[5].

That summer, blessed work took over again. After they had been turned down by Frank Loesser, who was busy writing his one and only opera, *The Most Happy Fella*, Feuer and Martin with whom Cole had worked so smoothly on *Can-Can* approached him. They offered him the musical version of the light comedy *Ninotchka*. Cole was not proud, he did not mind being

[5] The flower's developers overrode his suggestion that the splendid new flower be called 'The Mrs. Cole Porter Rose'.

second choice to write songs for what had been Garbo's first comedy. He knew his talent suited a light romance about a beautiful but unyielding Soviet commissar sent to Paris to investigate why a USSR composer had seemingly defected. He felt his Russian-Parisian-Jewish major-minor songs would be eminently suitable to her seduction by a handsome actor's agent with all the things (including *Silk Stockings*, the name of the show) a woman who has never been exposed to them desires. What he did not know was that the months ahead would be fraught with tension; what he never even suspected was that it would be his last Broadway venture.

It started auspiciously enough when the producers hired George S. Kaufman[6], king of the comedy playwrights, to fashion the script and direct the show. Kaufman collaborated on the libretto with his wife Lueen MacGrath, but Feuer and Martin felt there were not enough gags and laughs.

Noel Coward and Marlene Dietrich (a great friend of the German actress Hildegarde Neff, chosen for the Garbo role) came to Philadelphia to see a run-through. 'I'm told the show cost half a million dollars,' he said to Neff, 'in which case, I wonder why you have to wear clothes my charlady wouldn't be caught dead in.' When she shrugged her shoulders he added, 'You were quite delicious, but your first entrance had no build up, has to be changed. But before you get to New York they'll change practically everything.'

Noel's dire prediction was to come true, and while the show was still in Philadelphia, after much in-fighting, the Kaufmans bowed out and Abe Burroughs took over. Of course, his revisions caused much delay in the production reaching Broadway and the changes in the book inevitably necessitated Cole's re-writing much of the score.

At last, after Feuer himself took over the direction, a reasonably polished *Silk Stockings* eventually opened on Broadway on February 24, 1955. The birthpangs and postponements were exposed by all the critics, especially Walter Kerr who noted: '*Silk Stockings* was the end-product of a fabulous out-of-town sortie in which the authors were changed, the choreographers were changed, and the changes were changed.' Even Cole, who so adored opening nights, threw up his hands and left on a European tour once the show was 'frozen', four days before the opening.

In spite of all the re-writing the rest of the critics said that the book was heavy-handed and Feuer's direction lacked the gossamer touch of Ernst Lubitsch's *Ninotchka*. What allowed *Silk Stockings* to chalk up a run of 478 performances and, in spite of being one of the most expensive productions of its time, to turn in a profit was Cole's score. And everybody noted it.

---

[6] Kaufman had collaborated with Moss Hart on straight comedies including *Once in a Lifetime*, *You Can't Take It With You* and *The Man Who Came to Dinner*. As musical sketch-writer, director or librettist he had his hand in many Broadway hits including *The Coconuts*, *Animal Crackers*, *Strike Up the Band*, *Of Thee I Sing*, *Face The Music*, *Let 'Em Eat Cake*, *I'd Rather Be Right* and *Guys and Dolls*.

It was by no means one of his better efforts, but it had some successful numbers which helped lighten the dialogue. The title song, wandering between major and minor, is an attractive ballad. Other numbers, not hits, but more than serviceable, were 'Stereophonic Sound', 'Without Love', 'Paris Loves Lovers', and 'Satin and Silk'. But the hit of the show, and one of Cole's now-standard numbers, which was sung by Don Ameche as the actor's agent, was undoubtedly 'All of You'.

Fred Lounsberry, an eminent critic of popular lyrics, wrote some cogent remarks at the time the song was published. Excerpts from his essay are printed below the lyric.

Verse
After watching your appeal from ev'ry angle
There's a big romantic deal I've got to
   wangle,
For I've fallen for a certain luscious lass,
And it's not a passing fancy or a fancy pass.

Refrain
I love the looks of you, the lure of you,
I'd love to make a tour of you[7]
The eyes, the arms, the mouth of you,
The east, west, north and the south of you.
I'd love to gain complete control of you,
And handle even the heart and soul of you,
So love at least a small percent of me, do.
For I love all of you.

In a prudish community one might even be arrested for singing it ... the tour of you comes to an end at the 'south of you!' ... The opposites Porter had juggled for years in the relative privacy of theatres are publicly reconciled ... Beginning with a trait for which he is famous, there is Porter economy in 'All of You'. 63 of the 68 words in the refrain are mere monosyllables. The other 5 with 2 syllables each barely qualify as polysyllables at the minimum rate.

... Rhymes are intelligent, original and striking. The simple 'lure of you' rhymes with 'tour of you', and the simpler 'mouth of you' rhymes with 'south of you'. A child could spell the rhyming words, but he'd have to ask his parents what Porter's arrangement of them is all about.

This adult complexity with rudimentary materials is a sign of Porter's vital common touch. It's also a sign of his taste. No word is vulgar. No word, in itself, is even suggestive.

Samples of Porter's alliteration are included too: 'I love the looks of you, the lure of you.' Later on he has 'handle even the heart', and 'complete control'. ... The song is integrated ... to the story. Since it is sung to the Communist Ninotchka, well trained to pooh-pooh sentiment ...

How does the song apply to the man who sings it? 'All Of You' is sung by an American talent agent, and it's in precisely the terms an agent would use: After watching you *appeal* from every *angle*, there's a big romantic *deal* I've got to *wangle*. The italicized words are obviously the shop talk of an agent, and in the refrain ... *Handle* even the heart and soul of you and '... a small *percent* of me do. '*Complete control*' is an agent's phrase and even 'tour' has a theatrical flavour.

Cast in the language of a talent agent and applicable to Ninotchka, 'All Of

---

[7] For the movie version this line only became acceptable when Porter changed it to 'The sweet of you, the pure of you'.

You' fits *Silk Stocking* like a glove. It must accept the heavy honours of a lyric
masterpiece. Cole Porter's music for 'All of You' isn't bad either.

More than 'not bad' was the judgement of the American people, for 'All Of
You' was soon being played everywhere. Cole, by this time, was hard at work
in Hollywood on his score for *High Society*, MGM's musical adaptation of
Philip Barry's *The Philadelphia Story* which had starred Katharine Hepburn.

The stage play and film were about moneyed Philadelphians, and
emphasized sophistication, gloss and artifice over honesty. In the film the
setting became even more lavish and stuffy: Newport and its 200-room
mansions. Instead of a brittle, biting Hepburn we now had the softer and more
alluring Grace Kelly starring. As her ex-husband who will eventually win her
back from her tedious fiancé, Bing Crosby sang some of the finest songs ever
written for him: 'I Love You, Samantha', which Cole considered the best song
in the movie, and 'True Love'. Frank Sinatra and Celeste Holm who played a
pair of reporters and Louis Armstrong whose band was hired to provide the
music were not overlooked. Sinatra scored with 'You're Sensational', he and
Holm had an amusing duet called 'Who Wants to Be a Millionaire', and
Armstrong recorded the 'High Society Calypso' and 'Now You Has Jazz'. One
of the film's memorable moments was Sinatra and Crosby's rendition of
'Well, Did You Evah?', borrowed from *Du Barry Was a Lady*.

Bing Crosby, Grace Kelly
and Frank Sinatra, *High
Society*, 1956

When the picture was released in August 1956, 'True Love' immediately took off and eventually became one of the best-selling recordings of the year. Although Cole was never fond of the way Bing Crosby sang his song, he believed it had a chance to win the Academy Award. Frustrated because, in spite of all the wonderful songs he had turned out for the movies he had never won an Oscar, as soon as 'True Love' was nominated, Cole hired Stanley Musgrove, a publicity agent, who did his utmost to spur the song onward.

'True Love' sounds rather country-and-western because of its 3/4 loping rhythm. Its first theme (Fig 1, below) begins in that way, but, by the time we reach the third bar on the words 'give to me' and the introduction of a diminished chord, we realize we are dealing with a memorable Porterian motif.

Fig. 1

Then its bridge (Fig 2, below) wanders freshly in and amazingly out of a new key:

Fig. 2

Max Dreyfus[8], who certainly knew a good song when he saw one, wrote to Cole in late 1956 about his admiration for the song: 'In all my sixty-odd years of music publishing nothing has given me more personal pleasure and gratification than the extraordinary success of your "True Love". It is truly a simple, beautiful, tasteful composition worthy of a Franz Schubert.' He added. 'This also gives me a chance to tell you something that you must have known – that I have loved my association with you through all these years.'

Cole had hardly got back to New York after a tour of the Greek islands when he was on his way to Hollywood to do a new score, a film about a group of itinerant dancers called *Les Girls*. While there he would also write two new songs required for the film version of *Silk Stockings*. One of them, 'The Ritz Rock and Roll', was created after much research and listening to the then current dance craze, but beyond earning him marks for effort it was quite forgettable.

---

[8] In addition to Cole's songs Dreyfus's firm published the works of Jerome Kern, Sigmund Romberg, Rudolph Friml, Vincent Youmans, George Gershwin, Kurt Weill, Richard Rodgers among others.

Of the dozen songs Cole wrote for *Les Girls*,[9] most of them sounding like left-overs from *Can-Can* and *Silk Stockings*, five were used. One of them, 'Ca, C'est l'Amour' (replete with its phonetic pronunciation – Sah Say L'Amour – under the title), merited a fair amount of popularity, while the others could charitably be called serviceable.

That autumn Cole's sharp stomach pains, which had begun in the spring, grew worse and towards the end of the year he checked into Columbia-Presbyterian Hospital for a complete examination. A large lower stomach ulcer, the result of many years of heavy drinking, was discovered and in January 1957 much of the patient's intestine was removed. Two weeks later, Cole left the hospital feeling fit and ready to begin the usual meticulous research which always preceded a new project. This was to be his first television special – DuPont's *Show of the Month*. S. J. Perelman would write the libretto and Cole would set his songs into the story of *Aladdin*.

As it turned out, *Aladdin* was to be Cole's last score. Unfortunately it shows very little of the wit that Cole generally brought to fairy tales or fantasy. Perelman's script moved the hero into ancient China and owed more to slapstick than to his usual vitriolic wit, while Cole's music, except for one or two pentatonic-like melodies, did not even seem to try for the kind of elegant East-West fusion Richard Rodgers had achieved in *The King and I* and of which Cole was entirely capable. Because he was writing for the mass media, Cole wrote down, held back and produced lyrics that were only slightly naughty, which made them sound juvenile rather than adult.

A month before the show was to be put out on television, it was rumoured to be 'magical'. But Cole, whose stomach was acting up again and whose right leg was now deeply inflamed, seemed uninterested in *Aladdin*. He knew he had delivered a serviceable score, collected his fee, and closed the book on re-writes.

He re-entered Columbia-Presbyterian where examination revealed that now the *upper* part of his intestine was affected by a duodenal ulcer. But what was much more serious was the condition of his right leg. Not only was the tibia bone inflamed, but the leg, from the knee down, had badly degenerated and gangrene had set in.

The ulcer responded to treatment and a few days later the leg too reacted admirably to the thirty-second operation, the removal of a small piece of bone. But things were to be different after the thirty-third operation, an attempt to reconstruct the right leg. In spite of massive doses of antibiotics, this time the leg refused to heal and, after some weeks at home with Cole's

[9] Cole himself was hard on the score for *Les Girls*. First he said the only music necessary to the film was a song for the vaudeville act. Then he apologized for finishing the score, saying his songs were negligible – explaining that he already was suffering badly from an ulcer while writing it.

valet treating it, even he, who had been nursing Cole's leg for years, became unable to distinguish between the healthy and unhealthy tissue.

Cole was rushed back to the hospital, at which point Dr. Frank Stinchfield brought him the news that it was imperative to amputate his leg. Cole was dazed and shocked when the surgeon added that the operation could not be postponed for more than twenty-four hours. Asked whether he had any options, Dr. Stinchfield replied, 'Your options are you can keep your leg – or keep your life.'

On April 3, 1958, after twenty-one years and thirty-four operations, Cole Porter lost the battle to save his wounded limb. Although he healed quickly, was fitted with an artificial limb and was released from the hospital in late May he often bemoaned, 'I'm half a man now.'

All his friends came to visit, trying to cheer him up. Noel Coward came twice in the ten days Cole was in the hospital after the operation, and remarked that the 'lines of ceaseless pain have been wiped from his face. He is a bit fretful about having to manage with his new leg, but he will get over that. I think if I had to endure all those years of agony I would have had the damned thing off at the beginning, but it is a cruel decision to have to make and it involves much sex, vanity and many fears of being repellent. However it is now done at last, and I am convinced that his whole life will cheer up and that his work will profit accordingly.' But Noel was entirely wrong. Whatever Cole became after the surgery, he was no longer a composer or a lyricist, no longer a pianist, for he rarely opened the instrument, and after his sixty-eight birthday on June 9, 1958 not even a dinner guest – for that was the last time he went out to dine at a friend's house.

For the next five years until his death in 1962 he was occupied only by the past and his punctiliousness. An afternoon drive at 4.15; a cocktail at 5; a rest until 7. A single dinner guest at 8. Few friends came to see him, he alternated between Williamstown and Hollywood. In the last five years of his life he was frequently in hospital, never totally free from pain.

Cole Porter died in St. John's Hospital, Santa Monica, California at 11.05 on October 15, 1964. He is interred in the Mount Hope Cemetery in Peru, Indiana. He requested a simple private burial service, a quotation from the Bible followed by the Lord's Prayer. Although it was written lightly, Noel Coward's introduction to his Las Vegas club act seems to this writer a eulogy Cole would have approved of:

Mr. Irving Berlin	Richard Rodgers it's true
Often emphasizes sin	Took a more romantic view
In a charming way.	Of that sly biological urge,
Mr. Coward, we know,	But it really was Cole
Wrote a song or two to show	Who contrived to make the whole
Sex was here to stay.	Thing merge.

NOEL
1959-1973

OWARD VISITED COLE FREQUENTLY in the years before Porter's agonized passing. Invariably, some of the older man's morbidity rubbed off onto Noel's generally sunny disposition. Six years before Cole's tormented demise and shortly after he visited Porter in New York Coward began his own paean to old age and death; a serio-comedy called *Waiting in the Wings*. Amateur psychiatrists may say he had not written Violet's death out of his psyche, and that he had been plunged into the theatre world of intrigue and the nuisances of emigration before he had a full chance to express the tremendous loss he felt when his mother died. But, whatever it may have been, writing and producing this play coupled with the unavailability (or lack of interest) of both Ethel Merman and Rosalind Russell in his musical, *Later Than Spring*, kept Noel from the folly of starring an antiquated singer in yet another operetta.

Waiting in the Wings, which Coward had begun in 1958 and completed the next year, was to be his own catharsis, and although he dedicated the play to Dame Sybil Thorndike he might just as well have written Violet Veitch Coward on the flyleaf. The sentimental story which shows a remarkable understanding of actresses, their pride, their petty jealousies, their battles with old age and their desire to keep on acting takes place in The Wings, a home for retired professionals, and the writing is mature Coward.

Besides Dame Sybil, the play starred Marie Lohr, Mary Clare, Lewis Casson and a full complement of older performers, dear to the hearts of the British public. Plunged in among these old-timers was Graham Payn playing the youngish secretary of The Wings.

In his role of a former vaudevillian, Graham was given a fine song in the third act. There, Coward was even able to insert a brief musical interlude which does not seem forced, and wherein he had the denizens of the home perform some of their old music-hall numbers climaxing with one of Coward's best ballads, 'Come the Wild, Wild Weather[1]' which he gave to Graham.

'I have never received such abuse in my life,' Coward was to write after reading the critics on the morning after. 'I was accused of tastelessness, vulgarity, sentimentality, etc. To read them was like repeatedly being slashed in the face.'

Coward had poured out his heart in this play – for no other playwright had such respect, familiarity and love for the old troupers – and the critics

---

[1] See Musical Analysis Appendix.

greeted it with vitriol. To make matters worse, his novel *Pomp and Circumstance* which was published while *Waiting in the Wings* was still running was greeted with the same abuse. A light book, written with uncanny perception from the feminine viewpoint, it was dismissed as an 'island bagatelle' by the journalists who had a field day attacking his tax situation, his decision to become an expatriate and even his physical well-being.

'You cannot compare his vapid novel with the biting work of his early years,' said the *Sunday Express* on October 30, 1960. 'What then has happened? It is not just that Mr. Coward has picked the wrong medium, his plays and musicals of recent years have met with the same disappointed sighs which will greet this book. For all this I blame the inspector of taxes. For the last few years, in order to cut down on the taxes he pays to the crown he admires so extravagantly, Mr. Coward has wandered abroad – Bermuda, Jamaica, now Switzerland where no Colour can ever be Trooped. The exile may think that he misses his pageantry, but he misses much more. Since Noel Coward went away, the rest of us have moved on. We live no more in a world of cocktail patriotism, we live in the sharper world of the 60s. He has stayed where he was in a world which no longer exists, a world of droopy dukes. To sign off from the world is to lose the stimulus it gives. The tropics may not breed ulcers but they do not breed genius either. It might cost Mr. Coward many thousands of pounds to come back. The rewards might be greater; he might recapture the greatness he once had and we might regain a genius.'

But Coward had the last word. The public as always being the final arbiter, the novel, although it sold well in Britain, was a smash hit in America where it remained on the *New York Times* bestseller list for twenty-six weeks. *Waiting in the Wings* went on to run successfully for more than six months and toured to packed houses for another three. Not only could Coward laugh at the critics 'all the way to the bank', but the London *Sunday Times* offered him a soap box from which to answer those ever-present critical bashings in print. Noel sent in three long articles on the sorry state of the 'new' British drama from his chalet in Switzerland. This retreat had been purchased inexpensively and been totally refurbished with the large sums of money Coward had been paid for two cameo appearances the year before.[2]

The articles criticized the playwrights, the actors, and finally enabled Coward to aim his most pointed barbs at the reviewers themselves. In the first he cautioned the dramatists to 'consider the public ... Coax it, charm it, interest it, stimulate it, shock it now and then if you must ... but never, never, never bore the living hell out of it.'

---

[2] Noel played Hawthorn in *Our Man in Havana* and King in *Surprise Package*.

The actors, especially the method actors, known for their mumbled lines and slovenly appearance, were the next to be put on the carpet, but Coward saved his sharpest words for the critics who, he said, considered 'any successful play presented by a commercial management in the West End automatically inferior in quality to anything produced on a shoe string in the East End or Sloane Square'.

The critics, the playwrights and even the mumbling actors answered in angry print as was to be expected. Certainly, the attendant publicity only made the public flock to see Coward in cameo roles in films or rush to the bookshop or the theatre for another glimpse of his work.

But that winter Noel was too busy to answer back for he completed the balance of his score for *Sail Away* which was to be his first musical to have its première in New York rather than London. Again he would not only provide score and libretto but would direct the proceedings. He even went so far as to

Sail Away, New York

design the logo and draw the cover picture of the programme and record sleeve.

The birthpangs of most Broadway shows are well known, but Coward's project seems to have come in for more of its antic share in its transformation from *Later Than Spring* to *Sail Away*. Yet all looked fine at its opening in Boston on August 9, 1961.

Elaine Stritch and Jean Fenn co-starred. Again Noel could not seem to abandon his older operetta soprano, for Miss Fenn, on the roster of the Metropolitan Opera, was just that. Luckily, the veteran choreographer Joe Layton helped Coward see that these co-starring roles would be tantamount to sinking the cruise ship on which *Sail Away* takes place; even luckier was the fact that, when the company arrived in Philadelphia, half its then gigantic budget of $400,000 was still unspent, allowing Coward the luxury of re-writes and recasting in preparation for the Broadway opening. The *Philadelphia Inquirer* reported:

> SHAKEDOWN RUN OF SAIL AWAY HAS SHAKEN LOOSE ONE OF ITS STARS
> Jean Fenn plays a disillusioned married woman who goes on the fun cruise to forget and falls in love with a younger man. Co-starred with Elaine Stritch, the singer was entitled to have her role on a par with the comedienne's ... Miss Stritch gives a runaway performance that would be hard to match under any conditions, so the soprano part had to be built up out of proportion, and received critical rebuffs in Boston and here. With the New York opening only three weeks off, playwright Coward decided to reconstruct this play and write out the role ... Backstage gossip disclosed other frictions between the playwright and his singing star. *Sail Away* is Miss Fenn's first Broadway show and Coward's forty-fifth theatrical venture, but she insisted on choosing her own stage costumes. While directing a rehearsal, Coward was heard to remark, 'why does she insist on wearing the linen iron lung?'

But in spite of the re-writes, and although it looked like an instant hit, the show did not take Broadway by storm. It ran for a profitable six months, and then the public suddenly fell away. Curiously, it did the same when mounted a year later in London. Yet *Sail Away* is one of Coward's sunniest scores, and its songs are still valid.

The title song, of course, has become a standard. But one cannot overlook the musical's biggest hit 'Why Do the Wrong People Travel' ('When the right people stay back home/What explains this mass mania/To leave Pennsylvania/And clack around like flocks of geese/Demanding dry martinis on the Isles of Greece?'), especially as it brought the house down in Miss Stritch's deadpan delivery. She scored a bullseye too with my special favourite, not particularly memorable for its tune, but containing indelible lyrics. Anyone who has ever tried to comprehend a foreign language phrasebook cannot be immune to 'Useless Useful Phrases'. The lyrics of its choruses are printed below.

Refrain 1
Pray tell me the time,
It is six,
It is seven,
It's half past eleven,
It's twenty to two.
I want thirteen stamps,
Does your child have convulsions?
Please bring me some rhubarb,
I need a shampoo.
How much is that hat?
I desire some red stockings.
My mother is married,
These boots are too small,
My aunt has a cold,
Shall we go to the opera?
This meat is disgusting,
Is this the town hall?

Refrain 2
My cousin is deaf,
Kindly bring me a hatchet,
Pray pass me the pepper,
What pretty cretonne.
What time is the train,
It is late,
It is early,
It's running on schedule,

It's here,
It has gone.
I've written six letters,
I've written no letters,
Pray fetch me a horse,
I have need of a groom.
This isn't my passport,
This isn't my hatbox,
Please show me the way
To Napoleon's tomb.

Refrain 3
The weather is cooler,
The weather is hotter,
Pray fasten my corsets,
Please bring me a cloak,
I've lost my umbrella,
I'm in a great hurry, I'm going,
I'm staying,
D'you mind if I smoke?
This mutton is tough
There's a mouse in my bedroom,
This egg is delicious
This soup is too thick,
Please bring me a trout,
What an excellent pudding,
Pray hand me my gloves,
I'm going to be sick!

Sail Away had other gems. Chief among them were the entertainment director Mimi Paragon's (Stritch) opening songs, 'Come To Me' wherein Coward deftly introduced his characters without stopping the plot ('The work that I have chosen,/To be a professional pepper-upper/Isn't everyone's cuppa tea./ But I've wit and guile/And a big false smile/And the tourists rely on me'), and the sensitive ballad in which Mimi[3] reconciles and accepts her yen for a much younger man. Coward also invented a clever way to circumvent the old bugaboo of reprise. In *Sail Away*'s first act he introduces 'The Passenger Is Always Right', sung by the purser and crew, and uses the same song with the same singers dressed now as owners of a mid-Eastern bazaar to open the second act with 'The *Customer* is Always Right'.

By adding 'A Beatnick Love Affair' Coward attempted contemporaneity, but still the critics found the evening old-hat. Norman Nadell writing in the *World Telegram* impaled Coward with '*Sail Away* easily could have qualified as the musical of the year if it had opened in 1936'.

Noel, quite accustomed to these thrusts, had gone back to Jamaica disappointed that the American reviewers had been no kinder than their British counterparts. Since the box-office was doing well, and *Sail Away* had a

[3] Originally sung by Jean Fenn.

healthy advance, he thought he might take this opportunity to re-write the musical. But he put these thoughts aside to think out his next project when his future plans were interrupted by the news of Jack Wilson's death.

'He was a part of my life,' Noel was to enter in his dairy, 'for so very many years. I cannot feel sad that he is dead. He has been less than half alive for the last ten years ... Naturally, now that he is dead, my mind is inclined to skip the disintegration and fly back to when he was handsome, witty, charming, good company. What a hideous foolish waste of life! ... Of course, I am sad. Of course, I feel horrid inside. But not nearly so much as I might have. To me he died years ago.'

Jack's death coupled with the recent deaths of other intimate friends plunged Noel into a period of musing about his own eventual exit. 'One by one they go – a bit chipped off here, a bit chipped off there.' The gloom was relieved some ten days later after Cole Lesley and Noel discussed the subject with some humour. 'We decided we should have to get on with life until our turn came. I said, "After all, the day had to go on and breakfast had to be eaten," and he [Lesley] replied that if I died he might find it a little difficult to eat breakfast but would probably be peckish by lunch-time.'

But soon, with no prodding from Coward, future plans were to take care of themselves. Six months later, while the London production of *Sail Away* was being prepared, Noel received an offer from Herman Levin, its producer, to write the score for *The Sleeping Prince*. Although his experience with *Sail Away* had discouraged him from having anything to do with an American musical ever again, he had to admit that the story of a prince from Carpathia, a mythical country, who comes to London for the Coronation of George V in 1911 and falls in love with an American showgirl was his kind of story set in a period he knew well.

There was hardly much doubt that Coward would snap at the project, especially since it would mean working again with Joe Layton whose choreography had meshed so artfully with Noel's direction of *Sail Away*. Add to this Harry Kurnitz, a wag, friend and admirable librettist, who would be supplying the book. It was especially comforting because in his heart of hearts Coward believed the only thing that had kept *Sail Away* from a two-year run was his own failure as a librettist.

This musical which was eventually to be called *The Girl Who Came to Supper* took shape more quickly than *Sail Away* because Kurnitz and Coward were able to work *simultaneously*. Noel completed most of the nineteen songs – waltzes, lovesongs, comic songs, dances, soliloquy, invocations to London, and a national anthem for Carpathia (which, being mythical, never had one) – in the score within three months and by February 1963 the musical was ready for casting. Florence Henderson was chosen at the outset, but it was not so easy to settle on the star role of the Prince. Rex Harrison and Christopher Plummer both turned it down, while Keith Michell as well as Jose Ferrer accepted. Ferrer was finally chosen. And then the project had to be put on ice until a pregnant Florence Henderson delivered her baby in late August.

Yet, before the project even got to its first stage rehearsals, Noel was offered another plum. Hugh Martin, the composer, and Timothy Gray, the lyricist, asked Noel to direct *High Spirits*, a musical version of *Blithe Spirit* upon which they had been working for several years.

With most of these two scores complete, and waiting in the wings, Coward went off to Australia to direct *Sail Away*. The season certainly looked like a clean Coward sweep when a revival of *Private Lives* opened to splendid reviews at the Duke of York's Theatre in London. Exonerated from having written a decadent comedy, Coward crowed, 'It has suddenly been discovered, after thirty-three years, that it is a good play.'

At last, in September, *The Girl Who Came To Supper* was staged in Boston where it was greeted with unanimous raves. The reception in its next stop, Toronto, was deplorable, the *Toronto Star* claiming SUPPER MUSICAL IS MOSTLY LEFTOVERS, although all the papers admitted that the production, dancing and casting were imaginative.

By the time it arrived in Philadelphia, its next-to-last stop before Broadway, the cast was performing smoothly and the majority of reviews were so good that Noel went off to Jamaica. He was called back a few days later when President Kennedy was assassinated in Dallas.

Coward not only suffered a general loss, but a private one as well because of his closeness to Jack and Jacqueline Kennedy. The tragedy would have repercussions in his musical as well, since the opening number, 'Long Live the King – If He Can', with lines like

My uncle, the Grand Duke Stanislas   Everything went according to plan
Slept tight – in a bullet-proof nightshirt   And that, my friend,
Until one fatal Michaelmas   Was the end
His valet, like a stupid ass,   Of Uncle Stan.
Forgot to lay out the right shirt.

would now be out of the question. To make matters worse, Joe Layton was in hospital with hepatitis and, since the whole opening would have to be re-staged, Coward flew back and shepherded the production on its journey into Broadway.

New York's opinion was mixed. Kurnitz and Coward came in for the largest share of brickbats. Most of the critics noted that the title of the musical itself was a bastardization of *The Man Who Came to Dinner*. 'Even in his grave,' wrote the reviewer for *Time Magazine*, 'George S. Kaufman [*Dinner*'s play-wright] could think of funnier lines than Harry Kurnitz has been able to confect ... and Noel Coward could have given *Supper* some Noel Coward songs instead of the badly toasted marshmelodies he provided.'

The unexpected saviour of the evening, whose songs, like Mary Martin's in *Leave it to Me*, bore little relation to the plot, was making her American début. Her name was Tessie O'Shea and one critic wrote that 'her ovation sounded like the coronation of a new star', while another gushed, 'I'm in love with Miss O'Shea – every one of her two hundred or so pounds (at the old evaluation of $4.80 to the pound!)'

Once the show opened, Coward assessed its chances of survival. He said, 'Two factors militate against it [being a hit] are not enough heart in the book (particularly at the end of the play) and Jo Ferrer not being physically attractive enough.'

Coward was right *The Girl Who Came To Supper* managed to play 113 performances although some of its songs, especially 'Saturday Night at the Rose and Crown', a pub number (whose lusty opening phrase is printed below), and 'I'll Remember Her',[4] an exquisite bitter-sweet ballad, have gone on to become Coward standards. But for the next two years it nettled him to know that *Supper* was the only one of his musicals that never made it to London's West End.

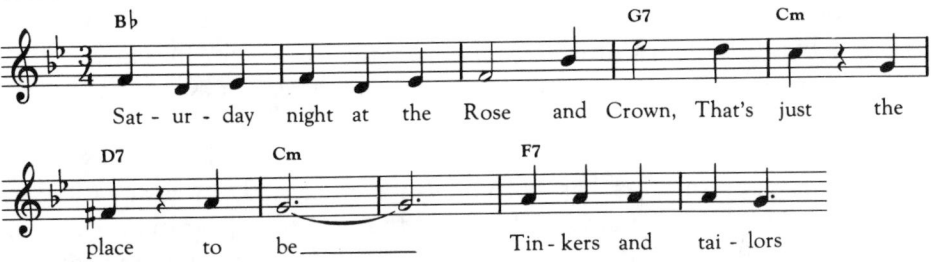

Although *The Girl Who Came to Supper* was to be Coward's last musical, Noel had no intention of abandoning the form, and it was with great relish that he took on the job of directing *High Spirits*. Noel, whose public knew he had never had anything to do with a musical that was not of his own making, warned Gray: 'No matter what I say, no matter what *you* say, everybody is going to believe I wrote the whole thing.' Actually, Coward's only contribution to the project was the closing lines of 'Home, Sweet Heaven'.

High Spirits starred Beatrice Lillie, Tammy Grimes and Louise Troy, and throughout rehearsals Miss Lillie, always mercurial and unreliable in lines, created such tension and offended Coward's sense of theatrical order so deeply that he believed he developed an ulcer from their frequent arguments. At last, with the opening only a few weeks off, when Tammy Grimes actually entered hospital because of 'self-induced hysteria', and the production was in

---

[4] See Musical analysis Appendix.

tatters around him, Gower Champion was called in to take over the direction.
Coward flew off to Jamaica in a state of near collapse.

Ironically, *High Spirits* was successful at the box office and ran for 375
performances. Beatrice Lillie single-handedly saved a mediocre score and
production. Norman Nadell, reviewer for the *World-Telegram and Sun*, wrote:

> Not that there's ever been the slightest doubt, but Beatrice Lillie's performance as
> Madame Arcati, the happy medium in *High Spirits*, re-affirms her place in the
> recorded history of the 20th century, along with the Battle of Jutland and Salk
> vaccine. When she is on stage, the musical achieves both the sublime and the
> uproariously ridiculous.

Unfortunately, while *High Spirits* was doing solid business at the Alvin Theater
in New York, it was decided to open the musical in London's West End. With
Cicely Courtneidge struggling valiantly in the part of Madame Arcati, the
production failed miserably and closed ignominiously – all this while *High
Spirits* continued to run blithely on 52nd Street.

As his sixty-sixth birthday neared, Coward was beginning to be
regarded as a 'national treasure', and revivals of his plays were everywhere. A
Noel Coward Repertory Company had even sprouted in New York and
scheduled three plays that had, by now, achieved classic status. Britain, not to
be outdone, was honouring its native son with a production at the Old Vic, the
first by a living dramatist under the new National Theatre management. *Hay
Fever*, Noel's great success of forty years ago, was chosen and Coward himself
agreed to direct it.

Meanwhile, by June 1965, he had written a new play inspired by many
creative impulses, not, as has been so often suggested, by a situation in
Coward's own life. Chief among them was the urge to appear once again on
stage, what Coward called his 'swan song'. But perhaps more important was
Noel's support for changing the Homosexual Bill which was then being argued
violently in the House of Lords.

The story itself, Noel admits, 'was suggested by a scene in David Cecil's
biography of Max Beerbohm when Constance Collier, after years of non-
contact, suddenly descends on him when he is an old man and flattens him
with her vitality'. Coward adds that Somerset Maugham, whose homosexuality was now widely publicised and who had written Noel a moving letter when
his lover, Gerald Haxton, died, was another source of inspiration for *A Song at
Twilight*.

In the play, a testy, revered, pompous older playwright, Sir Hugo
Latymer, is threatened with blackmail by an actress with whom he has had an
affair early in his life. The actress has a packet of homosexual letters and in the
course of the play she and the playwright's secretary-wife expose the hidden
character of Sir Hugo before the letters are finally returned to him.

This sensitive drama is as eloquent a plea for openness in human relationships, be they hetero- or homosexual, as has ever been staged. The critics, even Coward's most severe ones, noted this and the notices for A Song at Twilight were almost unanimously glowing.

Always interested in appearing in a repertoire of plays to stave off boredom, Coward added Shadows of the Evening and Come into the Garden, Maud, two shorter efforts. Since the setting for all three plays remained the same hotel suite in Switzerland, the plays were produced under the title of Suite in Three Keys, (presaging Neil Simon's Plaza Suite and California Suite). He played a variety of roles opposite Irene Worth and Lilli Palmer.

But it was an exhausting schedule, for on days when he gave both matinée and evening performances Coward would need to be at the theatre for a full eight hours. Not only did this tax his strength but Noel began to notice he was forgetting lines. Irene and Lilli covered for him adeptly and the public was none the wiser, but the situation, which was due to ever-accelerating arteriosclerosis, terrified Coward.

It was not unusual for Coward to decide after three months to close a play that was playing to near-capacity. What upset him more was the negative reply from his doctor as to the wisdom of acting in Suite in Three Keys[5] on Broadway. Coward, so accustomed to capitalizing on his successes on the other side of the ocean, accepted the opinion reluctantly. He was never again to appear on stage. But he did not stop acting.

That very year he was seen on television as Caesar in Richard Rodgers's musical version of Androcles and the Lion and soon with Elizabeth Taylor and Richard Burton in the cameo role of the Witch of Capri in Tennessee Williams's Boom (a version of his play The Milk Train Doesn't Stop Here Anymore). Early the next year he appeared in The Italian Job opposite Michael Caine.

Coward's creativity did not dry up during the winters in Jamaica and the springs and summers in Switzerland. In between filming Coward produced stories (Bon Voyage) and verse (Not Yet the Dodo), appeared on television, and radio, did recordings, interviews and, of course, supervised constant revivals of his earlier work. These years culminated in what Coward called 'Holy Week', his self-mocking term for seven days of celebration, a kind of mini-coronation, leading up to Noel's seventieth birthday. The BBC aired what seemed like its complete collection of Cowardiana during a week- long outpouring on radio and television; the National Film Theatre, not to be outdone, presented an entire season of his works. Even Broadway would not

---

[5] In 1974, the year following Coward's death, Come into the Garden, Maud and a shortened version of A Song at Twilight were produced on Broadway under the title of Noel Coward in Two Keys. They starred Anne Baxter, Jessica Tandy and Hume Cronyn.

be left out and mounted a new production of *Private Lives* with Tammy Grimes and Brian Bedford. All these accolades climaxed in Martin Tickner's gala birthday celebration from the stage of the Phoenix Theatre. A galaxy of performing stars sang his songs and recited his poems.

Coward did not leave the theatre until the final champagne toast was drunk on stage at five o'clock in the morning. When he did, his loyal fans were still waiting to greet him outside. One would imagine exhaustion setting in by noon but Noel was living on pure adrenalin at his birthday luncheon. It was planned by the Queen Mother, who unfortunately was under doctor's orders to stay in bed nursing a cold, and she left him a charming message 'hoping he would manage with her daughters'. With his usual gift for understatement Coward 'managed,' and was to record the festivities in his diary:

> My birthday lunch was given by the darling Queen Mother at Clarence House, where I received a crown-encrusted cigarette-box from her, an equally crown-encrusted cigarette-case from the Queen herself and some exquisite cuff-links from Princess Margaret and Tony. During lunch the Queen asked me whether I would accept Mr. Wilson's offer of a knighthood. I kissed her hand and said, in a rather strangulated voice, 'Yes, Ma'am.' Apart from all that, my seventieth birthday was uneventful.

Noel's knighthood, although many thought it at least twenty years too late, prompted a blizzard of telegrams and congratulatory letters from all over the world. No group was more pleased than Coward's theatrical colleagues. Alec Guinness summed it up for all his fellow knights when he cabled: 'We have been like a row of teeth with a front tooth missing. Now we can smile again.'

Always the royalist, Coward felt his knighthood was the pinnacle of his success and abruptly ceased writing his diary, saying he had nothing to write that could follow this honour. But for the rest of his life he never stopped collecting awards. Two special ones he cherished were the Tony for Distinguished Service to the American Theater and his Honorary Doctorate of Letters from Sussex University.

His last public appearance was on January 14, 1973, at a gala performance of *Oh, Coward*, a cornucopia of his songs, assembled by Roderick Cook in New York. This was the American counterpart to *Cowardy Custard* a revue devised by Sir Bernard Miles, which had been running for several months at the Mermaid Theatre in London. Four days later he flew off with Cole Lesley and Graham Payn for a holiday in the sun in his beloved Jamaica.

Noel, who by now drank very little, always looked forward to the end of the day, sitting and ruminating with his two close friends. Almost ritualistically they would gather on the verandah of Firefly Hill, sunset cocktails in hand, waiting for the appearance of the milk-white owl which signalled the onset of twilight.

So it was on that night of March 25. Cole Lesley records that he and Graham were halfway down the steps of Coward's verandah heading for their own lodgings at Blue Harbour when he called to them, 'Good night, my darlings. I'll see you tomorrow.'

Noel suffered a heart attack on the morning of March 26. His servant Miguel found him on the floor of his bathroom shortly after dawn. When Miguel offered to run down to fetch Graham and Cole from Blue Harbour, he replied, 'No, it's too early, they will still be asleep.' Holding on to Miguel's hand he gave a little smile and went back to a sleep from which he was never to waken.

With the Queen Mother, 1968

Postlude

COLE PORTER expired in Santa Monica shortly before midnight on 15 October 1964 and Noel Coward died in the hours before dawn on 26 March 1973 in his beloved Blue Harbour, Jamaica. Although each man was frequently accused of being sybaritic and careless about his future, both had carefully mapped out what was to become of their possessions, their estates and had planned for the future of their creative work.

Cole had set up a trust, a decade before his death, willing his manuscripts, scores and memorabilia to Yale, his Alma Mater.[1] Buxton Hill, the 200 acre estate, in his adopted town of Williamstown, Massachussets was to become (after Cole's death) a part of Williams College. It is not known whether the honorary doctorates that both Williams and Yale awarded Cole were instrumental in his decision to leave them these generous endownments.

Nor did Porter overlook his friends and those who cared for him. Years before he died he had prepared a twenty-nine page will detailing just which paintings, jewellery, studs and cigarette cases were to be left to whom. This document specified generous bequests to friends and employees and set up a trust fund to assist the two daughters of Paul Sylvain, a former valet. Although the bulk of his six million dollar property and cash as well as half the royalties from his songs went to his cousin Jules Omar Cole (and with Jules's passing to his son, James) he left the other half of the proceeds from copyright material to Ray Kelly.

Kelly had been a close friend of Cole's before the accident, and spent much time with him after the calamity. It was he and Paul Sylvain who often carried the songwriter into the theatre and both accompanied him on his trip to Cuba.

Since the last truly successful Porter musical had been *Silk Stockings*, written nearly a decade before, Cole's executors felt at the time he died that the estate would be despatched quickly. Speaking of the time in the mid-1960s when she was hired, Florence Leeds, Executive Secretary of the Trust told me 'John Wharton [Porter's lawyer] said it would be a temporary job. Two years and then the Trust would be closed. He never suspected Porter's music would have a continuing life and growth after its composer had died.'

Robert Montgomery, Jr, who has taken over Wharton's position attested to the continuing profitability of the Trust, citing, for example, a

---

[1] The Porter material is looked after with great care by the curators of the Beinecke Rare Book and Manuscript Library and the Yale Library in New Haven.

Coward at home in Les Avants, Switzerland

recording called *Red, Hot and Blue* (no relation to the musical) made in 1990 to benefit AIDS that netted over a million dollars to the charity. He said that the reason for the Trust's long-term success is the adaptability of Cole's songs. I would add that Porter's lyrics have contemporary concepts and a stinging smartness which refuse to date.

Although early in his career Porter sprinkled his lyrics with names of celebrities like Johnny Weissmuller, Elsie de Wolfe, Frank Harris and Irene Bordoni which would have little meaning to audiences on the brink of the twenty-first century, his later works avoided this topicality in favour of the elemental: how a lover thinks of his beloved 'night and day'; what happens 'every time we say goodbye'; or that nowadays 'anything goes'. These basic feelings are balanced in Porter's work by a risqué quality (that walks the fine line avoiding smuttiness) as exemplified in so many songs, among them 'But In the Morning, No', 'Let's Do It' 'Si Vous Aimez Les Poitrines', 'I Want to be Raided By You', or 'Always True To You In My Fashion'. By eliciting a smile rather than reaching for a guffaw. Cole's work stands up through repeated hearings.

Another aspect that keeps his songs fresh is the curiosity that led him to write songs in tempi common to the far flung corners of the globe and in this he was ahead of his time. He never wrote of the parochial American experience but used a saltarella, tarantella or a beguine rhythm to underpin his lyrics.

By perhaps the most memorable quality of the songwriter whose technique reached its zenith in the 1930s, a decade of worldwide depression, was his obliviousness to the disaster all around him and his refusal to settle for less than the top. He was super-rich and never tried to hide the fact. Because of it he became a glittering beacon for the cashless intelligentsia. Where other songwriters were touting 'a cup of coffee, a sandwich and you' or were boasting 'I've got five dollars' and claiming that life was just a bowl of cherries, Porter was chronicling those who were 'down in the depths on the ninetieth floor'. If he exhorted the disillusioned, post-Crash society to look up it was not to gaze at the silver lining the dark clouds hid but at the penthouse in the sky.

In that sense he was quite different from Noel Coward, whose elegance and gentility – although self-taught – were perhaps greater than Cole's. For while Cole's lasting gift to the world is his spiciness, exotica and chronicling of the rich, Noel's enduring value – certainly in his musical works, the subject of this book – is his handling of the warm, the small, the dramatic and especially the romantic.

As miniaturists, both men have never been more popular. Yet, although the works of Noel and Cole have frequently shared a cabaret evening in recent years, with the passage of time their dissimilarities become more apparent.

Where Cole was content to write of the present and his social circle, Coward's curiosity coupled with solid theatrical roots creates mini-short stories in song. Noel never forgets he is a dramatist whose métier compels him forever to ask 'Why?'. 'What's Going to Happen to the Tots?' he wonders, when their parents have blown themselves up or overdosed on pep and/ or sleeping pills. 'I Wonder What Happened To Him', or 'Why Must the Show Go On?' he enquires, as he makes tiny revue sketches out of a song.

Cole was a libertine who accepted people as he found them; Noel was a finger wagger, partly due to his directorial soul. He becomes preachy, moralistic and somewhat patronizing in songs like 'Dance, Little Lady', 'Poor Little Rich Girl', 'Parisian Pierrot' and 'Half Caste Woman'. Fortunately he grew out of the habit in his later songs.

Happily too, the epic quality in Coward's work – *Cavalcade*, *Operette* or *Pacific 1860* – was swept aside with the years leaving the touching intimacy of songs that suggest a tête-à-tête like 'A Room With A View', 'I'll Follow My Secret Heart', 'I'll See You Again' and 'Someday I'll Find You'. Noel, who was able to express his ardour in the dialogue of his best plays like *Private Lives*,

Hay Fever or *The Vortex*, had no need to display it in music. Unable to evince it in his private life, Cole put his considerable passion in his songs.

It is well known that his passion for songwriting dissipated late in his life. Following the amputation of his leg. Porter became a semi-recluse for the last six years. Quite the opposite is true of Coward who remained to the end as gregarious and spirited as ever. His circle was eclectic and enormous – but in spite of his worldliness we are struck, when listening to his songs, by his 'Englishness'. Perhaps that is why his music is so revered by older anglophiles the world over and dismissed by younger Britons who may feel his songs are jingoistic. Of his patriotism there can be no doubt. Once he achieved his knighthood he stopped keeping a diary, claiming nothing could surpass that honour.

Although he created little in the last years of his life, he continued to meet friends and to look after his work. Fortunately, he had Cole Lesley, who had handled his business matters during his life, to see to his estate's interests after his death, and then, upon Lesley's death, Graham Payn. One would not expect Payn, a singing-actor, to have much head for running a venture the size of the Coward legacy, especially since the handling of rights and productions went so swimmingly under Lesley's eye, but Graham Payn, with the dedicated help of Joan Hirst (who had inherited Lorn Loraine's job), certainly rose to the occasion.

Looking after Noel's work is a full-time job, for although Coward's operettas (with the exception of *Bitter Sweet*) seem to be unrevivable because of their dated libretti, this is not so of his plays. *Tonight at 8:30, The Vortex, Fallen Angels, Hay Fever, Easy Virtue, Private Lives, Design For Living, Present Laughter, Blithe Spirit* and *Relative Values* are constantly performed by theatre companies round the world and the number of productions shows no sign of diminishing. *Cowardy Custard* and *Oh, Coward*, revues based on Noel's songs, are equally popular.

Cole's most popular shows are *Anything Goes* and *Kiss Me, Kate*. (*You Never Know*, one of Cole's least favourite shows, has had several recent revivals because it requires a small cast, *Jubilee* and was mounted in 1991 to celebrate the centenary of Cole's birth.) But as with Coward's operettas, the revivability of most of Porter's musicals is done in by their books.

With their deaths, Cole Porter and Noel Coward left voids in musical theatre that are still unfilled today. Although each is totally different from the other, it is impossible not to recognize even wordless Porter or Coward melodies. Add the lyric and you have an unmistakable voice. A voice that summons up the '20s and '30s more clearly than a newsreel. Black tie, white tie, clipped, nasal, irreverent. Urbane.

Chronology

Year	Porter	Coward	USA	Britain	World
1891	Cole Porter born 9 June, Peru, Indiana.		US stage under the influence of London. Herman Melville born. Carnegie Hall opened.	Gilbert & Sullivan are most popular. Oscar Wilde publishes *The Picture of Dorian Gray*.	One could sense a separation into three distinct theatrical forms: operetta, musical comedy and revue.
1894			*The Passing Show*, a political revue.	Shaw's *Arms and the Man*.	Sino-Japanese War.
1897	Given his first pony.			Tate Gallery opens. Kipling publishes *Captains Courageous*. Queen Victoria celebrates her Diamond Jubilee.	
1899		Noel Pierce Coward, born December 16, Teddington, Middlesex.	First popular magnetic recordings of sound.	Gaiety Girl musicals; *San Toy* starring Marie Tempest.	The Boer War. The Dreyfus Case.
1901	'Song of the Birds', piano piece, dedicated to his mother.		Ziegfeld's *The Little Duchess* starring his wife, Anna Held.	*A Chinese Honeymoon*, Lavish musical that ran 1,075 performances. *Bluebell in Fairyland* (pantomime).	Death of Queen Victoria; accession of Edward VII.
1902	'Boblink Waltz', published privately.		De Koven's *Maid Marian*. Raymond Hitchcock in *King Dodo*.	*The Girl From Kay's*. Lionel Monckton in *A Country Girl*.	End of the Boer War. Phonographs spread recordings and popular music throughout the world.
1904			Kern: *Mr. Wix of Wickham*.	Gibson Girls, (imported from US) introduced to Britain.	Russo-Japanese War.

1905	Enters Worcester Academy.		Broadway's first neon signs. Herbert's *Mlle Modiste*.	Einstein's Theory of Relativity. Strauss-Wilde *Salome*.
1906			45 Minutes From Broadway by Cohan.	Aga Kahn founds All-India Muslim League.
1907		*The Merry Widow*	*The Merry Widow*; *The Talk of New York*.	China 'Open Door Policy'. Cubist show in Paris.
1908				Viennese operetta dominates both US and Britain. Art Nouveau emerging.
1909	Graduates Worcester Academy, tours Europe and enters Yale.	*The Dollar Princess*; Monckton's *The Arcadians*.	*The Chocolate Soldier*, adapted from Shaw's *Arms and the Man* is the most successful operetta.	Model 'T' Ford is introduced. Mahler's Symphony #9 debuts. *Carmen*, (French film).
1910	June: 'Bridget McGuire', his first published song. October: 'Bingo Eli Yale'.	Gerald du Maurier manages Windham's Theatre.	*Naughty Marietta*, by Victor Herbert is a great success.	Telephone in common use. George V accession to the British throne.
1911	First stage appearance as King Mussel in *The Goldfish*. Small part in *Where the Rainbow Ends*.	*The Count of Luxembourg*.	42 new musicals on Broadway. Irving Berlin publishes 'Alexander's Ragtime Band'. Al Jolson makes his debut at the Winter Garden Theater.	King George V coronation.
1912	April: *And the Villain Still Pursued Her*, presented for two performances. November: *Pot of Gold*.	Spring: Played an autumn leaf in ballet *An Autumn Idyll*. In music-hall sketch with Hawtree company.	Mostly revues, Gilbert & Sullivan *The Count of Luxembourg*. Friml: *The Firefly*.	Poetry Magazine founded. Cellophane invented. The liner Titanic sinks. Charles Pathé produces his first newsreel.

Year	Porter	Coward	USA	Britain	World
1913	April: *The Kaleidoscope.* Summer: Tour of Europe.	Begins collaboration with Esmé Wynne. Actor in Dean's company. December: Appeared as 'Slightly' in *Peter Pan.*	Herbert's *Sweethearts;* Friml's *High Jinks.*	Opening of the Birmingham Repertory Theatre.	Foxtrot craze sweeps the world. First ships pass through Panama Canal.
1914	April: *Paranoia.* May: *We're All Dressed Up and Don't Know Huerto Go.* June: Writes class reunion song. Autumn: Transfers to Harvard School of Music.	Meets Phillip Streatfield. Tours as 'Slightly' in *Peter Pan.* Collaborates (Coward writing the music) to 'Sea Poems' and on short stories with Esme Wynne.	Romberg's first, *Whirl of the World.* Kern's *The Girl From the Utah.* Berlin's *Watch Your Step.*	All Germanic operettas swept off the stage in favour of British fare: *Betty, The Bing Boys are Here* (hit song: 'If You Were the Only Girl in the World')	4 August: Britain declares war on Germany. US remains neutral.
1915	July: 'Esmarelda' is interpolated into the Broadway score of *Hands Up.* October: 'Two Big Eyes' interpolated into *Miss Information.* Begins work on *See America First.*	January: *Peter Pan,* return engagement. December: Reengaged for *Where the Rainbow Ends* but in an adult part. Esmé Wynne also in the cast.	*Katinka* score by Friml. Kern's *Very Good, Eddie.* Berlin's *Stop, Look and Listen.*	W. S. Maugham: *Of Human Bondage.* Gustav Holst: *The Planets.*	Lusitania is sunk. Charles Frohman, the great producer, drowns. *Birth of a Nation,* (film). Dada Movement begins.
1916	March: *See America First* opens on Broadway. 15 performances.	April: Charley in *Charley's Aunt,* and Esmé Wynne is Amy. Summer: Small part in *The Light Blues* with Cicely Courtnedge. Writes his first solo song, 'Forbidden Fruit'. Engaged as a dancer by the Elysee Restaurant.	*The Passing Show* introduces a George Gershwin song. Jazz sweeps the US.	*Chu-Chin-Chow* which ran 2,238 performances. *The Bing Girls.* Bolton-Wodehouse-Kern: *Miss Spring-time.*	Rasputin dies. G. B. Shaw publishes *Pygmalion.*

1917	Studies music in New York with Pietro Yon. Goes to work for the Duryea Relief Organisation.	*Ida Collaborates* (written with Esmé Wynne) is produced on a British tour. Engaged for various acting parts and as an extra in D. W. Griffith's *Hearts of the World*.	Victor Herbert is reigning king: *Maytime*, *Eileen*. London's hit is *Chu-Chin-Chow*. Kern's *Oh, Boy* and *Leave it to Jane*. Hitchcock's *Hitchy-Koo*.	J. M. Barrie: *Dear Brutus*. *Bubbly*, a revue with George Robey. Bolton-Wodehouse-Kern: *Have a Heart*.	7 April, US enters the war. Business off at operettas as a reaction to the Viennese type show. Women in munitions factories cut their hair; 'bobbed hair' becomes the fashion for American and British women. Tsar Nicholas abdicates.
1918	Attached to American Aviation Headquarters in Paris. Meets Linda Lee Thomas.	Writes his first solo play. *The Rat Trap*. Songs (collaborations): 'Tamarisk Town', 'When You Come Home On Leave', 'Peter Pan'.	*Sinbad*, starring Al Jolson, introduces 'Swanee' by Irving Caesar and George Gershwin, making Gershwin famous overnight. *Yip-Yip-Yahank*, Irving Berlin's war-time revue, is a huge success.	Kern's *Very Good Eddie* has song 'Alone With You', co-authored by Cole Porter interpolated into it. 'Altogether Too Fond of You', co-authored by Porter is interpolated into *Telling the Tale*. Britain's biggest hit is *The Lilac Domino*.	Armistice between allies and Germany. Original, US 'Dixieland Band' tours Europe.
1919	April: discharged from military service. Returns to US on boat and meets Raymond Hitchcock, who takes most of his songs for *Hitchy Koo of 1919*. It opens on Broadway in October, runs 56 performances. Marries Linda in Paris. They honeymoon in South of France and move into Linda's house in Paris.	Writes *I'll Leave it to You*. Begins work with Max Darewski and Esmé Wynne on opera *Crissa*.	*La, La, Lucille* first complete Gershwin score. *A Lonely Romeo*, introduces 'Any Old Place With You', first collaboration of Rodgers and Hart. Enormous growth of broadcasting.	*The Bing Boys on Broadway*. Bolton-Wodehouse-Kern collaborate on yet another hit: *Oh, Joy*. (*Oh, Boy* in US.)	Bauhaus Design Group is founded. Fritz Lang, *M* (Film). George Grosz (painting); Kurt Weil – *The Threepenny Opera*. Prohibition in US, 1919 to 1933.

Year	Porter	Coward	USA	Britain	World
1920	Studies counterpoint, harmony and orchestration at Schola Cantorum in Paris. 'Washington Square' published.	Continues to work on *Crissa* (never completed). Coward's *I'll Leave it to You* produced.	*Always You*, book and lyrics by O. Hammerstein. Ed Wynn's *Carnival*. Geo White's *Scandals* (Gershwin score). Rodgers & Hart's *Poor Little Ritz Girl*. Kern's *Sally*.	Edith Day in *Irene*. Paul Whiteman visits Britain and the rage for jazz becomes universal.	August: American women get the vote. Drastic change in fashion: men are clean-shaven and women are 'flappers', with short hair. First public broadcasting stations open in US and Britain.
1921	Charters a launch and they journey up the Nile. They rent a villa near Antibes to entertain in. Very little music or lyrics written.	The *Young Idea* and *Sirocco* written.	Vincent Youmans' first show, *Two Little Girls in Blue* (lyrics by Ira Gershwin writing as Arthur Francis). *Shuffle Along*, Sissle and Blake.	Kern's *Sally* conquers London.	Ireland to be a free state. President Harding declares ban on war. Famine in Russia. The Bauhaus style continues to hold sway. Art Deco begins to appear.
1922	Four of his songs interpolated into two London revues: *Mayfair and Montmartre*, and *Phi-Phi*. *Hitchy-Koo of 1922* (with a score mostly by Porter), opens and closes in less than 2 weeks.	Writes songs and sketches for *London Calling*.	The worst musical season in twenty years. Victor Herbert's *Orange Blossoms*. Stage debuts of Bobby Clark and Fred Allen.	With the World War behind and forgotten, operettas return: *Gypsy Princess* and *Lilac Time* are hits. Other influences are American musicals.	Last British troops leave Ireland. PEN (writers' association) is founded.
1923	Grandfather O. J. Cole dies, and Cole receives a large part of his estate from his mother. Collaborates with Gerald Murphy on *Within the Quota*, a ballet. The ballet is performed in Europe and in US.	Writes *The Vortex*, *Fallen Angels* and *Weatherwise* (sketch). *London Calling* (revue) is produced. *I'll Leave It To You*, (comedy) is produced in the US.	Revival of the Revue with major writers like George S. Kauffman and Marc Connely. Eddie Cantor in *Kid Boots*.	William Walton's *Façade* to poems of Edith Sitwell. Fred and Adele Astaire in *Stop Flirting*. *The Beauty Prize*.	Harding dies; Coolidge is US President. USSR is established.

1924	Porters rent Venice's Palazzo Papadopoli. Noel Coward and John Wilson visit. Porter writes songs for Greenwich Village Follies. September: Greenwich Village Follies opens in New York. During its run (127 performances) Porter's songs are gradually dropped.	Writes Hay Fever and Easy Virtue. Acts and tours in The Vortex.	Jack Buchanan, Beatrice Lillie and Gertrude Lawrence conquer Broadway in Charlot's Revue from London. The Marx Brothers debut with I'll Say She Is!	Toni starring Jack and Jane Buchanan (à la the Astaires). All the big hits are now coming from the US.	First Labour Government in Britain. 'Fono-Film', talking picture process is developed.
1925	Porters rent Palazzo Rezzonico. Start three years of party-giving and party-going, during which Cole writes occasional songs and receives occasional performances.	Writes music and lyrics for Cochran's On With The Dance. Stars in The Vortex in Britain and US. Writes poems of Hernia Whittlebot.	1925-1929 is the heyday of the song and dance musical. The Garrick Gaieties. (Rodgers & Hart); Scandals; Artists and Models; Follies; Operettas like The Vagabond King, and musical comedies like Sunny.	No, No, Nanette is a hit in Britain.	Hitler's Mein Kampf is published. Scopes' Darwinian Trial. The Charleston sweeps a dance-crazy world. Chaplin makes The Gold Rush.
1926	The Porters again summer at the Palazzo Rezzonico and winter in Paris, London and New York.	Tours the US in The Vortex. Writes Semi-Monde, This Was a Man, and The Marquise.	Charlot's Revue (second edition). Rodgers & Hart The Girl Friend; Romberg's The Desert Song. Gertrude Lawrence in Gershwins' Oh, Kay.	Most prominent British musical stars go to appear in the US. Lady Be Good, and The Student Prince are the major offerings.	Byrd establishes the North Pole. Lindburgh flies non-stop, New York to Paris.
1927	Summer at Rezzonico, but this time Cole begins to work. August: His father dies.	Writes songs for This Year of Grace.	Ziegfeld opens his most lavish new theatre with hit show, Rio Rita. Other successes in this banner year are Hit the	Biggest success was Hit the Deck, imported from US. Home grown musicals included Lady Luck and	Sacco and Vanzetti executed in US. German financial crisis. C. B. De Mille produces Kings of Kings (film).

Continued overleaf

Year	Porter	Coward	USA	Britain	World
1927 (contd)	November: Fanny Brice introduces 'Weren't We Fools', (briefly) into her act.		*Deck, Good News, My Maryland, A Connecticut Yankee, Funny Face* and *Show Boat*.	*The Blue Train*.	Talking movies arrive with Al Jolson in *The Jazz Singer*.
1928	*Paris* opens in February in US, tours, is polished and eventually achieves a Broadway run of 195 performances. *La Revue des Ambassadeurs* opens in Paris.	Writes, directs and stars in *This Year of Grace* which is produced in Britain and US. Writes scenario for *Concerto*, an unproduced film.	*Rosalie, Blackbirds of 1928*, score by Jimmy McHugh and Dorothy Fields; *Hold Everything* in which Bert Lahr debuts; *Animal Crackers* with the Marx Brothers; *Whoopee* with Eddie Cantor.	*Funny Face* (with the Astaires) and *Show Boat* from America. British musicals: *Lumber Love, Lady Mary,* and *Virginia*.	Amelia Earheart flies the Atlantic. Hoover is elected President of US. Women suffrage in Britain. Weill-Brecht: *The Threepenny Opera*. First Disney 'Mickey Mouse'; First radio 'soap-opera'.
1929	March: *Wake Up and Dream*; London. November: *Fifty Million Frenchmen*, US. *The Battle of Paris* (film) released. December: *Wake Up and Dream* opens in New York.	Writes and directs *Bitter Sweet* which is a great success in Britain, but, because of the stock market crash, only a mild success in New York.	*The Little Show*, (debut of Schwartz and Dietz). *Sweet Adeline*, a big old-fashioned musical of Kern.	*Mr. Cinders*.	Stock market crash affects the world. Hardest hit is the theatre. Admiral Byrd flies over South Pole. Toscanini takes over New York Philharmonic.
1930	November: *The New Yorkers*.	Writes, directs, produces and stars in *Private Lives*. Writes *Some Other Private Lives*, and *Post Mortem*. Begins score for *Cavalcade*.	*Strike Up the Band* first musical to win the Pulitzer Prize. Debut of Ethel Merman in Gershwins' *Girl Crazy*.	A dreary season saved only by Rodgers and Hart's *Ever Green*.	Depression. Ghandi and civil disobedience. Photoflash invented.
1931	Works on *Stardust*, (musical never completed or produced).	Acts in *Private Lives*, New York. Completes score of *Cavalcade*.	*The Bandwagon, The Ziegfeld Follies, The Cat and the Fiddle, Of Thee I Sing*.	Jack Buchanan and Elsie Randolph are a dancing team to rival the Astaires in *Stand*	Worldwide depression continues. Britain suspends gold payments.

1932	Private Lives is filmed.	November: The Gay Divorce, US production.	Writes book, music and lyrics for Words and Music. Writes Design For Living; The Queen Was in the Parlour. Cavalcade is filmed.	Walk a Little Faster with music by Vernon Duke. Through the Years, music by Vincent Youmans. Face The Music with a score by Irving Berlin.	Up and Sing. Gracie Fields in Walk This Way; The White Horse Inn and Noel Gay's Hold My Hand.	Evelyn Laye in Helen.	Roosevelt elected US President. Lindbergh kidnapping. Death of Ziegfeld. Debut of Shirley Temple.
1933		September: Nymph Errant, London. November: The Gay Divorce, London.	Acting in Design For Living. Writes Conversation Piece. Film of Design For Living.	As Thousands Cheer, with Irving Berlin score.		London's big hits are the two Cole Porter shows.	Hitler becomes Chancellor of Germany.
1934		Writes score or Once Upon a Time, (never produced). Summer: An extended boat trip on the Rhine. October: Gay Divorce film released as Gay Divorcée. All of Porter's score cut except 'Night and Day'. November: Anything Goes, a smash hit. December: writes six songs for film Adios, Argentina (never produced).	Directs and stars in Britain as the Duc de Chavigny-Varennes in Conversation Piece. Writes Point Valaine. Conversation Piece opens in New York.	Spectacle rules the day. Revenge With Music (Dietz and Schwartz) and The Great Waltz. New Faces introduces Imogene Coca and Henry Fonda. Life Begins at 8:40 features dancer Ray Bolger.		Vivian Ellis' Jill Darling and Mr. Whittington.	Hitler becomes Führer. The Thin Man series in films.

Year	Porter	Coward	USA	Britain	World
1935	Porters, Monty Woolley and Moss Hart on a round-the-world trip ostensibly to write *Jubilee*. June: *Anything Goes* opens in London. June: Porters and Hart go to Hollywood to cast *Jubilee*. October: *Jubilee* opens in New York.	*The Scoundrel* (film) Directs *Point Valaine* in New York. *Bitter Sweet* opens on US West Coast. Writes, directs and appears with Gertrude Lawrence in *Tonight at 8:30* in London.	*At Home Abroad* with Beatrice Lillie; Gershwin's *Porgy and Bess* opens.	Ivor Novello's *Glamorous Night*. *The Flying Trapeze* with Jack Buchanan.	Saar restored to Germany. The 'Swing' era begins. Jazz of 'Negro or Jewish' origin is banned from German radio. Garbo appears in *Anna Karenina*.
1936	January-June: In Hollywood working on score of *Born To Dance*. October: *Red, Hot and Blue* opens in New York. December: Contributes a song to the Lunt's show *O Mistress Mine*.	*Tonight at 8:30* in Boston, Washington, New York. *Private Lives* is filmed in French.	*On Your Toes* is directed by George Abbott. Johnny Johnson, Kurt Weill's first US musical.	Ivor Novello's *Careless Rapture*. *This'll Make You Whistle* with Jack Buchanan. *Anything Goes* with Jeanne Aubert.	German troops enter the Rhine; the Rome-Berlin axis. Abdication of Edward VIII in Britain. Frank Lloyd Wright architecture is in demand. BBC begins TV service.
1937	January-June: in Hollywood, working on *Rosalie*. Cole and Linda separate unofficially. September: works on score of *Greek to You* (uncompleted and unproduced). October: severe riding accident and both legs are crushed. Linda and Cole are reunited. October: works on score of *You Never Know*. December: *Rosalie* released.	Writes *Operette*. Directs Gerald Savory's *George and Margaret* for Broadway. Publishes first volume of his autobiography *Present Indicative*.	George Gershwin dies in July. *Pins and Needles*, a labour organisation revue. *I'd Rather Be Right*, a topical musical. *Hooray for What!* is a collaboration of Harold Arlen and 'Yip' Harburg.	*Crest of the Wave* by Ivor Novello. *Me and My Girl* by Noel Gay. *On Your Toes*, a Rodgers & Hart's musical is the hit of London.	German aggression worsens. British continue policy of appeasement. Spanish Civil War. Paris World's Fair. *Lost Horizon* (film).

1938	March-September: You Never Know embarks on a lengthy pre-Broadway tour. Abandons Greek to You. The Sun Never Sets, extravaganza using one Porter song opens in London. November: Leave It To Me is a hit in New York.	Operette is presented in Manchester and London. Writes Set To Music, an adaptation of Words and Music which is successful in Boston and Washington. Beatrice Lillie is the star.	Rodgers & Hart's I Married an Angel; Hellzapoppin; Knickerbocker Holiday, a collaboration of Kurt Weill and Maxwell Anderson.	No new musical successes.	Germany annexes Austria. The New York World's Fair. The Lambeth Walk becomes the latest dance craze. Snow White and the Seven Dwarfs (Disney animated feature.)
1939	Works on Broadway Melody. October: interpolates a song into The Man Who Came to Dinner. December: Du Barry Was a Lady opens in New York.	Writes Present Laughter and This Happy Breed. Directs Set To Music in New York. His book of short stories, To Step Aside is published.	Too Many Girls – Rodgers & Hart. Very Warm For May Kern & Hammerstein. Kern and Hammerstein also collaborate on 'The Last Time I Saw Paris' which sweeps free-thinking world.	The Dancing Years by Ivor Novello has great success in London and will run for five years. Pop song: 'Roll out the Barrel' is an enormous hit.	Germany invades Poland. Gone With The Wind (film).
1940	January: Porters and friends sail to Central America and South Seas. February: Broadway Melody of 1940 is released. July: Porters buy a large estate in Massachusetts. October: Panama Hattie opens in New York.	Coward decides to give up all creative and performing work except in the service of his country: he tours Australia entertaining the troops. In spite of his resolve he writes Time Remembered.	Very few good shows, only Louisiana Purchase, (Irving Berlin) and Pal Joey (Rodgers & Hart).	Mostly revivals like Chu-Chin-Chow, one newcomer, New Faces of 1940 (featuring 'A Nightingale Sang in Berkeley Square').	Churchill is prime minister. The fall of France. Films: Fantasia and Chaplin's The Great Dictator.

Year	Porter	Coward	USA	Britain	World
1941	March-May: works on *You'll Never Get Rich* (film). October: *You'll Never Get Rich* is released. October: *Let's Face It* opens on Broadway. November: Hospitalised for further leg surgery.	Writes individual songs for the War: 'Bren Gun', 'London Pride,' etc. Writes the screenplay for *In Which We Serve*. Writes *Blithe Spirit*.	Broadway mostly mounts 'escape' shows. *Lady In the Dark* is the only solid hit.		Lend-lease. December: US enters the War. After attack on Pearl Harbor US and Britain declare war on Japan. Film: *Citizen Kane*.
1942	March-May: works on *Something to Shout About* (film). July-August: works on *Something For the Boys*. November: *Du Barry Was A Lady* opens in London. December: *Something For the Boys* opens in Boston.	Acts in, directs, and composes score for *In Which We Serve*. Acts in *Blithe Spirit*. *We Were Dancing* is filmed.	Wartime shows: *Let Freedom Sing* and *Something For the Boys*. Escape shows: *By Jupiter* and films like Irving Berlin's *Holiday Inn*.	*Waltz Without End*, Ivor Novello.	The atomic age begins. Germans reach Stalingrad. Magnetic tape for recording is invented.
1943	January: *Something For the Boys* opens in New York. February: *Something to Shout About* is released. February-July: Works on *Mississippi Belle* (film never released). December: *Mexican Hayride* opens in Boston.	Tours in *Blithe Spirit*, *Present Laughter* and *This Happy Breed*. *This Happy Breed* is filmed.	*Oklahoma* revolutionises the American musical. Other successes are *One Touch of Venus* and *Carmen Jones*.	*The Lisbon Story*; A touring company of Irving Berlin's *This Is the Army*.	Germans surrender North Africa; Mussolini falls. *Stage Door Canteen* (film); *For Whom the Bell Tolls* (film). Sinatra is the idol of teenagers.
1944	January: *Mexican Hayride* opens in New York. December: *Seven Lively*	*Middle East Diary* published. Tours the Far East performing for troops.	*Bloomer Girl*, with a Rich Arlen score. *On the Town*, the first Broadway work of	Very little of lasting value.	Normandy landing. FDR's third term. Laurence Olivier's *Henry V*.

Year	Cole Porter	Noël Coward	American theatre	London musicals	The world
1945	Arts opens in New York.	Appears at the Stage Door Canteen. Blithe Spirit filmed.	Comden & Green with a Leonard Berstein score.	Operettas are popular: Three Waltzes; Gay Rosalinda, also Under Your Hat.	Germany surrenders; FDR dies; US drops the atomic bomb; Japan surrenders. Bebop becomes a world-wide craze.
1946	January-March: Hospitalised for further leg surgery. Summer: Supervised script for film biography, Night and Day. May: Around the World opens in New York. August: Night and Day opens nationally. Summer: Writes most of the score for The Pirate (film.)	Sigh No More, (writes book, music and lyrics.) Begins work on Pacific 1860. Brief Encounter is filmed. Directs Pacific 1860. Writes Peace In Our Time. Blithe Spirit is presented (in French) in Paris.	Call Me Mister a mustering out revue. Annie Get Your Gun, Irving Berlin's most acclaimed score.	Big Ben by Vivien Ellis.	First meeting of the UN. Xerography developed. British Arts Council is inaugurated. BBC Third Programme begins transmitting.
1947	February-November: Filming The Pirate. This was generally a quiet year, for after a series of flops, Porter has trouble getting contracts for new shows.	Present Laughter in London. Writes Long Island Sound.	US theatre finds its voice with Allegro, Brigadoon, High Button Shoes and Street Scene.	American musicals take London: Oklahoma and Annie Get Your Gun are biggest hits.	Truman doctrine; Marshall Plan. Indian independence. A Streetcar Named Desire. First Edinburgh Festival.
1948	February-May: writes the score for Kiss Me, Kate, most highly acclaimed and longest running of all Porter shows. December: Kiss Me, Kate opens to glowing reviews.	Stars in Joyeux Chagrins, (Present Laughter) in Brussels and Paris. Writes screenplay for The Astonished Heart. Directs Tonight at 8:30 in New York.	A season aiming for charm: Hits are Lend an Ear, (revue) and Where's Charlie? (musical version of Charlie's Aunt).	The American invasion begins with Brigadoon and Lute Song. British: Cage Me a Peacock.	End of the British mandate in Palestine. In art it is the era of Jackson Pollock and Henry Moore. Laurence Olivier's Hamlet, (film).
1949	Writes most of score for Out of This World.	Writes music and lyrics for Ace of Clubs. Writes Island Fling,	The big shows take over: South Pacific, Miss Liberty, Regina,	British musicals: Ivor Novello's King's Rhapsody.	NATO established. China becomes communist.

continued overleaf

Year	Porter	Coward	USA	Britain	World
1949 (contd)		(later called *South Sea Bubble*). Acts in *The Astonished Heart*.	and *Gentlemen Prefer Blondes*.	Also *Tough At the Top*.	
1950	December: *Out of This World* opens in New York.	Records leading role in *Conversation Piece*. Writes *Relative Values*. *Ace of Clubs* is produced and tours.	Irving Berlin's hit, *Call Me Madam*. Frank Loesser's *Guys and Dolls*.	American hit: *Carousel*. British musical: *Take it From Here*, (revue); *Dear Miss Phoebe*, (musical version of *Quality Street* and *Blue For a Boy* (farce).	The Korean War. UN Building completed. Menotti's opera, *The Consul* has a run on Broadway.
1951	March: *Kiss Me, Kate* opens in London. Cole is severely depressed and suffers mental breakdown.	Records narrative for *Carnival of the Animals*. Readies a night-club act and has an enormous triumph as a cabaret entertainer at the Café de Paris. Writes *Quadrille*. *Relative Values* tours. *Star Quality* (short stories) is published in London and New York.	Rodgers & Hammerstein's *The King and I* and Lerner & Loewe's *Paint Your Wagon*. Also burlesque: *Top Banana*.	From US: *Kiss Me, Kate*. British: Ivor Novello's *Gay's the Word*, and Vivian Ellis' *And So to Bed*.	Electric power from atomic energy. Britain begins rating system for films. *The Archers* sitcom. Johnny Ray and Elvis Presley are singing sensations.
1952	May-August: completes most of score of *Can-Can*. His mother, Kate Porter, dies at age of 90.	Additional engagements at Café de Paris. Three plays from *Tonight at 8:30* are filmed as *Meet Me Tonight*. Directs *Quadrille* on tour.		*Call Me Madam* and British hits: *Zip Goes a Million* and *Bet Your Life* (adapted from *Brewster's Millions*).	Contraceptive pill is developed. Elizabeth II's coronation. *The Mousetrap* opens. Chaplin's film *Limelight* released.
1953	*Can-Can* opens in New York.	Writes many special songs for his cabaret act. Writes *After The Ball*.	A dreadful season which produced only mild successes, *Me and Juliet* and *Kismet*.	From US: *Guys and Dolls*, *Paint Your Wagon*, *The King and I* and holdovers, *Porgy*	Death of Stalin. Korean armistice. Rosenbergs executed.

		Acts in Shaw's The Apple Cart. Publishes The Noel Coward Songbook.		and Carousel. Two superb British shows: The Boy Friend and Salad Days.	
1954	May: Linda Porter dies at the age of 70. October: Can-Can opens in London. November: Silk Stockings opens in Philadelphia.	More cabaret material. Does a Royal Command Performance. Writes Nude With Violin.	Small shows like The Threepenny Opera, The Boy Friend and The Golden Apple vie with extravaganzas like Pajama Game and House of Flowers.	Can-Can and Wedding in Paris.	Salk polio vaccine developed. The H-bomb. High court bans segregation. End of Vietnam War. McCarthy censured.
1955	February: Silk Stockings opens in New York. May: Receives Honorary Degree as Doctor of Music from Williams College. July-November: Works on score of High Society.	Has an outstanding cabaret success in US at Las Vegas. Writes and performs TV special Together With Music for himself and Mary Martin. Performs cameo role in Around the World in 80 Days.	Wholesome, home-spun shows: Plain and Fancy, Damn Yankees and Pipe Dream.	The Pajama Game. The Water Gypsies.	The Khrushchev era. Churchill steps down. US launches satellite. Perón overthrown.
1956	February-June: Takes a long European trip. July: Works on Les Girls (film). October: High Society is released.	Blithe Spirit is adapted for TV. This Happy Breed is adapted for TV. He records Noel Coward in New York.	My Fair Lady, Mr. Wonderful, The Most Happy Fella and Candide. Also a snappy revue from London: Cranks.	Fanny and Grab Me a Gondola.	Eisenhower wins second term. The Hungarian Revolt. Maria Callas takes Milan and New York by storm.
1957	January: Undergoes surgery for gastric ulcer. July: Silk Stockings (film) is released. August-November: Writes score for Aladdin (TV special). November: Les Girls is released.	Directs Nude With Violin and plays Sebastian on tour and in New York. Conversation Piece is revived off-Broadway.	West Side Story and The Music Man. (Music Man wins the Tony Award.)	Damn Yankees and Bells Are Ringing.	Shake up in the Kremlin. Sputnik.

Year	Porter	Coward	USA	Britain	World
1958	February: *Aladdin* is shown on coast-to-coast TV. April: Porter's right leg is amputated at the hip.	Composes *London Morning*, a ballet. Tours US in *Nude with Violin and Present Laughter*. Writes and directs *Look After Lulu*.	*The Body Beautiful*, the debut of Bock & Harnick. Other shows are *Flower Drum Song*, *Goldilocks* and *La Plume de Ma Tante*.	British: *Valmouth*, *Irma La Douce* and *Expresso Bongo*.	De Gaulle is premiere of France. Alaska is US 49th state.
1959		Acts in *Our Man in Havana* and *Surprise Package* (films). Writes *Waiting in the Wings*. Directs *Look After Lulu* in New York.	A banner year: *Red-head*, *Destry Rides Again*, *Once Upon a Matress*, *Gypsy* and *The Sound of Music*.	*The World of Paul Stickey*.	Hawaii becomes US 50th state.
1960	Receives Honorary degree/(Doctor of Humane Letters) from Yale University.	*Pomp and Circumstance*, a novel.	Another banner year: *Bye, Bye, Birdie*, *The Fantasticks*, *The Unsinkable Molly Brown*, *Camelot* and *Wildcat*.	Lionel Bart's ever green classic, *Oliver*. *Lilly White Boys*.	Princess Margaret marries Antony Armstrong-Jones. J. F. Kennedy is elected President of the US.
1961	Frequently hospitalised.	*Sail Away* produced in Boston and New York; Coward records score. *This Happy Breed* is produced on BBC TV.	Jerry Herman's first hit: *Milk and Honey*. Also *How To Succeed In Business Without Really Trying*.	An onslaught from Broadway: *The Music Man*, *The Sound of Music*, *Bye, Bye, Birdie*, *Do Re Mi*, and *The Fantasticks*. British musical success: Newley's *Stop The World*.	Soviet and US astronauts orbit the earth. Mississippi riots. Berlin Wall erected.
1962		Writes book, music and lyrics for *The Girl Who Came to Supper*. *Sail Away* is presented in London and on tour.	*All American*, *A Funny Thing (Happened on the Way to the Forum)*, *Stop the World* and *Little Me*.	*Blitz*.	The Cuban blockade. John Glen orbits the earth.

1963	Reclusive.	Cameo role in Paris When it Sizzles. Supervises production of Sail Away in Australia.	She Loves Me and 110 In the Shade.	Three lasting British musicals: Pickwick, Half a Sixpence and Oh, What a Lovely War.	Civil rights marches. Kennedy assassinated.
1964	Dies 11:05 pm, 15 October, St. John's Hospital, Santa Monica, California.	High Spirits, a musical based on Blithe Spirit opens in New York. Hay Fever is revived in London.	Hello, Dolly, Anyone Can Whistle, Fiddler on the Roof and Oh, What a Lovely War.	Robert and Elizabeth and Maggie May.	US attacks north Vietnam. Khrushchev is ousted. Lyndon Johnson is re-elected. Beatles's US début.
1965		The Lyrics of Noel Coward is published. Writes Suite in Three Keys. Acts in Bunny Lake is Missing (film).	Baker Street, Do I Hear A Waltz, On a Clear Day and Man of La Mancha.	Charlie Girl.	Space rendezvous.
1966		Acts in Suite in Three Keys. Writes Pretty Polly Barlow.		Mame and Cabaret. Jarrocks.	Floods damage Florence, Italy. Mao's Cultural Revolution.
1967		Acts Caesar in Androcles in US TV and the Witch of Caprin in Boom (film). Bon Voyage (stories) and Not Yet the Dodo are published in New York and London	A dreadful season: only Hallaluja, Baby is a mild success.		
1968		Acts Mr. Bridget in The Italian Job (film).	Off-Broadway takes over: Your Own Thing, Jacques Brel is Alive, Hair, Noel Coward's Sweet Potato. Also Zorba and Promises, Promises.	The Young Visiters, The Canterbury Tales.	Martin Luther King and Robert F. Kennedy assassinated. Czechoslovakia invaded by Russians.

Year	Porter	Coward	USA	Britain	World
1969		Records *Back to Back* with John Betjeman, (poems).	*Coco.*	*Two Cities.*	Men walk on the moon.
1970			*Purlie*, a white gospel show is a semi-hit. Also *Applause* and Sondheim's *Company*.		
1971		*The Grand Tour*, a score for the Royal Ballet.	*Follies*, *Jesus Christ Superstar*.		Communist China admitted to UN.
1972		*Cowardy Custard* at the Mermaid Theatre in London. *Oh, Coward* in New York.	*Grease.*		Israeli Olympic team murdered. Nixon is re-elected. European Common Market.
1973		Dies – 8 am, 26 March, Blue Harbour, Jamaica.	Sondheim's *A Little Night Music* and *Raisin.*		Vietnam peace. Nixon resigns.

Analysis of Selected Songs

ANALYSIS OF PORTER SONGS

I'VE A SHOOTING BOX IN SCOTLAND

(*Paranoia* and *See America First*)
Written in 1913, published in 1916. Sung by
Dorothie Bigelow and John Goldsworthy.

This song is the earliest of the immature Porter
songs to show the saucy erudition that would
later become his hallmark. In performance it
became so successful that additional verses and
choruses had to be created. The song was the first
Cole Porter work to be recorded.

Form: Verse – 32 bars, consisting of two 8-bar
couplets followed by a 16 bar modulatory
section.
Chorus – 32 bars, ABAC.

Lyrics: This is a list song *par excellence*, with the
admixture of contemporary and antique, clas-
sic and voguish that was to become a Porter
trademark. But more importantly, it was
Porter's first effort to tie things up with a
'punch line'. Once Cole saw how the public
applauded the idea, he used it frequently and
the surprise ending was to become a trademark.

Nowadays it's rather nobby
To regard one's private hobby
As the object of one's tenderest affection.
Some excel at Alpine climbing,
Others have a turn for rhyming,
While a lot of people go in for collections.
Such as prints by Hiroshigi
Edelweiss from off the Rigi
Jacobean soup tureens
Early types of limousines
Pipes constructed from a dry cob,
Baseball hits by Mr. Ty Cobb.
Locks of Missus Browning's hair
Photographs of Ina Claire,
First editions still uncut,
Daily pranks of Jeff and Mutt,
Della Robia singing boys,
Signatures of Alfred Noyes
Fancy bantams,
Grecian vases,
Tropic beetles,
Irish laces
But my favorite pastime
Is collecting country places.

Refrain 1
I've a shooting box in Scotland
I've a chateau in Touraine
I've a silly little chalet
In the Interlaken Valley
I've a Hacienda in Spain.
I've a private fjord in Norway
I've a villa close to Rome,
And in traveling,
It's really quite a comfort to know
That you're never far from home!

Verse 2
Now it's really very funny
What an awful lot of money
On exorbitant hotels a chap can squander
But I never have to do so,
Like resourceful Mister Crusoe
I can find a home however far I wander.

Refrain 2
I've a bungalow in Simla
I've an island east of Maine,
If you care for hotter places
I've an African oasis
On an uninhabited plain.
I've a houseboat on the Yangtse
I've an igloo up at Nome
Yes, in traveling
It's really quite a comfort to know
That you're never far from home!

Verse 3
Having lots of idle leisure
I pursue a life of pleasure,
Like a rolling stone in constant agitation.
For, tho' stay-at-homes may cavil
I admit I'd rather travel
Than collect a crop of mossy vegetation.

Refrain 3
I've shanty in the Rockies,
I've a castle on the Rhine,
I've a Siamese pagoda
I've a cottage in Fashoda
Near the equatorial line.
On my sable farm in Russia
O'er the barren steppes we'll roam,
And in traveling
It's really quite a comfort to know
That you're never far from home!

Parody: (Cole often parodied his own work. Sometimes the results were scatological, but more often they were simply clever lyrics with a new point of view. The following parody was recalled by Porter's friend Lieutenant Rex Benson. Its authenticity was corroborated by Dorothy Bigelow who sang it in Porter's first Broadway show, *See America First*.)

I've had shooting pains in Scotland,
I've had measles in Touraine
I've had horrible malaria
When going through Bavaria
That suddenly turned to ptomaine.
I've had Bright's disease in Denmark
I've had whooping cough in Rome
But when traveling the Continent
It's pleasant to know
That there's leprosy at home

Melody: The verse seems more like an afterthought, and not a very successful one at that. The first half, with its upward scale-line, owes a lot to Sullivan. Its range makes it difficult to sing. The second half (although it modulates) seems to be stuck in a groove and merely at the service of a clever lyric. But the chorus is a charmer. Repeatedly leading to an appoggiatura on the word 'in', Porter creates a memorable motive. The line of the 8th through 12th bar ('I've a silly little chalet/In the Interlaken valley') seems to be settling down into a glen; a remarkable example of Porter's sense of prosody. The melody reaches its climax in its penultimate phrase, and settles down for its punch line.

Harmony: As mentioned before, the modulation from the key of C to Ab in mid-verse, while daring, impresses me as somewhat conservatory show-off and rather pointless. But there is nothing superfluous in the chorus. The diminished cliche works charmingly with the melodic line, and at the climactic 3/4 point of the song the fresh (and always logical) settling down on the expected subdominant is most satisfying.

Rhythm: Porter had not found his great rhythmic stride yet, but in bar 14 he inserts a rest in mid-word and gives his tune a little rhythmic somersault.

WEREN'T WE FOOLS
Written during the summer of 1927 supposedly for Fanny Brice, and published later that year. The song was performed by Miss Brice during her engagement at New York's Palace Theatre that November.

The work, in simple 4/4, in the key of Eb, is one of Porter's most moving and simplest and has had a revival in the 1990s as a favorite of the neo-torch song singer.

Form: 2 verses (each leading to a repeated chorus): 24 bars (8-bar phrase, consequent 8-bar phrase; 4-bar modulation to the key of the mediant; 4-bar lead in on the dominant). Chorus: 32 bars, A1, A2, bridge, A3.

Lyrics: This is one of the rare songs in which Cole does not try to be clever. This lyric displays none of the smartness, the brittleness or placing the love object on a pedestal for which Cole was so often criticized. Being almost entirely written in monosyllables this song maintains an unusual honesty.

Verse I
Ev'ry time I see you, dear,
I think of days when you were near
And I held you close to my heart.
Life was like a perfect dream,
And, yet, so real, it didn't seem
That we two could ever drift apart.
I know that all you said to me was true,
And you love me still, as I love you.

Chorus
Weren't we fools to lose each other?
Weren't we fools to say goodbye?
Though we knew we loved each other
You chose another,
So did I.
If we'd realized our love was worth defending,
Then the story's broken threads we might be
   mending,
With perhaps a diff'rent ending,
A happy ending,
Weren't we fools?

Verse II
Think of all the plans we made,
The schemes we had,
The plots we laid
To work out a life of our own.
All of them were thrown away,
Yet when we meet again today
The crowd disappears and we're alone.
I long to put my arms around you now!
But it wouldn't be the same somehow.

(Repeat chorus)

Melody: The first motive with its downward chromatic slide on the first three titular notes followed by similar slide in the second phrase creates a theme that suits the first few words of the chorus.

Eb   Bm/D   Bbm6Db   C7   F9

Weren't we   fools_____   to   lose   each – oth – er?

The bridge, as in all good songs of this type has a rising line and is sequential. For the A3, the climax is reached on a dominant 13th, an appoggiatura on the word 'ending' is truly poignant.

Harmony: The verse is interesting, for it uses the diminished cliché and treats it melodically with an appoggiatura, but it is the innovative harmonic scheme of the first two bars of the chorus that elevates this song above most of Porter's ballads. The harmony Eb, Bbm/D, Bbm (an entire bar of suspended harmony on the key word, 'fools') which finally, in the 3rd bar settles down on a C13, and eventually a C7 is truly breathtaking. The bridge, using II and V of the subdominant followed by II and V of the dominant creates the proper elevation of line.

Rhythm: This song does not have a strong rhythmic pulse, although it should be noted that Porter enlivens the melody with anticipations of the beat. They may have been afterthoughts but they do help to give the song a certain 'kick'.

LET'S DO IT, LET'S FALL IN LOVE (Paris)
Published in 1928, it was introduced by Irene Bordoni and Arthur Margetson.

As one of the half dozen best known songs by Cole, it has been the most often parodied. Perhaps the most famous take-off was written by Noel Coward and used in his Las Vegas act.

Form: 16-bar verse followed by a 32-bar chorus in A¹, A², bridge and A³.

Lyrics: Each of the five choruses that comprise the song deals with a specific grouping: the first is an ethnic one, (although Cole himself, realizing the words 'Chinks' and 'Japs' might offend, diluted the opening lines with the familiar, 'Birds do it, bees do it, ...'), the second is limited to birds, the third to fish, the fourth, insects and the last to mammals.

Verse
When the little bluebird
Who has never said a word
Starts to sing, 'Spring, spring.'
When the little bluebell
In the bottom of the dell
Starts to ring 'Ding, ding,'

When the little blue clerk
In the middle of his work
Starts a tune to the moon up above,
It is nature, that's all
Simply telling us to fall
In love.

Refrain I
And that's why Chinks do it, Japs do it,
Up in Lappland, little Lapps do it,
Let's do it, let's fall in love.
In Spain the best upper sets do it,
Lithuanians and Letts do it,
Let's do it, let's fall in love.
The Dutch in old Amsterdam do it,
Not to mention the Finns,
Folks in Siam do it,
Think of Siamese twins,
Some Argentines without means do it,
People say in Boston, even beans do it,
Let's do it, let's fall in love.

Refrain 2
The nightingales in the dark do it,
Larks, k-razy for a lark, do it,
Let's do it, let's fall in love.
Canaries caged in the house do it,
When they're out of season, grouse do it,
Let's do it, let's fall in love.
The most sedate barnyard fowls do it
When a chanticleer cries,
High-browed old owls do it,
They're supposed to be wise.
Penguins in flocks, on the rocks, do it,
Even little cuckoos in their clocks, do it,
Let's do it, let's fall in love.

Refrain 3
Romantic sponges, they say, do it,
Oysters down in Oyster Bay do it,
Let's do it, let's fall in love.
Cold Cape Cod clams, 'gainst their wish, do it,
Even lazy jellyfish do it,
Let's do it, let's fall in love.
Electric eels, I might add do it,
Though it shocks them, I know,
Why ask if shad do it,
Waiter, bring me shad roe.
In shallow shoals English soles do it,
Goldfish in the privacy of bowls do it,
Let's do it, let's fall in love.

Refrain 3 (British Production)
Young whelks and winkles in pubs do it
Little sponges, in their tubs do it,
Let's do it, let's fall in love.
Cold salmon quite 'gainst their wish do it,

Even lazy jellyfish do it,
Let's do it, let's fall in love.
The most select schools of cod do it,
Though it shocks them, I fear,
Sturgeon, thank God, do it,
Have some caviar, dear.
In shady shoals English soles do it,
Goldfish, in the privacy of bowls do it,
Let's do it, let's fall in love.

Refrain 4
The dragonflies in the reeds do it,
Sentimental centipedes do it,
Let's do it, let's fall in love.
Mosquitos, heaven forbid, do it,
So does ev'ry katydid, do it,
Let's do it, let's fall in love.
The most refined ladybugs do it,
When a gentleman calls,
Moths in your rugs do it,
What's the use of moth balls?
Locusts in trees do it, bees do it,
Even educated fleas do it,
Let's do it, let's fall in love.

Chorus 5
The chimpanzees in the zoos do it,
Some courageous kangaroos do it,
Let's do it, let's fall in love.
I'm sure giraffes, on the sly do it,
Heavy hippopotami do it,
Let's do it, let's fall in love.
Old sloths who hang down from twigs do it
Though the effort is great.
Sweet guinea pigs do it,
Buy a couple and wait.
The world admits bears in pits do it,
Even pekineses at the Ritz do it,
Let's do it, let's fall in love.

NOEL COWARD'S PARODY

Verse I
Mister Irving Berlin
Often emphasises sin
In a charming way.
Mister Coward, we know,
Wrote a song or two to show
Sex is here to stay.
Richard Rodgers, it's true
Takes a more romantic view
Of that sly biological urge,
But it really was Cole
Who contrived to make the whole
Thing merge ...

Chorus I
He said that Belgans and Dutch do it,
Even Hildegard and Hutch do it,
Let's do it, let's fall in love.
Monkeys, whenever you look do it,
Aly Kahn and King Farouk do it
Let's do it, let's fall in love.
The most recherché cocottes do it,

In a luxury flat,
Locks, Dunn's and Scott's do it,
At the drop of a hat.
Excited spinsters in spas do it,
Duchesses when opening bazaars do it,
Let's do it, let's fall in love.

Verse 2
Our leading writers in swarms do it,
Somerset and all the Maughams do it,
Let's do it, let's fall in love.
The Brontës felt that they must do it,
Mrs. Humphrey Ward could just do it,
Let's do it, let's fall in love.
Anouilh and Sartre – God knows why – do it
As a sort of a curse,
Eliot and Fry do it,
But they do it in verse.
Some mystics, as a routine do it,
Even Evelyn Waugh and Graham Greene do it.
Let's do it, let's fall in love.

Verse 2
In the spring of the year
Inhibitions disappear
And our hearts beat high.
We had better face facts,
Ev'ry gland that overacts
Has an alibi.
For each bird and each bee,
Each slap-happy, sappy tree
Each temptation that lures us along
Is just nature elle-même
Merely singing us the same
Old song ...

Refrain 3
Girls from the R. A. D. A. do it
B. B. C. announcers may do it,
Let's do it, let's fall in love.
The Ballet Joos to a man do it,
Alfred Lunt and Lynn Fontanne do it,
Let's do it, let's fall in love.
Well-made young actors in tights do it,
Without mentioning names,
Glamorous knights do it
With theatrical dames.
Critics as sour as a quince do it,
Even Emile Littler and Prince do it,
Let's do it, let's fall in love.

Melody: Porter, ever vigilant that his verse be an interesting contrast to his refrain, uses one here that sings like an upward rising arpeggio. It is a perfect foil for the motive of the refrain, comprising three sly descending chromatic pitches. (Curiously like 'Weren't We Fools', but here the effect is totally different.) Even in the bridge these three decending tones persist, but the effect is one of flattening or 'blue notes', rather than lugubriousness. In the A3 section the melody climaxes on D flat rising to D and E flat in succeeding bars. The entire span of the chorus, (although it feels much more rangy) is slightly over an octave.

Harmony: The harmony is not intense, mostly I's II's and V's but the choice of melodic notes against these simple chords create 13s and flat 9s everywhere. The bridge reveals a nice circular pattern moving from Bb7 through Eb to Ab7 into Db before heading home through an F7/C

Rhythm: The rhythmic motive is a simple syncopation, twice repeated. In the 3rd bar Cole deviates by putting a rest on the first beat. This pattern is followed throughout *except* for the A3, here the rest is gone and the line extended. (Fig. 1 and 2 below) The effect is surprising and masterful.

Fig.1

Birds do it,— Bees do it,— E-ven ed-u-ca-ted fleas do it—

Fig 2

Some Ar-gen-tines with out— means do it,— Peo-ple say, in Bos-ton ev-en

YOU DON'T KNOW PAREE (Fifty Million Frenchmen)
Written in 1929. Sung by William Gaxton in the show and by Irene Bordoni in her solo night-club act after her divorce from Ray Goetz.

Form: Verse: 8 bars (8 phrases); Chorus: 28 bars divided into A1 (6 bars), A2 (6 bars), bridge (8 bars) and A3 (8 bars). Sheet copy written in the key of C.

Lyrics: This is one of Cole's least rhymed, least 'clever' songs, however each word seems carefully chosen and trenchant with meaning. The alliteration (laughed a lot, learned a lot, loved a lot, lost a lot) seems a satisfying substitute for the rhymes. The punch line comes at the end of the verse, while the most moving thought is expressed in the penultimate line of the chorus.

Verse
You come to Paris,
You come to play,
You have a very good time,
You go away.
And from then on,
You talk of Paris knowingly;
You may know Paris,
You don't know Paree.

Chorus
Though you've been around a lot,
And danced a lot, and laughed a lot,
You don't know Paree.
You may say you've seen a lot,
And heard a lot and learned a lot,
You don't know Paree.
Paree will still be laughing
After every one of us disappears,
But never once forget her laughter
Is the laughter that hides the tears.
And, until you've lived a lot,
And loved a lot, and lost a lot,
You don't know Paree,
You don't know Paree.

Voice

You come to Pa-ris, you come to play;

Piano

You have a won-der-ful time, you go a-way.

And, from then on, you talk of Pa-ris know-ing-ly;

You may know Pa-ris, you don't know Pa-ree.

Melody: The instructional verse is almost par-lando yet it takes a big range and leads into the first motivic phrase of the chorus which is a remarkable example of setting words to music. Full of short, skipping, gasped phrases the melody mirrors a teacher's speech. This leads to a memorable bridge, basically a descending scale line and a contrasting (4-bar) long line which is immediately repeated. The A3 returns us to the first motive, maintains its climax on high G and plunges the song into an almost two octave range. In an era when most popular music did not venture beyond an octave or a tenth at the outside this was daring indeed.

Harmony: The main harmonic interest is in the bridge, one of Cole's most daring and modulatory. Beginning on the dominant (G) it uses II, V, I of F (Gm7, C7, F) followed by II, V, I of Eb (Fm7, Bb7, Eb). A simple G7 pulls us back to start the A3 section.

Rhythm: This song has always seemed to me to be a waltz masquerading as a 4/4 ballad. I believe the shortened A sections betray its natural 16-bar 3/4 genesis, and that it was poured into its present rhythmic jacket because of 'Paree, What Did You Do To Me?' a sweeping waltz which 'You Don't Know Paree' directly followed in the score. Nonetheless, it fits fairly well into its printed form although the song has no great rhythmic interest.

Incidental Information: Cole, an ardent oper-aphile inserted as a fill-in, (chorus, bar 6 and again, bar 12) a direct quote from *Louise*, Charpentier's threnody on the wicked ways a big city like Paris worked its magic to corrupt a naive suburban girl. The situation in *Louise* paralleling the one in *Fifty Million Frenchmen* made the borrowing appropriate. The motive would certainly have been used to pay homage to a composer and opera Cole and Linda Porter would have seen many times.

THE TALE OF THE OYSTER (Misc.1925-6)

This song written, in Venice as 'The Scampi' was created to spoof German lieder and to amuse his friends on the Lido, particularly the Princess San Faustino, (born Jane Campbell in New Jersey). So successful was it that Porter sought wider dissemination. With the lyric rewritten as 'The Tale of the Oyster' it was introduced by Helen Broderick into 'Fifty Million Frenchmen' in 1929. Although well sung by Miss Broderick, the noted critic Gilbert Seldes – missing the whole point of the jibe – singled out only the final lines, finding this song 'about regurgitation' offensive, and it was dropped shortly after the opening. The song languished in oblivion until rescued by Kaye Ballard who included it in the 'Ben Bagley Revisited' album.

Form: Set up like a Schubertian lied, this song in seven stanzas, each containing ten bars: an eight bar melodic line, a one bar comment by a supposed narrator. The tenth bar piano solo not only rounds out the form, but it allows a lieder singer to ready herself for the next verse and the audience to chuckle. The form is very close to theme and variations.

Lyrics: The rhyme scheme is pure AABB (with the added non-rhyming observation) throughout:

Down by the sea lived a lonesome oyster	A
Ev'ry day getting sadder and moister	A
He found his home life awf'lly wet	B
And longed to travel with the upper set	B
Poor little oyster	Commentary, unrhymed

The language, never forced or inverted, is mostly monosyllabic. When it comes to the narration, it is intellectual without being stuffy.

Melody: Small, close with a rocking sea effect, staying around the pitch of 'G', the flexible 3rd of the scale. Words and music climax in the seventh bar of every section and settle down to a low vocal comment. By the fourth and fifth verse, the tune, transposed and raised, is reaching for a climax. This it finds in the sixth variation where Porter abandons his original theme. The seventh verse returns us to the rocking and serves as a final coda.

Harmony: The key is Eb and the chord scheme is essentially I, I + , II, V for the first 2 verses. By the third verse Porter takes the ever-present 'G' and harmonizes his tune in G minor. For the next one he moves us into C major, bright proud and strong. In the middle of it the commentator slides us into the super-bright key of E. In verse 5, we are rolling on the sea and Porter throws us between the waves of A minor and E7. Verse 6 is an even more animated version of the preceding one which leads to the punch line. After the comment of 'Up comes the oyster!' the composer uses his one bar to modulate back to his original key of Eb for his next words are 'Back again where he started from'. The song ends stating the lyric's quiet wisdom very much the way it began.

Rhythm: The rhythm is purposely square and plodding except for a lilting syncopation in each verse's seventh bar. This always seems to coincide with some new twist in the story.

Incidental Information: Porter was fascinated by animated underwater creatures. As early as 1922 he had written 'The Sponge' wherein a mother sponge cautions her daughter to keep away from artist's bathtubs.
The lyrics of 'The Scampi' are too good not to

be reprinted here. The tune is the same as 'The Tale of the Oyster'.

Once there lived a nice young Scampi
In a canal that was dark and damp, he
Found his home life much too wet,
And longed to travel with the supper set.
Poor little Scampi.

Fate was kind for very soon a-
Long came the chef from the Hotel Luna,
Saw that Scampi lying there,
And said, 'I'll put you on my bill of fare.
Lucky little Scampi.

See him on his silver platter
Hearing the queens of the Lido chatter,
Getting the latest in regard
To Elsa Maxwell and Lady Cunard.
Thrilled Little Scampi.

See that ambitious Scampi we know
Feeding the Princess San Faustino.
Think of his joy as he gaily glides
Down to the middle of her Roman insides.
Proud little Scampi.

After dinner the Princess Jane
Said to her hostess, 'I've got such a pain.
Don't be cross, but I think I shall
Go for a giro in a side canal.'
Scared little Scampi.

Off they went through the troubled tide,
The gondola rocking from side to side.
They tossed about 'till that poor young Scampi
Found that his quarters were much too crampy.
Up comes the Scampi.

Back once more where he started from
He said, 'I haven't a single qualm,
For I've had a taste of the world, you see,
And a great princess has had a taste of me.'
Wise little Scampi.

NIGHT AND DAY (*The Gay Divorce*, published 1932, sung by Fred Astaire and danced by Astaire and Claire Luce)

This song, along with 'Begin the Beguine', is perhaps Porter's best known single work. It was written to accommodate the voice of Fred Astaire.

Form: Verse: 16 bars, consisting of 4–8 bar sections. The chorus comprising 48 bars is divided into A1 (16 bars), A2 (16 bars), bridge (8 bars) and A3 (forshortened into 8 bars).

Lyrics: The Verse of this song is indispensible and is one of the best known verses in all popular music. Its lyric ideas would have had to dictate the static quality of its melody, and the way it leads directly into the chorus. Both verse and chorus display little of the Porter glib smartness but have instead an ardent poetic quality. Perhaps it's carping but the phrase 'under the hide of me', (which Cole was to use again in 'I've Got You Under My Skin' as 'deep in the hide of me') inserted obviously to rhyme with 'inside of me' strikes me as unworthy of

the man who could write such an insouciant inner rhyme as 'there's an, oh, such a hungry yearning burning inside of me' in the very next line.

Verse
Like the beat, beat, beat of the tom-tom
When the jungle shadows fall,
Like the tick, tick, tock of the stately clock
As it stands against the wall,
Like the drip, drip, drip of the raindrops
When a summer show'r is through;
So a voice within me keeps repeating
You, you, you ...

Refrain
Night and day you are the one,
Only you beneath the moon and under the sun.
Whether near to me or far,
It's no matter, darling, where you are,
I think of you night and day.
Day and night why is it so,
That this longing for you follows wherever I go?
In the roaring traffic's boom,
In the silence of my lonely room.
I think of you night and day.
Night and day under the hide of me

There's an, oh, such a hungry yearning burning
  inside of me,
And its torment won't be through,
Till you let me spend my life making love to you
Day and night,
Night and day.

Melody: From the verse's opening melodic
pitch of G which must set some sort of record,
being used 35 times in a row, (Rodgers & Hart's
'Johnny One Note' with its 16 consecutive Cs
would not be written until 5 years later) to the
refrain's repeated Gs on the title words, this
melodic line uses the persistence of this one
note brilliantly. G is even used to release the
tension of the bridge. As in other Porter songs,
this G is the highest pitch achieved in the A1.
By the A2, Porter has cleverly increased the
span to G (sharp) and A natural (see Fig. 1
below).
  By time we reach the bridge, the tessitura
has been raised. Now the melodic line hovers
around Bb and takes on an intensity which
makes it perfectly logical to have the foreshortened A3. Except for the intense ending, most
of the song hovers around G or below, with
most of its movement chromatic and downward. However at the end there is that one
octave skip on 'let me spend my life making

(skip) love to you' that creates the perfect emotional ending to the song.

Harmony: The verse, with its never changing
melodic pitch is an interesting set-up for the
constantly varied harmony. From its twelveth
through sixteenth bar and right into the chorus
Porter begins a descending bass line that moves
by half steps creating oblique motion[1] (he
would use this technique again at the end of 'In
the Still of the Night' and 'So In Love' pulling
the line as taut as a slingshot (see Fig. 2 below).
  The bridge is built on two chords: the I and
bIII. The I creates a strong elemental feeling,
the bIII a freshly exotic one.

Rhythm: Although often successfully performed in Beguine tempo, 'Night and Day' is
actually a straight fox-trot, with not a great deal
of novelty in its rhythmic treatment. Porter
saves the song from rhythmic tedium by substituting quarter note triplets in the A2 at 'follows
wherever I go' where there had been straight
quarter notes in the A1. He creates similar
rhythmic interest at the end of the bridge with
'Oh, such a hungry yearning burning inside of
me'.

Fig. 1

...long-ing   for   you   fol-lows where ev - er   I   go.....

Fig. 2

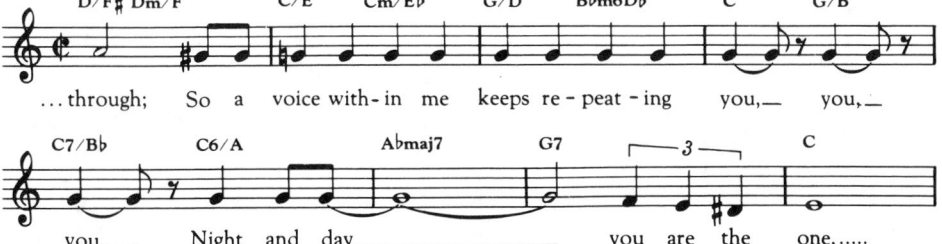

...through;   So   a   voice with-in   me   keeps re - peat - ing   you,__   you,__
you,__   Night   and   day_____   you   are   the   one,.....

WHY SHOULDN'T I (Jubilee) 1935
Sung in the show by Margaret Adams, the
ingénue. This is one of Porter's most engaging
and yearning songs; simple and complex by turns,
it never seems to lose its youthful freshness. It
was not immediately successful, but in time it has
grown to be one of his most frequently
performed works.

Situation in the Show: The naive princess who
has a yen for playwright, Eric Dare, (a take-off
of Noel Coward,) sings this to her girlfriend.

Form: 16-bar verse, marked *Moderato* followed by a 32-bar refrain, marked *Slowly, with
tender expression.* The verse divides itself into 2

[1] See Musical terms appendix

8-bar sections, while the chorus is A1, A2, bridge, A3 (*Not* A B C A2 as misstated by Alec Wilder).

Lyrics: Except for the rather arty lines of the verse and some of the interlude this lyric is pure golden simplicity and very affecting. The A3 section with its rhymes about debutantes and Hollywood is especially charming.

Verse
All my life I've been so secluded
Love has eluded me.
But from knowing second hand what I do of it
I feel certain I could stand a closer view of it.
Till today I studied love discretely,
But now that I'm completely free,
I must find some kind persona grata
To give me data personally.

Refrain
Why shouldn't I
Take a chance when romance passes by
Why shouldn't I know of love?
Why wait around
When each age has a sage who has found
That upon this earth
Love is all that is really worth thinking of.
It must be fun, lots of fun,
To be sure when day is done
That the hour is coming when
You'll be kissed and then
You'll be kissed again.
Each debutante says it's good

And ev'ry star out in far Hollywood
Seems to give it a try,
So why shouldn't I?

Interlude
What kind of man will I discover
When I embark upon my quest?
The ordinary type of lover
I feel would never pass the test.
For I want a man who's creative, a man who writes,
A man to his fingertips an artist,
A man who can give a girl Arabian nights,
Nevertheless in pajamas quite the smartest
Who will know just when and when not to make
    love to me
A man with that certain flair,
In fact, a man like Eric Dare.[1]

Melody: The melodic line of the verse is somewhat unnecessarily intricate, hard to sing and not very memorable. It sounds like it was written as an afterthought. But the melody of the refrain is memorable on first hearing. Its melodic motive (5, 4, 3 of the scale or G, F, E) seems as assertive as the title. The range which seems small is actually an octave and a fourth, but the outer pitches are only touched upon (Fig. 1).

Harmony: The characteristic that makes this song most beloved of professional musicians is perhaps its harmony. Beginning innocuously enough in the A1 with I, II and V chords, the A2 modulates so smoothly we are hardly aware

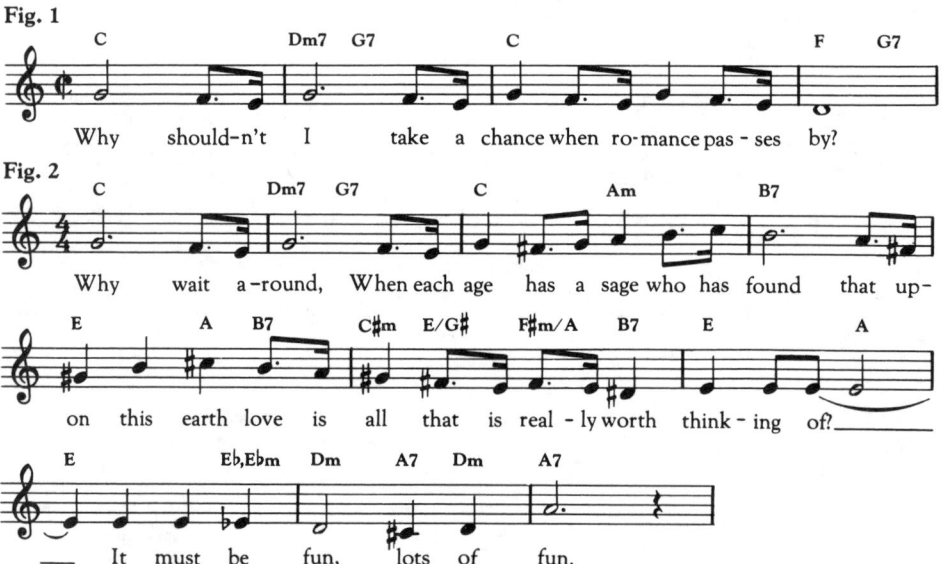

[1] Eric Dare was a character in *Jubilee* modeled after Cole's friend Noel Coward.

of it and ends up a major third above (from C to E). This change is obviously planned so the bridge, full of yearning, beginning with D minor can be approached tenderly through Eb. After a moment in the key of D minor we are led back through the diminished chord into the key of C. The A3 is typical Porter; warming as it heads towards the subdominant and a bright VI, II, V, I. (Fig. 2).

Rhythm: The recurring rhythm of dotted half followed by dotted eighth and sixteenth gives the song a certain backbone. This occurs so often throughout the body of the song that it becomes a kind of motif. Because of the delicious modulation in the A2, there are necessarily more notes in this section, and here the rhythms become kind of square. Yet syncopations at the end of the bridge relieve it, and with the words 'seems to give it a try' coupled with an ascending scale, Cole introduces quarter note triplets leading to the climax pitch. The rhythmic motif returns again at the very end.

IT'S DE-LOVELY[1] (Red, Hot and Blue)
Written in 1936. Sung in the show by Ethel Merman and Bob Hope. It has since been frequently interpolated into the many revivals of *Anything Goes.*

Form: Since this is a duet, the 20-bar verse is cast into an 8-bar section sung by the man and an answering 8-bar section sung by the woman. After a 4-bar lead-in we move directly to the refrain. Form of the refrain is a typical A1, A2, bridge and extended A3. The interesting exception here is that the A2 is built a melodic and harmonic tone higher than the A1.

Lyric: With its 2 verses (the second of which is rarely sung, but which has a marvelously saucy lyric) and 5 refrains, 'It's De-Lovely' is a good example of the story song, a category the mature Cole Porter used rarely. The fourth and fifth refrains were obviously requested encores dealing with the further adventures of a loving couple. Since the title is so well known, one is

struck at once by the alliterative tour de force in the A sections of the song: (In the first and last it is the 'de' sound, later it is the 'vee', then the 'dr' and the 'pee' sounds.) But for me it is the bridges wherein Cole seems to have lavished his best invention that are most pleasing. As an example of Cole's fastidiousness in inner rhyming one should not overlook at every bridge's end the single added rhyming syllable that seems to glue the bridge to the returning A3. Take any one for analysis; Cole sticks to the same scheme throughout:

You can tell at a glance
What a swell night this is for romance
You can hear dear Mother nature murmuring *low,*
'Let yourself *go.'*
So please be sweet, my chickadee,

Verse 1
He: I feel a sudden urge to sing
The kind of ditty that invokes the spring
So control your desire to curse
While I crucify the verse.
She: This verse you've started seems to me
The Tin-Pantithesis of melody,
So to spare me, please, the pain,
Just skip the damn thing and sing the refrain.
He: Mi, mi, mi, mi,
Re, re, re, re,
Do, sol, mi, do, la, si.
She: Take it away.

Refrain 1
The night is young, the skies are clear,
So if you want to go walking, dear,
It's delightful, it's delicious, it's de-lovely,
I understand the reason why
You're sentimental, 'cause so am I,
It's delightful, it's delicious, it's de-lovely,
You can tell at a glance
What a swell night this is for romance
You can hear dear Mother nature murmuring low,
'Let yourself go.'
So please be sweet, my chickadee,
And when I kiss you just say to me,
It's delightful, it's delicious,
It's delectable, it's delirious,
It's dilemma, it's delimit, it's deluxe

---

[1] Porter gave two semi-contradictory versions of the origin of the title of this song.

(1)'I took a world tour a couple of years ago, and I was in Java with Monty Woolley and Moss Hart. We'd just been served that famous Eastern fruit the mangosteen – and were all enjoying it mightily. Moss Hart said, "It's delightful!" I chimed in with "It's delicious!" And Monty Wooley said, "It's de-lovely!" and there's the title of the song.'

(2)'In 1935 when my wife and I and Monty Woolley were approaching the harbor of Rio de Janeiro by boat, it was dawn. My wife and I had risen especially for the event, but Mr. Woolley had stayed up all night to see it and during the night had enjoyed a few whiskey-and-sodas. As we stood on the bow of the boat, my exclamation was "It's delightful!" My wife followed with "It's delicious!" and Monty, in his happy state, cried, "It's dee-lovely!" This last exclamation gave me the title for the song.'

Verse 2
She: Oh, charming sir, the way you sing
Would break the heart of Missus Crosby's Bing
For the tone of your tra-la-la
Has that certain je ne sais quoi.
He: Oh, thank thee kindly, winsome wench,
But 'stead of falling into Berlitz French
Just warble to me, please,
This beautiful strain in plain Brooklynese.
Mi, mi, mi, mi
Re, re, re, re,
Do, sol, mi, do, la, si.
She: Take it away.

Refrain 2
Time marches on and soon it's plain
You've won my heart and I've lost my brain,
It's delightful, it's delicious, it's de-lovely.
Life seems so sweet that we decide
It's in the bag to get unified,
It's delightful, it's delicious, it's de-lovely.
See the crowd in that church,
See the proud parson plopped on his perch,
Get the sweet beat of that organ sealing our doom,
'Here goes the groom, boom!'
How they cheer and how they smile
As we go galloping down the aisle,
'It's divine, dear, it's diveen, dear,
It's de-wunderbar, it's de victory,
It's de vallop, it's de vinner, it's de voiks,
It's de-lovely.'

Refrain 3
The knot is tied and so we take
A few hours off to eat wedding cake,
It's delightful, it's delicious, it's de-lovely.
It feels so fine to be a bride,
And how's the groom? Why, he's slightly fried,
It's delightful, it's delicious, it's de-lovely.
To the pop of champagne
Off we hop in our plush little plane
Till a bright light through the darkness cozily calls
'Niag'ra Falls.'
All's well my love, our day's complete,
And what beautiful bridal suite,
'It's de-reamy, its de-rowsy,
It's de-reverie, it's de-rhapsody,
It's de-regal, it's de-royal, it's de-Ritz,
It's de-lovely.'

Refrain 4
We settle down as man and wife
To solve the riddle called 'married life,'
It's delightful, it's delicious, it's de-lovely.
We're on the crest, we have no cares,
We're just a couple of honey bears,
It's delightful, it's delicious, it's de-lovely.
All's as right as can be,
Till one night, at my window I see
An absurd bird with a bundle hung on his nose.
'Get baby clothes,'
Those eyes of yours are filled with joy

When Nurse appears and cries, 'It's a boy!'
'He's appalling, he's appealing,
He's a pollywog, he's a paragon,
He's a Popeye, he's a panic, he's a pip,
He's de-lovely.'

Refrain 5
Our boy grows up, he's six feet three,
He's so good-looking, he looks like me,
It's delightful, it's delicious, it's de-lovely.
He's such a hit, this son of ours
That all the dowagers send him flowers,
It's delightful, it's delicious, it's de-lovely.
So sublime is his press,
That in time L. B. Mayer, no less,
Makes a night flight to New York and tells him he
    should
'Go Hollywood.'
Good God! Today he gets such pay
That Elaine Barrie's his fiancée,
It's delightful, it's delicious,
It's delectable, it's delirious,
It's dilemma, it's delimit, it's deluxe,
It's de-lovely.

Melody: The special brightness of this melody is due in large measure to its harmony, (see below). There seems to be nothing extraneous in this tune; the A sections are merely 3 rising chromatic notes and a bouncing back and forth on the interval of the third. The bridge uses the broken chords tone of the 'commercial bridge'.[1]

Harmony: The I, I aug, I6 sequence, which Porter uses in the A1 section of this song is a strong positive harmonic device that has been effectively used by songwriters as diverse as Berlin and Sondheim. Adapting the idea for the A2 into II, II aug, (although purists will avow there is no such chord) II6 keeps the A sections from becoming dull. But what appeals most to musicians is the final section with its descending bass. This oblique motion[2] with the tune fixed in mid register against a rubber band-like pulling bass line creates the necessary tension.

Rhythm: The syncopated rhythm of the basic motive (Bar 1) gives way to a different syncopation (Bar 5). The bridge uses an entirely fresh rhythmic design, but again, what is most exhilarating and original happens in the final section. At the penultimate bar an unsuspected eighth-note rest moves everything over just enough to add an exciting rhythmic freedom to one of Cole Porter's most daring songs.

[1] See Musical Terms appendix
[2] See Musical Terms appendix

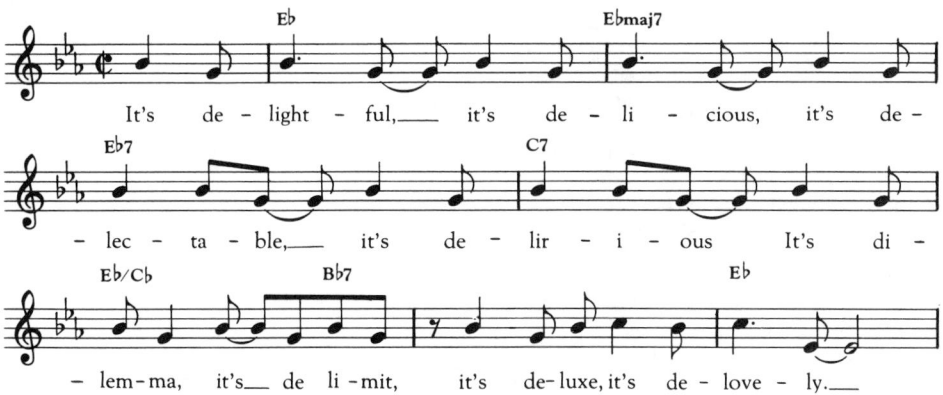

It's de - light - ful,___ it's de - li - cious, it's de - lec - ta - ble,___ it's de - lir - i - ous It's di - lem - ma, it's___ de li - mit, it's de - luxe, it's de - love - ly.___

IN THE STILL OF THE NIGHT (*Rosalie*)
Published 1937. Sung in the film by Nelson Eddy.

Form: One of the few verseless songs Porter wrote, the form here is a very free A1, A2, bridge, A3. The A1 and A2 are 16 bars while the bridge is 24. The A3 which is 16 bars *only* reiterates the opening motive. Porter also wrote a long piano postlude which is almost never performed.

Lyric: Except for the n(ight) sound and its rhyming with 'flight' and 'sight', this lyric relies on gentle 'i' and 'a' vowel sounds as befits its title. The rhyming scheme is deceptively intricate, the use of an interrogatory bridge coupled with the rise in pitch creating the necessary intensity. The slow-moving elongated A3 wherein Cole rhymes 'dim', 'rim', 'hill', 'chill' and 'still' almost makes us forget the coming last word of the song, 'night', which rhymes with 'sight' heard 16 bars ago as the last word of the bridge.

In the still of the night
As I gaze from my window
At the moon in its flight
My thoughts all stray to you.
In the still of the night,
When the world is in slumber

Oh, the times without number
Darling, when I say to you.
'Do you love me
As I love you?
Are you my life to be
My dream come true?
Or will this dream of mine
Fade out of sight
Like the moon growing dim
On the rim of the hill
In the chill,
Still of the night.'

Melody: Perhaps because of its range which is wider than most popular songs this composition has become a favourite of recital singers (who invariably come out with 'In the steel of the night'). Cole marked the A sections to be sung 'mysteriously', and the memorable motive settling on the sixth of the key seems to create just that. It is not remarkable that the A1 section ends on the 5th of the scale, but it *is* unique that the A3 *section ends on the fifth* without sounding forced, in fact, ending on the tonic or any other pitch in this case would sound forced. The bridge which is marked *Appassionato* lets out all the emotional stops. This is due partly to the high tessitura used and the harmonic intensity (see fig. A below). The A3 simply repeats the motive with fresh harmony bringing the song to a pianissimo close.

Fig. A

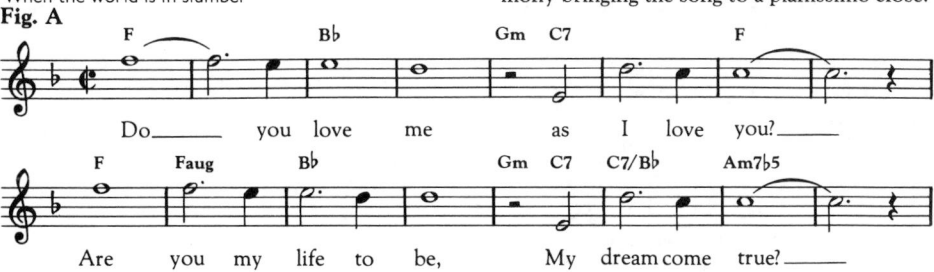

Do___ you love me as I love you?___

Are you my life to be, My dream come true?___

Harmony: Porter's sense of harmony never seems to have been used to better advantage. The A1 sets the stage with rudimentary chords, the only interest being the change from major to minor. But in the A2 we have a full-fledged modulation to the key of the mediant (F to A minor) yet the composer comes right back creating further interest by his return to the tonic key for the bridge. This bridge (which is reputed to have made stony-hearted Louis B. Mayer cry) carries us, for the first time in the song, into the subdominant harmony. Cole cleverly saves the extra zinger of the I to I augmented to subdominant for the 9th and 10th bar of the bridge, the repetition of the first theme. Musicians have long admired Porter's sense of descending harmony and nowhere is it

more gorgeously apparent than in the A3 section of this song, (Fig B below) where his bass journeys downward from the word 'fade' on D flat to the word 'chill' where it finally arrives on G.

Rhythm: This is not a particularly lively song having not the slightest sense of syncopation or rhythmic anticipation, but one can see a clever compositional trick at work here in Porter's use of aumentation[1]. It is apparent, if one compares the motive as it is first introduced in the A1 (Fig. A) to the way it appears to be stretched out in the A3 (Fig. B), that Porter aimed for a gentle slowing down without adding extra bars. And he succeeded.

Fig. B

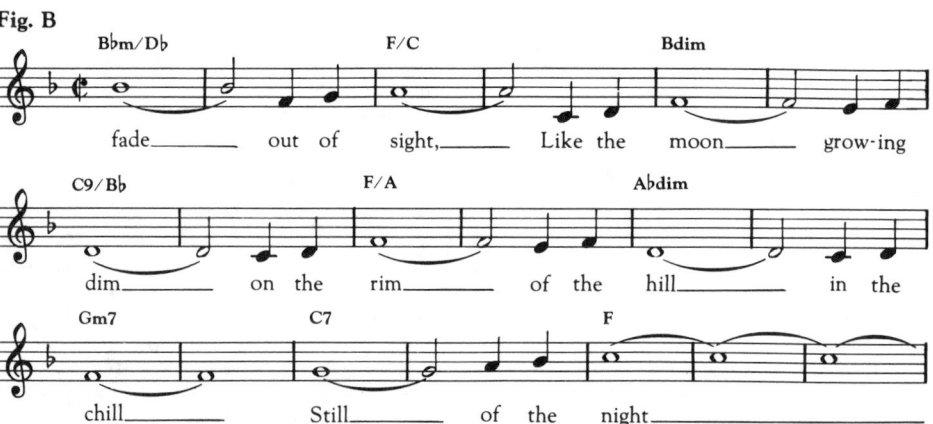

ACE IN THE HOLE (*Let's Face It*)
Published 1941. Sung by Mary Jane Walsh with back-up by Sunnie O'Day and Nanette Fabray.

This is one of my favourite songs because it represents the essence of Cole Porter. The minor opening, the circular harmonic design, the witty and timely (then) lyrics, the advice given freely and the optimistic point of view on how to conquer adversity.

Situation in the Show: Smart-alec ingénue tells her 2 friends how to make the men in their lives behave.

Form: There is a long (28-bar) verse, followed by an ABAC chorus. ABAC is common for a show tune, but here the division is unusual, even for Porter. A1 = 12 bars; B = 4 bars; A2 = 12 bars; C = 4 bars.

Lyrics: The verse sets the stage for us to believe in the forthcoming advice. Porter frequently

cautions neophytes (as in 'Experiment'). Most often it is a wise grandmother who councils: 'When I'm in a spot it's true, I always know what to do'. (A similar verse is to be found in 'Never Give Anything Away', 'Opportunity Knocks But Once,' and elsewhere).

The chorus states the concept at the outset. 'Bad times may follow your tracks' followed immediately by a typical Porter concept, 'Sad times may bar you from Saks'. Any other lyricist would have illustrated the opening line with some obvious deprivation, but only Porter would consider the times dire when one is unable to shop at the world's (then) most luxurious department store. As one would expect, there are many topical references: *Abie's Irish Rose*, a long-running play; Gable-Lombard, a torrid Hollywood affair, and so on.

[1] See Musical Terms Appendix

There is a patter section whose concept I find a bit obtuse and not consistent with the main feeling of the song. The lyric explains how a girl might make jealous a boyfriend who won't give her a tumble: 'Say you talked to Barbara Hutton and she's sending you Cary Grant'. Then there is a return to the second half of the chorus with an added short coda (not printed in the sheet music) full of inner rhyme:

'Always try to arrive at
Having an *ace* some *place* private'

Melody: The long verse has a parlando quality, almost like a recitative with the duo answering the singer back. In the chorus, the line is a lovely combination of the big skip and lower passing tone which breaks the old bugaboo rule of turning and going in the opposite direction after a big skip. The first phrase is sequenced 3 times and this is what makes the song memorable (Fig. A). The twelfth-sixteenth bars have a rhythmic snap that leads to the dominant (Fig. B). Then Porter plunges back to the relative minor again and does the same thing for 4 bars. Now, since the harmony is the same as in the first half, the melody is built a third higher for

intensity. The melody ends, after all its skippiness and lower appoggiaturas with a welcome contrasting ascending scale[1]. This is another example of Porter's remarkable sense of prosody. If you try to sing the ultimate line, 'Always have an ace in the hole', it would be unnatural to come out with any other pitches than the ones Porter chose (Fig. C)

Harmony: The key relationship is very free. The verse starts in F, a simple recitative and then goes to Ab (where it looks like it was headed for Fm), then to F and a long C7, dominant pedalpoint to the chorus. In the chorus, the unprepared entrance into Dm at the opening is slightly reminiscent of 'Easy to Love' and totally fresh. The design is circle of fifths[1] but, except for the opening, all bright dominant 7ths. Of course it ends in major – as most songs of that period that began in minor. The patter section has a wonderful 8-bar pedal point on the II chord.

Rhythm: The rhythmic contrast between the verse which is straightforward and the chorus, highly syncopated, creates as much interest as delight. After the patter section when the chor-

Fig. A

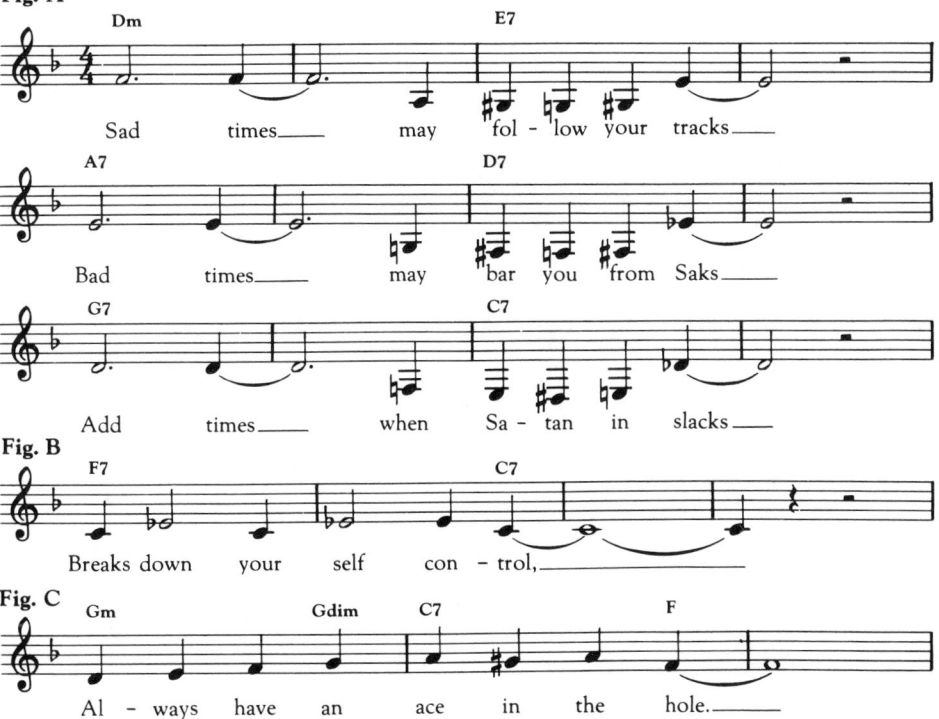

us reprises the back-up singers have an intricate rhythmic line.

Incidental Information: The low key of D minor was suitable for the belting chest voice of Mary Jane Walsh. When the song was readied for sheet music publication, it was decided to transpose it up a fifth to A minor. Perhaps because of its wide (almost an octave and a half) range the song was never one of Porter's great money makers. Porter was obliged by censors to change the verse line before the New York opening from:

'Each night little granny
Would plop on her fanny
And give me this good advice'

to

'Each night grandmummy
Would pat on my tummy
And give me this good advice'

Research: The complete piano-vocal score is to be found in the Cole Porter Trust, Library of Congress, Yale Beinecke Library and Lincoln Center Library.

SO IN LOVE (*Kiss Me, Kate*)

Published 1948. Sung by Patricia Morrison, later reprised by Alfred Drake.

Form: This is one of Porter's few songs that lacks a lead-in verse. The form is simple A1, A2, bridge, A3, (with a 4-bar extension on the A3) each section being 16 bars rather than the usual 8. The song is written alla breve, clearly indicating only 2 pulses per bar.

Melody: The sinuous melody, one of Porter's best, ranges over an octave and a 4th. Beginning low in the minor, it soon makes its effect by skips of a fifth, always to an appoggiatura,[1] and always ending in the major. Each section climaxes a bit higher, an effect that gives the song a growing power. A1 reaches its top on the word 'fill', (Db) (Fig. 1); A2 on the syllable 'dar-' (Eb) (Fig 2); the bridge on the word 'joy' (Fb) (Fig. 3) and the A3 on the word 'till' pitched on the highest note in the song, an F natural.

Lyric: Until its final section this lyric uses no fresh ideas, but it is so utterly romantic, and marries so well with the tune that one is not aware of awkward inverse speech ('the night mysterious', instead of 'the mysterious night', 'my joy delirious' instead of 'delirious with joy'). The final A3 section works wonderfully for the characters in the show, because Fred *has* deceived and deserted Lilli, and equally well as anybody's torch song.

[1] See musical terms appendix

Fig. 1

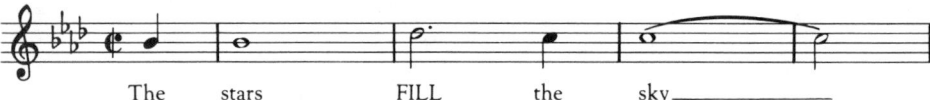

The   stars   FILL   the   sky_____

Fig. 2

You   know   DAR – ling   why_____

Fig. 3

In   love   with   my   JOY   de – lir – i – ous_____

Fig. 4

I'm   yours   TILL   I   die_____

Strange, dear, but true, dear,
When I'm close to you, dear,
The stars fill the sky,
So in love with you, am I.
Even without you
My arms fold about you
You know, darling, why,
So in love with you, am I.
In love with the night mysterious,
The night when you first were there.
In love with my joy delirious
When I knew that you could care.
So taunt me, and hurt me,
Deceive me, desert me,
I'm yours till I die.
So in love,
So in love,
So in love with you my love, am I.

Harmony: The Porter sense of harmony accented by *le mot juste* seems to be working hand in hand in this song. The very first 2 pitches, C and D flat, a semitone apart, harmonized first with a sinuous F minor ('Strange, dear') and immediately after with an urgent C7 ('but true, dear'), seem a perfect setting of these words. Beyond these measures, the ninths created by the appoggiaturas in the 5th and 7th bars add to the emotional intensity of the harmony. The bridge, beginning on the subdominant sets a new fresh, brighter tone, but the Fb at its climax creates a flat ninth chord that smacks again of the super romantic. After a 2 bar break, we are plunged again into the minor, this time almost masochistically with the lyrics 'taunt me, and hurt me, deceive me, desert me', (usually played in bolero tempo) until we reach the coda, this time with an evaded ending. The curious and beautiful harmony in this coda has an *alto* line (from the 61st measure) that

descends inexorably from F through Fb, Eb, D natural, Db to end as the song concludes on C. A triumph.

Rhythm: There is little of rhythmic interest here except to mention the harmonic rhythm that works in 2 bar phrases and the clever way Porter achieves variety in the bridge, by introducing it on an upbeat, (In *love*, the *night*) so that the ensuing 'taunt' and 'hurt' can contrast strongly on their downbeats.

WHERE IS THE LIFE THAT LATE I LED?

(*Kiss Me, Kate*)
Sung by Alfred Drake. Although introduced in 1948, the song was not published until the following year.

Form: This most amusing song is a polyglot and its mercurial change of moods and section probably accounts for much of its humour. It shares with many of the *Kiss Me, Kate* songs a form borrowed from native Italian dances, especially the Venetian boat song, and the canzones of Sorrento. Beginning with a 24-bar verse, (16 fast and 8 slow), that leads to the lively tarantella chorus, a perfect 32-bar A1, A2, bridge and A3. Then comes a repeated interlude, full of mock seriousness. Chorus and interlude are twice repeated ending with the rousing chorus and an almost operatic cadenza.

Melody: Falling somewhere between an aria and a show-tune, the verse of this song which sits happily between major and minor could have come from Napoli, while the chorus (Fig A) with its melisma on the word 'I' is purely Sicilian. The patter section, half in the relative

Fig. A

Fig. B

minor and half in the parallel major, sounds like a Venetian boat song (as noted above), and, surprisingly, this vocal *tour de force* including the splendid cadenza, (Fig B) – written for Alfred Drake's flexible voice – uses only the range of an octave and a fifth.

Lyric: Probably among Cole's most erudite and witty lyrics. Mixing styles, anachronisms and showbiz and Elizabethan terms, it never fails to stop the show.

Verse
Since I reached the charming age of puberty,
And began to finger feminine curls,
Like a show that's typically Shuberty
I have always had a multitude of girls.
But now that a married man at last, am I
How aware of my dear departed past, am I.

Chorus I
Where is the life that late I led?
Where is it now? Totally dead!
Where is the fun I used to find?
Where has it gone? Gone with the wind.
A married life may all be well,
But raising an heir
Could never compare
With raising a bit of hell,
So I repeat what first I said,
Where is the life that late I led?

Patter I
In dear Milano, where are you, Momo?
Still selling those pictures of the scriptures in the Duomo?

And Carolina, where are you, Lina,
Still peddling your pizza in the streets o' Taomina?
And in Firenze, where are you, Alice
Still there in your pretty, itty-bitty, Pitti Palace
And sweet Lucretia, so young and gay-ee,
What scandalous doin's in the ruins of Pompeii!

Chorus 2
Where is the life that late I led?
Where is it now? Totally dead!
Where is the fun I used to find?
Where has it gone? Gone with the wind.
The marriage game is quite all right
It's easy to play
During the day
But, oh, what a bore at night.
So I repeat what first I said,
Where is the life that late I –?

Patter 2
Where is Rebecca, my Becki-weckio?
Again is she cruising that amusing Ponte Vecchio
Where is Fedora, the wild virago?
It's lucky I missed her gangster sister from Chicago.
Where is Venetia, who loved to chat so?
Could still she be drinkin' in her stinkin' pink palazzao?
And lovely Lisa, where are you Lisa,
You gave a new meaning to the leaning tow'r of Pisa.

Refrain 3
Where is the life that late I led?
Where is it now? Totally dead!
Where is the fun I used to find?
Where has it gone? Gone with the wind.
I've oft been told of nuptual bliss,
But what do you do,

Fig. C

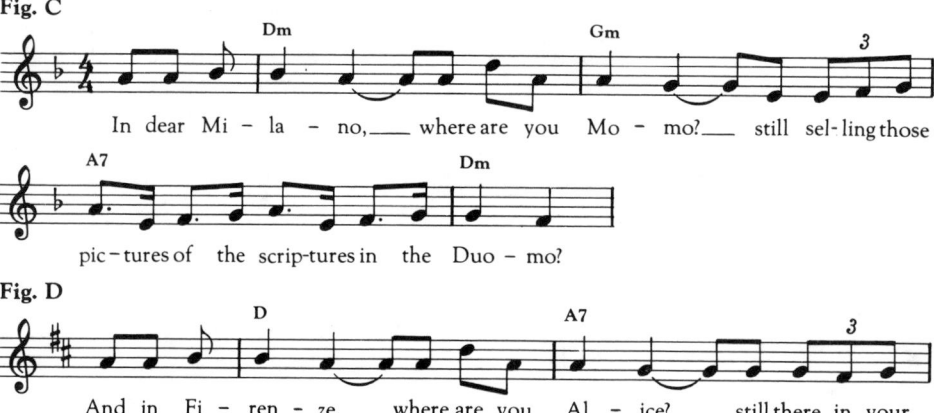

Fig. D

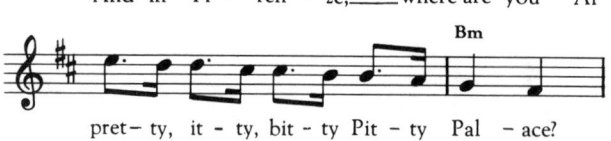

A quarter to two
With only a shrew to kiss?
So I repeat what first I said,
Where is the life that late I led?

Harmony: Beginning in C and using a liberal sprinkling of minor sub-dominants, the verse of this song merely sets the stage for the chorus in F. (And one cannot overlook Porter's use of the Neopolitan sixth chord 3 bars before the verse's end. Was Cole pulling our leg?) A1 and A2 use mostly tonic and dominant chords, while the A2 brings about a little excursion to the relative minor (D minor). But the real joy and humour of this number lies in the patter section. The theme is quoted below (Fig. C) and deliciously majorized 4 bars later (Fig. D)

Rhythm: The use of so many Italianate rhythms and tempi gives this canzone a great variety. The most obvious change is the rhythmic alternation which comes from having the chorus in 6/8 and the patter in 4/4. Additionally one finds here a great variety in harmonic rhythm, that is, sometimes the chords last for 2 bars, sometimes they shift every half bar.

IT'S ALL RIGHT WITH ME (*Can-Can*)
Sung by Peter Cookson. A late addition to the score, added before the Philadelphia previews. Published in 1953.

When Richard Rodgers was asked to name his favourite Porter, he answered unhesitatingly, 'It's All Right With Me', pointing out that 'all of us in the business of writing songs are only too aware of the near impossibility of making a new approach to a love situation by means of words and music'. This lyric, (see below) Mr. Rodgers points out, 'represents a basic reaction that all of us have experienced at one time or another, one of almost rueful pleasure. It's all simple and direct, but there's a fairly intellectual concept accompanying the emotion that makes for something refreshing and moving. To describe a tune in terms of its attractiveness is almost

impossible, but this one with its criss-crossing of minor to major and the insistence of its rhythm, makes it just about irresistible. With this song Cole Porter was never better, and there is no higher praise.'

Form: A1 (16 bars), A2 (16 bars), bridge (16 bars), A3 (16 bars) with extension (8 bars). Porter often preferred this double length commercial form when reaching for an emotional wallop. Long enough to convey his message *without* resorting to a repeat of the chorus, and yet not so long as to risk becoming tiresome (as 'Begin the Beguine',) or exceeding the three minute allotted time of the 78 RPM shellac record with a long 'list song' such as 'Can-Can' or 'You're the Top'.

Melody: This unforgettable song approaches natural speech throughout. Because of the *tour-de-force* Porter has accomplished here, one should be aware of the pitch placement of its lyrics in any discussion of its melodic line. Running the gamut of heart-wrenching emotionality, one is struck on first hearing by its economy of range – merely a minor tenth. But its climax points are chosen for maximum effect. The first 8 bars of the A1 (Fig. A) state the premise of the song in lyrics and melody with a rising line; the second 8 bars descend. The same thing happens with a more intensified lyric in the A2, but in the bridge, the higher tessitura creates an increased tension until the question, 'don't you want to forget someone too?' returns the voice to a seductively conspiratorial mid-range and segues into the A3. The extension, commencing with low 'D' actually follows the concept of the song which throws better judgement and caution to the winds in reaching up over an octave – and staying there.

Lyric: Like 'So In Love' this song is another of the few lacking a verse or a second chorus. Porter's notes show no alternate lines, indicating that the lyric he kept and published was the

Fig. A

one he was sure of. Certainly, the song displays a logical growth within its rueful few lines, the protagonist mentioning by turns the face, the smile and then the illegitimacy of the proposed assignation – perhaps a one-night stand. Although it catapulted the song into wide popularity, Cole never approved of Lena Horne's up-tempo version of the song, saying it was 'not to be played too fast' and adding 'you should cry when you sing it'.

It's the wrong time and the wrong place,
Though your face is charming, it's the wrong face,
It's not her face, but such a charming face,
That it's all right with me.
It's the wrong song, in the wrong style,
Though your smile is lovely it's the wrong smile,
It's not her smile, but such a lovely smile.
That it's all right with me.
You can't know how happy I am that we met,
I'm strangely attracted to you.
There's someone I'm trying so hard to forget,
Don't you want to forget someone too?
It's the wrong game with the wrong chips,
Though your lips are tempting, they're the wrong lips,
They're not her lips, but they're such tempting lips
That if some night you're free,
Dear, it's all right,
It's all right with me.

Harmony: Perhaps of all of Porter's songs this has the most exciting harmonic possibilities. Porter's original harmonization using an alternation of C minor and F9 against the same motive is brilliant and adds greatly to the harmonic tension that makes this song, with its alternation between minor and major such a favourite of jazz musicians.[1] In the bridge, (which is built largely on the subdominant with liberal sprinklings of diminished chords) the tension that the Eb pedal-point creates finally becomes unbearable and the bass descends though a strong II and V to plunge us into the A3 section. One should not overlook the extension which happens so inevitably on the melodic leading tone, the word 'free', and a Bb minor seventh chord followed by an Eb *seventh* (which sends us into the key of A flat at this late stage in the song) and the final high melodic Eb which is held for more than 2 bars, harmonized with an F9, and a Bb 11 (suspension) going daringly directly to I.

Rhythm: What rhythmic complexity there is in this song occurs because of inevitable hesitations in natural speech. The rhythm of the tune starts to become syncopated in the fifth full bar on the words 'though your face is *charming*' a phrase which interestingly recurs again in the 11th with 'such a *charming* face'. Since syncopation creates accent, Porter is able through this technique to accent 'lovely smile', and 'tempting lips' in later sections.

Perhaps this is Porter's best song, never going over-the-top while encompassing all of his virtues: combining in its lyric and music, seduction, romance, sexuality, urbanity, up-to-dateness, fitting the show and fleshing out the character who sings it and universal in that it expresses the feeling of men and women everywhere who fantasize or verbalize an extra-relationship affair.

ANALYSIS OF COWARD SONGS

FORBIDDEN FRUIT

(1917) This is the first song in which Noel Coward takes credit for having written both music and lyrics. Claiming it was created when he was only sixteen, it shows a worldliness and a cynicism far beyond his years.

Form: The use of several verses and several refrains in his patter songs was to become a Coward hallmark. In 'Forbidden Fruit' the twelve bar verse beginning with two 4-bar phrases followed by a 4-bar lead-in to the chorus is reminiscent of Kern. However, the sixteen bar chorus, built in ABAC form, most popular in 1917 feels like it comes straight out of music-hall. Combining the obvious form with the cheeky lyrics (see below) gives the song a remarkable freshness.

Lyrics: These lyrics are unique in concept (eloping with a woman and then being 'knocked down' by her husband; sacrificing

---

[1] One often hears the first eight bars of this song, especially when performed as an instruemental reharmonized as Cm; Cm/B; Cm/Bb; Cm/A natural; Cm/Ab; Cm/G; Fm (2 bars).

'honour' for a small string of pearls' as well as the technique of inner rhymes. Sometimes young Coward indulges in the crutch of inverted English which can make for bad poetry and worse lyrics ('blasé he will quickly be; on the side his lady love is shoved; anxiously through life they prowl). Notice that Coward already uses the word 'make' in its sexual connotation and that he saves his best punch line for the end of the song. These knowing tricks which had to be self-taught, are also found in the early works of Cole Porter.

Verse 1

Ordinary man invariably sighs
Vainly for what cannot be,
If he's in an orchard, he will cast
    his eyes
Up into the highest tree,
There may be a lot of windfalls
Lying all around
But you'll never see a man
Enjoy the fruit that's on the ground.

Refrain 1

Ev'ry peach out of reach is attractive,
'Cos it's just a little bit too high,
And you'll find that ev'ry man
Will try to pluck it if he can
As he passes by,
For a brute loves the fruit that's forbidden
And I'll bet you half a crown.[1]
He'll appreciate the flavour of it much, much more
If he has to climb a bit to shake it down.

Verse 2

If a man's engaged and feels that he is loved,
Blasé he will quickly be,
Often on one side his lady love is shoved
While he goes upon a spree,
Then perhaps she'll marry
And you can bet your life
He'll want her very badly
When she's someone else's wife.

Refrain 2

Ev'ry peach out of reach is attractive,
'Cos it's just a little bit too high,
Though it isn't very sane
To make the things you can't attain,
Still you always try,
If you find that you're blind with devotion,
For delightful Mrs. Brown,
You'll appreciate eloping with her much, much
    more,
If her husband comes along and knocks you down.

Verse 3

Women haven't altered since the days of Eve,
Anxiously through life they prowl,
Always try'ng to better what their friends achieve,
Either by fair means or foul,
A girl may be quite careful
Of the sort of life she picks
But to be a real success she's got to know a lot of
    tricks.

Refrain 3

Ev'ry peach out of reach is attractive
'Cos it's just a little bit too high,
Even well brought up young girls
Will look at other women's pearls
With a yearning eye.
If they fight day and night persevering
And a small string they collect,
They'll appreciate the colour of them much much
    more,
If they'd sacrificed a little self respect.

Melody: The catchy tune of this chorus is preceeded by a rather sing-songy verse (Fig. 1) whose last two bars (Fig. 2) have a descending line showing that even at this early age, Coward tried to illustrate his lyric through his melodic line. In this case, talking about taking down the fruit in the orchard coming down, (and later in the chorus with the lines 'He'll appreciate the flavour of it much, much more if he has to climb a bit to shake it down,) he uses a long

Fig. 1

Fig. 2

---

[1] Speaking of the meager wager of half a crown, Coward wrote in an introduction to 'Forbidden Fruit' that a bet of fifty pounds 'or at least a fiver would be more in keeping with the general urbanity of the theme ... but it must be remembered that to the author, half a crown in 1916 was the equivalent of five pounds in 1926.'

skippy scale-line that ranges over an octave and a third.

The charm of the melody of the refrain is brought about by the downward skips of, first, a third and then, a second. Coward is consistent in the use of these intervals throughout the rest of the refrain – a musical device that creates great unity.

Harmony: Coward's harmony, self-taught, but nevertheless often quite daring is only occasionally displayed in this song which relies pretty much on II's V's and I's to make its point. In the last bar (12th) of the verse he uses the IV chord in minor, soon to become a staple of the '30s, but one that would give a dated sound to his music beyond that decade.

Rhythm: The persistent dotted eight and sixteenth rhythm used slavishly throughout this song give it both its lilt and are responsible for its somewhat monotonous rhythmic sameness. Coward was soon to grow out of such monotony as well as the constant two bar phrases which give this early gem such squareness.

Incidental Information: Although written in 1916, the song was not published until 1953. Besides its correct title of 'Forbidden Fruit', it has been known as 'Every Peach', and originally, 'If He Has To Climb a Bit To Shake It Down'. The song was used in the film 'Star', sung by a young Daniel Massey who was portraying an even younger Noel Coward at an audition.

Ev-ry peach out of reach is at-tract-ive   Cos it's just a lit-tle bit too   high

WHEN MY SHIP COMES HOME (*London Calling*) 1923
The song was introduced by Winifred Satchell. This sensitive lyric coupled to a yearning melody shows a great advance over 'Forbidden Fruit'. Although written in 1923, the concept (that the ship laden with jewels won't mean anything without bringing the singer love) is delicately handled and was to be used again in 'My Ship', the pivotal song of another important show, *Lady In The Dark* (1941), starring Gertrude Lawrence. In its imagery and mood as well, Kurt Weill and Ira Gershwin's song owes a great deal to Coward's much earlier one. On the whole, the song is so beautifully balanced that one is surprised it never became better known.

Form: The verse has an 8-bar body with a 4-bar lead in to the chorus, which has 16 bars, ABAC. This form, being the same used in 'Forbidden Fruit', is less reminiscent of music-hall and closer to the American showtune.

Lyrics:

Verse 1
Sometimes when I'm weary
And the world seems grey,
And the firelight flickers blue,
Somewhere in the future,
Maybe far away
There are dreams that may come true,

Cinderella's story is so lovely to pretend,
Someday soon, my story too,
May have a happy end.

Refrain 1
When my ship comes home,
When my ship comes home,
Silks and velvets and cloth of gold,
Caskets bursting with wealth untold,
When my ship comes home
Through the world I'll roam,
Open skies above me,
Someone dear to love me,
When my ship comes home.

Verse 2
Life is nothing
But a game of make believe
Until true love comes your way.
Such a dreary pattern
Through the years you weave,
If you can't afford to pay.
Fate is sometimes cruel
And a new dawn soon may break,
Ev'ry single jewel
I'll be wearing for your sake.

Refrain 2
When my ship comes home,
When my ship comes home
No more waiting thru empty years,
Pearls and diamonds
In place of tears,
When my ship comes home
Through the world I'll roam

Open skies above me,
Someone dear to love me,
When my ship comes home.

Melody: The simple verse with its naïve, almost parlando character, sets the fairy-tale story and again shows Coward's ability to match words to music.

Although the entire song lies within the economical range of a tenth, great yearning is built into this rising melodic line of the refrain. In the repeat, Coward replaces the climatic D in bar 4 see* with an emotional F in bar 12 see**, thereby creating a beautiful climax for the song.

Harmony: Exoticism is suggested, beginning with an introduction that juxtaposes the chords of B and Eb (although one may suspect this may be the work of an over zealous arranger). Beyond that, except for a somewhat overused augmented chord (again, to create an exotic effect), the harmony is fresh and endearing. The harmonic rhythm is well contrasted, especially in bars 4 to 8 (see example below).

Rhythm: There is very little rhythmic interest here, but that does not mean the song is boring in that department. Coward uses fresh combinations of quarters and eighth notes keeping each of the sections surprisingly unhackneyed.

A ROOM WITH A VIEW (*This Year of Grace*)
1928
Introduced by Jessie Matthews and Sonnie Hale.
This song, the hit of the show, is one of Coward's most popular. It was the favourite composition of Edward VIII when he was Prince of Wales, who reportedly requested it to be played nine times non-stop at the Ascot Cabaret Ball – a gruelling test for any melody. In *This Year of Grace* it was not only used as a charming duet for ingénue and

juvenile, but was plugged again by the entire company (with different words[1]) at the finale.

Form: With the verse cast into A1 (8 bars), A2 (8 bars), a release (4 and 4 bars) and an A3 (8 bars again) and *especially* the refrain, cast in the same AABA form, 'A Room With A View' is quite a departure from the songs, mostly ABAC, that Coward had been writing before.

[1] see parody lyric (p. 314)

The AABA form (practised in the late '20s and throughout the '30s by the Gershwins and most other American songwriters) is far more commercial.

Lyrics: From its title onward, this song captures the youthful urge – just becoming a pattern the world over of leaving the family and striking out on one's own. When Coward's lyric states 'no one to give advice,/ That sounds a paradise/ few could fail to choose' it is not unlike Lorenz Hart's concept for 'Mountain Greenery' (written two years earlier), with lines like 'how we love sequestering/ where no pests are pestering,/ No dear mama holds us in tether'. Coward's music and lyric never complemented each other so perfectly. The complete lyric follows.

Verse I
He: I've been cherishing
Through the perishing
Winter nights and days,
A funny little phrase
That means
Such a lot to me
That you've got to be
With me heart and soul
For on you the whole
Thing leans.
She: Won't you kindly tell me what you're
Driving at?
What conclusion you're arriving at?
He: Please don't turn away
Or my dream will stay
Hidden out of sight
Among a lot of might
Have beens.

Refrain I
A room with a view and you
And no one to worry us,
No one to hurry us through
This dream we've found.
We'll gaze at the sky and try
To guess what it's all about
Then we will figure out why
The world is round.
She: We'll be as happy and contented
As birds upon a tree,
High above the mountains and sea.
Both: We'll bill in and we'll coo-oo-oo
And sorrow will never come,
Oh will it ever come to
Our room with a view?

Verse 2
She: I'm so practical
I'd make tactical
Errors as your wife,
I'd try to set your life to rights.

I'm upset a bit
For I get a bit
Dizzy now and then
Following your mental flights.
He: Come with me and leave behind the
Noisy crowds,
Sunlight shines for us above the clouds
She: My eyes glistened too
While I listened to
All the things you said.
I'm glad I've got a head for heights.

Refrain 2
A room with a view, and you
And no one to give advice,
That sounds a paradise few
Could dream to choose.
With fingers entwined we'll find
Relief from the preachers who
Always beseech us to mind
Our p's and q's.
He: We'll watch the whole world pass before
us
While we are sitting still.
Leaning on our own windowsill.
Both: We'll bill and we'll coo-oo-oo,
And maybe a stork will bring
This, that, and the t'other thing to
Our room with a view.

PARODY VERSION
Entire cast: You've seen our revue, right
through
We hope you're applauding too,
For it's according to you,
The money speaks.
We hope you can rouse Keith Prowse
Something sensational,
Their approbation 'll
House us here for weeks.
We thought it best to have a tryout
We're not allowed to shirk.
Please don't let us fly out of work.
The best we can do, it's true
May not make you yearn again
Soon to return again to
The Cochran revue.

Melody: From its verse onwards, this song uses an economy of range unlike many of Coward's previous ones. The A sections of both verse and chorus only encompass an octave and even their B sections add only another tone to the total. The charming melody succeeds, in addition to its obvious rhythmic interest, because of two important melodic elements: (1) the catchy motive ending on the romantic third of the key (see*) and (2) especially in the refrain, the fresh use of the leading-tone (see**). (See excerpts from Verse and Refrain below.)

Harmony: The chorus of this song is charged with personal vigour and youth, from its lead-in on the V augmented to its A1 ending on the leading-tone (see***). The bridge of the refrain, built around the subdominant, while hardly new-hat is very bright. Yet Coward is extremely fussy, going so far as to change a single pitch to a 'blue note' when the words of the verse seem to call for it.

Rhythm: Coward's contrast between verse and chorus and the latter's fresh rhythm contributes to the infectious quality of this song. Throughout the verse the rhythm has been

extremely 'square', and fallen into matching 2-, 4- and 8-bar phrases. Suddenly in the chorus we have a syncopated lead-in (bar 1), held notes (bars 2, 3), jumpy rhythm using sixteenth notes (bars 4, 5), followed by slow notes that finally settle down on the leading tone (bars 6, 7, 8).

As was noted earlier, the set of music to lyric is indeed remarkable here. One has only to look at the opening of the release of the refrain to hear the 'birds upon the tree'.

I'LL SEE YOU AGAIN (*Bitter Sweet*) 1929
This duet, Coward's best known romantic composition, was sung in the original London production by Peggy Wood (Sara) and George Metaxa (Carl) and in the Broadway version by Evelyn Laye and Gerald Nodin. The duet allows for some bravura singing in its verse before settling down to one of Coward's most beautiful waltzes in its refrain.

Form: What first appears like a long, rambling verse is carefully built throughout its 68 bars on three ideas: the teacher's request (Fig. 1), the student's answer (Fig. 2) and the love theme (Fig. 3). The refrain is a pure 32-bar song in the theatrical form.

Lyrics: Although the verse is wonderfully specific, as a song of parting, the lyrics of the refrain are more general and poetic. The implication is that the illusion of presence will appear to each of them every spring.

Carl Now, Miss Sarah, if you please,
Sing a scale for me,
Sarah Ah –
Carl Take a breath and then reprise
In a diff'rent key,
Sarah Ah –
Carl All my life I shall remember knowing You
All the pleasure I have found in
Showing you
The diff'rent ways
That one may phrase,
The changing light and the changing shade
Happiness that must die,
Melodies that must fly,
Memories that must fade
Dusty and forgotten by and by.
Sarah Learning scales will never seem so sweet again
Till our destinies shall let us meet again
Carl The will of fate
May come too late

Fig. 1

Fig. 2

Fig. 3

Sarah When I'm recalling the hours we've had
Why will the foolish tears
Tremble across the years?
Why shall I feel so sad,
Carl Treasuring the mem'ry of these days
Always?

Refrain (Together)
I'll see you again
Whenever spring breaks through again.
Time may lie heavy between
But what has been is past forgetting.
This sweet memory
Across the years will come to me
Tho my world may go awry,
In my heart will ever lie
Just the echo of a sigh,
Goodbye.

(Altered ending lyric for 3rd Act)
Tho my world may go awry,
Tho the years my tears may dry
I shall love you till I die
Goodbye.

Melody: This melodic line, one of Coward's best, divides itself – as do most waltzes –into 4-bar and 2-bar phrases. The quality that sets this graceful song apart is that in the early, 4-bar phrases the climax falls consistently on the second bar (I'll *see* ... spring *breaks* etc.), while in the later 2-bar ones the accent is now on the *second beat* (though my *world* ... in my *heart*). Additional poignancy is achieved through the liberal use of appoggiatura (indicated with asterisks).

Harmony: Coward's harmony was never more interesting. After the carefully created artificiality of the singing lesson in the first 8 bars of the verse, the contrasting passion of the lovers shines through in the rich harmony built around the II, V, I sequence, peppered with accented neighbouring tones (see *). Coward's frequent and favourite key change, up a minor third, works well throughout this verse, and even his over-use of the augmented V chord does not seem cloying in this operetta setting.

Rhythm: There is nothing remarkable about the typical waltz rhythm Coward has chosen here. What *is* interesting is the harmonic rhythm of the duet – harmonies that change sometimes every 4 bars, 2 bars, singly or even within the bar, cleverly keep the music interesting and compelling.

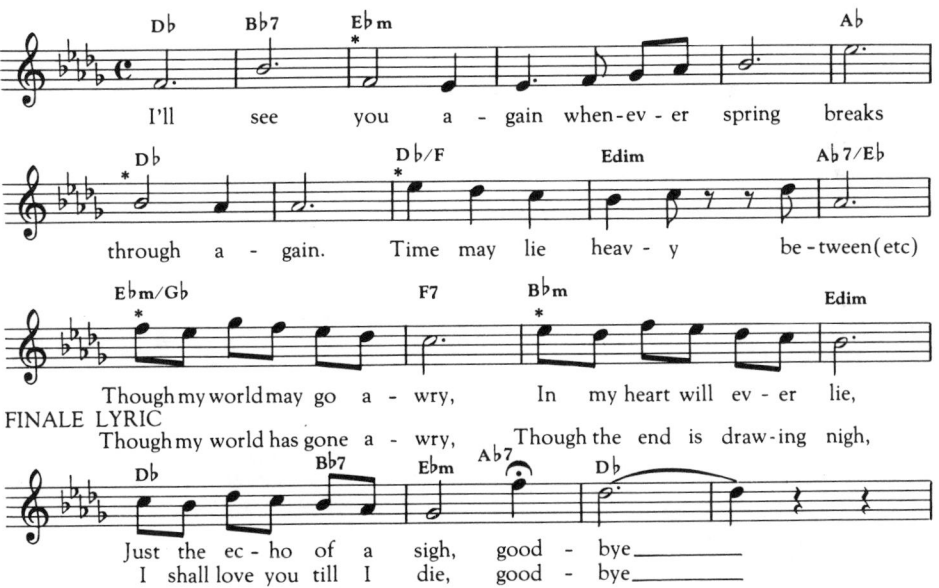

MAD ABOUT THE BOY (*Words and Music*)
1932

A scene in the revue, performed on a revolving stage, in which a society lady (Joyce Barbour), a street-walker (Steffi Duna), a schoolgirl (Norah Howard) and a Cockney servant (Doris Hare) sing of their passion for a movie star. At the end of the sketch, the 'boy' who, rumour has it, was modelled after heart-throb Douglas Fairbanks, comes on and is shown to be a self-centred chap, throwing their fan letters into the waste-paper basket. The early performances of the sketch had a teenage Graham Payn (in his first performances) hawking papers while the crowd queued up to buy tickets to the cinema star's latest triumph. This was later cut.

Form: The form is a usual 16-bar verse followed by a 32-bar refrain built in the popular form of A1, A2, Release, A3. For the schoolgirl's segment, Coward dispensed with the published verse and substituted a mooning recitative sung over her sister's piano practice. For the servant's solo, he used a jig in 6/8 time. These changes kept the rather lengthy scene varied and interesting.

Lyrics: They are a masterpiece of character development. The rhyming technique is ingenious especially when rhyming the word 'boy'. Coward finds 'toy' 'cloy' 'destroy' and others, including my favourite, 'corduroy'.

Society Woman
I met him at a party just a couple of years ago,
He was rather over-hearty and ridiculous,
But as I'd seen him on the screen
He cast a certain spell,
I bask'd in his attraction for a couple of hours or so,
His manners were a fraction too meticulous,
If he was real or not I couldn't tell,
But like a silly fool, I fell –
Mad about the boy,
I know it's stupid to be mad about the boy,
I'm so ashamed of it
But must admit
The sleepless nights I've had about the boy,
On the silver screen
He melts my foolish heart in ev'ry single scene,
Although I'm quite aware
That here and there
Are traces of the cad about the boy,
Lord knows I'm not a fool girl,
I really shouldn't care,
Lord knows I'm not a schoolgirl
In the flurry of her first affair.
Will it ever cloy?
This odd diversity of misery and joy,
I'm feeling quite insane
And young again
And all because I'm mad about the boy,

School Girl
Homework, homework,
Ev'ry night there's homework;
While Elsie practises the gas goes pop,
I wish, I wish she'd stop,
Oh dear, oh dear,
Here it's always 'No, dear,'
You can't go out again; you must stay home;
You waste your money on that common
                    Picturedrome,
Don't shirk, stay here and do your work,
Yearning, yearning,
How my heart is burning.
I'll see him Saturday in *Strong Man's Pain*
And then on Monday and on Friday week again.
To me he is the sole man
Who can kiss as well as Coleman.
I could faint whenever there's a closeup of his lips,
Though Barrymore is larger,
When my hero's on his charger,
Even Douglas Fairbanks Junior hasn't smaller hips.
If he could only know
I adore him so.

Mad about the boy
It's simply scrumptious to be mad about the boy,
I know that quite sincerely
Houseman really
Wrote *The Shropshire Lad* about the boy,
In my English prose
I've done a tracing of his forehead and his nose,
And there is, honour bright,
A certain slight
Effect of Galahad about the boy,
I've talked to Rosie Hooper,
She feels the same as me,
She says that Gary Cooper
Doesn't thrill her to the same degree,
In *Can Love Destroy?*
When he meets Garbo in a suit of corduroy
He gives a little frown
And knocks her down,
Oh dear, oh dear, I'm mad about the boy,

Streetwalker
It seems a little silly
For a girl of my age and weight
To walk down Picadilly
In a haze of love.
It ought to take a good deal more
To get a bad girl down.
I should have been exempt,
For my particular kind of fate
Has taught me such contempt
For ev'ry phase of love,
And now I've been and spent my last half-crown
To weep about a painted clown.

Mad about the boy,
It's pretty funny but I'm mad about the boy
He has a gay appeal
That makes me feel
There's maybe something sad about the boy.
Walking down the street,

His eyes look out at me from people that I meet,
I can't believe it's true,
But when I'm blue,
In some strange way I'm glad about the boy.
I'm hardly sentimental,
Love isn't so sublime.
I have to pay my rental
And I can't afford to waste much time.
If I could employ
A little magic that would finally destroy
This dream that pains me
And enchains me
But I can't because I'm mad about the boy.

Cockney Maid
Ev'ry Wednesday afternoon I get a little time off
   from three to eleven.

Then I go to the picture house and taste a little of my
   particular heaven.
He appears in a little while,
Through a mist of tears I can see him smiling above
   me.
Ev'ry picture I see him in,
Ev'ry lover's caress,
Makes my wonderful dreams begin
Makes me long to confess
That if ever he looked at me, and thought perhaps it
   was worth the trouble to
Love me,
I'd give in and I wouldn't care however far from the
   path of virtue he'd
Shove me,
Just suppose our love was brief,
If he treated me rough

REFRAIN

Mad a-bout the boy,___ I know it's stu-pid to be mad a-bout the boy,___ ___ I'm so a-shamed of it But must ad-mit The sleep-less nights I've had a-bout the boy.

I'd be happy beyond belief,
Once would be enough.

Mad about the boy,
I know I'm potty, but I'm mad about the boy,
He sets me 'eart on fire
With love's desire,
In fact I've got it bad about the boy
When I do the rooms,
I see 'is face in all the brushes and the brooms,
Last week I strained me back
And got the sack
And 'ad a row with dad about the boy,
I'm finished with Novarro,
I'm tired of Richard Dix
I'm pierced by cupid's arrow
Ev'ry Wednesday from four till six,
'Ow I should enjoy
To let 'im treat me like a plaything or a toy,
I'd give my all to him
And crawl to him;
So 'elp me Gawd, I'm mad about the boy.

Melody: The verse, with its parlando quality, is pure introduction. It is the refrain, his first (and only) important song in a minor key – a total departure for Coward – that has made this a standard. The melody, with its frequent shifts to the major, is not unlike Cole Porter's minor

ones. The melodic line, obviously conceived after the harmonic one, a II chord with a flattened fifth (see below), creates its own intensity by wandering up a scale, and (again borrowing a Porter trick) reaching higher for each of its endings. The release has a poignant and fresh tune, but like the A sections it is the adventurous harmony that leads the way.

Harmony: IV, V, I – the strongest possible harmonic sequence – underlines this entire song. The modulatory release, one of Coward's most moving, uses IV, V, I in G minor followed by IV, V, I in F minor, settling down at last on IV, V, I in C minor, before introducing the obligatory V of V (D7) leading to V (G7). (See analysis of the release below.)

Rhythm: As in most torch songs rhythm is not of paramount interest. Coward indulges in his oft-used conversational style of dotted eighth and sixteenth.

YOU WERE THERE (*Tonight at 8.30*) 1935
This song, from *Shadow Play*, which was the finale to the second programme of one-act plays in this series, is one of Coward's most interesting fox-

trots. Although typical of the crooner-ballads of the mid-'30s, it goes beyond the ordinary, and its melody, harmony and language could have been written by no one but Noel. In the context of the play, 'You Were There' is the thematic love song the two principals, Victoria and Simon, sing when they have their first fateful meeting. It reappears with their love scene and creates a happy close to the evening by repeating the karmatic inevitability of their love.

Form: Replete with 16-bar verse, this typical show tune is true to that form. The refrain is a perfect A1 (8 bars divided into two 4-bar similar phrases), B (8 bars, several shorter phrases), A2 (8 bars again, an exact repetition of A1), C (8 bars, short excited phrases leading to a return of the title).

Lyrics: Perhaps Coward alone, with his sense of theatrical description, could get away with lines like 'your eyes looked into mine and faltered', rhyming with 'the color of the whole world altered', making them sound inspired.

Verse 1
Was it in the real world?
Or was it in a dream?
Was it just a note in some eternal theme?
Was it accidental
Or accurately planned?
How could I hesitate
Knowing that my fate
Led me by the hand?

Refrain
You were there,
I saw you and my heart stopped beating
You were there,
And in that first enchanted meeting
Life changed its tune,
The stars and moon came near to me.
Dreams that I dreamed
Like magic seemed to be clear to me,
Dear to me.
You were there,
Your eyes looked into mine and faltered,
Everywhere
The colour of the whole world altered,
False became true,
My universe tumbled in two,
The earth became heaven,
For you were there.

Verse 2
How could we explain it,
The spark and then the fire?
How add up the total of our heart's desire?
Maybe some magician

A thousand years ago
Wove us a subtle spell,
So that we could tell,
So that we could know.

(Repeat Chorus)

Melody: Coward created one of his most memorable melodies by contrasting the first two static title bars with the ascending scale of next two. Then from bar 25 onwards, the persistence of the high F on the words 'false', 'tumbled' and 'heaven' constantly repeated and achieved, through what seems like a broken chord, gives the whole ending an excitement and inevitability.

Harmony: It was only natural, being self-taught, that Coward's sense of harmony should develop more strongly as he matured. One only has to examine the verse, contrasting the second and tenth bars and the fourth and twelfth bars, to notice that in each case he made a purposeful change in the harmony which *necessitated* a melodic change. Coward loved the augmented chord and its over-use often gave his music a saccharine quality. Here, used in the second bar of the refrain, it seems perfectly appropriate.

Rhythm: Beyond the opening phrase, with its obvious contrast of half notes followed by a series of quarters, the B theme (bars 9-16) has a wonderfully syncopated feeling.

THE STATELY HOMES OF ENGLAND

(*Operette*) 1938
Originally planned as a gentle slap on the noble wrists of the British peerage, and inserted into this operetta's 'show-within-a-show' as a diversion, this subtle charmer supplied one of the few moments when the evening came alive. The tune, quasi-minor, is very Gilbert & Sullivan, while the lyrics (especially in the third refrain), contain topical coruscating references that only Coward could get away with. No wonder he was not given a knighthood until the very end of his life - at which point his evaluation of royalty could do no further harm to the monarchy or its standard bearers!

Form: An 8-bar prelude, introducing the four Lords (with the remarkably descriptive names of Elderley, Borrowmere, Sickert and Camp) who sing the song, leads directly to the 6/8 verse (32 bars) and then to the refrain (32 bars). Both verse and refrain are built in ABAC form, the one important difference being that the verse talks about the ineffectuality of the men themselves, while the refrain talks about the sad state of their *homes*.

Lyrics: Coward, always the chronicler of the state of the monarchy, was never more coruscating. The second verse contains an antisemitic slur, but one assumes it comes from the esprit of these nincompoops, rather than the mind of Noel. As an example of Coward's superb lyrical technique, one should not overlook the unexpected, extra inner rhyme in the two penultimate lines ('grand' and 'stand', 'might' and 'fight', etc.). With 3 verses and 5 refrains, by the time we have reached the last, slightly smutty one we are beyond the point of diminishing returns.

Introduction

Lord Elderley, Lord Borrowmere,
Lord Sickert and Lord Camp
With every virtue, every grace,
Are what avails the sceptred race.

Verse I

Here you see the four of us,
And there are so many more of us,
Eldest sons that must succeed.
We know how Caesar conquered Gaul
And how to whack a cricket ball;
Apart from this our education
Lacks coordination.
Though we're young and tentative
And rather rip-resentaive
Scions of a noble breed,
We are the products of those homes serene
and stately
Which only lately
Seem to have run to seed!

Refrain I

The stately homes of England
How beautiful they stand,
To prove the upper classes
Have still the upper hand;
Thought the fact that they have to be
      rebuilt
And frequently mortgaged to the hilt
Is inclined to take the gilt
Off the gingerbread,
And certainly damps the fun
Of the eldest son.
But still we won't be beaten
We'll scrimp and scrape and save.
The playing fields of Eton
Have made us frightfully brave,
And though if the Van Dycks have to go
And we pawn the Bechstein Grand,
We'll stand
By the Stately Homes of England.

Verse 2

Here you see the pick of us
You may be heartily sick of us,
Still with sense we're all imbued.
Our homes command extensive views
And with assistance from the Jews
We have been able to dispose of
Rows and rows and rows of
Gainsboroughs and Lawrences,
Some sporting prints of Aunt Florence's
Some of which were rather rude.
Although we sometimes flaunt our family
      conventions
Our good intentions
Mustn't be misconstrued.

Refrain 2

The Stately Homes of England
We proudly represent.
We only keep them up for
Americans to rent.
Though the pipes that supply the bathroom burst
And the lavat'ry makes you fear the worst,
It was used by Charles the First-
Quite informally,
And later by George the Fourth
On a journey north.
The State Apartments keep their
Historical renown.
It's wiser not to sleep there
In case they tumble down;
But still, if they ever catch on fire
Which, with any luck, they might,
We'll fight
For the Stately Homes of England.

Refrain 3

The Stately Homes of England
Though rather in the lurch,
Provided a lot of chances
For psychical research.
There's the ghost of a crazy younger son
Who murdered in thirteen fifty one,
An extremely rowdy nun,
Who resented it,
And people who come to call
Meet her in the hall.
The baby in the guest wing
Who crouches by the grate.
Was walled up in the west wing
In fourteen twenty-eight.
If anyone spots
The Queen of Scots
In a hand-embroidered shroud,
We're proud
Of the Stately Homes of England.

Verse 3

Behold us in our hours of ease,
Uncertain, coy and hard to please.
Reading in Debrett of us,
This fine patrician quartet of us,

We can feel extremely proud
Our ancient lineage we trace
Back to the cradle of the race
Before those beastly Roman bowmen
Bitched our local yeomen.
Though the new democracy
May pain the old aristocracy
We've not winced nor cried aloud
Under the bludgeonings of chance
What will be – will be.
Our heads will still be
Bloody but unbowed.

Refrain 4
The Stately Homes of England
In valley, dale and glen.
Produce a race of charming,
Innocuous young men.
Though our mental equipment may be slight
And we barely distinguish left from right,
We are quite prepared to fight
For our principles,
Though none of us know, so far,
What they really are.
Our duty to the nation
It's only fair to state,
Lies not in procreation
But what we procreate;
And so we can cry with kindling eye
As to married life we go,
What ho!
For the Stately Homes of England!

Refrain 5
The Stately Homes of England
Although a trifle bleak,
Historically speaking.
Are more or less unique.
We've a cousin who won the Golden Fleece
And a very peculiar fowling-piece
Which was sent to Cromwell's niece,
Who detested it

And rapidly sent it back
With a dirty crack.
A note we have from Chaucer
Contains a bawdy joke
We also have saucer
That Bloody Mary broke
We've two pairs of tights
King Arther's Knights
Had already worn away,
Sing Hey!
For the Stately Homes of England!

Melody: Here, as in so many of Coward's patter songs, the tune of the verse goes nowhere. The melody of the chorus, however, almost wandering into a pure minor key, is a truly charming. By using upper and lower neighbours (marked u. n. and l. n. on the score), Coward creates a built-in Gothic elegance that perfectly matches the melody.

Harmony: There are some beautiful, fresh harmonic devices, such as the D7 chord at the end of the first phrase and its change to a C7 chord at the end of the second, in *exactly* the same place (see bars 4 and 8 above); but then because Coward often goes so far afield, harmonically, there are awkward places, such as the change from F7 to B7, where we see him struggling to come back. In spite of these, one gladly welcomes this number into the pantheon of Coward patter songs.

Rhythm: As in most patter songs, especially those in 6/8 rhythm, there is very little rhythmic interest. Luckily, we are involved with a fresh melody here and interesting, if not always satisfying, harmonies.

LONDON PRIDE (1941)

This is one of the 4 special songs Coward wrote as a contribution to his country and its people during World War Two. As he matured he was to write, with increasing frequency, occasional songs that had no place in shows. Noel's command of his technique and his inspiration, coupled with his fervent nationalism, makes this one of his best.

Form: The construction of 'London Pride' is unique in Coward's output. Treated as a sort of folk-song, the refrain is ABA, but the A sections, being 8 bars in length, divide themselves naturally into 4 and 4. The B section of the refrain (Fig. B), acts somewhat like a bridge. An 8-bar contrasting interlude is inserted following each refrain, making the completed form: refrain, interlude, refrain, interlude, refrain.

Lyric: The concept of the song originates from equating the lavender flower's street name, London Pride, with the actual pride that Londoners take in their city. The lyric is not only a hymn to London as a city, but halfway through Coward adds a morale-building element: the indomitable spirit of the British people. One should not overlook the exquisite rhyming at the endings of each refrain and the way Coward ties the bouquet with a ribbon in the last one: 'Nothing ... replace ... grace'; 'Nothing ... harm ... charm'; 'Nothing ... override ... pride'.

Refrain 1

London Pride has been handed down to us.
London Pride is a flower that's free.
London Pride means our own dear town to us,
And our pride it forever will be.
Woa, Liza, see the coster barrows
Vegetable marrows and the fruit piled high
Woa, Liza, little London sparrows
Covent Garden Market where the costers cry.
Cockney feet mark the beat of history
Ev'ry street pins a memory down.
Nothing ever can quite replace
The grace of London Town.

Interlude 1

There's a little city flow'r ev'ry spring unfailing
Growing in the crevices by some London railing
Tho it has a Latin name in town and countryside
We in England call it London Pride.

Refrain 2

London Pride has been handed down to us.
London Pride is a flower that's free.
London Pride means our own dear town to us,
And our pride it forever will be.
Hey, lady, when the day is dawning,
See the p'liceman yawning on his lonely beat.

Gay lady, Mayfair in the morning.
Hear the footsteps echo in the empty street.
Early rain and the pavements glistening,
All Park Lane in a shimmering gown.
Nothing ever could break or harm
The charm of London town.

Interlude 2

In our city darkened now – street and square and
    crescent.
We can feel our living past in our shadowed present
Ghosts beside our starlit Thames who lived and
    loved and died
Keep throughout the ages London Pride.

Refrain 3

London Pride has been handed down to us.
London Pride is a flower that's free.
London Pride means our own dear town to us
And our pride it forever will be.
Grey city, stubbornly implanted,
Taken so for granted for a thousand years
Stay city smokily enchanted,
Cradle of our memories and hopes and fears.
Ev'ry Blitz your resistance toughening
From the Ritz to the Anchor and Crown,
Nothing ever could override
The pride of London Town.

Melody: The hymn-like strength of this melodic line is obvious from the outset (Fig. A). This is further amplified when the second bar opens on the fourth tone of the scale, which only impels the melody downward. The B section (Fig. B) not only provides strong, melodic contrast, but pulls the voice into a much higher tessitura so that it can eventually settle down into the returning A section. The modal beginning to the interlude (Fig. C) gives the whole song the feeling of a folk-song from a much earlier time.

Harmony: Whether created by Coward or his frequent musical amanuensis, Elsie April, this number is beautifully harmonised. In most cases, as in the beginning of the bridge (Fig. B), the harmony seems to spring naturally from the melodic line, but sometimes as in the interlude (Fig. C), it is layered on top. The last bars (Fig. D), heroically reharmonised, are stirring indeed.

Rhythm: Although it tries to pass itself off as a folk-song, 'London Pride' is enormously varied rhythmically. The stolid rhythm of the first melody is followed by the bridge, with its syncopation and jerkily descriptive notes. In the modal interlude there is a rather standard eighth note rhythm that works well with the refrain.

Fig.A

Fig.B Lon-don Pride has been han-ded down to us. Lon-don Pride is a flow-er that's free.

Woa Li - za, see the cos - ter bar-rows, Veg - e - ta - ble mar-rows and the

fruit piled high.

Fig.C

There's a lit - tle ci - ty flow'r ev' - ry spring un - fail - ing,

Grow - ing in the cre - vi - ces by some Lon - don rail - ing.

Fig.D

No - thing ev - er could ov - er - ride The pride of Lon - don Town.

SIGH NO MORE (*Sigh No More*)

Sung by Graham Payn with (and to) a chorus of 19 'ladies' this is one of Coward's most daring and finest melodies. Its lack of popular success is primarily due to its optimistic lyric – talking about grey clouds that fill the sky no more – seeming not to fit its romantic, but quite sad melody. But there are other things that make this song a favourite of musicians: its lack of repetition (making it sound almost through-composed), its free and wide range and, most of all, its harmonic freedom.

Form: This is 20 bars of verse, comprising 2 sequential 4-bar phrases, leading to 3 free-form phrases, which move directly into the refrain. The unusual chorus, as noted above, is closest to ABAC form with an extension.

Lyric: The stilted quality of this lyric suggests a period far earlier than 1945. This, coupled with long phrases that seem to pause at awkward moments, is somewhat nettling (See*). But there is no denying that the lyric is all one operetta-like piece. Coward's technique allows

him to get away with this and a great deal of appropriate sibilance ('sigh', 'sky', 'spring', 'sweet').

Verse
Poor mournful ladies are you weeping for a dream
          once dreamed?
Are you still list'ning for some remembered theme
          that seemed*
To promise happiness and love and gentle years
          devoid of fears?
Sweet music starts again,
Lift up your hearts again and dry,
Ah, dry those tears.

Refrain
Sigh no more, sigh no more,
Grey clouds of sorrow fill the sky no more.
Cry no more
Die no more,
Those little deaths at parting,
New life and new love are starting.
Sing again, sing again –
The winter's over and it's spring again.
Joy is your troubadour.
Sweet and beguiling ladies sigh no more,
Sigh no more.
Sweet and beguiling ladies sigh no more.

REFRAIN *Not too slow, very legato*

Sigh no more, sigh no more. Grey clouds of

mp - mf

sor-row fill the sky no more. Cry no more,

Die no more, Those lit-tle deaths at part-ing, new life and new

love are start-ing, Sing a - gain, sing a - gain,

Melody: The 4 to 3 suspension is one of the strongest in all of music. Coward sets this on the very first bar of the refrain; it occurs again in the fifth bar. By the time we reach the seventh bar (on the word 'sky'), we are dealing with a flat 2 to 1 suspension which increases the mournful sound of this melody. By the eighth bar (on the word 'cry') the harmony (C minor followed by F minor) has taken over, thus increasing the melancholic feel. One should note the operatic range of this song, an octave and a sixth, which adds to its moving legato line. The first 20 bars of the refrain are quoted above.

Harmony: In this kind of composition it is hard to know if the melodic line was an outgrowth of the harmonic concept or not, but here Coward seems at his most adventurous in both categories. Bars 13 to 16 show a particular freedom.

Rhythm: Although the rhythm follows the word value of dotted half, quarter and whole, used many times throughout the refrain, it never becomes static, because short phrases alternate with long ones. Sometimes long phrases made up entirely of quarter notes come pouring out (bars 12 to 16) followed by short groups. This rhythmic contrast helps to give the song an improvised feeling.

MATELOT (*Sigh No More*) 1945
This almost mystical song, one of the most controversial Coward ever wrote because it is open to so many interpretations, has the quality of an art song at the same time as having the appeal of a sea shanty. In performance it often *seems* overlong because generally sung too slowly.

Form: One notices Coward's freedom at once in a 9-bar verse. This is followed by the refrain, which breaks down to a 4-bar section followed by *two* 4-bar sections, acting as a a a double bridge. Thus this non-conventional refrain falls into A (4 bars), B (4 bars), C (4 bars) and A (4 bars).

Lyric: The singer of this poem (because of its inner rhymes, poetic language and subject matter, it's hard to call this a lyric to a popular song), which is written in the first person, could be a lover, of the same or opposite sex, or – as most have assumed – the mother of the sailor of the title. In my opinion, there are too many 'in'

clues for it to be other than a homosexual song. But no matter; most of the best material is open to several interpretations. And the poem is exquisitely constructed.

Verse 1
Jean Louis Domnic Pierre Bouchon
True to the breed that bore him
Answered the call
That held in thrall
His father's heart before him.
Jean Louis Domenic sailed away
Further than love could find him
Yet through the night
He heard a light
And gentle voice behind him say

Refrain 1
Matelot, Matelot,
Where you go
My thoughts go with you
Matelot, Matelot,
When you go down to the sea.
As you gaze from afar
On the ev'ning star
Wherever you may roam,
You will remember the light
Through the winter night
That guides you safely home.
Though you find
Womenkind to be frail
One love cannot fail, my son
Till our days are done.
Matelot, matelot,
Where you go my thoughts go with you
Matelot, matelot,
When you go down to the sea.

Verse 2
Jean Louis Domnic Pierre Bouchon
Journeyed the wide world over,
Lips that he kissed
Could not resist
This loving, roving rover.
Jean Louis Domenic right or wrong
Ever pursued a new love,
Till in his brain
There beat a strain
He knew to be his true love song.

Refrain 2
Matelot, matelot,
Where you go my heart goes with you,
Matelot, matelot,
When you go down to the sea.
For a year and a day
You may sail away
And have no thought of me,
Yet through the wind and the spray
You will hear me say
No love was ever free.
You will sigh when horizons are clear,
'Something that is dear to me
Cannot let me be.'

Matelot, matelot,
Where you go my heart goes with you.
Matelot, matelot,
When you go down to the sea.

Refrain 3
Matelot, Matelot,
Where you go
My heart will follow
Matelot, Matelot,
When you go down to the sea.
When there's grief in the sky
And the waves ride high
My heart to yours will say,
'You may be sure that I'm true
To my love for you,

Though half the world away.
Never mind
If you find other charms,
Here within my arms you'll sleep
Sailor from the deep.
Matelot, matelot
Where you go my heart will follow
Matelot, matelot,
When you go down to the sea.

Melody: Again, the quasi-art song seems to apply, with Coward's use of eighth notes sixteenths almost exclusively for this narrative song. The most interesting aspect of the melodic line happens from the ninth bar on. Modality takes over, leading us back to the main theme by bar 12. But this time the song shifts melodically, and arbitrarily, into the parallel minor, moving back and forth. The trick, often used by Cole Porter, gives the tune a haunting ambivalence.

Harmony: Most of the harmonic construction is not exceptional until we arrive at the second bridge (bar 9). Suddenly, the bright modality, the use of F minor followed by Bb7, lifts the entire song out of the ordinary. The change back a forth into the minor, as noted above, also works to supply harmonic richness.

Rhythm: The rhythm is foursquare. The piano copy uses a simple rolling arpeggio, contrasted with the chordal bridges. The arpeggio is as implacable and relentless as the sea.

SAIL AWAY

Originally written for *Ace of Clubs*, this song has had 2 lives. In its first incarnation, stuck in as an extra song sung by sailor Harry when his love affair is going awry, and reprised at the finale, it was not greatly admired. A decade later, as the title song of Coward's musical cruise, now sung poignantly by the leading man, Johnny, who is sailing away to forget an unhappy love affair, it was somewhat more – but not wildly – successful. It is one of Coward's very best songs and its philosophy, appropriate to Noel, is perhaps even more suitable for Cole.

Form: The refrain is cast into the usual 32 bars, using A (8 bars), A (8 bars), B (8 Bars), A (8 Bars). The *Ace of Clubs* verse has a 10-bar lead-in[1], while the more intense one used in *Sail Away* has 16.

Lyric: This is one of Coward's least arty, most moving lyrics. One should pay special attention to the second refrain and observe the cliché rhyming of 'rise above' and 'worn-out glove' in the earlier version. In the later rendering this is altered to the more natural and moving 'noisy town' and 'let you down'. The first release, with the words 'when you feel your song is orchestrated wrong', has become a favourite of musicians everywhere.

Verse 1

Ace of Clubs Version
When a sailor goes to sea,
Though he leaves his love behind,
Time and tide will set him free
From the grief inside him

Sea and sky will ease his heart
Regulate his troubled mind,
Ev'ry sailor has a chart,
And a star to guide him – home.

Verse 2
Love is meant to make us glad,
Love can make the world go round,
Love can drive you raving mad,
Torment and upset you.
Love can give your heart a jolt
But philosophers have found
That it's wise to do a bolt
When it starts to get you – down.

Verse I

Sail Away Version
A dif'frent sky,
New worlds to gaze upon,
The strange excitement of an unfamiliar shore.
One more goodbye,
One more illusion gone,
Just cut your losses and begin once more.

Refrain I
When the storm clouds are riding through a winter
    sky
Sail away – sail away.
When the love light is fading in your
        sweetheart's eye,
Sail away – sail away.
When you feel your song is orchestrated wrong
Why should you prolong
Your stay?
When the wind and the weather blow your dreams
        sky-high, sail away
Sail away – sail away.

Refrain 2

Ace of Clubs
When you life seems too difficult to rise above,
Sail away – sail away.
When your heart feels as dreary as a worn-out glove,
Sail away – sail away.

Refrain 2

Sail Away
When you can't bear the clamour of the noisy town
Sail away, – sail away,
When the friend that you counted on has let you
        down,
Sail away – sail away.

(Both Versions)
But when soon or late
You recognize your fate,
That will be your great, great day.
On the wings of the morning with your own true
        love,
Sail away – sail away – sail away.

---

[1] One sees many more syllables in this verse than the later one because of the sea-shanty theme, heavy with eighth notes.

Melody: A glance at the sea hornpipe – like verse in the first version (Fig. 1) shows how appropriate it was to the character singing it; the second version (Fig. 2) equally reveals the personality of the sophisticated man who is singing it.

The jaunty melody of the refrain (Fig. 3) has to be one of the most catchy Coward ever wrote. The first 16 bars are quoted below:

Harmony: Even though this tune is bright and light, Coward gave it a meaningful touch of melancholy in its harmonization, at the least the 1950 version. Here, the crucial third bar (Fig. 4) is harmonized in major, as contrasted with the same passage in the eleventh bar (Fig. 5), heading towards the minor. This was unfortunately not observed in the 1960 version (Fig. 6 and 7).

Rhythm: As mentioned above, the eighth note rhythm of the 1950 version sets this song as a hornpipe. The later version treats the verse as a proper Broadway lead-in.

COME THE WILD, WILD WEATHER

(*Waiting in the Wings*) 1959
There is very little raison d'être in the play for the intrusion of this song about deep and enduring friendship. But the musical interlude (of which it forms the cornerstone) is followed by a spritely dance, culminating in the death of one of the inmates of the home for retired actresses. This provides a highly melodramatic moment in the middle of the third act of this gentle tragi-comedy. This song itself is fresh, moving and because it is about friendship, rather than love or comedy, rather unique in the Coward canon.

Form: Beginning with a 16-bar chorus in folk-tune style, this is divided into a 4-bar flowing theme (A1), repeated (A2). This is followed by a 4-bar bridge (B), which leads to the return of the first theme (A3). What Coward called the 'verse' is really an 8-bar interlude, which seems to have been inserted because the number would be too brief otherwise.

Lyric: This is one of the rare Coward songs where the melodic idea seems far superior to the lyric. It is known that Coward was aiming for forthrightness, but what he seems to have come up with is cliché.

Come the wild, wild weather,
Come the wind, come the rain,
Come the little white flakes of snow,
Come the joy, come the pain.
We shall still be together
When our life story ends,
For whenever we chance to go
We shall always be friends.
We may find while we're travelling through the
years
Moments of joy and love and happiness,
Reason for grief, reason for tears.

Fig. 1

When a sail - or goes to sea, Tho' he leaves his love be - hind,

Time and tide will set him free from the grief in - side him.

Fig. 2

A diff' - rent sky, New worlds to gaze up - on,

The strange ex - cite - ment of an un - fa - mil - iar shore.

Fig. 3

When the storm clouds are ri-ding thru a win-ter sky, Sail a-

-way,_____ sail a-way._____ When the

love-light is fa-ding in your sweet-heart's eye, Sail a-

-way,_____ sail a-way._____

Fig. 4

REFRAIN

storm clouds are rid-ing through a win-ter sky, Sail a-way._____
life seems too dif-fi-cult to rise a-bove Sail a-way._____

_____ Sail a-way._____ When the love-light is fad-ing in your
_____ Sail a-way._____ When your heart feels as drear-y as a

Fig. 5

sweet - heart's eye Sail a - way_____ Sail a - way._____
worn out glove Sail a - way_____ Sail a - way._____

_____ When you feel your song is or - ches - tra - ted wrong
_____ But when soon or late You re - cog - nize your Fate

Just cut your loss - es and be - gin once more.

Fig. 6 REFRAIN *(brightly)*

1. When the storm clouds are rid - ing through a win - ter sky, Sail a-
2. (When you) can't bear the clam - or of the nois - y town, Sail a-

Come the wild, wild weather,
If we've lost or we've won
We'll remember these words we say
Till our story is done.

Verse
Time may hold in store for us
Glory or defeat
Maybe never more for us
Life will seem so sweet.
Time will change so many things,
Tides will ebb and flow,
But wherever fate may lead us
Always we shall know ...

(Repeat Refrain)

Melody: This charming song has two qualities
that are a departure for Coward: its pentatoni-
cism (meaning that it might have been composed using only the black keys) and the smallish range, at least of the refrain, which is

little more than an octave. Written in the key of
Db, which in itself is a departure for Coward,
the small release section moves into F and
returns felicitously to the parent key.

Harmony: The beautiful descending bass that
accompanies the initial motive, the melodic use
of the diminished seventh, which pulls the lis-
tener back from the key of F to the key of Db
and the appogiaturas in the verse all show a rich
harmonic invention, proclaiming Coward in
masterful form. I have quoted the release
below.

Rhythm: Stylistically, as mentioned before,
this song has some of the lilt of Scotland or
Ireland about it (see*). Although the verse is
dull rhythmically because it is so foursquare,
its very rigidity contrasts beautifully with the
repeat of the chorus (fig. 8).

Fig. 7

Fig. 8

We may find while we're tra - vel -ling through the years.   Moments of

joy and love and hap-pi - ness, Rea-son for grief, rea-son for tears,

I'LL REMEMBER HER (*The Girl who Came to Supper*) 1963

This, the last song Coward wrote, or at least the last song sung in his final musical, has all the sensitivity of a Lerner-Loewe 'after she's gone' confession. It has the additional attributes of possessing a moving punch-line and accomplishes the totally unexpected when, near the end, its melody changes to the subdominant key and ends in this foreign tonality. Coward accomplishes this musical somersault without once making the ending sound forced.

Form: Although written in 4/4 and comprising 16 bars, the form of this song is basically akin to the 32-bar show-tune, ABAC. There are two refrains and no verse, which was common to musicals of the '60s.

Lyric: Full of tenderness and inner rhymes, this lyric has the hallmark of what makes a superior theatre song: applicable to the characters in the play, yet full of meaning to anyone who has had an unforgettable brief encounter and is amazed that they have made an indelible impression on the *other person*.

Refrain 1

I'll remember her;
How incredibly naive she was;
I couldn't quite believe she was sincere.
So alert, so impertinent and yet so sweet,
My defeat was clear.
I'll remember her;
Her absurd exaggerating,
And her utterly deflating repartee,
And the only thing that worries me at all
Is whether she'll remember me.

Refrain 2

I'll remember her;
In the ev'nings when I'm lonely
And imagining if only she were there.
I'll relive, oh so vividly
Our sad and sweet incomplete affair.
I'll remember her;
Heavy hearted when we parted
With her eyes so full of tears she couldn't see;
And I'll feel inside a foolish sort of pride
To think that she remembers me.

Melody: This melody has the sort of *sprech-stimme*, half-sung quality that somehow contains echoes of Rex Harrison's voice singing 'I've Grown Accustomed to Her Face'. This is no accident, since Coward had Harrison in mind for the leading role and Herman Levin, the musical's producer, had also produced *My Fair Lady*. But 'I'll Remember Her' (see*) creates a lot more tension when Coward placed the syllables 'member her' on an unresolved melody note, before his lyric goes blithely off to list his inamorata's qualities (Fig. 1).

One cannot leave this melodic line without observing the moving way Coward changes key before the ultimate phrase. He ends the phrase before ('eyes so full of tears she couldn't see') on an Ab. This allows him to finish the song in the key of Eb (Fig. 2).

Harmony: That Coward had captured the American musical idiom is nowhere more apparent than in this song. One only has to check the ins and outs of its B section with its 'diminished cliché', followed by I, VI, II, V (Fig. 3)[1].

Rhythm: Because it is trying hard to resemble speech patterns, and the singer is babbling excitedly when he is involved in description, this song is full of dotted eighth and sixteenth notes. When he is sing-talking about his own feelings, we find straight half, quarter and eighth notes. Although there is no syncopation, because of these mercurial changes, the song has constant rhythmic interest.

Fig. 1

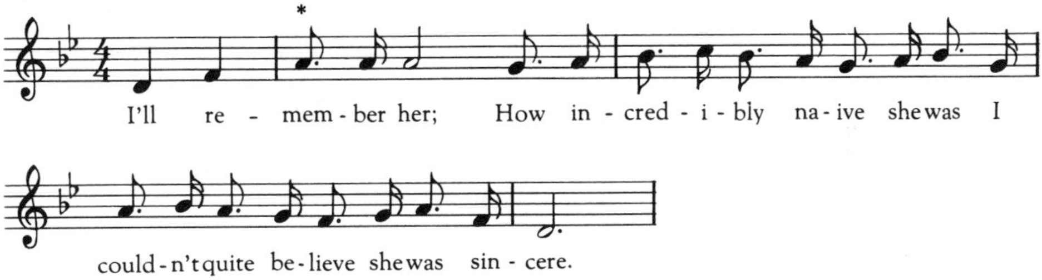

Fig. 2

Fig. 3

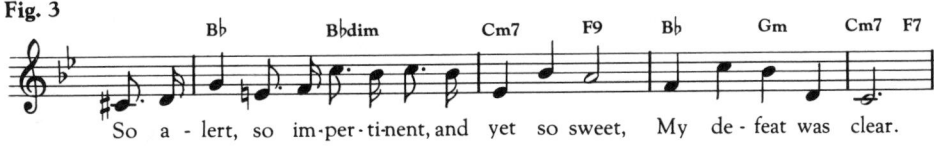

---

[1] See Glossary of Musical Terms

Glossary of Musical Terms

AABA A common song form in which the first theme (usually eight bars in length) is repeated and followed by a contrasting theme. This second statement is followed by a return to the first theme. All the 'A's must be essentially the same; however, their endings may vary.

A1, A2, bridge, A3 A preferred way of referring to the AABA.

Alberti bass Alberti, a contemporary of Mozart, is remembered mostly for the manner in which he broke chords to make them sustain on the harpsichords of his time.

alla breve 4/4 time played rather quickly so that there are only two counts to the bar. Popular musicians call this 'cut time'.

appoggiatura From the Italian word meaning 'to lean'. A decorative pitch, not belonging to the indicated chord, usually approaching the resolution from above. Appoggiaturas create mild dissonance and can add great intensity to a melodic line.

arpeggio From the Italian word for harp, *arpa*. An arpeggio is a chord whose members are sounded individually.

augmented 1) Raising the pitch a half-tone. 2) A triad with its fifth raised a half-tone.

beguine A sensual languid dance said to be of Tahitian origin. Its accent is on the second eight-note (quaver) in the bar.

belting Using the chest voice rather than letting air pass over the diaphragm, to create what is known as a soprano or 'head sound'.

blue note The flattened 3rd, 5th, 6th or 7th of the scale when used in conjunction with a major harmony creates a distinctly biting (some consider it melancholy) sound typical of the blues.

bridge The B section of an AABA song. A contrasting section also called 'release' or 'channel'.

cadence A series of chords leading to a conclusion. The typical interminable (and sometime laughable) V – I cadence can be found at the end of most Rossini overtures.

chromaticism The use of accidental tones falling outside the prevailing key signature.

circle of chords The natural progression of dominant sevenths to tonics. The series of

chords is usually written in circular fashion:

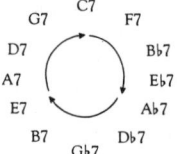

contrary motion (see motion, contrary)

crotchet The British term for quarter note.

cut time see alla breve

cycle of chords (see circle of chords)

diminished cliché My own term for a series of four chords comprising the tonic (I), a diminished seventh (usually built on the tonic or the lowered supertonic, I dim or # I dim), the minor supertonic (II) and the dominant (V). These four chords are as common in popular music as the I, VI, II, V series.

fox-trot A dance that spawned many songs popular from 1914 to 1925. The dance, which uses a box-step, is always in 4/4 time, often with a hesitation on the 3rd beat of the bar. This dance developed during a period of animal-named popular dances, such as the turkey-trot, monkey-slide and bunny-hug, and is still a favourite of the older generation.

hemiola The deceptive change of metre achieved by false emphasis. Ex: One *two* three, *one* two *three*.

leading tone The seventh note of the scale, so called because it leads smoothly back into the tonic.

legit A shortening of the term **legitimate**, implying proper or operatic singing using resonating head tones rather than chest or 'belt' singing.

measure 1) A musical unit divided by a barline. 2) A synonym for **bar**.

melisma The use of several pitches on a single literary syllable. Melismatic passages are most often associated with the baroque, but are also frequently found in Middle Eastern, Hebraic, and 'soul' music (see example of Cole Porter's 'Solomon' below).

modulation Changing from one key to another. Modulation is not done to accommodate a singer (**transposition**), but to create interest in a composition or an arrangement.

SO - - - O-LO-MON had a thou - sand wives —

motion The movement of melodic as against harmonic lines. Usually referred to as the treble or soprano line against the bass line. There are three kinds: **parallel**, which applies to bass and soprano moving in the same direction; **contrary**, as the word would indicated, is movement in opposite directions and **oblique**, when one voice stays on the same pitch while the other moves.

motive (or *motif*) The basic germ of a musical idea. A series of notes set in a rhythm that will be used again and again in various ways throughout the song.

oblique motion (*see* motion: parallel, contrary, oblique)

one-six-two-five a harmonic pattern usually expressed as I, VI, II, V, indicating a series of chords (succeeding tonic, submediant, supertonic, dominant triads) upon which countless melodies have been constructed. As the underpinning of songs from 'Heart and Soul' to many of the rock & roll songs of the '60s and beyond, this cliché is the granddaddy of them all.

parallel motion (*see* motion, parallel)

prosody The blending of words and music. Good prosody coupled with an artist's clear diction will make a lyric understandable.

punch line song One whose lyric contains a surprise at its conclusion, preferably in the very last syllable.

quarter note The basic pulse of most popular songs. The British term is 'crotchet'.

quaver International term for eighth-note.

ragtime A rhythmic style popular between 1890 and 1914 famous for syncopation and anticipation.

range The vocal palette. In popular songs before the '60s this was limited to a tenth (an octave and a third). Showtunes were permitted a somewhat wider latitude, but it was not until works by Bernstein, Bacharach, Sondheim and Lloyd Webber, who employed well-trained singers, that a singer's full range was utilized.

refrain The main body of the song, sometimes interchangeable with 'chorus'.

reprise A custom of repeating a song, often in several parts of a show, in order to make it indelible.

segue Italian for 'follow'. A musical direction, meaning 'to proceed to the next section without a pause or break'.

semitone A half tone, the next nearest pitch. In the Western musical system the octave is divided into twelve semitones.

skip A musical interval that is more than a whole step.

story-song A song whose narrative is its most important feature.

subdominant The fourth degree of the diatonic scale. The subdominant chord is one of the three principal triads.

suspension A non-chord member that formerly had to resolve to a chord member. Contemporary popular music uses suspensions more liberally than most harmony books permit and does not oblige them to resolve. The most frequently used suspension is the 4th.

syncopation Misplacing accents that are normally felt on the 1st and 3rd of the bar.

tag An extension to a song, sometimes called the 'coda'.

tessitura The general range of a composition. Songs that remain largely around the top of their range are said to have a high tessitura, those that keep punching out the middle or bottom notes are said to have low tessitura.

transposition Changing key of a song or composition. Music is generally transposed to place it within the best possible vocal range of the artist.

tremolo A piano technique popular during the Victorian period. The right hand trembles, breaking the intervals of octave or sixth. This technique later became the mainstay of tear-jerking scenes in the old Nickelodeon movies.

triad A chord of three notes; two superimposed thirds.

trio The middle section of a song, originally performed on three instruments. In contemporary language this is called an 'interlude'.

tritone The interval of the diminished fifth (or augmented fourth.) The tritone was known as the sound of the devil's violin (achieved by retuning) and is assiduously avoided in all exercises in harmony or composition.

upbeat A lead-in or pickup. The beat before the bar-line and downbeat. Upbeat is so named for the position of the conductor's arm.

vamp A repeated chord pattern usually ad-libbed until the entrance of the solo artist.

verse Before 1960 the mood-setting, expendable introductory section preceding an ABAC or AABA chorus.

waltz Although usually written 3/4 time, the waltz is generally performed with one beat to the bar.

whole tone A full step; two half steps.

whole tone scale A scale made up of full steps. Only two whole-tone scales are possible in our musical system, one beginning on B and the other beginning on C. All others, no matter where they begin, are repetitions of these.

Bibliography

AGATE, JAMES, *Egos, Vols 1–9* Hamish Hamilton, Gollancz, Harrap, London 1932–48

ALDRICH, RICHARD, *Gertrude Lawrence as Mrs A.* Greystone Press, New York, 1954

ASTAIRE, FRED, *Steps In Time*, Heineman, London, 1959

ATKINSON, BROOKS, *Broadway*, Macmillan, New York, 1970

BANKHEAD, TALLULAH, *Tallulah*, Gollancz, London, 1952

BARKER, FELIX, *The Oliviers*, Hamish Hamilton, London, 1953

BOARDMAN, GERALD, *American Musical Theatre*, Oxford University Press, New York, 1978

BOWEN, EZRA, (editor) *This Fabulous Century*, 1921–1930, Time-Life, New York, 1969

BRAHMS, CARYL AND SHERRIN, NED, *Song By Song*, Ross Anderson, Bolton, 1984

BRIERS, RICHARD, *Coward & Company*, Robson Books, London, 1989

BROWN, JARED, *The Fabulous Lunts* Atheneum, New York, 1988

CLARK, GERALD, *Capote*, Simon & Schuster, New York, 1988

COCHRAN, CHARLES, *I Had Almost Forgotten*, Hutchinson, London, 1932

COURTNEY, MARGARET, *Laurette Taylor*, Reinhart, New York, 1955

COWARD, NOEL, *Plays*, Volumes I through V, Methuen, London, 1983

COWARD, NOEL, *Lyrics*, Overlook Press, Woodstock, New York, 1965

—*Collected Verse*, Methuen, London, 1984

—*Autobiography*, Methuen, London, 1986

—*Collected Sketches and Lyrics*, Hutchinson & Co, London, 1931

—*The Noel Coward Songbook*, Michael Joseph, London, 1973

—*A Noel Coward Gala*, Chappell, New York, 1973

—*Sir Noel Coward, His Words and Music*, Chappell, New York, 1973

DAMASE, JACQUES, *Les Folies du Music-Hall*, Spring Books, London, 1960

DE MILLE, AGNES, *Speak To Me, Dance With Me*, Little, Brown, Boston 1973

EDWARDS, ANNE, *Vivien Leigh*, Simon & Schuster, New York, 1976

EELLS, GEORGE, *The Life That Late He Led*, Putnam, New York, 1967

ENGEL, LEHMAN, *The American Musical Theater*, Macmillan, New York, 1975

EVERETT, SUSAN, *London: The Glamour Years* 1919–39, Bison, London, 1985

GASSNER, JOHN, *The Theater in Our Times*, Crown, New York, 1954

GOTTFRIED, MARTIN, *Jed Harris*, Little, Brown, Boston, 1984

GRAFTON, DAVID, *Red, Hot and Blue*, Stein & Day, Briarcliff Manor, New York, 1987

GRAHAM, SHEILAH, *A State of Heat*, W. H. Allen, London, 1972

GREEN, BENNY, *Let's Face the Music*, Michael Joseph, London, 1989

GREEN, STANLEY, *Encyclopedia of the Musical Theatre*, Da Capo, New York, 1984

HARRISON, REX, *Autobiography*, Morrow, 1975

HART, MOSS, *Act One*, Random House, New York, 1959

HAWTREE, CHARLES, *The Truth At Last*, Butterworth, London, 1924

HOLDEN, ANTHONY, *Laurence Olivier*, Atheneum, New York, 1988

HUGGETT, RICHARD, *Binkie Beaumont*, Hodder & Stoughton, London, 1989

KERR, WALTER, *Thirty Plays Hath November*, Simon & Schuster, New York, 1969

KIMBALL, ROBERT, (editor) *Cole*, Holt, Rinehart & Winston, New York, 1971

—(editor), *The Complete Lyrics of Cole Porter*, Knopf, New York, 1983

—(editor) *The Unpublished Cole Porter*, Simon & Schuster, New York, 1975

KNEF, HILDEGARD, *Gift Horse*, Dell, New York, 1971

LAHR, JOHN, *Coward: The Playwright*, Methuen, London, 1982

LAWRENCE, GERTRUDE, *A Star Danced*, Doubleday, New York, 1945

LESLEY, COLE, *The Life of Noel Coward*, Jonathan Cape, London, 1976

LOGAN, JOSHUA, *Josh*, Dell, New York, 1976

MANDER, RAYMOND AND MITCHESON, JOE, *Theatrical Companion to Coward*, Rockliff, London, 1957

MASSEY, RAYMOND, *A Hundred Different Lives*, Little, Brown, Boston, 1979

MAXWELL, ELSA, *The Celebrity Circus*, W. H. Allen, 1964

MEREDITH, SCOTT, *George S. Kaufman and His Friends*, Doubleday, New York, 1974

MORGAN, TED, *Maugham*, Simon & Schuster,

New York, 1980

MORLEY, SHERIDAN, *A Talent To Amuse*, Michael Joseph, London, 1969

—With Cole Leslie and Graham Payn, *Noel Coward and His Friends*, Weidenfeld & Nicholson, London, 1979.

—With Graham Payn, *The Noel Coward Diaries*, Weidenfeld & Nicolson, London, 1982.

—*Gertrude Lawrence*, McGraw-Hill, New York, 1981

—*Shooting Stars*, Quartet, London, 1983

—*Spread a Little Happiness*, Thames & Hudson, London, 1987

NICHOLS, BEVERLEY, *The Sweet and Twenties*, Weidenfeld & Nicholson, London, 1958

NOBLE, PETER, *Ivor Novello*, Falcon Press, London, 1951

OLIVIER, LAURENCE, *On Acting*, Simon & Schuster, New York, 1986

PEARSON, JOHN, *The Sitwells*, Harcourt, Brace, Jovanovich, New York, 1978

PORTER, COLE, *The Cole Porter Songbook*, Simon and Schuster, New York, 1959

RODGERS, RICHARD, *Musical Stages*, Random House, New York, 1975

RUSSELL, JACQUI, *File on Coward*, Methuen, London, 1987

SCHWARTZ, CHARLES, *Cole Porter*, Dial, New York, 1977

SHEED, WILFRID, *Clare Booth Luce*, Dutton, New York, 1982

STAGG, JERRY, *The Brothers Shubert*, Random House, New York, 1968

SUSKIN, STEVEN, *Opening Night on Broadway*, Schirmers, New York, 1990

TEICHMAN, HOWARD, *George S. Kaufman*, Atheneum, New York, 1972

TREWIN, J. C. *Theatre Since 1900*, Dakers, London, 1951

WILDER, ALEC, *American Popular Song 1900-1950*, Oxford University Press, New York, 1972

WYNNE-TYSON, JON, *Marvelous Party*, Calder, London, 1989

Credits
QUOTED MUSIC AND LYRICS

Ace in the Hole © 1941
All of You © 1954
Almiro © 1928
Anything Goes © 1934
At Long Last Love © 1938
Baby, Let's Dance © 1928
Be a Clown © 1946
Bianca © 1948
But in the Morning, No © 1939
Can-Can © 1952
Cocotte, The © 1933
Experiment © 1933
Extra Man, The © 1927
Fountain of Youth © 1928
Georgia Sand © 1933
Get Out of Town © 1938
Hans © 1928
Hello, Miss Chapel Street © 1971
How Could We Be Wrong © 1933
If I Were Only a Football Man © 1983
I, Jupiter © 1949
I Love You © 1943
I'm a Gigolo © 1929
In a Moorish Garden © 1928
In the Still of the Night © 1937
It's All Right With Me © 1953
It's Bad For Me © 1933
It's De-Lovely © 1936
I've a Shooting Box in Scotland © 1916
Let's Do It © 1928
Let's End the Beguine © 1966

Little Skipper From Heaven Above, A © 1936
Looking at You © 1929
Lost Liberty Blues, The © 1928
Member of the Yale Elizabethan Club, A © 1971
My Cozy Little Corner in the Ritz © 1919
My Houseboat on the Thames © 1976
Neuville-Sur-Mer © 1933
Night and Day © 1932
Physician, The © 1933
Si Vous Aimez les Poitrines © 1972
So In Love © 1948
Solomon © 1933
Sweet Nudity © 1979
Tales of the Oyster © 1966
Thank You So Much, Mrs Lowsborough Goodbye © 1934
That Zip Cornwall Cooch © 1983
That Black and White Baby of Mine © 1919
They're Always Entertaining © 1971
True Love © 1955
Two Little Babes in the Wood © 1928
Use Your Imagination © 1949
Wake Up and Dream © 1929
Well, Did you Evah? © 1956
Weren't We Fools? © 1927
Where is the Life that Late I Led? © 1949
Where, Oh Where © 1949
Where Would You Get Your Coat? © 1966
Why Shouldn't I? © 1935
You Don't Know Paree © 1929

Asparagus, The © 1917
Boy Actor, The © 1917
Call of Life, The © 1929
Carrie © 1924
Chase Me, Charlie © 1950
Children of the Ritz © 1932
City © 1931
Come the Wild, Wild Weather © 1960
Could You Please Oblige Us With a Bren Gun? © 1941
Countess Mitzi © 1938

Dear Little Cafe © 1929
Don't Let's Be Beastly to the Germans © 1943
Don't Put Your Daughter on the Stage, Mrs Worthington © 1935
First Love © 1925
Footmen Quartet © 1929
Forbidden Fruit © 1927
Girls of the CIV, The © 1931
Green Carnation © 1929
Half Caste Woman © 1931
Has Anybody Seen Our Ship? © 1935

If Love Were All © 1929
If You Could Only Come With Me © 1929
I'll Follow My Secretary Heart © 1934
I'll Remember Her © 1963
I'll See You Again © 1929
Imagine the Duchess's Feelings © 1941
Island of Boolamazoo, The © 1938
It Doesn't Matter How Old You Are © 1928
I've Been to a Marvellous Party © 1939
I Wonder What Happened to Him © 1945
Josephine © 1952
Let's Do It © 1944
Let's Live Dangerously © 1932
Let's Say Goodbye © 1932
London Pride © 1941
Love Ditty to a Turnip © 1917
Mad About the Boy © 1932
Mad Dogs and Englishmen © 1932
Matelot © 1945
My Kind of Man © 1950
Never Again © 1938
Nevermore © 1934
Nina © 1945
Nothing Can Last Forever © 1950
Oldest Postmistress, The © 1932

Onion, The © 1917
Opening Chorus © 1932
Party's Over Now, The © 1932
Regency Rakes © 1934
Room With a View, A © 1928
Rug of Persia © 1938
Sail Away © 1950
Sentiment © 1924
Sigh No More © 1945
Something on a Tray © 1954
Something To Do With Spring © 1932
Stately Homes of England © 1938
That is the End of the News © 1945
There is Always Something Fishy About the French © 1934
This Could Be True © 1950
Three White Feathers © 1939
Tomato, The © 1917
Twentieth Century Blues © 1931
Vegetable Verse © 1917
When My Ship Comes Home © 1924
Wife of the Acrobat, The © 1932
You Were There © 1935
Zigeuner © 1929

ILLUSTRATIONS
The author gratefully acknowledges the following for permission to reproduce photographs and illustrations:

The Cole Porter Trust: pp.9, 34, 51, 60, 80, 81, 95, 102, 140, 143, 166, 187, 191, 240 243; the Noel Coward Estate: pp.19, 23, 26, 99, 180, 229, 263; the Raymond Mander and Joe Mitchenson Theatre Collection: frontispiece, pp.44, 45, 65, 71, 88, 89, 96, 115, 122, 125, 154, 158, 200, 227, 234; James Cole: pp.10, 28; the Hulton-Deutsch Collection Ltd: pp.129, 146; Guttenburg Studios: p.108; the Miami County Historical Society, Inc., Cole Porter Collection p.57; Billy Rose Theatre Collection, the New York Public Library for the Performing Arts, Astor, Lenox and Tilden Foundations: p.111; © 1956 Turner Entertainment Co., All Rights Reserved: p. 246; Elman & Glover: p.196; Angus McBean: p. 207; Mark Swain: p. 233; Friedman Abeles: p. 252; Barry Swaebe: p.261.

Every effort has been made to trace copyright holders. If, however, there are inadvertent omissions, these can be corrected in any future editions.

Index

Titles in bold refer to films, literary works, plays and shows; those in italics refer to songs. Figures in italics refer to captions.